0026300

National Party Platforms of 1980

National Party Platforms of 1980

Supplement to
National Party Platforms, 1840-1976

compiled by Donald Bruce Johnson

UNIVERSITY OF ILLINOIS PRESS Urbana Chicago London

Library of Congress Cataloging in Publication Data

Johnson, Donald Bruce, 1921-
    National party platforms, 1840-1976. Supplement
1980.

    1. Political parties—United States—History.
I. Johnson, Donald Bruce, 1921-   . National
party platforms. II. Title.
JK2255.J643   324.2′3′0973   81-10448
ISBN 0-252-00923-1   AACR2

Contents

CAMPAIGN OF 1980

In 1980, more than 225 persons, at one time or another, were candidates for the presidency of the United States. As late as August, more than thirty were still listed as candidates, as defined by the Federal Election Campaign Act Amendments of 1979, although several had publicly withdrawn from the competition.

The election of 1980 brought to the polls more than eighty million voters who elected Republican Ronald Reagan, of California, as president and George Bush, of Texas, as vice-president with 43,901,812 popular votes and 489 electoral votes. They defeated Democratic incumbents President Jimmy Carter, of Georgia, and Vice-President Walter Mondale, of Minnesota, who received 35,483,820 popular votes and 49 electoral votes. John B. Anderson, a congressman from Illinois running with former Wisconsin governor, Patrick J. Lucey, under the banner of the National Unity Campaign, acquired 5,719,722 votes in all fifty states but no electoral votes. Also on the ballot in all states was the Libertarian Party, whose candidates, Edward E. Clark of California for president and David Koch of New York for vice-president attracted 921,188 popular votes. A new Citizens Party, with Barry Commoner of New York and LaDonna Harris of New Mexico as its candidates, featured a platform that originally had 325 planks which were submitted to its known supporters in a national referendum. The planks ratified are presented here. The Citizens Party polled 234,279 votes.

The American Independent Party that first appeared in 1968 again was divided in 1980. Percy L. Greaves, Jr., of New York and Frank Varnum of California ran on the American Party platform adopted by the American Party National Convention in Pasadena, California, in December of 1979. John Rarick of Louisiana and Eileen M. Shearer of California were the candidates for the American Independent Party which held its convention in Sacramento, California, in August of 1980. Mr. Greaves and Mr. Varnum received 6,647 votes and the Rarick-Shearer ticket was endorsed by 41,268 persons.

The Socialist Party candidates in 1980 were David McReynolds of New York and Sister Diane Drufenbrock of Wisconsin. They polled 6,895 votes on November 4. The Socialist Workers nominated Andrew Pulley of Illinois for president and Matilde Zimmerman of New York for vice-president; they received 6,271 votes. The Communist Party again nominated Gus Hall of New York for president; Angela Davis of California was his running mate. They were supported by 44,954 voters. Deidre Griswold of New Jersey and Larry Holmes of New York were the candidates of the Workers World Party and they polled 13,300 votes. In 1980, the National Statesman Party, with Benjamin Bubar of Maine for president and Earl F. Dodge of Colorado for vice-president replaced the Prohibition Party that had been on various state ballots for many years. The ticket garnered 7,212 votes. The platforms of all of these parties appear below. The election returns presented here were compiled by the *Congressional Quarterly*.

The American Labor Party of 1976 did not reemerge as an organization in 1980. Its 1976 candidate, Lyndon LaRouche, ran unsuccessfully for the nomination of the Democratic Party. Finally, the Socialist Labor Party chose not to nominate candidates for the presidency and vice-presidency in 1980.

American Platform 1980

PREAMBLE

Members of the American Party believe that the original Constitution of the United States and the Bill of Rights were prepared and adopted by men acting under inspiration from Almighty God, that they are solemn compacts between the people of the states of this nation which all officers of government are under oath to obey, and that the eternal moral laws expressed therein must be adhered to or individual liberty will perish.

— from the Constitution of the American Party

The American Party offers the following platform in the sincere belief that these stands on the most important issues of the day are both right and necessary for peace, prosperity, justice and domestic tranquility.

DOMESTIC POLICY

Agriculture

A competitive free market is the best means of assuring a fair return to the farmer for the crops he produces. We therefore favor the phased termination of government production and price controls, subsidies, and government-owned reserves which depress farm prices. We favor the withdrawal of similar subsidies from other areas of economic life. While free two-way trade is essential for agricultural prosperity, we recognize the need for protection against foreign imports produced by slave labor or government subsidy.

Business

The federal government is notoriously inept at running a business. The Postal Service and Amtrak are two current flagrant examples. Both are inefficient and expensive. The history of government-run enterprises in all ages and nations makes it clear that no possible reforms or reorganizations can salvage such enterprises from insolvency and poor service. The solution is to divest the government of all commercial enterprises and turn them over to competitive free enterprise.

Since the government does not know how to run a business, it should not have the power to tell businessmen how to run theirs. Regulatory agencies such as the Interstate Commerce Commission and the Occupational Safety and Health Administration intervene arbitrarily, unwisely, and despotically in the day-to-day conduct of most legitimate businesses. In so doing, they cost the citizens of this nation billions of dollars in taxes, higher prices, and the countless man-hours required to fill out senseless forms. They should be abolished except in those few instances where, subject to judicial review, they carry out the only constitutional function of government in relation to business affairs, which is to prevent fraud and enforce legitimate contracts.

Bank accounts should be immune to inspection by the federal government.

We oppose the legislation of such things as conversion to the metric system. Those who find the metric system advantageous are free to adopt it but have no right to use government to force it at great cost and inconvenience on everyone else.

Consumer Protection

Government has the duty and the right to safeguard the people of America against fraud and the sale of dangerous products. In all cases, however, violators must be found guilty in a court of law, not an executive tribunal of an enforcing agency. Furthermore, agencies which monitor the safety of products and the honesty of claims made for them must limit their concerns narrowly to bona fide dangers and misrepresentations. They are not to expand the context of their responsibilities to such things as the unwarranted banning of ammunition as a "dangerous substance" or the specification of the size and shape of cereal boxes, etc. The

American consumer is sufficiently market-wise to make his own choices and his right to do so is not by leave of any federal bureaucrat.

Crime

The primary concern of government at all levels should be the safety of the lives and property of law-abiding citizens, not the rights of criminals. Deterrence is the chief weapon against crime and the most effective deterrent is the certainty of apprehension, speedy conviction and fitting punishment. Fitting the punishment to the crime requires restoration of the death penalty for crimes of violence and for treason. It also rules out plea bargaining and demands greater uniformity of sentencing for convictions for the same crime. We support the autonomy of local law enforcement.

We favor restitution laws, where possible, requiring criminals to reimburse those injured by their crimes. They should also be required to perform useful work to defray the costs of their imprisonment.

One of the weakest aspects of present penology is an over-permissive parole system which reduces sentences actually served to sometimes nominal terms. Paroles should be earned with difficulty. Because of the high incidence of crime committed by prisoners on furlough, felons should not receive special privileges. Prisoners have the right to expect humane treatment and nothing more.

Child Care

Child care is not a legitimate function of the federal government but is an unwanted intrusion into the domestic affairs of American families. Working mothers should make their own arrangements for the care of their children during working hours.

Present state and local juvenile authorities have the authority and the responsibility to make certain that no children suffer neglect or maltreatment. Americans do not need federal child advocates to set acceptable standards of child-raising and tell parents how to bring up their children.

Drug Abuse

America is suffering from a drug epidemic which must be brought under control by eliminating the source of supply. As with other criminals, pushers and suppliers must be deterred by certainty of apprehension, speedy trial, and stiff mandatory sentences.

Since the Communist Chinese regime is the source of roughly three-fourths of the world's illicit hard drugs, the United States should discontinue all diplomatic and commercial relations with Red China.

Education

The present crisis in education must be solved in stages and at several levels. First, so that no parents need defy the law by refusing to send their children to schools of which they disapprove, compulsory attendance laws should be repealed. Second, the control of schools should be returned to the local system by Congressional limitation of the jurisdiction of federal courts and by an end to busing for racial balance. Third, the federal government should be eliminated entirely from interference in local schools by putting an end to federal aid with its inevitable guidelines.

Fourth, the only permanently satisfactory solution to the many problems of general education—busing, curricula, discipline, drugs, the ban of prayers in the schools—is decentralization of the educational system and the adoption of free enterprise methods. To this end, we favor instituting the voucher system wherein it is parents' unconditional right to enroll their children in schools of their own choice—public, private or parochial—to be financed by equal per capita vouchers drawn against school tax revenues.

We oppose any federal prohibition of voluntary nondenominational prayers in the public schools.

Elections

The manner of conducting elections is the prerogative of the states according to the Constitution and this right is not to be usurped by federal government.

The appropriation of tax money to finance conventions and candidates is using money paid under compulsion to promote programs and persons to which and to whom many taxpayers are strongly opposed. Such use of public funds is therefore immoral and should be stopped at once.

Energy Policy

The free enterprise system will automatically adjust to available energy resources and supply consumers in the optimum way if the producers of oil, gas, and coal are not hamstrung by punitive or politically motivated price controls and taxes on the production and distribution of energy.

The development of nuclear and solar power as major energy sources of the future will also take place naturally and smoothly if such development is not stifled by bureaucratic regulation.

The Department of Energy should be abolished without delay.

Environmental Protection

The Environmental Protection Agency is an outstanding example of a tyrannical bureaucracy operating beyond the reach of popular control and should be abolished. Its automobile pollution and insecticide control programs have been costly blunders. Where governmental regulation is shown to be necessary, let each state assume its proper responsibility to pass whatever laws are required.

Equal Rights Amendment

The proposed so-called Equal Rights Amendment will not assure women of rights they either do not have or cannot attain more simply and directly. It would, however, abolish privileges and immunities which most Americans believe should be accorded women, such as exemption from combat duty. Ratification of the Equal Rights Amendment should be opposed or repealed.

The Congressional extension of the limiting date of the Equal Rights Amendment is patently unconstitutional and should be voided.

Executive Orders

The Constitution specifies that only Congress may enact laws and that it may not delegate its legislative powers. Therefore, though the President may issue executive orders to administer the executive branch of government, neither the President nor any other officer may create laws by executive order. All such existing so-called laws should be declared void and further executive edicts forbidden. The alternative is tyranny.

Federal Judiciary

Federal courts have for too long indulged in widespread judicial legislation which is a clear usurpation of power. They should be returned to their proper function of interpretation and adjudication by any or all of several means. The simplest is Congressional limitation of the powers of the Supreme Court and other federal courts, as provided in Article III, Section 2 of the Constitution.

Gun Control

The right of citizens to keep and bear arms, whether for sporting purposes or personal defense, is guaranteed by the Second Amendment of the Bill of Rights and is not to be abridged. The purpose of government is not the control of law-abiding gun owners but the control of gun-wielding criminals. We therefore favor heavy mandatory state penalties for crimes committed with a gun. We oppose all laws existing and proposed for the registration of guns and ammunition.

Health Care

Not only does the federal government have no Constitutional authority for general health care programs, but experience has already demonstrated that such programs are inefficient, slow, wasteful, and corruption-prone. Federal health care programs should be phased out while at the same time private medical insurance and hospitalization plans should be permitted to operate free from governmental interference.

One of the many serious objections to government intrusion into health care is the unwarranted interference with the confidential doctor-patient relationship. Such interference is already being practiced by the federal Professional Services Review Organization, which should be abolished.

Another infringement of the doctor-patient relationship is the legal harassment of doctors and patients who employ bureaucratically prohibited treatments and medications which are admittedly not harmful and possibly beneficial. We favor freedom of choice in all health care.

By the same token, and as a part of such freedom, we oppose involuntary mass medication. Specifically, nothing may be added to public water supplies except chemicals intended for their purification.

With the grim examples of state-directed medical programs available to us in Canada and Europe, we oppose any similar trend toward socialized medicine in this country.

Illegal Aliens

Illegal aliens should be identified and dealt with according to law.

Inflation

Inflation is an insidious regressive tax for which only the government is to blame. The reckless deficit spending of the past four decades and the self-serving monetary manipulation of the Federal Reserve System have brought America to the brink of fiscal disaster. We must return to balanced federal budgets and fully redeemable currency in which a dollar is defined as a specific weight of gold for which "paper money" may be exchanged at any time. When this is done, the Federal Reserve System will be superfluous and should be abolished.

Labor

Workers have a right to form and join unions which promote their specific interest. Union dues and membership must be entirely voluntary. Local unions should be controlled by local members and the law should guarantee the exercise of that control.

Unions should not have the power to prevent non-union workers from accepting employment. Wage rates and working conditions should be determined by the forces of the free market. Union bosses must be prevented from the use of force or the threat of force to attain their ends. The use of labor, donations, equipment, and of money obtained from union dues and pension funds to control political candidates of the major parties is both immoral and illegal. Those guilty of giving and receiving such funds should be prosecuted just as certainly as corporations which break laws concerning political campaign contributions.

Workers must be allowed the same freedom of access to their employer's case in collective bargaining discussions as to the union case.

Government workers hold their jobs as a privilege, not a right, and essential government services cannot be interrupted by strikes or threats of strikes by public employees. Collective bargaining for public employees must therefore be made illegal.

Land Use

Land use laws are federal zoning laws or federally instigated state zoning laws. As such, they effectively confiscate or reduce the value of privately owned land without due process. We oppose such laws as tyrannical and oppressive and because they are an invitation to wholesale corruption. We also oppose compulsory federal flood control insurance and its built-in land use provisions.

The Northwest Ordinance of 1787 required that all new states be admitted on a basis of equality with the original thirteen, but in practice the federal government has usurped the rights of many states by retaining vast areas under its control. Federally controlled lands such as those under the Bureau of Land Management, the National Forest Service and the National Park Service, which are held contrary to Article 1, Section 3, paragraph 17 of the U.S. Constitution, should be deeded to the respective states.

National Security

The United States must defend itself against espionage, sabotage, subversion and sedition, or it will succumb to its foreign and domestic enemies. The full power of the federal government should be applied to the apprehension, conviction and punishment of persons guilty of these high crimes. We call for the reestablishment of and vigorous support for the House Internal Security Committee, the Senate Internal Security

Subcommittee, and the Subversive Activities Control Board. All loyalty and security risks should be dismissed from government service.

Treason is defined by the Constitution and specified as a capital crime. We call for the enforcement of this provision of the Constitution.

Open Housing

The sale of any property must be a voluntary transaction by both buyer and seller. The seller may not be coerced to sell to anyone for any reason and no private buyer may be subsidized with public money.

Public Morality

Neither Congress nor the federal courts should infringe the rights of states and local governments to enact constitutional laws restricting obscenity, pornography, and illicit sex acts, especially prostitution and homosexuality.

Quotas

Qualifications for admissions, hirings or promotions within private organizations should only be by mutual agreement of the parties concerned. Tax-supported organizations should not determine admissions, hirings or promotions on the basis of race, religion or national origin, but on merit alone.

Regional Government

Regional and metro government run by appointed bureaucrats is a device to impose direct federal control upon metropolitan areas and to bypass state and local sovereignty; backers of the scheme themselves admit it. As such it is a blow against local control of representative government and should be abolished. We believe that no appointed official should have authority equal to that of elected officials within the same jurisdiction.

Revenue Sharing

Until the federal government gets out of debt, it has no revenue to share. Borrowing money to give to the states upon conditions set by the federal government is immoral and should be stopped at once. The states could raise their own revenues by taxes if the federal taxes were lower.

Sanctity of Life

The duty to protect the life of each citizen is the paramount duty of any government. Though it may be superficially plausible that a pregnant woman should have complete control over her own body, neither she nor anyone else may extend that right of control to the body of the unborn child she carries. Government is obligated to protect the life of both child and mother and, if necessary, to protect the life of the child from the mother.

A life may be taken according to the law only after conviction for a capital offense, or to save the mother's life.

Social Security

Social Security is a bad bargain for those not already drawing benefits; future benefits will return only a small fraction of the amounts paid in and there is no guaranteed minimum, no cash value. Unless the entire system is soundly funded, it should be phased out. Much more advantageous insurance and retirement plans are offered by private programs.

As long as Social Security remains in force, all earnings limitations should be removed and all federal employees, including Congress and the President should be required to participate.

Taxes

Government which taxes some of its citizens in order to win elections by subsidizing favored factions of the electorate is incompatible with freedom and prosperity. It encourages fraud, sloth and disrespect for the law, and at the same time discourages potential employers, savers and investors. All taxes should be direct, highly visible and proportional in order that everyone have an equal interest in keeping them minimal. They should be levied and collected solely for the payment of the Constitutional functions of government.

We would accomplish this by phasing out the Marxist progressive feature of the federal income tax by gradually reducing the rates on the higher bracket incomes and, by steps, eliminating exemptions. Everyone would then bear their fair share of government expenditures and there would no longer be a built-in inducement for any group to seek special favors at the expense of the taxpayers.

To encourage people to save and invest, we would remove double taxation on dividends and further reduce taxes on capital gains.

We would require the IRS to operate in accordance with normal Constitutional legal procedures whereby the papers and property of all taxpayers would be safe from seizure until the taxpayer has been found guilty of a crime in a court of law.

We call for an impartial, thoroughgoing investigation of the large tax-exempt foundations which have in effect served as questionable tax dodges for multimillionaires while fronting as charitable or educational organizations.

Urban Renewal

Urban renewal uses the power of government to condemn private property for resale to new private owners and is therefore immoral. It has been an expensive failure and has resulted in the forcible displacement of millions of citizens from their homes, the destruction of hundreds of thousands of low-rent housing units. Its harmful effects have fallen most heavily on the poor and minorities. Urban renewal should be abolished.

Unemployment

Persistent unemployment is caused by unrealistic minimum wage laws enforced by government, abuse in payment of unemployment compensation, and exorbitant wage rates imposed by some unions. Unemployment may be made minimal by restoring freedom in the job market so that every potential worker will be free to compete for any job for which he is qualified.

Welfare

Federal welfare programs are unconstitutional, needlessly expensive, and riddled with corruption. They should therefore be abolished, leaving such concerns to the several states, counties, municipalities and private charity.

Much unemployment is caused by the federal government through its minimum wage laws and unemployment insurance. Abolishing or phasing out these pernicious laws will reduce the need for welfare to a level with which state and local governments can cope.

FOREIGN POLICY

Communist Nations

All Communist dictatorships have achieved power by force, deception and bloodshed and survive in power through terrorist rule. They do not represent the people they have enslaved and are therefore illegitimate. The United States should withdraw diplomatic recognition of these regimes.

We favor a discontinuation of all trade and commerce with any countries which do not allow the emigration of any citizen who wishes to leave or prohibit

his taking his possessions with him.

Foreign Aid

Foreign aid is an international welfare scheme by the federal government. It is wasteful and more often than not retards the sound economic growth of the people supposed to be aided. It has so far cost Americans over $250 billion. Foreign aid must be stopped at once.

Hemispheric Defense

Failure to assert and apply the Monroe Doctrine led to the establishment of the first Communist totalitarian state in the Western hemisphere. The Monroe Doctrine must be reasserted by giving every possible non-military form of assistance to Cubans seeking to restore a free government to Cuba.

We condemn the present and previous national administrations for their ceaseless efforts to embarrass, weaken and overthrow anti-Communist governments in Central and South America. We call for an about-face which would lead to the displacement of Marxist regimes in Nicaragua, Cuba, Guiana, etc., and their replacement by governments which rest upon genuine popular support rather than external subversion and rule by terror.

Middle East

The U.S. must pursue America's true interests in all parts of the world. In the Middle East this requires non-intervention and non-involvement. The U.S. must not orient its foreign policy primarily to conform to the interests of any foreign nation.

This nation's vexing humiliation in Iran would not have occurred had not the Carter administration meddled disastrously in Iran's internal affairs. Only a more credible military establishment and a less supine and misguided foreign policy can prevent unlimited repetitions of this fiasco.

Military Strength

International Communism is an implacable enemy which has declared and repeated its fixed purpose to destroy America and the free world. It is suicidal for this country to disarm. We must have a military establishment able to defend us against any combination of enemies.

We must denounce and repudiate both SALT I and SALT II as open invitations to Communist conquest and enslavement rather than the means to peace. Since the U.S. can win any arms race, we should not lose our freedom by surrender and default.

Offshore Resources

We must protect and enforce exclusive private American claims to offshore oil, gas and mineral resources, as well as fishing rights to a distance of 200 miles. Stern measures should be taken against communist ships' harassment and destruction of American fishing in American waters.

Panama Canal

The Panama Canal and the Canal Zone are American territory every bit as much as Florida, Alaska or the Louisiana Purchase. The Hay–Bunau-Varilla Treaty gives the United States full sovereignty over the Canal Zone in perpetuity.

We call for the abrogation of the recently passed disgraceful treaties with the Marxist Panamanian regime and the reassertion of U.S. ownership and control.

Secret Diplomacy

Ours is not a government of, by and for the people if we allow Presidents or Secretaries of State to bind us with secret treaties. We declare that no treaty or agreement should be honored unless it is made public and ratified by the U.S. Senate as required by the Constitution.

State Department

For more than three decades the Department of State has been a scandal-ridden haven for known loyalty and security risks. Though presidential candidates have routinely promised to clean up the State Department, no effective action has yet been taken. The existing situation is intolerable, since it makes the effective functioning of patriotic members of the State Department not only most difficult, but also detrimental to their professional advancement and hazardous to their personal safety. Loyalty and security risks should be identified by a careful and thorough investigation and dismissed from government service.

The State Department is vastly overstaffed and should be cut back drastically.

Treaty Law

Americans are not secure in their Constitutional rights if such rights can be superseded by provisions of any treaty. We therefore call for ratification of the Bricker Amendment which would assert the primacy of the U.S. Constitution.

The President does not have the Constitutional authority to terminate treaties without the consent of the Senate. We call for the establishment of normal diplomatic relations with the Republic of China on Taiwan and for the reactivation of the mutual defense treaty with the government of Nationalist China.

United Nations

During the more than thirty-five years the United Nations has been in existence, more people have lost their lives, homes, possessions and freedom than in any similar period in history. Totalitarian Communist regimes cast hundreds of vetoes in the UN Security Council to make the world safe for leftist dictatorships and they and their satellites control the UN's General Assembly while the American taxpayer foots the lion's share of the bill for keeping the UN going. The UN is a compact with tyrants and therefore cannot under any circumstances secure freedom, justice or peace. We should withdraw from the United Nations and every other organization which infringes the sovereignty of the United States.

War

Our military involvements in both Vietnam and Korea were undeclared wars. We therefore would require that foreign military actions cannot be pursued more than 72 hours without a declaration of war by Congress. We denounce any no-win policy as treasonous. It is immoral to draft anyone to fight an undeclared war.

American Independent Platform 1980

PREAMBLE

The American Independent Party, gratefully acknowledging the Lord God as the creator and protector of the nation, hereby appeals to Him for continuing guidance in its efforts to preserve this nation as a government of the people, by the people, and for the people in this time of peril.

In order to preserve our liberties and our republic, we reaffirm the principle of individual rights upon which the United States of America was founded:

—that every man has, inherent in his being, an inalienable right to his life, his liberty, and the pursuit of his own interests;

—that the right to own, use, exchange, control, protect, and freely dispose of property is a natural, necessary, and inseparable extension of these rights;

—that the proper function of government is the safeguarding of these rights through the preservation of internal order, the provision of national defense, and the administration of justice;

—that an examination of history reveals that governments generally have failed in their obligations, becoming themselves the major violators of individual rights;

—that, therefore, government's powers must be carefully divided and limited.

In consequence whereof, we call upon all men who value their liberty to join us in pursuit of these political ideals.

STATE AND NATIONAL POLICIES

Individual Rights

The American Independent Party speaks for individual freedom; the right of each citizen to the ownership of property and the control of his own property, the right to engage in business, or participate in his labor union without governmental interference.

We shall steadfastly oppose Federal legislation permitting the Federal bureaucracy to tell a businessman whom he must hire or fire, tamper with union seniority lists and apprenticeship programs, or invade the individual's right of privacy.

We call for the elimination of government competition with free and competitive businesses and institutions.

We believe that any promulgation or revision of rules or regulations by Federal governmental agencies, prior to becoming effective, must be submitted to and approved by Congress.

The American Independent Party reaffirms its support of the constitutional right of Americans to travel, especially by automobile, without governmental interference, and strongly opposes unnecessary Federal restrictions and harassments such as the 55 mile-per-hour speed limit, compulsory, expensive, and unduly restrictive "pollution" controls, and all Federal policies which create or encourage gasoline shortages and/or artificially high prices for gasoline.

Secrecy in Government

The American Independent Party believes that government must be conducted in the full light of public scrutiny. Secrecy is the tool of dictatorship, not of government of, by and for the people. We pledge our full support to all necessary legislation to assure full disclosure to the people of the activities of their government, excepting for matters clearly in the interest of national security.

We have witnessed the massive misuse of governmental power to harass citizens and interfere with their basic constitutional rights. The American Independent Party condemns all such abuses by government, including illegal surveillance and wire-tapping, creation of enemy lists, burglary, IRS harassment, and conspiratorial interference with citizen participation in the election process.

We support legislation providing for the prompt and adequate punishment of any government official who violates the rights of any citizen, and to provide for just indemnification to such citizen if he or she has suffered loss and/or deprivation of rights by a government official.

The Census

The American Independent Party believes that the census, as presently administered, is an unconstitutional invasion of privacy, and that the census is being misused to provide the government with information to support unnecessary spending. We call upon Congress to fund the Census Bureau only to the extent necessary to achieve the Bureau's sole constitutional purpose: enumeration of the citizenry in order to reapportion the legislature.

We further hold that an enumeration of the citizenry for purposes of reapportionment does not properly include non-citizen residents.

Local Government

The American Independent Party is totally committed to the governmental framework embodied in the Constitution of the United States with its emphasis on a maximum of individual freedom and local autonomy. We are unalterably opposed to Federal domination of local institutions, particularly our public schools.

We realize that any and all programs of Federal aid to states and municipalities have strings attached to force compliance with Federal demands; that any money which goes through Federal channels greatly shrinks before getting back to the state level. We believe that, rather than being returned by the Federal government to the states, money for state and local programs should be left at the state and local levels. Therefore, the American Independent Party is unalterably opposed to so-called Federal Revenue Sharing.

Regional Government

The American Independent Party is opposed to the creation of regional government entities which exercise tax and police powers without direct responsibility to the voters and the taxpayers which such agencies are alleged to serve. Too often, the objective of those seeking to create such regional bodies is the destruction or usurpation of the authority of local or state governments.

Regionalism causes the loss of control by elected officials, with unlimited power reverting to appointees, and adds to the ever increasing tax burden. Regionalism seeks to dissolve county governments; transfer state powers to a central authority in Washington; administer the affairs of United States citizens through a network of Federal Regions and State Regional subdivisions; seize control of the land and production facilities; change our form of government; and reduce Americans to the status of economic serfs on the land which was once theirs.

We hold that Congress cannot legally grant funds for Federal regional programs.

In connection with necessary vigilance on the subject of regional government, we encourage a re-examination of the concept of zoning laws, which frequently are a thinly veiled transfer of power from private property owners to local collectivist planners.

We call for the elimination of oppressive governmental agencies which impose unreasonable restrictions on the right of property owners to use and to develop their own real property.

Natural Resources and Protection of the Environment

The American Independent Party is deeply concerned with the protection of our environment and the conservation of our natural resources.

We support all reasonable efforts to solve the problems of air and water pollution, and America's other environmental maladies, but oppose arbitrary, costly, or unreasonable interference by bureaucratic governmental agencies in the right of property owners to use and develop their own property.

We do not believe that pollution problems can be resolved by destroying the private capital investment system, but rather by state and local enforcement of the common and statutory laws on this subject, and by the inventive genius of a free people operating in a competitive economic system.

We advocate repeal of the Environmental Protection Act.

The American Independent Party opposes the establishment of a Federal Land Use Policy. We acknowledge the importance of ecological considerations, but these considerations are not properly used as a device to usurp the inalienable right of private ownership of property.

We are opposed to the Federal acquisition of state land through such legislation as the Alaska Land Use Bill. The Federal government should not be allowed to take land from the states without full payment, and state legislative approval.

We propose that dams be built to produce smog-free hydroelectric power, as well as to provide flood control, water supply, irrigation systems, and recreation.

We oppose the extension of Federal authority to regulation of water rights matters which have traditionally been the concern and prerogative of the several states.

Safe nuclear power is available today. We favor the development of such power and oppose restrictive laws designed to prohibit the construction and operation of nuclear power plants, including any prohibition of the use of nuclear waste, which is a present, fully developed technology, as an energy source.

Energy

The American Independent Party is deeply concerned by the need of our society for sufficient energy to sustain our standard of living, and to provide food for our use.

We propose diligent pursuit by private enterprise of all possible solutions to the current energy crisis, including hydroelectric power, solar energy, home insulation, wind generators, ocean energy conversion, nuclear energy, use of coal, shale, and oil sands for the production of power or conversion to gas, and use of coal and shale for conversion to synthetic liquid fuels.

We are aware of opposition by certain groups to the development and use of nuclear power, but believe such opposition lacks scientific foundation. There is no record of loss of life, either in this country or abroad, as a result of use for peaceful purposes of nuclear energy.

We support conservation by individuals and industry to extend our available energy supply.

The Oil Monopoly

The American people have chosen the privately owned automobile as their principle means of transport. The freedom and mobility of Americans, made possible by their ability to own their own automobiles, is a major element of our high standard of living.

The American Independent Party rejects the use by government and the giant oil companies of the artificially produced gasoline crisis as an excuse to force a reduction in the standard of living of Americans.

We propose that:

—the United States take immediate steps to reduce this country's dependence on foreign oil by encouraging domestic production of oil, and development of alternate fuel supplies such as conversion of coal to oil;

—the oil industry be freed of government regulations which deter increased production;

—the anti-trust laws be strictly applied to the giant

oil companies to assure that American consumers are, in fact, receiving the benefits of a free competitive market;

— laws be enacted to prohibit the giant oil companies from diverting their profits from resolution of the "oil crisis" to the acquisition of business ventures unrelated to production of oil;

— any tax on gasoline which is designed to penalize the consumer for use of his automotive vehicle be repealed.

The American Independent Party opposes the diversion of gasoline taxes from development and maintenance of our highway system to impractical and unwanted rapid transit systems.

We further propose that gasoline be conserved by the elimination of all school busing for racial purposes.

We further propose that there be no prohibition on the development of small or large, individual or joint, novel or conventional alcohol stills, or similar energy source factors.

Consumer Protection

The American Independent Party supports reasonable programs to provide protection for consumers and wage earners against hazards to their health and safety, but points out that, in many instances, the government has gone too far in its regulatory activities, creating a cure more destructive than the disease. These excesses should be curbed.

Believing in free competitive enterprise, we are unrelenting in our opposition to government-maintained monopolies which stifle competition. Where these monopolies exist, they must be strictly regulated to protect the public from unfair and arbitrary rate increases.

We are opposed to the use by those monopolies, such as the telephone company, of consumer-derived revenues for political purposes for the direct or indirect influencing of elections.

Interstate Commerce Commission

The Interstate Commerce Commission, which was created on the pretense that it would protect the consumer, has totally failed in its purpose. The effect of its regulations has been to strangle interstate commerce as a whole, including the independent truckers; stifle free enterprise; and maintain unreasonably high prices for the consumers.

Therefore, the American Independent Party calls for the abolition of the Interstate Commerce Commission.

Inflation

The average family in America today is the victim of government-created inflation which robs the working man of the advantage achieved by high wage standards.

Government created the problem of inflation by deficit spending, indiscriminate issuance of fiat money, and sanctioning as lawful the world control enterprise known as fractional reserve banking, and government must be curbed in such further activity.

The American Independent Party supports all steps necessary to halt the inflationary spiral, including reductions in Federal spending, putting the government on a pay-as-you-go basis, and restoring a sound monetary standard.

The American Independent Party advocates the abolition of the Federal Reserve System (a private corporation), and the return to the gold and silver standard.

We propose that immediate steps be taken to repeal all Federal laws and regulations which discourage or inhibit the reopening of gold mines, and that silver be restored in our coinage.

The right to own and exchange gold, or any precious metal, is a basic right and a protection against inflation. Never should this right be denied to the American people.

We object strongly to the policy of present and past administrations in blaming either the working man or the businessman for the problems of inflation.

The imposition of wage and price controls, ostensibly established to curb inflation, would constitute a fraud upon every citizen of America. We oppose such controls.

Taxation

Through ever-increasing tax rates, the average man in America carries the full burden of the cost of a reckless and wasteful government. The able-bodied who refuse to work produce no income, pay no taxes, and draw lavish welfare subsidies. The ultra-rich acquire vast sums, but use tax loopholes and tax-exempt foundations to evade the payment of taxes.

The American Independent Party supports immediate tax reduction for the lower and middle-income citizens of America, a closing of the tax loopholes for the ultra-rich, and taxation of the presently exempt foundations unless their purposes are narrowly limited to charitable pursuits.

The American Independent Party believes that the Federal government should be restricted to its constitutional functions, and that, if this were done, it would be financially feasible to eliminate the Federal personal graduated income tax, estate and gift taxes. Such a program, if adopted, would provide a profit of 20 percent to the average American wage earner. This proposal is contained in the Liberty Amendment, a proposed constitutional amendment, which has been introduced in Congress as House Joint Resolution 23, and the text of which follows:

Section 1. The Government of the United States shall not engage in any business, professional, commercial, financial or industrial enterprise except as specified in the Constitution.

Section 2. The constitution or laws of any state, or the laws of the United States shall not be subject to the terms of any foreign or domestic agreement which would abrogate this amendment.

Section 3. The activities of the United States Government which violate the intent and purpose of this amendment shall, within a period of three years from the date of the ratification of this amendment, be liquidated, and the properties and facilities affected shall be sold.

Section 4. Three years after the ratification of this amendment, the sixteenth article of amendments to the Constitution of the United States shall stand repealed and thereafter Congress shall not levy taxes on personal incomes, estates, and/or gifts.

The American Independent Party opposes the adoption of the European style hidden sales tax known as the value added tax, either as a new tax measure, or as a replacement of any existing tax.

We propose repeal of all taxes imposed on retirement pensions.

The Federal telephone tax is a nuisance, and an unwarranted tax on speech. We call for its immediate repeal.

We support revision of the tax laws to protect the consuming public from piracy by the multi-national oil companies, which use increased foreign royalty payments as an excuse to raise gasoline prices while writing those same royalties off dollar for dollar against their U.S. income tax returns.

Agriculture

The American Independent Party supports the phased complete withdrawal of government controls, restrictions, and subsidies from agriculture, but only as, and if, we withdraw similar subsidies from other areas of American economic life.

We propose that the 160-acre limitation, limiting the land which a farmer may irrigate with water from Federal projects, be repealed.

Labor

The American Independent Party fully supports the advances made by the working people of America. We shall continue to support the right of workers to organize, bargain collectively, and control the internal affairs of their union organizations without Federal government interference. We oppose compulsory,

Federally enforced arbitration on local unions.

The American Independent Party will resist enactment of any law impairing the hard-won rights of working people.

The American Independent Party recognizes that all retirement and pension programs are a deferred part of every worker's wage or salary. As such, all participation in retirement and pension programs should remain the property of every participating employee, regardless of where he may be employed. We strongly support legislation, union agreements, or other private action to guarantee such interest. Every working man, union or non-union, waged or salaried, should be allowed to take his pension benefits with him, wherever he may be employed, from his first job to his last.

We support the right of rank and file union members to control the destiny of their own local unions through democratic processes and the secret ballot in union elections. We support the right of local unions to call on state election officials to assist in monitoring elections for national and international union officials.

The creation of job opportunities for our citizens is an essential requirement of today's economy. We believe this goal can best be accomplished by the free enterprise system rather than through government-sponsored makework programs. The elimination of unreasonable government restrictions on businesses would permit creation of unlimited employment opportunities for American working men and women.

Equal Rights Amendment

The "Equal Rights Amendment" will, if ratified, have the effect of nullifying present laws providing special protection for women in the social and economic fields.

American women traditionally have been free to do whatever befits their individual talents. We strongly support equal pay for equal work, and believe that the solution to this problem already has been, or can be, accomplished by statute.

We oppose the ratification of the Equal Rights Amendment by any more states, and will support all state movements to rescind it. We oppose any further extension of time for ratification of the Equal Rights Amendment by state legislatures, and urge that recognition be given to past and future rescissions of ratification by state legislatures.

Housing

The opportunity of each individual citizen to own his or her own home is a fundamental premise of the American economic system. This opportunity is now being denied to our citizens by a combination of artificially high prices, unreasonable governmental regulation of land use and residential construction, and exorbitant interest rates fostered and approved by .government.

The American Independent Party believes that America's housing needs can be met in a competitive, free enterprise environment, unhampered by arbitrary, counter-productive government regulation. To this end, we support legislation to curb inflation and reduce interest rates, and to eliminate costly, unreasonable and non–safety-related governmental regulation of land use and/or residential construction.

Provision of an adequate supply of rental housing is also essential to meet the total housing needs of our communities. We believe that the provision of such rental housing can and will be supplied under a system of free, competitive enterprise. Rent controls are counter-productive in that they deter investment in rental property development, and foster deterioration of existing rental units. Therefore, the American Independent Party opposes any imposition of rent controls on rental property owners.

We oppose the concept of Federally funded or subsidized public housing.

Welfare

The American Independent Party is sensitive to the needs of America's aged, blind, and disabled citizens, and fully supports state and local programs to enable these citizens to live in dignity and economic security.

We are unalterably opposed to tax-supported subsidies to able-bodied persons who refuse to work, engage in welfare fraud, or utilize their reproductive capacities for the purpose of securing ever larger welfare payments.

We support all statutory and administrative amendments necessary to achieve the complete elimination of rampant fraud in public assistance programs.

We oppose all Federal funding of public assistance programs, and support repeal of the food stamp program.

We propose that:

— the complete responsibility for administration of all tax-supported welfare be returned to the counties, to be administered by an elected official;

— all welfare rolls be opened for public inspection;

— welfare workers be made responsible for their own negligence; and that

— a penalty for perjury clause be included in all applications for welfare to protect the public from fraud.

We are opposed to the payment to any welfare recipient of benefits in excess of what that recipient could earn by working.

We further propose that the Congress of the United States enact legislation to remove the appellate jurisdiction of the Supreme Court in matters relating to social welfare.

Social Security

The American Independent Party fully appreciates the rightful aspiration of the aged to live in dignity and economic security.

The aged have been the principal victims of an irresponsible government-fostered inflation. We support legislation to require the Federal government to protect Social Security funds as a special trust, using those funds solely for the purpose of providing benefits to the beneficiaries. We support the removal of the earnings limitation on persons 62 and over in order that they may earn any amount of additional income.

We support the right of those entering the labor market to elect to participate in approved private retirement plans as an alternative to the Federal Social Security Program. Current studies establish that, at present rates, the same funds paid into Social Security over the average worker's productive life would produce, if paid into a private investment trust fund, a principal sum sufficient to provide the worker a retirement income at least several times larger than present Social Security benefits.

Health Care

The average man today is threatened in his economic security by the high cost of medical care. We believe that the advantages of our scientific achievements in the medical field should be available to every citizen, the productive and gainfully employed as well as those on welfare.

We support cooperative efforts between state and local governments, private insurance carriers, and private charitable institutions to provide low-cost medical insurance for the average citizen.

The American Independent Party favors legislation to assure freedom of choice of practitioner, and treatment for all citizens with any health problem.

We believe that every citizen is entitled to seek health treatment of his choice, and every health care practitioner is entitled to give his patient a mutually agreed upon treatment, and such treatment should be restricted only if it is conclusively proved harmful to the patient.

We are particularly sensitive to the special needs of the handicapped, and support state-administered programs which offer these citizens the educational and employment opportunities to lead productive lives.

We oppose compulsory mass medication in any form.

Education

The American Independent Party fully supports the concept of quality education for every American child. We believe that education is a local responsibility and we are unalterably committed to the preservation of the neighborhood school without Federal control or interference. The Federal Government has no constitutional authority to be involved in education. We, therefore, support the repeal of the law which created the Federal Department of Education. We believe that the educational dollar should be spent for improved classroom instruction, not for unproductive busing of pupils for purposes of racial balance, for bilingual education, or for social experimentation. We strongly reaffirm our opposition to the described busing, and to the transfer of teachers for similar purposes.

We support all necessary legislation to encourage the development of systems of private education, including tax setoffs for parents who choose to place their children in private schools.

We support the adoption of all necessary policies to assure high academic standards in the public schools.

We support the concept of voluntary non-denominational prayer in the public schools. We would protect the right of an individual not to participate, but do not believe the minority has the right to bar participation by the majority in desired religious exercises. We will resist any and all attempts by governmental agencies to use our educational systems to experiment with the lives of our children through such programs as sex education, sensitivity training, and drug experimentation. We believe that public schools should be required to reflect the moral standards of the community.

We favor placing our schools under the jurisdiction of local school boards, and the financing of schools by state and local taxation only.

Civil Rights Laws

Human dignity is a basic right recognized in the Constitution by our Founding Fathers. We reaffirm our belief that all men are created equal in the eyes of God, and, therefore, should be evaluated on their individual merits.

We recognize, however, that much of government's interference in the economy has come about through the enactment of so-called civil rights laws opposed by the majority of Americans.

Therefore the American Independent Party proposes the immediate repeal of the FEPC and forced housing laws in accord with the wishes of the people.

The American Independent Party is unalterably opposed to any program of reverse discrimination under which quotas of ethnic minorities, regardless of qualification, are admitted to our academic institutions if it means denying admission to better qualified majority group applicants.

We are equally opposed to such reverse discrimination practices in employment, promotion of employees, and financial transactions. We point out that Congress, in enacting the Civil Rights Act of 1964, specifically prohibited preferential treatment as specified in U.S. Code, Title 42, Section 2000e-2, paragraph J. Affirmative action, which is totally contrary to the concept of equal opportunity, should be abandoned.

We reaffirm our belief in the Tenth Amendment to the Constitution of the United States, which provides that "the powers not delegated to the United States by the Constitution, nor prohibited by it to the States, are reserved to the States respectively, or to the people."

District of Columbia

Congress has adopted, and submitted to the state legislatures for ratification, a proposed constitutional amendment to provide representation in Congress for the District of Columbia, "as if it were a state."

The American Independent Party is strongly opposed to such amendment, and urges its rejection by the several state legislatures.

Communism

The American Independent Party expresses its undying opposition to the criminal Communist conspiracy. We propose that:

—all identified Communists be removed from employment by our academic institutions, all branches of government, and our defense plants; and that

—the United States Department of Justice reinstate and maintain its list of subversive organizations to include the more recently formed subversive groups.

It is imperative that subversive and terrorist activities be thoroughly investigated and exposed in view of their increasingly violent nature. Therefore, the American Independent Party supports the reinstatement of the House Committee on Internal Security, the Senate Internal Security Subcommittee, the Subversive Activities Control Board, and urges adoption by Congress, at the earliest possible date, of appropriate resolutions to accomplish this objective.

Protection from Crime and Violence

The law-abiding citizens of the United States have a right to be protected from crime, violence and lawlessness.

The American Independent Party pledges full support to local law enforcement in its effort to control crime, and encourages all citizens to assist law enforcement on a voluntary basis whenever necessary. We support reforms in our judicial system to provide a speedy and just determination in criminal cases, and retention of the historic constitutional right of each state and the Federal government to impose capital punishment for aggravated criminal offenses.

We support local control and financing of our local police forces, and oppose attempts to establish Federal control over local police.

We support strengthened laws to prohibit lenient sentencing of felony repeaters, including mandatory life sentences without probation or parole for individuals convicted three or more times on felony charges.

We support the rehabilitation of felons where possible, but this shall not be construed to mean that efforts at rehabilitation should be continually extended to habitual repeaters when the result is to increase the number of hard-core criminals released to continue depredations against society.

We support the imposition of maximum penalties on those convicted of the crimes of skyjacking, political assassination, or attempt to commit such crimes.

Gun Control

The Second Amendment to the Constitution of the United States affords to every citizen the right to keep and bear arms.

The American Independent Party supports the right of all citizens to be fully protected in their homes, persons, and property, and opposes the registration of guns and ammunition, or any other attempt to outlaw specific types of arms. We believe that registration of guns will deprive the citizenry of the power to insure freedom from political oppression.

We further assert that the 1968 Gun Control Act is an infringement of our constitutional right to keep and bear arms, and said Act should be repealed.

We point out that the lawless always acquire weapons, and the result of disarming our citizens, coupled with judicial emasculation of local police protection, would be to leave the average citizen without protection from the lawless.

The Judiciary

The American Independent Party would end judicial usurpation of the constitutional process by re-quiring Federal judges at the district court level to be directly elected by the people; by requiring Federal judges at the appellate level, including Supreme Court Justices, to be reconfirmed in their appointments every four years; by limiting the appellate jurisdiction of the Federal courts in state constitutional cases; and by requiring all state and local judges to be directly elected by vote of the people.

We believe that Congress should enact legislation to remove the appellate jurisdiction of the Supreme Court in matters relating to prayer in schools, abortion, school busing, and racial or sexual quotas.

Juries

When the United States Constitution was written, it was the recognized right of juries to decide both the facts and the law of a case. This was recognized as a proper power and moral right of juries to protect citizens against tyrannical acts of wrongful prosecution by government. By a process of judicial usurpation, most jurors today are wrongfully sworn to uphold the law as the judge gives it, rather than sworn to uphold the Constitution and the rights of the citizen. Jurors thus become unwitting puppets to uphold unjust laws. The American Independent Party supports legislation to restore the full rights of the juries, and to provide effective punishment, including dismissal from office, for judges who set themselves above the rights of the citizenry said judges are supposed to serve.

Drug Abuse

The American Independent Party asserts that drugs are a serious problem in our nation, particularly among our youth, threatening the physical and mental health and/or the lives of the users, and leading to many crimes, accidents and other misfortunes.

We oppose legalization of any narcotic except for prescribed medical purposes. We favor strong local and state laws making it a criminal offense, with a mandatory jail sentence, to illegally sell or supply drugs to any person.

The ultimate source of most hard drugs in the United States is found in foreign nations. We support all legislation and administrative action necessary to stop the flow of hard drugs from these countries to the United States.

Law and Morality

The American Independent Party supports laws providing maximum legal penalties for the criminal distribution, publication or exhibition of obscenity.

We further oppose legalization of homosexuality, special privileges, government appointments, or other favorable recognition of known or admitted homosexuals.

Respect for Life

A companion to the rise of crime in America has been the growing lack of respect for life and the institutions of home, marriage and family.

The American Independent Party recognizes that the first and most important role of government at any level is the protection of the right to life. We support reinstatement of all anti-abortion laws, which laws, by their very nature, protect the lives of those innocents least able to defend themselves.

We support the efforts of those who seek enactment of the human life constitutional amendment, which will specifically mandate every branch of government to protect this right for every human being at every stage of its development.

We are opposed to euthanasia, the so-called "mercy killing" of the aged, ailing, or infirm, by the administration of drugs or the withholding of medication essential to the patient's comfort or possible recovery.

Elections

The development of the American Independent Party is dependent upon an opportunity to fully participate in the election process in the several states. We shall work for the elimination of discriminatory state laws which make it difficult or impossible for new parties to participate in the election process. We support judicial or legislative action, wherever necessary, to achieve this objective.

We oppose the present system under which the Federal government provides matching funds for political campaigns and the present Federal income tax check-off provisions for contributions to political parties. If such statutes remain in force, they should be amended to provide equal participation for the American Independent Party.

We support full disclosure of campaign contributions and expenditures.

We further propose that:

—the equal time and fairness doctrines, applicable to the broadcast media, be strengthened and enforced;

—the Federal mandate for multilingual ballots be rescinded; and that

—the Voting Rights Act of 1965, which discriminates against certain states, be repealed.

The American Independent Party welcomes America's young voters and invites them to participate in our activities. We encourage our newly enfranchised young voters to play an active part in the leadership and development of the American Independent Party.

Foreign Policy

National Sovereignty

The United States is a free and sovereign republic which desires to live in friendship with all nations, without interfering in their internal affairs, and without permitting their interference in ours. We are, therefore, unalterably opposed to entangling alliances—via treaties, or any other form of commitment—which compromise our national sovereignty, or commit us to intervention in foreign wars. To this end, we shall:

—steadfastly oppose American participation in any form of world government organization;

—call upon the President and Congress to terminate United States membership in the United Nations and its subsidiary organizations; and

—propose that the Constitution be amended to prohibit the United States Government from entering any treaty or other agreement which makes any commitment of American military forces or tax money, compromises the sovereignty of the United States, or accomplishes a purpose properly the subject of domestic law.

World Government by Back Door

Just as we are opposed to world government by direct action, so we are opposed to world government by the back door by bestowal of statehood on remote insular territories. The present American territories should, upon qualification, be granted commonwealth status—not statehood.

Pacts and Agreements

Since World War II, the United States has increasingly played the undesirable role of an international policeman. Through our involvements abroad, our country is being changed from a republic to a world empire in which our freedoms are being sacrificed on an altar of international involvement. The United States is now committed by treaty to defend some 42 foreign nations in all parts of the world, and by agreements other than treaties to defend at least 19 more. Therefore, we:

—call upon the President and the Congress to immediately commence a systematic withdrawal from these treaties and agreements, each of which holds the potential to plunge America into a war in some farflung corner of the earth; and

—reaffirm our support of the Monroe Doctrine under which the United States has clearly stated its perpetual interest in the independence from foreign domination of the several republics of the Western Hemisphere, so that all expansionist powers will be forewarned of our commitment to the freedom of the Western Hemisphere from foreign domination.

Unconstitutional, Undeclared Wars

Since World War II, the United States has been involved in tragic, unconstitutional, undeclared wars in Korea and Vietnam, which cost our country the lives of many thousands of young Americans. These wars were the direct and forseeable result of the bipartisan interventionist policy of both Democrat and Republican administrations.

The American Independent Party is opposed to the continuation of the same interventionist policy, under either Jimmy Carter or Ronald Reagan, with that policy's capacity to involve our country in repeated Vietnam-like wars.

Acknowledging the lesson of Vietnam and Korea, we demand that:

—never again shall United States troops be employed on any foreign field of battle without a declaration of war by Congress as required by the United States Constitution;

—Congress refuse to fund unconstitutional, undeclared wars pursuant to presidential whim or international obligations under which American sovereignty has been transferred to multi-national agencies;

—the War Powers Act be further strengthened to preclude American involvement in undeclared wars; and that

—such other statutes be enacted as may be required to achieve these objectives.

Foreign Involvements

The American Independent Party is opposed to American involvement in the Middle East conflict between Israel and the Arab states, and to intervention in Africa, Asia, or Europe. The United States has no interest in these areas which would justify the sacrifice of our sons on foreign battlefields. Nor is our country properly cast as a merchant of death in a Middle Eastern or other international arms race.

At a time when we have extricated ourselves from involvement in the Indo-China war, it is shocking to find both Democrat and Republican politicians thrusting us toward war on other foreign battlefields. We are not prepared to exchange the slaughter of our sons in the jungle for their slaughter in some other foreign locale.

We, therefore, propose that the United States:

—declare American neutrality in such places as the Middle East;

—repudiate any commitment, express or implied, to send U.S. troops to participate in any conflict arising there; and

—cease financing or arming of belligerents in the world's troubled areas.

We are unalterably opposed to any continued commitment to place American civilian technicians at early warning surveillance centers on the Sinai Peninsula.

Iran

The American Independent Party condemns the action of Iranian rebels, backed by the Iranian government, in seizing and holding captive the personnel of the U.S. Embassy in Teheran. This violation of the sanctity of our diplomats constitutes an irresponsible, criminal act.

We further express our disgust at the inept and bungling manner in which President Carter has conducted the efforts to secure release of the American hostages. If proof was needed of his lack of leadership qualities, the handling of the Iranian affair has provided it.

We propose that:

—the United States government warn all of our nationals living in Iran to vacate that country at the earliest possible date;

—the United States government take such steps as may be necessary to secure immediate release of the hostages, acting in strict conformity with our laws;

—care be taken not to take any steps beyond those necessary to achieve this immediate and limited objective;

—under no circumstances should the hostage problem be misused to justify a permanent military presence in the Middle East-Persian Gulf region for any period after the return to the United States of the hostages; and that

—the United States treat Iran as an outlaw nation, imposing the maximum economic and diplomatic sanctions against Iran, including permanent confiscation of all Iranian assets in this country, and immediate deportation of all Iranians sympathetic to the present government of that country.

Relations with Communist Nations

The American Independent Party is deeply concerned by the United States government's current policy of accord with Communist China.

Instead of consorting with communist governments, we believe that the United States should terminate all trade with, and aid to communist countries. It has been estimated that the entirety of the communist empire would collapse if absolutely without aid and trade from the free world. We should provide moral encouragement to the people of captive nations whose homelands are presently oppressed by the communist tyranny. We specifically urge the United States to reiterate its friendship for Nationalist China. We are opposed to any recognition of the Castro communist government in Cuba.

In addition, we pledge the repudiation of any agreement to which the United States is a party which recommends or approves the communist enslavement of people.

We condemn the Soviet invasion of Afghanistan, and wish the people of Afghanistan success in their effort to free their land from communist tyranny.

Being spiritually united with our Christian brethren in Poland, we pray God, as they do, that they may throw off the yoke of communism.

Foreign Aid

Since World War II, the United States has engaged in the greatest international giveaway program ever conceived by man, and is now spending over $48,000,000,000 a year to aid foreign nations. These expenditures have won us no friends and constitute a major drain on the resources of our taxpayers. Therefore, we demand that:

—no further funds be appropriated for any kind of foreign aid program;

—United States participation in international lending institutions, such as the World Bank and the International Monetary Fund, be ended;

—the Export-Import Bank be abolished;

—all government subsidies and investment guarantees to encourage U.S. businesses to invest in foreign lands be immediately terminated; and

—all debts owed to the United States by foreign countries from previous wars be collected.

We are particularly opposed to any American aid to North Vietnam or other communist nations.

Impact of Foreign Aid on Consumer Prices

No subject is of more immediate concern to the American people than inflation, and the ever-higher prices our people are compelled to pay for necessities such as food and gasoline. In a land which produces plenty, food and other basic commodities are being priced beyond the ability of the average American to buy them.

Much of the frightening cost of food in America can be directly attributed to the Federal government's international manipulation with our agricultural produce. As a result of the export of our agricultural commodities—such as wheat, rice, and corn—the domestic prices of wheat, rice, and corn products have skyrocketed.

Not to be overlooked is the influence of the infamous Russian wheat deal on the price of food in America. As our wheat supply was shipped abroad, the price of wheat increased drastically, being reflected in tremendous increases in the consumer prices of meat, bread, and cereal products.

Similarly, while the gasoline shortage was acute in America, and while local gasoline prices were rising at an alarming rate, this country shipped millions of gallons of fuel oil abroad.

The American Independent Party believes that our government should represent the interests of the hard-working, taxpaying citizens of the United States, not those of huge multi-national corporations, Russian communists, international financial manipulators, and self-interested foreign nations. We pledge a responsible international economic policy which places the interests of the American people first, and assures the use of our resources to promote the economic well-being of our own consuming public.

We are unalterably opposed to the loan of American money to foreign governments and concerns at interest rates lower than those available to the American worker, businessman, and investor.

Tariffs and Trade

Since the adoption of the 1934 Trade Agreements Act, the United States Government has engaged in a selective free trade policy which has destroyed or endangered important segments of our domestic agriculture and industry, and has jeopardized the wages of our working men, and totally destroyed jobs for many. This free trade policy is being used to foster socialism in America through welfare and subsidy programs. Therefore, we urge that:

—Congress take all necessary action to protect American workers, farmers, and businesses threatened by slave labor foreign competition, and by imports subsidized by foreign governments;

—the United States cease participation in international tariff-cutting organizations such as the General Agreement on Tariffs and Trade (GATT);

—the United States Government establish a firm policy that U.S. businesses investing abroad do so at their own risk, and that there is no obligation by our government to protect those investments with the lives of our sons, or the taxes of our citizens; and that

—Congress reassume its constitutional power over tariffs, utilizing a Tariff Commission responsible to the Congress to set specific tariff rates on a flexible basis, with all such rates representing the difference in production costs here and abroad, thus protecting American labor, agriculture, and industry from unfair foreign competition; and that domestic and hemispheric self-sufficiency be encouraged to assure the United States an adequate supply of critical materials and strategic commodities in time of war.

In setting tariffs on foreign goods, the Tariff Commission should also consider foreign trade practices which have an adverse impact on the balance of payments of the United States. These practices include quotas and unfair inspection rules imposed on products imported from the United States, and foreign government subsidies on exports to the United States.

We support restoration of America's place as a major sea power with a far-ranging merchant fleet. We favor modernization and enlargement of our existing merchant fleet.

Fishing Rights and Other Sea Resources

The American Independent Party supports extension of United States territorial sovereignty over fishing rights and sea bed resources to the 200-mile limit, and calls for strengthening the U.S. Coast Guard to the extent needed for adequate control and protection of this area.

We hold that boats from communist nations should not be allowed to fish in U.S. waters.

We oppose all "favored nation" or "sweetheart" agreements which would permit foreign fishing, detrimental to our own fishing industry, within the 200-mile limit.

Since the sea beds contain the world's greatest wealth in the form of food and minerals, and the waters of the oceans have always been open to all the peoples of the earth, the American Independent Party believes the oceans should be kept free beyond the 200-mile limit, and not at any time be put under control of the United Nations.

Immigration

Liberalization of American immigration laws is upsetting the labor balance in our country, and having an adverse effect on our economy. The mass importation of peoples with low standards of living threatens the wage structure of the American working man and, frequently, the political subversion of our American institutions. Therefore, we recommend that:

—United States immigration laws be rewritten to limit immigration to modest quotas of immigrants from European and Western Hemisphere countries, and other people who share our general cultural traditions and background;

—the United States discontinue all special immigration programs such as that under which Vietnamese and Cuban refugees are being admitted to swell our welfare rolls;

—all other immigration be prohibited except in individual hardship cases or other individual special circumstances;

—all immigrants be carefully screened to guarantee the loyalty to the United States of all persons entering this country; and that

—laws be enacted and enforced to deport illegal aliens, withhold from them all unemployment and welfare benefits, and penalize employers knowingly hiring them.

We support the reorganization and strengthening of the Immigration and Naturalization Service for the purpose of apprehending and deporting illegal aliens.

The American Independent Party is generally opposed to the employment of aliens by tax-supported agencies, believing that tax-funded employment should be reserved for American citizens in all cases where there is a qualified citizen to fill the job.

State Department

The State Department, for almost 50 years, has been actively engaged in the promotion of internationalism contrary to the best interests of the United States. Therefore, we recommend that:

—all necessary legislative and administrative action be taken to assure that every person serving in the State Department adheres to the objectives set forth in this platform; and that all persons found to be security risks be summarily discharged, defining sexual deviates and subversives as "security risks per se";

—expenditures by the Department be reduced sufficiently to limit its activities to the purposes set forth in this platform;

—all non-conforming functions, such as the Peace Corps and U.S. Information Agency, be eliminated; and that

—our Government be prohibited from conducting secret negotiations or entering into secret treaties or agreements in any way binding on the United States.

In addition, we recognize the Council on Foreign Relations and the Tri-Lateral Commission as the principal organizations influencing our State Department and the foreign policy of the United States in the drive to make America a part of a one-world socialist government. We pledge full exposure of this conspiratorial apparatus.

Panama Canal

The sovereign right of the United States to the United States Territory of the Canal Zone has been jeopardized by the recent treaties entered into between the United States and Panama. Inasmuch as the United States bought both the sovereignty and the grant ownership of the ten-mile-wide Canal Zone, we propose that the government of the United States maintain and protect its sovereign right and exclusive jurisdiction of the Canal Zone in perpetuity, and repudiate the new treaties with Panama.

Furthermore, the American Independent Party stands opposed to United States construction of a sea level canal in Panama as a replacement for the present canal.

South Africa

As it is not the prerogative of foreign nations to determine the internal policies of the United States, so it is not our prerogative to dictate the internal policies of foreign countries. We should, therefore, declare our friendship with all nations who genuinely desire friendship with us. Consequently, we:

— call upon our government to cease its acts of hostility toward the Republic of South Africa and, indeed, all other non-communist countries who have by word and deed demonstrated their friendship for the United States;

— urge our government to encourage trade on a favored nation basis with all friendly, non-communist nations.

The American Independent Party condemns all efforts to impose an economic boycott of South Africa, or the boycott of businesses investing in South Africa.

We further oppose the current effort to impose a terrorist-dominated government on Southwest Africa (Namibia), and recognize the validity of South Africa's claim to Walvis Bay as an integral part of the Republic of South Africa.

We oppose any manipulation of the gold supply by the United States for the sole and specific purpose of injuring the economy of South Africa.

Defense Policies

The defense of the United States is a primary responsibility of government. The American Independent Party supports all necessary measures to provide full protection of the United States from any foreign threat.

We recognize that it is impossible to restore fiscal responsibility to government without a complete reappraisal of defense expenditures. We believe such expenditures can be reduced and still maintain an independent defense capability fully sufficient to protect the United States.

We insist that all so-called defense programs not directly related to the protection of our nation be eliminated; that every item of expenditure be carefully reviewed to eliminate waste, fraud, theft, inefficiency, and excess profits from all defense contracts and military expenditures.

We oppose the imposition of the draft, except as may be required during times of declared war. We are opposed to compulsory military training, but support a well-trained and highly organized volunteer state home militia.

Since World War II, the domestic prosperity of the United States has been built upon a hot and cold war economy. In this context, war has become an integral part of the domestic economic policy of both Democrat and Republican administrations. Therefore, we urge that:

— the United States government take immediate steps to encourage the reorientation of the economy to provide domestic prosperity without the artificial and inflationary stimulus of war and threats of war;

— the United States government continue to recognize the contribution of our servicemen to the national welfare by the extension of liberal benefits to all veterans;

— in any war in which our country engages, sufficient taxes be imposed to take the profit out of war, and to equalize the sacrifices of those at home with those called upon to fight on the battlefield abroad;

— a new Neutrality Act be adopted to eliminate the conditions designed to involve the United States in foreign wars. Such act should include the prohibition of arms sales to belligerent nations, use of U.S. military personnel and facilities to train troops for belligerents, private loans by American banking interests to warring powers, and sales by foreign governments of their bonds in the United States;

— individuals and organizations who advocate American involvement in foreign conflicts be required to register as agents of the country whose interest they represent; and that

— all persons actively aiding any foreign enemy be interned and tried for treason against the United States.

Disarmament

The principle of universal disarmament is a desirable goal. It can be achieved, however, only if all nations conform equally to disarmament agreements. There is no current evidence of a sincere desire by major world powers to disarm. Therefore, we recommend that:

— Public Law 87-297, otherwise known as the Arms Control and Disarmament Act, be repealed;

— the Strategic Arms Limitation Treaty — Salt II — be rejected;

— no further disarmament treaties be adopted in the absence of full evidence of good faith by all concerned powers, including the right of inspection and true equality of arms reductions;

— no disarmament treaty be adopted involving the express or implied obligation of the United States to go to war to enforce arms limitations, or to protect foreign nations jeopardized by powers violating disarmament agreements; and that

— no disarmament treaty be adopted granting to the United Nations the power to establish an international police force to enforce the provisions of such treaty.

Citizens Platform 1980

PREAMBLE

1. The commanding heights of the American economy are occupied by giant corporations whose grip on the nation's economic and political life has brought our society to the verge of national crisis. The politicians of the two old parties have lost their independence. Congress itself is immobilized. Unprecedented inflation haunts the economy. Unprecedented interest rates have placed home ownership beyond the reach of an entire generation of young Americans. Mass unemployment threatens intolerable social tensions in our industrial heartland. A major depression has become a distinct and immediate possibility.

2. The democratic heritage which has nurtured and sustained us as a people seems, at this moment in history, to be in disarray. Yet the men, women and children who, as the families of America, are the soul of the nation, have continued to strive for a life of dignity for themselves and for our country. They ask themselves and each other: What has gone wrong?

3. We Americans know that for two hundred years our nation has given sustenance to mankind's ancient quest for a democratic way of life. We have taken pride in knowing that all the world's peoples who dared to dream of freedom from old tyrannies have looked to the United States for democratic ideas and practices.

4. But somehow things have changed. The young of the world now proclaim America as their enemy. The defenders of inherited forms of oppression around the world — the military dictators, old landed families who profit from the toil of peasants — often remain in power with American help. In Asia, Latin America and Africa, the aspiring young see their hopes blocked as the United States props up failing dynasties and military dictatorships. Though this is done in the name of protecting "American interests," the result is precisely the opposite: many people of the Third World develop hatred of the U.S. Here also the American people ask themselves: What has gone wrong?

5. Out of these historic circumstances, then, the Citizens Party has been born in the belief that our nation must mobilize its deepest strength: the American people itself. Only we can save ourselves. Only we, the people, can give new life to our democratic traditions, for we are America. Though we do not now run our country, we are the living evidence of the democratic heritage.

6. The American people — not petrochemical companies — must save our rivers and our air. The American people — not nuclear power producers — must commit the nation to solar power. The people — not multinational oil executives — must bring the country's economy under democratic governance. The people — not corporate agribusiness — must prevent the disappearance of the world's most efficient agricultural producer, the American family farmer. And it is only the American people — not the military/industrial complex — that can put the nation on the path to genuine peace, not the mere absence of war.

7. The Citizens Party knows how difficult it is to recruit millions to a party that is, as yet, largely unknown. We know who influences Congress, the economy, the media. We know who writes the laws, who determines which Americans profit from inflation and unemployment and which Americans suffer terribly from both. We know that many of our fellow citizens are resigned, feeling after years of frustration that "you can't fight city hall." We know the meaning of the phrase, "you have to play the game . . ." but we say that somebody, somewhere has got to stop playing games and instead decide to erect a house where all Americans can come to participate in the shaping of their own lives — on the job, in the marketplace and in the city halls and capitals of our land.

8. Only a party of the people, one free of corporate control, can do this. Only such a party can bring democratic values to bear on the necessities of life — on matters of health, housing and jobs. Only such a party can carry the nation beyond rhetoric about minority rights and women's rights to attain justice in our everyday lives. Only such a party can truly work toward peace and disarmament.

9. What kind of Americans are we to dream such dreams? We are no different than those we ask to join us — people who work in offices and factories to produce the necessities of life, people who work in homes and schools to raise the young into democratic citizenship, people who have suffered discrimination.

10. Do we have the right to dream such dreams? Of course we do. Was it not our predecessor Thomas Jefferson who first proclaimed that "all men are created equal"? It was, two hundred years ago, a bold new idea. We have not yet lived up to it fully, but the idea itself continues to light the way, even as we try to ex-

pand its meaning. It is in this tradition, then, that we in the Citizens Party begin in 1980 to build a new mass democratic party of Americans, one that can grow to become a national force.

11. We ask the help of all citizens, Democrats, Republicans and independents, those who are concerned, those who have almost given up, and those who have been waiting for a chance to help build a democracy that works. To those millions we say, "Come, help us build a party of the American people . . . help us shape a more secure future for humanity." We ask all Americans to recognize that our planet is now too small, too crowded, too dangerous and too fearful for any of us to sit on the sidelines any longer.

The time to go to work is now.
We, the people, have to start now.

Economy

12. Three watershed moments in the modern American economy bear directly on the platform planks that follow. The first moment came before World War I, when large-scale business concentration first aroused the American people to mount an "anti-trust" crusade. That effort failed. Though new layers of regulatory agencies were added to the federal bureaucracy, it soon became clear that these agencies were subservient to the industries they were supposed to regulate. As a result, financial and industrial concentration continued unimpeded. The idea of doing something about it quietly died.

13. This "golden age" of business, one that lingers in national politics in the nostalgia of the Reagan Republicans, was shattered by its own excesses in the Great Depression. This catastrophe brought the nation to the second watershed, the "Keynesian Revolution" of Franklin Roosevelt's New Deal. The new remedy was simple: unemployment and deflation caused by the Depression were to be corrected by government spending. As in the earlier period, structural change designed to restrain corporate concentration was avoided. It was only World War II that ended the Depression. Deficit spending followed the war, providing for a time a measure of credence to the New Deal approach.

14. But Keynesian liberalism died in America in the 1960s. Vietnam War spending was not of the magnitude to have the same economic effect that World War II spending had achieved. But, instead of the unemployment and deflation of the 1930s, the United States entered into a frightening new situation: unemployment and inflation. This unprecedented circumstance left the government paralyzed. Any move to cope with inflation heightened the miseries of unemployment; any attempt to cut unemployment through spending lit the fires of further inflation. The contradiction of liberal economics stood starkly revealed, and the American economy entered a state of permanent crisis.

15. Today, the economic experts, though discredited, do understand one truth: a balanced budget in the 1980s means upwards of twenty million unemployed Americans, and an anxiety-ridden society transfixed by social tension and street muggings.

16. The striking thing about all of this is that no one associated with the major parties — not Carter, not Reagan and not Anderson — has found the strength of purpose to carry out the national resolve as it was in 1910: to try and treat the underlying cause of a dysfunctional and unjust economy. Both the Democrats and the Republicans hide from the fact that large corporations siphon too much of the Gross National Product into too few hands. Instead, Reagan — sounding like William McKinley in the robber baron era — calls for a return to the 1890s; Carter sounds like an uncomfortable New Dealer who has lost the faith; and Anderson mutters old pieties that he hopes will qualify him as a "moderate." All can be summarized in one phrase: these are the varied sounds of corporate politics in the late 20th century. It is a politics of tired old men, a politics of decay.

17. The Citizens Party rejects these responses as economically suicidal and ethically bankrupt; they will plunge America into a major depression. The economic policies of the Citizens Party are designed as a first step in placing central economic issues on the agenda of public discussion in the United States.

18. The Citizens Party asserts, as a guiding principle, that individual enterprise and the willingness of American men and women to attempt, at their own risk, to provide desirable new goods and services, has been and remains an essential impetus to the economic growth and health of the nation. The monopolistic structure of the American political economy today, and the dominance of multinational firms in every essential sector of the economy, threaten this classically American mechanism. Therefore, the Citizens Party will give the highest priority to the task of removing the institutionalized advantages that oligopolies have developed in relation to tax structures, access to venture capital, and other sources of impetus for private enterprise. These efforts will be directed toward the goal of reestablishing conditions favorable for the competitive growth of a vigorous sector of small and independent private enterprises. The issue here, as throughout, is economy democracy.

19. The Citizens Party calls for building a new economy, one in which workers and consumers exercise

democratic control over the economic decisions that, today, separate the promise of American society from its reality. This task requires a direct challenge to established corporate and privileged interests. Economic decision-making must be made part of the democratic process. The people must have an effective voice in deciding such essential questions as what goods and services shall be produced; where and how they shall be produced; what prices shall be charged; and toward what ends the wealth of the nation shall be invested.

20. We reject the policies of both the Democratic and Republican parties to lower the living standards, increase unemployment, relax anti-pollution standards, and reduce the economic rights of the majority of the nation's working people in order to fight inflation or increase military expenditures.

21. Inflation, the most serious immediate problem of the American people today, has been caused primarily by: (1) expenditures of vast sums on uneconomic military programs that have caused enormous budgetary and balance-of-payment deficits; (2) administered prices in the oil, steel, auto, rubber, cereal and many other industries, by the three or four major companies in those industries which collude to set prices, in violation not only of the economic law of supply and demand but of federal anti-trust laws; (3) an economic system based on non-renewable energy sources; and (4) excessive increases in the money supply.

The Citizens Party proposes to deal with this problem by:

22. Imposing an immediate freeze on prices, profits, interest rates and rents; and simultaneously beginning to restructure key inflation-driving industries such as food, energy, housing, medical care and finance.

23. When these policies are implemented, wages can be controlled without weakening the purchasing power of workers.

24. Reducing the military budget drastically, recognizing that many of the current and proposed defense expenditures do nothing to improve the real defense capacity of this country, but instead insure profits for certain American corporations.

25. Beginning to shift the economy from the use of non-renewable to development and use of the full range of renewable energy sources.

26. A gradual and sustained reduction in the growth of money and credit.

27. The Citizens Party is committed to providing employment at a living wage for all who seek to work, in the communities, where possible, in which they live. To this end, we propose that the various levels of government begin an extensive social investment through public institutions that are directly account-

able to the people: in housing; renewable energy production; environmental cleanup; public transportation; disease prevention and health care; and education and day-care. We also call for the conversion of uneconomic segments of our defense industries to peaceful and productive efforts directed toward the goals of improving the quality of life for our people and providing an array of new jobs.

28. To rebuild our economy and provide employment requires commitment to increased capital accumulation to support new growth sectors, revitalize our basic industries, and provide much needed housing. To increase savings and investment we support:

—ending the corporate income tax and requiring all large corporations to pay out all profits and dividends with the profits taxed at the tax rate of stockholders to prevent large corporations from holding cash, takeovers, or from putting their profit in other nonproductive investments

—creating a public development bank to invest the funds saved by cuts in the military budget in productive areas of the economy

—increasing interest rates on smaller savings accounts

—providing all income maintenance, including Social Security, through a negative income tax

—implementing a progressive value added tax (VAT) and ending the regressive Social Security payroll tax; the VAT would be made progressive by providing income tax credit to completely shield low-income families and further tax credits to partially shield middle-income families—thus the full tax would be felt only by high-income families based on their consumption; VAT proceeds would be used to replace the income needed for income maintenance programs previously funded by the regressive Social Security tax.

29. The Citizens Party is pledged to redistribute income away from the giant corporations and the rich, in favor of the working people of this nation and in favor of social investment. To this end we pledge to:

30. Encourage and support the American working people in their struggle to obtain wages that provide for a dignified standard of living.

31. Provide an adequate minimum income to all Americans who are unable to work or are temporarily out of work.

32. Significantly increase the legal minimum wage and extend it to include all workers.

33. Restructure the American system of taxation to provide sharply progressive taxes on those with large amounts of income, wealth or profits, to reduce the burden on the lower and middle income class members of our society.

34. Provide no welfare for Big Business—no tax

abatements or federal aid; halt corporate control of job programs; close tax loopholes and eliminate cost-plus contracts.

35. Corporations exist only by virtue of charters granted by governments that are supposed to represent the interests of the people. Recent years have seen unprecedented abuse of the privileges granted to large corporations. It is past time to pursue an alternative.

36. The Citizens Party pledges to place irresponsible corporations and industries under social control; or, if these efforts fail, under social ownership. Social control and responsibility must be established for the public interest and welfare, as well as for the interests of national security. If it can be done by public regulation alone, we propose to do so. In cases where it can be done effectively only by direct public ownership, we stand prepared to take that step at the least centralized level feasible.

37. We also propose that corporate executives, including top management, be held criminally liable for health, threats to safety and environmental injury resulting from actions of their firms.

38. Specifically, it is time to pursue the appropriate alternatives with regard to the oil and energy industries, utilities of all types, bank and credit institutions, and the railroads.

39. The Citizens Party supports broad initiatives in social control of business: worker self-management, producer and consumer cooperatives, community-based and community-owned firms. We support small businesses which operate in a decentralized, democratic manner. We also support the creation of socially-owned and nationally-operated businesses where that is appropriate: for example, railroads. We support the inclusion of significant worker and consumer representation on the boards of directors of all corporations.

The Citizens Party supports the development of democratic economic planning; for example, to:

40. Plan for the renovation and redesign (where possible) or the elimination (where necessary) of inefficient and obsolete production facilities, including portions of our defense industries; together with retraining and relocation assistance for displaced workers, to protect the interests of those workers and their communities.

41. Develop a rational and energy-efficient system of public transportation within and between our urban centers.

42. The Citizens Party recognizes that, under the influence of large United States-based multinational corporations, the economies of both the U.S. and many Third World nations have been fundamentally distorted, resulting in tragic hardship for millions of people. Therefore:

43. The Citizens Party supports the New International Economic Order adopted by the General Assembly of the United Nations, and calls for the strict limitation of the powers of global corporations throughout the world economy.

44. It is clearly necessary for the American people to restrict the ability of corporations to export capital from this country, if we are to stop the dismantling of much of our industrial base and the export of jobs abroad.

45. The Citizens Party supports increased economic aid to those countries that respect the economic and political rights of their people.

ENERGY, ENVIRONMENT AND NATURAL RESOURCES

46. The American people must play a much more central role in formulating energy policy. This requires, as in other areas of national life, that political institutions be made more democratic. But in energy policy, yet another requirement is clear: the American people must become much more informed about what is involved in using energy produced from oil, gas, coal, nuclear, solar and other sources.

47. The history of the United States is one of over-consumption of non-renewable resources, particularly oil and gas. With less than one-twentieth of the world's population, we presently consume more than one-sixth of the world's energy production. Moreover, Americans waste more fuel annually than is used by two-thirds of the world's population.

48. Our economy has been built on cheap, non-renewable energy. It is dependent on unstable and frequently autocratic regimes for oil supplies; on all-too-stable and autocratic oil and gas companies for supply, exploration and distribution of energy; and on a private transportation system (supported by public funds) which has made it more profitable to produce large, energy-inefficient cars than small, efficient cars and public transportation.

49. The cost of depending on the oil companies, the OPEC cartel and private transportation companies is far too high—not only in the direct costs of exploration, but also the increasing costs to our environment and economy. We now import about 52 percent of our domestic petroleum supplies, and rising oil prices have been the largest single cause of the increase in the Consumer Price Index, as well as the major factor in the nation's negative balance of trade.

50. The United States must devise a massive program (at least comparable in scope to the far less important space program) to integrate into our economy both new and sadly-neglected old technology: solar, photovoltaic, geothermal, wind turbine, low-head hydro and other sources of renewable energy.

51. The Citizens Party believes that we must re-assert effective social control over national energy resource development, production, marketing mechanisms and pricing now dominated and manipulated by private corporations. We must establish social control and responsibility for the public interest and welfare as well as for the interest of national security. In energy, as elsewhere in the economy, if social control can be established by public regulation alone, we propose to do so. If it can only be done by direct public ownership, we stand prepared to do that. Over the next several years the Citizens Party will develop a comprehensive set of proposals along these lines. Some principles and policies are already clear.

To bring the energy industries under public control, the Citizens Party proposes:

52. Price controls on crude oil, natural gas and petroleum products, until reasonably priced alternatives are available, so that Americans of ordinary means will be able to meet their basic energy needs at a cost they can afford.

53. To require that energy conglomerates horizontally divest themselves of coal, solar and uranium production, and vertically divest themselves of distribution systems, shipping facilities and retail sales outlets.

54. To provide a public oil import authority to purchase and distribute all crude oil and petroleum products imported into the United States.

To protect Public Lands and resources, the Citizens Party proposes:

55. To reassert the national public interest as the controlling value in the management of Public Lands and resources, and to create national support and citizen participation mechanisms to insure that policies and practices serve the public interest, not private speculators.

56. To establish a public authority to develop (in accordance with sound ecological principles) all non-renewable energy reserves on federally controlled lands and in offshore waters. This authority may contract with private enterprise for development of these resources. Native American tribal lands are not subject to such federal authority.

57. To direct those agencies responsible for Public Lands and resources to plan cooperatively; to make all decisions in relation to the long-term public interest; and to safeguard resources from wasteful, inappropriate and dangerous development and use.

58. To require users and developers of Public Lands to demonstrate that their existing and proposed resource uses are clearly in the public interest. The archaic 1872 Mining Law, enacted in a frontier era to provide opportunity to prospectors and developing mines on Public Lands, should be repealed because it is used to resist environmental, economic and social controls over the operations of large corporate mining interests.

59. To provide adequate funding for the Bureau of Land Management from its leases and fees, rather than from appropriations of general funds, in order to make possible the effective implementation of the Public Lands and Policy Act of 1976.

60. As currently practiced, regulation of utilities has failed to provide energy at affordable and stable prices, a healthful environment, and insured energy resources for the future. The Citizens Party, therefore, calls for social governance of utilities.

To protect the environment, the Citizens Party calls for:

61. An immediate moratorium on new nuclear power plant construction, and the phase-out of all existing plants within five years. We also support an accelerated research program into the problems of handling and containing radioactive materials and the disposal of radioactive wastes.

62. A National Environmental Bill of Rights, protecting the rights of all to a healthful and productive environment, including the rights to clean air and water; safe, renewable energy systems; freedom from involuntary exposure to toxic materials; freedom from excessive noise; protection from acid rain; protection of open spaces, scenic resources and archeological sites; and protection of animals and their natural habitats.

63. Immediate attention to creating safe, healthful urban environments, whose residents have adequate income, housing, transportation and recreation, in addition to well-maintained sewer and tunnel systems and garbage and waste disposal to reduce rodent infestation and disease.

64. A national land-use policy, with emphasis on preservation of prime wilderness and agricultural lands, to protect farmlands, expand wilderness areas and establish controls on rivers and wetlands.

65. Control of the use and disposal of toxic substances and wastes.

66. Legislation to hold companies and corporations (and their executives, including top management) liable for health, safety and environmental damage resulting from actions of their firms.

To promote conservation and the development of renewable energy sources, the Citizens Party supports:

67. A national program for the recycling of reusable materials.

68. Expanded federal assistance and direct grants for low-income households to weatherize owner-occupied homes.

69. Increased funds to state and local governments to develop conservation/renewable–energy-resource plans, such as changing building codes to require con-

servation and use of solar energy.

70. Selective imposition of mandatory requirements reducing the use of non-renewable energy, such as gasoline efficiency standards increased to an average of 30 miles per gallon by 1982 and the use of alcohol fuels in all state and federally owned vehicles.

71. Transferral of all research funds from breeder reactors and fossil-derived synthetic fuels to development of renewable energy resources.

72. Repeal of the Price-Anderson Act, a combined government/utility/insurance carrier pool that drastically limits the liability of the nuclear power industry for major accidents.

73. Expanded subsidies, tax incentives and direct allocations to encourage conservation and social measures (such as mass transit) and the development of renewable resources (such as gasohol, geothermal and solar power). All subsidies and incentives which support the exploitation of non-renewable resources should be phased out.

74. Support of the development of alcohol fuels, particularly small-scale, farm-based applications in accordance with sound soil conservation practices.

75. Production and use of methane gas and cogeneration of electricity.

76. Federal financing of conservation and alternative energy projects which favor decentralized investment.

77. Institution of programs to improve forest productivity, and to stimulate better forest management and planning for selective use of wood as an energy resource.

[Paragraphs 78, 79, and 80 were not ratified by members of the party.]

Foreign and Military Policy

81. American foreign policy should be democratic. The Citizens Party recognizes that United States foreign policy traditionally has been formulated by elites closely allied with corporate interests, and does not truly represent the interests of the majority of the American people.

82. The Citizens Party believes that the time has come to develop a foreign policy which clearly distinguishes between the legitimate interests and security of the American people and those of private corporate interests.

83. The Citizens Party seeks a truly strong United States. Both major parties, however, have defined "strength" solely in terms of increased defense spending. The term "national security" has been used to justify increased military spending which actually creates far fewer jobs than socially useful forms of spending, and causes much of the inflation we are now suffering. Thus we grow weaker — not stronger — under the defense and foreign policies of the two major parties.

84. The Citizens Party believes there is no goal more important than world peace, a genuine peace — not merely the absence of war — that will release, to meet basic human needs, the vast physical, financial and human resources now wasted in the illusory attempt to gain national security through military strength.

85. Thus, the Citizens Party calls for a genuine and untiring effort towards mutual, step-by-step disarmament worldwide. The nuclear arms race is suicidal and threatens the very survival of the human race. Therefore, the Citizens Party urges an immediate international moratorium on research, testing, manufacture, deployment and sale of new nuclear weapons and technology, and calls on the United States to take this initiative.

86. The Citizens Party pledges itself to oppose any movement toward first-strike capability. We also oppose the development of weapons systems such as the MX.

87. It is a tragedy that the productive genius and power of the American working people have been diverted from urgent human needs and bent toward waste and destruction. We believe American arms should be sold abroad only in exceptional circumstances. Since we believe international disputes can and must be settled without force of arms, we advocate the conversion of a significant proportion of the American weapons industry to socially useful production. Those who can make extraordinary missile systems can also make extraordinary solar conversion and mass transit systems.

88. No amount of military aid can enhance the credibility or stability of a government that does not have the support of its own people. The Citizens Party opposes United States support of dictatorial governments anywhere in the world; in particular we oppose American support of white minority rule in southern Africa. We are also opposed to any form of U.S. military intervention, by aid or force, in the emerging civil wars of El Salvador and any of its Central American neighbors.

89. The Citizens Party recognizes that both the Soviet Union and the United States continually seek to expand their spheres of influence. Based on the observable record of the past generation, neither is committed to the creation of democratic governments abroad. We oppose all attempts by either superpower to extend hegemony over any part of the globe. We condemn Soviet intervention in Afghanistan as we, individually, have condemned American interventions of a similar kind.

The Citizens Party pledges:

90. To commit U.S. foreign and military policy to the principles of non-intervention in the internal affairs of other countries, and the inviolability of the right of all people to self-determination.

91. To join with other nations in strengthening international standards of human rights and ratification of international human rights covenants.

92. To constrain the power of multinational corporations to exploit the workers and national resources of underdeveloped nations, and to finance dictatorial governments which favor the short-term interests of the global corporations.

93. To support the economic development of Third World countries struggling for democratic rights, self-determination and majority rule. While foreign trade is vital to the American and international economies, the Citizens Party believes it should not be conducted for the profit of global corporations but for the benefit of the peoples of the world. Therefore, we believe that the nations of the world should be paid fair prices for their raw materials, other exports and labor, rather than administered prices set and controlled by the international cartels of the multinationals; that they should not be condemned to being producers of cheap raw materials and consumers of expensive manufactured goods.

94. To encourage the development of international means of conflict resolution, and to recognize that only a fairer distribution of economic and social resources within and between countries can reduce conflicts to peacefully manageable dimensions. Therefore, we favor strengthening and reforming the United Nations and the World Court toward the goals of establishing an effective, just world order and a global democratic community.

95. The Citizens Party is opposed to both a peacetime draft and compulsory national service for both men and women.

96. The CIA and all other intelligence agencies must be rigorously overseen by Congress, so that never again will there be a repetition of the extreme transgressions, at home and abroad, which have characterized the past few decades. We believe that covert activities and espionage should be abolished, since the gains are usually illusory while the costs, in terms of violated principles, are all too real. Therefore, the Citizens Party rejects the proposed Foreign International Charter Act of 1980 (S 2284) because we believe that it sanctions such illegal activities, reduces Congressional oversight, and attempts to undermine the present provisions of the federal Freedom of Information Act.

97. The Citizens Party favors the normalization of United States relations with Cuba and the Democratic Republic of Vietnam, recognizing that refusal to do so has increased the dependence of these countries on the Soviet Union.

98. We condemn the taking of the hostages in Iran. We also sympathize with the Iranian struggle to bring the Shah to justice and to make clear the role of the United States in Iran. The assets of the Shah should be collected and returned to the people of Iran. We believe the embassy staff is hostage also to President Carter's refusal to acknowledge American involvement in Iran. The United States should freely acknowledge such involvement, which is known to the whole world.

99. The Citizens Party believes the right of the State of Israel to exist is not only a fundamental prerequisite to lasting peace, but a matter of human justice. It is equally a matter of human justice that the rights of the Palestinian people to a homeland be clearly, freely and unmistakably acknowledged. So far, these two realities have confounded and defeated the world. The problem, in our opinion, cannot be realistically addressed by a party platform, but it can be made less rigid, less volatile and less unresolvable by an American government determined to support all those committed to patient and peaceful negotiations. The prerequisites for resolving the Middle East crisis will be found in a genuine effort to respond to the yearning for peace and basic human needs of the two peoples, rather than through continued defense of the stalemated policies of partisan leaders.

100. The Citizens Party opposes the use of chemical and biological weapons.

FOOD AND AGRICULTURE

101. The American family farm is the most efficient unit of agricultural production in the world, yet today our agriculture is increasingly dominated by vertically integrated and tightly concentrated agribusiness corporations. For rural America this control of our food economy means soaring farm production costs; unfair and widely fluctuating prices for agricultural products; credit available only at exorbitant rates; oppressive market power wielded by a small, select circle of competing corporate interests; and a national farm debt of $160 billion. At the same time, corporate agribusiness, having lobbied for special tax concessions denied family farmers, is producing high-priced synthetic and chemically adulterated foods which are then marketed through packaging and franchising chains sustained by expensive advertising. For consumers this means that the food we eat is produced for profit, not people. A noticeable deterioration in food quality and a decreasing freedom of choice are the sad and inevitable results.

102. The Citizens Party believes people should understand the nature of our current food crisis, foster alternatives and encourage a coalition of farmers, workers and consumers, motivated by legitimate self-interest, to demand a major role in determining how our food is produced and who will control the land. To date, worker has been played against farmer, farmer against consumer, and taxpayer against everyone. The Citizens Party seeks to reunite all people for our common good.

The Citizens Party supports:

103. A parity program based on a fair return to farmers as a fundamental goal.

104. A fair share of national income for farm families and a fair exchange value for farm products.

105. Conservation and use of agricultural resources which are environmentally and socially accountable and responsible.

106. Safeguarding consumer supply and quality of food and fiber.

107. Encouragement of the rapid development of alcohol fuels, gasohol and methane in small-scale and farm-based enterprises, consistent with sound soil conservation principles, to help supply the nation's energy needs.

108. Stability of farm commodity prices and promotion of national economic stability.

109. The intent of the Family Farm Development Act (HR 6295), which seeks to reverse the demise of the family farm system and to encourage its growth; and the National Reclamation Lands Opportunity Act (HR 3393) which will enforce the 1902 Reclamation Act and make available thousands of acres in the West to a new generation of family farmers.

The Citizens Party supports efforts to:

110. Structure the tax laws to discourage speculative corporate investors.

111. Strengthen and enforce national and state antitrust and disclosure laws as they relate to agribusiness.

112. Make the land-grant college system responsive to family farms rather than agribusiness.

113. Curtail the use of dangerous chemical pesticides and promote integrated pest management programs.

114. Protect independent seed development and preserve genetic diversity.

115. Support member-based production and marketing coops and direct marketing programs.

116. Encourage diversified regional food systems.

117. Put an end to multinational exploitation of Third World resources through cash cropping.

118. Encourage soil conservation practices and the preservation of farmland.

119. Establish a system of national and international grain reserves for the purposes of relief of famine and price stabilization. The assets of this grain bank should be made available for use by starving peoples anywhere.

120. Reverse the loss of Black, Native American and other minority-owned farmlands.

121. Organize farmworkers and support their right to bargain collectively.

122. Establish a national food and nutrition policy that includes comprehensive programs designed to meet interests of consumer nutrition, education and research rather than agribusiness.

123. Abolish tax deductions for brand name advertising; direct the Food and Drug Administration to establish stricter standards for food additive use; require that all food labels display complete ingredient lists; establish an office within the Department of Agriculture to promote consumer food coops; and increase funding of the Food Stamp program.

URBAN POLICY

124. We do not protest current national urban policy. There is none to protest. The United States desperately needs a comprehensive urban policy which addresses the interrelated housing, transportation, education and service needs of our urban populations, and provides a national context for the presently random development of cities. In the absence of such a national context, the cities of the Northeast will continue to decline while the cities of the Sunbelt swell into boomtowns which will inevitably go bust.

125. We oppose the current attitude that, except for an occasional splashy mall or fancy plaza, abandons development and maintenance of our cities to the very market forces which have been responsible for the crisis in the first place. Over the next several years the Citizens Party will be developing a comprehensive set of proposals along these lines.

126. Two general principles inform all of our policy initiatives: commitment to social equality and decentralization of decision-making authority, wherever possible, to the neighborhood level.

Some particular aspects of our program are already clear:

127. A primary concern of any housing policy shall be to prevent the forced displacement of existing residents while their neighborhoods are being "improved." In particular we deplore the human dislocations which accompany the "gentrification" of many of our cities.

128. We favor removal of tax incentives which encourage speculation and promote windfall profits in the real estate market.

129. Existing housing stock must be preserved and, where necessary, rehabilitated and expanded.

130. To the extent that the private market is failing to alleviate drastic housing shortages, government should move to fill the vacuum through financing and building programs. For example, programs may be developed which involve the unemployed and others in planning and construction, at union wage levels, of energy-efficient housing.

131. Tenant rights need to be protected with regard to condominium/cooperative conversion, arson, rent gouging, eviction and segregation.

132. People need to be protected from the redlining practices of bankers and insurance companies which tend to devalue and segregate their communities.

133. While rent control, by itself, can never be a solution to a community's long-term housing problems, it may be appropriate as a holding action while other policies are developed and implemented. If undertaken, however, rent control must be implemented with particular care so as not to crush smaller landlords while disciplining larger ones.

134. We endorse the concept of equal housing opportunity for all families, households and individuals, regardless of race, religion, nationality, age, sex, disability, affectional preference or family composition.

135. In transportation we favor policies that emphasize the most advanced technologies in mass transit. Federal support for such systems needs to be expanded within a transportation policy conceived on a national scale, but appropriate to and implemented by local communities.

136. Land-use policies must contribute to the stability and self-sufficiency of the community. Development ought not to be allowed in areas where housing will require extraordinary governmental expenditures in order to be protected from natural forces; for example, in flood plains, chaparral hills and along fault lines.

[Paragraph 137 was rejected.]

HEALTH

138. The United States has the most inequitable health care system of any industrialized nation in the world. Health care needs to be democratized and made accessible and affordable to all citizens. The Citizens Party supports the establishment of a national health service that stresses preventive care, is financed progressively from national and local revenues, makes personal health services available to all citizens as a matter of entitlement, and assures all Americans adequate health services. These principles are best embodied in HR 2969 as originally introduced by Rep. Dellums.

139. Health is not an accident of nature. Poor health is largely the product of an environment which penalizes millions of Americans with occupational hazards, poor housing and inadequate diets. While we as a nation must work to correct these underlying causes, we also recognize the need for immediate remedies. National health policies and programs should be directed toward the prevention of illness and injury by improving conditions in the home, the workplace and the community, in order to provide the essentials for health: adequate income, nutritious food, adequate housing and clothing, clean air and water, safe working conditions, safe transportation, and adequate recreation.

140. We recognize the need for redress in the distribution of our national health resources. Priority must be given to those people—the poor, the elderly, the disabled, racial minorities, and those living in rural and central city areas—who have traditionally been deprived of adequate health services.

141. Medical institutions are for people, not the reverse. Cost-effectiveness must be measured in terms of the patient's interest, not the bureaucracy's. We must encourage the development and use of the simplest, safest, most cost-effective level of care and technology appropriate to prevent and treat health problems, including home health care.

142. We need to break up the corporate and professional monopolies of our health care system. Programs should be implemented to train and use teams of health care workers, including midwives, physicians' assistants, nurse practitioners, qualified counselors and family physicians, with access to specialists and non-traditional helpers as appropriate or preferred.

143. The American people want—and should have—more control over their own health care and increased independence from self-serving medical institutions.

144. We must insure that the health system becomes faithful to its true purpose of promoting health. The health care system must be made accountable to the people it serves through such devices as governing boards controlled by consumers.

145. The Citizens Party desires to insure the financial integrity of health care for all Americans, at the same time protecting freedom of choice for those Americans who, while participating in the funding of the nation's health service, prefer to participate in private services.

146. Safe, effective contraception and abortion should be available to all.

147. Mental health services should be an integral part of a comprehensive health system. Drug education, counseling and other community mental health services are vital to the maintenance of a mentally healthy population.

148. We must expand, clarify and enforce the legal rights of mental patients, especially those which protect individuals from involuntary treatment such as psychosurgery and electro-shock.

149. We should support the development of humane and adequate opportunities for community living and treatment for mental patients, including mentally disabled persons and those who have been institutionalized. We oppose the involuntary incarceration, on the basis of mental health considerations, of persons who have not been charged with or convicted of a crime, and who do not present an immediate and substantial danger to themselves or other persons.

EDUCATION

150. Quality education is a major goal of the Citizens Party. We pledge to support a public educational system which provides opportunity for children of all classes and social conditions; encourages personal development, intellectual growth and critical exploration of the world; and nurtures an understanding of human rights, responsibilities and freedoms.

151. We are committed to challenge racism as it is manifested within the educational system. We support efforts to include the history, contributions and struggles of Black, Hispanic, Asian and Native Americans in public school curricula. We support the desegregation of the educational system and efforts to expand multicultural and bilingual education.

The Citizens Party supports policies which:

152. Allocate educational resources according to a principle of redress: greater expenditure of public monies and effort to those born into disadvantage.

153. Fund public education from general state and federal monies rather than from property taxes.

154. Reorganize the reward system within the teaching profession and offer incentives to encourage teachers to remain in classroom instruction, rather than seek higher pay and status in administrative work; to encourage excellence; and to encourage teachers to choose more challenging assignments.

155. Vigorously support adequate educational programs for the physically, mentally or emotionally disabled.

156. Eliminate all ROTC and military training programs from public education institutions.

157. Ban corporal punishment in the schools.

158. Insure academic freedom.

159. Support the lifelong pursuit of learning for all Americans.

160. Affirm the right of students to influence the decision-making processes affecting them.

161. Affirm the First Amendment rights of students.

162. Eliminate cultural biases from standardized tests.

163. Recognize that education occurs everywhere: in families, churches, schools, the media, playgrounds, workplaces, prisons and public libraries. The Citizens Party supports policies that promote and enhance the diversity and quality of educational experience wherever it occurs.

164. Ensure due process with respect to student suspensions and expulsions.

LAW AND JUSTICE

165. The Citizens Party recognizes that law-breaking by corporate and government institutions is as much a threat to the public well-being as the more commonly feared "street crime." OSHA and other government studies verify that over 100,000 workers per year die from occupationally related diseases and preventable accidents in the workplace—five times the number estimated to die annually from street crimes. White collar crimes, including corporate crimes, are estimated to cost the public up to $160 billion per year—more than ten times the estimated $15 billion cost per year of street crimes.

166. The Citizens Party recognizes that the dangerous problem of street crime is inseparable from serious social and economic problems—especially unemployment and underemployment. The criminal justice system and its agents are powerless to remedy these sources of crime. We propose to give priority to crime reduction through preventive economic and social programs: full employment for all who are willing and able to work, and other social programs designed to meet the needs of those least well-off.

167. To encourage social justice, the law must serve and protect the rights and interests of individuals, the community and the environment, rather than those of corporate, governmental and other institutions. The law should be a useful tool accessible to everyone equally.

Therefore, the Citizens Party pledges to:

168. Restructure the criminal justice system so that the corporate and governmental violence and harm and street crimes are prosecuted in proportion to the magnitude of the harm inflicted.

169. Reduce reliance on the criminal law where it has been shown to be ineffective. While we recognize that there are indeed victims of certain so-called victimless crimes and that there are social costs involved, we believe that such problems must be addressed outside criminal adjudication.

170. Redraw the sentencing provisions of criminal law to give priority to a wide range of non-incarcerative sentencing options, such as restitution, money

fines proportional to income, community service and remedies to the victims.

171. Advocate policies aimed at halting the construction of all new prisons, save those designed to replace larger, obsolete facilities.

172. Help protect the citizens' right to walk the streets safely and without fear, by working to eliminate the social and economic sources of crime. In the short run, however, we should establish escort services, adequate street lighting, self-defense training and other such programs.

173. Develop humanistic retraining and move toward demilitarization of police. We endorse the establishment of civilian police review boards wherever supported by the community.

174. Develop simple, informal and inexpensive means for dispute resolution without resort to the court system.

175. Impose no punishment on law-breakers greater than separation from society. Although it is often necessary to send offenders to prison, we must still respect the absolute inviolability of their rights to life, privacy, health and safety. Prisoners have the right to work at decent wages, to maintain family and other ties and obligations, to communicate freely and to be involved in the determination of their living conditions.

176. Abolish capital punishment in all cases as unworthy of a humane society.

177. Support the enactment and strict enforcement of a national hand gun control law.

178. Oppose repressive legislation such as the omnibus federal criminal code revision bill (S 1722) and the proposed FBI Charter (S 1612).

LABOR

179. American labor is under attack. In 1979 real wages fell by 5.3 percent, and now in 1980 the current administration is deliberately creating unemployment in order to fight inflation. Employers have mounted a new offensive against worker rights. Pattern bargaining is being disrupted by employer attempts to remove groups of workers from industry-wide standards. Business is frequently demanding takeaways of previously-won contract provisions. Union busting is again becoming an accepted practice in industrial relations. Meanwhile, labor's legislative program has been decimated by the growing anti-worker policies of the corporately controlled Presidency and Congress.

180. The Citizens Party identifies with the aspirations of working men and women, and is committed to policies which provide decent standards of living and improved conditions for workers. To this end, we support unionism as a just and necessary response to the inadequacies of the present corporate state, and commit ourselves to a full employment economy that provides decent jobs, at a living wage, for all Americans able and willing to work. We support such measures as a shortened work week, lengthened vacations, limitations on forced overtime, and socially useful public works to create jobs.

181. We support expanded job training programs for the young, the disabled, minorities, women and workers displaced by technological change.

182. No more Youngstowns! We favor restrictions on plant closings which threaten the viability of communities. We support programs that enable communities to propose alternatives to closings, such as federally guaranteed loans to enable workers and communities to purchase plants and modernize them, and company or government guarantees of wages and benefits until workers affected by plant closings can find suitable employment.

183. We support broadened and strengthened occupational safety and health rights. OSHA provisions should be enforced to protect workers from workplace dangers.

184. We support significantly increasing the minimum wage and extending it to all workers.

185. We call for the reform of the Federal Unemployment Compensation program so as to provide adequate income protection for workers who are temporarily out of work.

186. We support worker control over workplace conditions, such as job design, production and work standards, as well as control over health and safety standards.

187. We support affirmative action and equal employment rights to integrate work forces, including opening the crafts.

188. We call for the repeal of the Taft-Hartley Act and the Hatch Act; we urge passage of labor law reform; we favor protecting the Davis-Bacon Act.

WOMEN IN SOCIETY

189. The Citizens Party wants to create an open, non-sexist, non-racist society in which all people will be free to develop to their full potential. Historically, women's contributions have been fundamental to the development of our society and yet continue to be undervalued. Women have not been treated as equal members of society, distorting self-perceptions and all human relationships. Women's liberty is severely restricted by the ever-present threat of violence. We reject the acceptance of violence as normal in male-female relationships.

190. The Citizens Party opposes the use of sex, class and race as obstacles to the enjoyment of a decent income, good housing, adequate diet and medical care, and the development of one's full potential.

Therefore, we support policies which provide:

191. Affordable quality childcare for all.

192. Better distribution of childcare facilities, including childcare in workplaces.

193. Childcare facilities governed by parents and workers.

194. In a society where leadership is almost exclusively male, we support active efforts, including quotas, to create opportunities for full participation for women.

195. Rape is an act of violence. We support programs which provide strong, effective measures to combat rape, including rape within marriage; active reform of existing rape laws (including enlargement beyond traditional legal concepts the circumstances under which the crime is considered to have occurred); and legal and medical support for rape victims.

196. At least one out of four women is physically beaten by a male partner. We must provide help for battered families, including legal resources, psychological counseling, and accessible centers and programs which aid women in achieving freedom from economic dependence on men.

197. We support school programs which train women to defend themselves against rape.

198. We support transportation systems which would provide greater safety and freedom of movement for women.

199. We oppose sexual harassment on the job, in schools and in prisons.

200. We oppose the portrayal of women as sex objects and victims in the media.

201. Women must have full access to jobs at all levels in a full-employment economy.

202. Women and men must receive equal pay for work of comparable value.

203. We support the organization of women workers at all levels, among all groups (including domestic workers, who suffer from exclusion from minimum wage standards).

204. We support strong, effective affirmative action programs, including programs within unions, to bring about full representation of women.

205. We support on-the-job training and employment training programs for the unemployed.

206. We support strong occupational safety and health standards, and condemn the practice of exposing workers to deadly toxins. We oppose any corporate or government attempts to avoid cleaning up workplace hazards to male and female reproductive abilities by excluding women from high-paying industrial jobs or forcing them to be sterilized.

207. We call for the recognition of volunteer work as job experience.

208. Job discrimination against women with children must be eliminated, and we therefore propose such programs as flexible work hours, workplace childcare and part-time employment at all job levels.

209. Social Security and pension benefits for single and married people should be equalized. People not previously covered by such benefits, including homemakers, should be included.

210. Safe, effective, low-cost contraception and abortion (including federal funding for abortion, as for other health care needs, for public assistance recipients) must be available.

211. We call for an end to sterilization abuse, and the development and enforcement of guidelines requiring informed consent for sterilization.

212. We favor sex education and educational programs for parenting.

213. We support programs offering pregnancy, maternity and paternity benefits.

214. We support the decriminalization of prostitution.

215. We support protection of the rights of women prisoners.

216. We support the ratification of the Equal Rights Amendment, and the adoption and implementation, at all levels of government, of programs and policies consistent with the proposed Amendment.

BLACK AMERICANS

217. The most pervasive social and political issue confronting American society is racism. The struggle for democracy has been continuously and systematically frustrated by racist assumptions and practices which affect every institution of American life. This dynamic is the basis of the oppression of Black Americans and other minorities, as well as the means by which an overwhelming majority of Whites also lose in the quest for democratic governance.

218. Racism has prevented working people from developing a common conception of their condition and moving to realize their common social and political interests. The profits derived from the oppression of Blacks and other minorities and the exploitation of White workers have contributed to the corporate domination of American life.

219. The Citizens Party recognizes that the rights and gains made by Black Americans over the last quarter-century in court decisions, legislation, policies and procedures have not produced economic and political equality for Blacks.

We pledge to:

220. Pursue, as a paramount goal, the just and equitable redistribution of wealth and power in this country, insuring that the lives of Black Americans reflect this redistribution.

221. Pursue full employment to assure jobs for everyone willing and able to work, with special em-

phasis on programs for younger Black and minority workers.

222. Support the full implementation of affirmative action programs in both public and private sectors of the economy.

223. Respect, defend and support the culture and institutions of Black communities which nurture and promote self-pride, self-determination and Black consciousness.

224. Support policies, legislation and procedures which prohibit discrimination in housing. We also support legislation and practices that end the displacement of minorities and poor people in our urban areas.

225. Support the desegregation of the educational system.

Hispanic Rights

226. The historic presence of Hispanic peoples in the United States has been heightened in recent years by the migration of Mexicans, Puerto Ricans, Cubans and other Latin Americans.

227. Much of America is becoming a bilingual society. In regions of the country where Hispanic people live in substantial numbers, the Citizens Party supports bilingual, bicultural education, and the publication of government documents in both Spanish and English.

228. We deplore the treatment of undocumented immigrants and the exploitation of migrant workers, many of whom are Hispanic. We favor the enactment of legislation to protect all people living within the boundaries of the United States against unjust and exploitative treatment.

229. We advocate the rigorous enforcement of all civil rights statutes on behalf of Hispanics who are victims of unlawful discrimination and segregation.

230. We support self-determination for the Puerto Rican people, and pledge to abide by any decision they make democratically with respect to statehood, independence or commonwealth status.

231. Sin Fronteras—No Borders. Open up the United States border. Abolish the Texas Rangers, the Border Patrol, the Immigration authority. Stop the arbitrary, brutal and racist treatment of Mexican people and Mexican Americans.

Native American Rights

232. Honor the historic, legal and moral commitment of the people and government of the United States to their treaty agreements with Native American peoples.

233. Restore to Native American nations their rights to self-determination and self-government, independent of Washington-based bureaucracies. However, hold the appropriate government agencies responsible and accountable for honoring their trust responsibly and respecting the right of tribal nations to exercise their rights of self-determination and self-government.

234. Establish a permanent Native American Treaty Review Commission to arbitrate and mediate all disputes between Native American peoples and non-Indian political entities, and also those occurring among disputing parties within Native American communities.

235. To Native American peoples Mother Earth is sacred. End the desecration of this sacred Mother Earth. End the exploitation of natural resources on Native American lands by private and public companies, and the destruction and pollution of those lands by mining and waste-dumping practices. Honor the right of Native American nations to protect their Mother Earth in the best interests of their peoples.

236. Vigorously protect the rights of Native American people to participate in and celebrate their own cultures. Terminate once and for all those practices which contribute to the destruction of the cultures of Native American peoples.

237. We assert the inviolable right of all people to be free from incarceration or execution on the basis of their political beliefs.

238. Make available health care of the quality necessary to compensate for and restore the health of all Native American persons who have been victimized by waste dumping, unhealthy working conditions and environmental pollution caused by public and private corporations which have imposed these predicaments on or near Native American lands.

Welfare Rights

239. The problems of the present welfare system are reflections of the maldistribution of wealth and power in our society. The Citizens Party program for restructuring the economy and the health care system is aimed at more effectively meeting the human needs of all Americans and reducing the need for welfare programs.

240. The Citizens Party believes the overwhelming majority of poor people prefer a job to welfare, including the elderly, the disabled and parents with children. We are committed to providing a decent job at living wages for every American who is able and willing to work, and a guaranteed minimum income for those who are unable to work.

241. Until full employment and a guaranteed income are achieved, the Citizens Party proposes to pro-

ceed conservatively with welfare reforms. During the transition, the primary purpose of welfare should be to provide the basic necessities: income adequate to purchase food, shelter, clothing, health care and transportation.

242. We support policies to increase cash grant levels to a federally defined minimum standard higher than the present, inadequate "poverty line."

243. Welfare payments should be provided through procedures that are simple; require a minimum of intrusion into people's lives; and convey that welfare is a right under law, equitably available to all.

244. We support a federally financed General Assistance category to aid those not meeting the AFDC and SSI requirements.

[Paragraph 245 was not approved.]

246. We support wage supplements to low income workers who earn less than a living wage.

247. We support establishing unemployment or underemployment of either parent as eligibility factors for welfare in all states, and insuring that all rules and regulations are clearly aimed at encouraging and supporting efforts to work and creating and maintaining families.

248. The Citizens Party deplores the stigmatization of welfare recipients as unproductive members of society, and calls for public education about the rights of people to receive welfare.

YOUTH RIGHTS

249. The Citizens Party affirms the young people of America as a capable and vital force with important contributions to make to all aspects of society. We support their right to influence decisions that affect them.

250. We reject peacetime registration and the draft, and all forms of compulsory national civilian service for youth.

251. We call for supporting and expanding important social programs for youth such as family planning, drug abuse prevention and rehabilitation, halfway houses, vocational and general counseling, daycare centers, infant and toddler programs, extracurricular activities, safe playgrounds, and programs meeting special health needs of young people.

252. We support emphasis of the rehabilitative and nonpunitive functions of the juvenile justice system.

253. We affirm the right of children to be free from emotional, physical and sexual abuse by their parents, relatives and other adults.

254. We recommend appointment of a commission to study the arbitrary nature of the legal and social distinctions between the ages of minority and majority, and examine their implications for the issues of "status offenses."

255. We encourage the portrayal of youth contributions to and achievements in the arts and sciences, politics and social change movements.

256. We support the right to work for all youth by providing jobs and job training where necessary.

257. We affirm the right of young people to a quality education, regardless of economic conditions.

258. We support efforts that actively foster interaction between people of different ages, and reject age discrimination.

259. We support removal of all children from adult jails and prisons.

260. We demand that involuntary commitment of young people to mental institutions not occur without due process.

FREEDOM OF SEXUAL PREFERENCE

261. Millions of people are subject to severe social, economic, psychological and legal oppression because of their sexual orientation. We recognize that all people have the right to define and express their own sexuality.

262. We call for insurance of the rights of all people striving for freedom of choice in sexual expression to full participation in the social, political and economic life of the country, without fear of prejudice or reprisals based on sexual orientation.

263. The ultimate invasion of the dignity of human beings by government is to intrude on their private sexual lives. We support repeal of all laws covering private sexual conduct between consenting adults when no harm to others is suffered or threatened, and release of all those now incarcerated under such laws.

264. We support adoption of legislation to prohibit discrimination in housing, employment, public accommodations and public services, where such discrimination is based on sexual orientation.

265. We support a ban, by executive order, of discrimination based on sexual orientation in the federal government, the military and federally contracted private employment.

266. The military should be prohibited from using other-than-honorable discharges for homosexuality, and should upgrade to fully honorable all discharges previously issued for homosexuality.

267. Discrimination based on sexual orientation and marital status in child custody, adoption and inheritance cases should be ended.

268. The banning of homosexuals from entry and immigration into the United States should be ended.

269. Work to eliminate biased attitudes against gay men and lesbians which occur in public programs, including public schools.

ELDERLY RIGHTS

270. Our older citizens have special problems. All Americans need to work together to enhance and prolong the independent life of older citizens and make it less difficult for them to participate in the social, economic and political life of our nation.

In so doing, we must recognize that:

271. Most elderly Americans are well and relatively few need institutional care.

272. The family is the primary helper of its older members and should be aided in caring for the infirm elderly.

273. At a time when the dehumanizing consequences of institutionalization are beginning to be recognized for the young, the mentally ill and the criminal population, warehousing is increasing for the elderly. This prevents elderly Americans from participating in the life of the nation and deprives society of their experience and wisdom.

Therefore, we recommend:

274. Seating elderly citizens on boards of agencies and of programs affecting their lives, including health care.

[Paragraph 275 was not ratified.]

276. That programs for the elderly seek the advice of organized senior citizen groups and of professional organizations which have addressed themselves to these causes.

The Citizens Party also recommends that we:

277. Guarantee adequate income to every elderly citizen and support the right to a part or full time job, and to job training.

278. Discourage mandatory retirement age rules.

279. Work for community support systems that prolong independent living for the elderly, such as self-help programs, homemaker services, hot meal deliveries, security checks, escorted shopping, accessible transportation, recreation and education.

280. Support short-term and emergency care to prevent a loss of independence because of temporary illness and disability.

281. To the extent possible, government programs should not segregate people according to age.

282. In this area of national life, as in so many others, we must not fall victim to destructive stereotypes.

DISABLED RIGHTS

283. Disabled persons, both physically and mentally, are subjected daily to blatant forms of discrimination which prevent them from full participation in society. Through institutionalization and other forms of discrimination, federal, state and local governments invest large sums of money to prevent handicapped persons from contributing to society. The attitudinal and legal barriers of society constitute the greatest disabling condition of handicapped people.

284. The Citizens Party recognizes that the struggle of disabled persons to achieve full participation in the social, political and economic life of our society is, in very real terms, a civil rights movement. We advocate the inclusion of disabled persons as a protected class under the Civil Rights Act of 1964.

285. We advocate full implementation of all sections of the 1973 Rehabilitation Act as amended in 1978.

286. We support the removal of all of the provisions of the Social Security Act which prevent disabled persons from engaging in substantial gainful employment.

287. We support reform of the Supplemental Security Income program to provide disabled persons unable to work with a decent standard of living, and advocate the extension of this coverage to disabled children.

288. We endorse increased funding for community-based supportive services which promote independent living for disabled persons.

289. We are committed to full accessibility for disabled persons and believe that meaningful accessibility is achieved only when transportation and communication barriers are removed along with architectural barriers.

VIETNAM VETERANS

The Citizens Party believes the nation has a responsibility to:

290. Correct long-standing inadequacies in Vietnam veteran benefits in employment, health and education.

291. Extend indefinitely the period of time within which GI educational benefits can be claimed.

292. Support readjustment counseling and other mental health services for Vietnam veterans and their families in community health centers, in addition to existing VA programs.

293. Support the presumption that any Vietnam veteran who was exposed to Agent Orange or other chemical agents, and presents specific symptoms, was disabled by service-related causes and is entitled to compensation.

294. Expand training and career development programs for Vietnam veterans.

295. Support redress of actions based on racism in the military, such as less-than-honorable discharges for minor infractions.

296. Support an end to all destruction of military records of veterans.

[Paragraph 297 was rejected.]

298. End discriminatory employment practices against Vietnam veterans.

299. Review records of all Vietnam veterans in prison or on parole, whose incarceration may stem from service-related psychological or drug abuse problems.

MEDIA AND COMMUNICATIONS

300. Free and independent media (press, radio, television, etc.) are necessary to insure a well-informed and responsible citizenry and are essential to democratic governance.

301. Independent and competitive news reporting and diversity in programming have been crippled by concentration of corporate power in the media. Large media empires have grown through mergers and acquisitions; manufacturing and financial conglomerates are continually acquiring radio and television stations and publishing companies; and corporations further dominate popular culture through advertising.

Therefore, the Citizens Party supports policies which:

302. Encourage wide diversity in media offerings.

303. Promote technologies which make competing entertainments and viewpoints widely available at low cost.

304. Root out all forms of censorship by government and advertisers, specifically including those which suppress unpopular minority viewpoints or cultural expressions.

305. Significantly expand public and local access, affirmative action and citizen participation in programming decisions of broadcasters and cable programmers.

306. Protect the right of reporters, publications and broadcasters to disseminate information to which they have access, so long as they do not infringe on the privacy rights of individuals; and protect their right to keep their files and information sources confidential.

307. The Citizens Party deplores the use by the media of negative stereotyping of people on the basis of their race, sex, age, sexual preference, marital status, ethnic or national origin, etc.

ARTS AND CULTURE

308. The Citizens Party recognizes that, in an impersonal industrial society such as ours, art is more important than ever, for it enriches the mind and spirit and heart in essential ways that counter the sterility of the corporate state. Thus, art in its many forms must be available to all.

309. We are committed to foster participation in the creation and experience of art and other cultural activities as a basic human right, access to which shall not be denied on the basis of income, class, age, disability, sex, race, ethnic or regional background, or political belief.

310. The governing boards of all artistic and cultural organizations aided by public funds should be constituted so that qualified professionals and representative members of the community exercise effective control over policy. When federal funds are involved, policies should be consistent with general national guidelines intended to assure quality and necessary economy, not uniformity of methodology or taste. Although private support should be welcomed as well, it must never be allowed to control policy.

SPORTS AND RECREATION

311. The Citizens Party supports sports and recreation policies which assure that participation in sports and recreational activities is encouraged and is available to every citizen without prejudice as to age, sex, race, income or disability.

312. Currently existing sports franchises must be considered the same as other private corporations, and are subject to all Citizens Party policy on private corporate conduct. We support public control of sports franchises using facilities built with public funds.

313. We further support policies which insure that the poorest neighborhoods have public recreational facilities and opportunities to participate in sports and recreation equal to those in wealthy neighborhoods.

314. We support assuring that the elderly have the opportunity to enjoy parks free of fear, and to participate in sports programs geared to their needs.

315. We support insuring that women have the opportunity to participate in all recreational and competitive programs available to men, and have equal access to all facilities.

316. We encourage universities to insure that athletes whom they recruit for their teams are given needed supportive services, encouraged to earn degrees, and acquire substantial academic skills.

317. We encourage creation of cooperatives and consortia to promote community recreation.

STATEHOOD FOR THE DISTRICT OF COLUMBIA

The Citizens Party will support efforts to:

318. Extend full constitutional rights to all United States citizens residing in the District of Columbia.

319. Support the rights of citizens of the District of

Columbia to self-governance under the Constitution.

320. Support a constitutional amendment which would grant statehood to the District of Columbia.

321. End taxation without representation for Washington, D.C. residents, and insure their right to elect voting representatives to the U.S. Senate and House of Representatives.

322. Distribute equally to all citizens of the Union the burden of supporting federal property and activity in the District of Columbia.

Communist Platform 1980

A PEOPLE'S PROGRAM . . .

1. Ratify Salt II, End the Arms Race

Peace is crucial. A new war would mean nuclear holocaust. Therefore we must normalize relations with the Soviet Union, restore detente and negotiate mutual arms reduction. Cut the U.S. military budget by $100 billion and transfer the funds to domestic needs. End the blockade of Cuba. Independence for Puerto Rico.

2. Jobs for All. Stop Plant Closings

Enact the 6-hour day with no cut in pay, no speed-up or forced overtime. Federal takeover of closed factories under democratic trade union and community control. Convert these plants to useful production. An emergency government program to create new jobs. Raise unemployment compensation to 75 percent of prevailing wage.

3. A Labor Bill of Rights

Pass the Labor Reform Bill. Repeal Taft-Hartley and Landrum-Griffin Acts. End all restrictions on the right to organize and strike. Affirmative action programs at all levels of hiring, training and upgrading. Full rights for all foreign-born workers with or without documents.

4. Defend Farm Workers and Family Farmers

Full civil and trade union rights for farm workers. Government guaranteed low-interest loans, free crop insurance and 100 percent parity prices for family farm operators. End trade restrictions and embargoes against socialist and developing countries.

5. Fight Racism, Defend Democratic Rights

Take emergency measures to enforce civil rights laws and genuine affirmative action programs in employment, housing, education, health care and political representation. Make racist acts a criminal offense. Outlaw the KKK and Nazis. Defeat S. 1722 — the repressive anti-labor federal criminal code bill. Outlaw the death penalty. Padlock the CIA and FBI. Guarantee equal access to the ballot and the mass media for independent candidates and political parties.

6. Raise Family Living Standards

End all taxes on first $25,000 of family income. Guarantee $15,000 minimum income for family of four. No evictions or forced repossessions. No shutoff of utilities for families unable to pay.

7. Full Equality for Women

Pass the Equal Rights Amendment. Equal pay for comparable work. Prosecute employers who discriminate in hiring and upgrading or who harass women on the job. Federally funded, comprehensive child care accessible to all. Safe, affordable family planning and abortion. No involuntary sterilization. Full representation of women at all levels of government.

8. Fight for the Needs of Youth

Pass a National Youth Act to provide jobs, education and training, cultural and recreational opportunities for young people. No military registration, no draft. Free education through college. Unemployment compensation for first-job seekers.

9. Strengthen the Rights of Senior Citizens

Increase social security payments to meet inflationary living costs. No taxes on social security income. Free public transportation for seniors. Special aid on rent, utilities and mortgages for the needy. Reduce Medicare deductible to zero. Remove restrictions on seniors' jobs.

10. Health Care — A Human Right

Pass a National Health Act to provide free comprehensive quality health care for all as a basic human right. Public ownership of the health care industry.

Stop hospital closings. Expand public health facilities. Strengthen and enforce the Occupational Safety and Health Act (OSHA).

11. Clean The Environment

Force the monopolies to pay the costs to clean up our air, water and land. Strengthen and enforce anti-pollution standards. Full compensation to victims of pollution, at corporate expense.

12. Nationalize the Energy Industry

Put the oil monopolies and all energy production under public ownership. Stop price rip-offs. Federal support for alternative energy sources. Close all nuclear plants until independent scientist-consumer-trade union committees decide they are safe to operate.

Democratic Platform 1980

PREAMBLE

In its third century, America faces great challenges and an uncertain future. The decade that America now enters presents us with decisions as monumental and fundamental as those we faced during the Civil War, during two World Wars, and during the Great Depression. Our current task is different from each of these historic challenges. But in many ways the challenge is the same: to marshall the talents and spirit of the American people, to harness our enormous resources, and to face the future with confidence and hope.

The task now before us is as global as the worldwide energy shortage, and as local as the plight of children in Appalachia. It reaches from the condition of older Eastern cities and the industries of the snowbelt, to the complex new demands of our sunbelt region and the special needs of our Western states. It is as basic as the entitlement of minorities and women to real equality in every aspect of the nation's life. It is as immediate as the refugee crisis in Miami and the natural disaster at Mount St. Helens. It is as futuristic as the exploration of space and the oceans. It is as idealistic as the spirit of liberty which imbues our Constitution. It requires nothing less than a continued dedication to Democratic principles by each element in our society — government, business, labor, and every citizen — to the promise and potential of our nation.

We live in a time when effective policy requires an understanding of the web of competing values and interests which exist in our country. We must combine compassion with self-discipline. We must forego simplistic answers for long-term solutions to our problems.

With the Republican leadership closing its eyes to the realities of our time and running for the Presidency on a program of the easy answer, of the pleasant-sounding political promise, it is time to take a page from Adlai Stevenson's 1952 presidential campaign — it is time "to talk sense to the American people." It is time to talk bluntly and candidly about our problems and our proposed solutions; to face up to our problems and respond to them.

If we fail in this important task . . . if we fail to lay the issues squarely before the American people, we could well allow the federal government to revert to four years of Republicanism — neglect of the poor and disadvantaged, disdain for working men and women, compassion only for the rich and the privileged, failure to meet the challenges of energy, inflation and unemployment, and a breakdown of the partnership among local, state and federal governments. We as Democrats must not let this happen.

After nearly four years in office, we Democrats have not solved all of America's problems.

Most of these problems we inherited. Eight years of Republican politics left this nation weak, rudderless, unrespected and deeply divided.

As a result of this legacy, despite our progress, inflation still erodes the standard of living of every American.

As a result of this legacy, despite our progress, too many Americans are out of work.

As a result of this legacy, despite our progress, complete equality for all citizens has yet to be achieved.

As a result of this legacy, despite our progress, we still live in a very dangerous world, where competing ideologies and age-old animosities daily threaten the peace.

As a result of this legacy, our nation is still subject to the oil pricing and production decisions of foreign countries.

We will not run from these problems, nor will we fail. The record of the past four years is a testament to what the Democrats can do working together.

Time and time again in these past four years, a Democratic Congress and a Democratic President proved that they were willing to make the tough decisions.

Today, because of that Democratic partnership, we are a stronger nation.

Today, because of that Democratic partnership, we are at peace.

Today, because of that Democratic partnership, we are a more just nation.

Today, because of that Democratic partnership, honor and truth and integrity have been restored to our government and to our political process.

And so this party looks to the future with determination and confidence.

We have been and we shall remain the party of all Americans. We seek solutions that not only meet the needs of the many, but reaffirm our commitment to improve the conditions of the least fortunate in our society.

In this platform we offer programs and solutions that represent our dedication to Democratic principles. They define a spirit as well as a program . . . a set of beliefs as well as a set of ideas. Time and events may alter their priority or prospects. But nothing will alter the defining spirit and values of the Democratic Party.

The platform of the Democratic Party is a contract with the people. We believe that accountability for Democratic principles goes hand in hand with dedication to those principles. The Democratic Party is proud of its historic heritage of commitment to the people of America. Fulfilling this platform will permit us to keep faith with that tradition.

CHAPTER I: THE ECONOMY

A Commitment to Economic Fairness

The Democratic Party will take no action whose effect will be a significant increase in unemployment — no fiscal action, no monetary action, no budgetary action — if it is the assessment of either the Council of Economic Advisers or the Congressional Budget Office that such action will cause significantly greater unemployment.

In all of our economic programs, the one overriding principle must be fairness. All Americans must bear a fair share of our economic burdens and reap a fair share of our economic benefits. High interest rates impose an unfair burden — on farmers, small businesses, and younger families buying homes. Recession imposes an unfair burden on those least able to bear it. Democratic economic policy must assure fairness for workers, the elderly, women, the poor, minorities and the majority who are middle income Americans. In 1980, we pledge a truly Democratic economic policy to secure a prosperous economic future.

ECONOMIC STRENGTH

While the past three and a half years of Democratic leadership have been years of growth for our economy, we now find ourselves in a recession.

The Democratic Party is committed to taking the necessary steps to combat the current recession. However, we cannot abandon our fight against inflation. We must fight both of these problems at the same time; we are committed to do so. We will continue to pursue the fight against inflation in ways not designed or intended to increase unemployment.

Our current economic situation is unique. In 1977, we inherited a severe recession from the Republicans. The Democratic Administration and the Democratic Congress acted quickly to reduce the unacceptably high levels of unemployment and to stimulate the economy. And we succeeded. We recovered from that deep recession and our economy was strengthened and revitalized. As that fight was won, the enormous increases in foreign oil prices — 120 percent last year — and declining productivity fueled an inflationary spiral that also had to be fought. The Democrats did that, and inflation has begun to recede. In working to combat these dual problems, significant economic actions have been taken.

Two tax cuts have been enacted, in 1977 and 1978, reducing taxes on individuals and businesses by an amount equal, this year, to about $40 billion.

While meeting our national security and pressing domestic needs, the Democratic Partnership has restrained the increase in government spending in ways which have steadily reduced the deficit we inherited.

Airline and banking regulatory reforms have been enacted; further regulatory reforms are now under consideration.

In the effort to restrain inflation, a voluntary pay advisory committee has been established with labor, business, and public representatives pursuant to a National Accord.

The first national export policy was developed; export and trade responsibilities were reorganized and strengthened; the Multilateral Trade Negotiations were completed; and the MTN Agreement was approved by the Congress.

To ensure a greater impact for scarce federal dollars, grant and loan programs have been redirected to the areas of greatest need, and the formula programs have been redesigned to *target* the areas with the most serious problems.

As a result of these economic actions:

Employment — More than 8.5 million new jobs have

been added to the workforce; about 1 million of those jobs are held by Blacks, and nearly an additional 1 million are held by Hispanics. Gains have been made by all groups—more men, more women, more minorities, and more young people are working than ever before in our history. Despite these gains, current unemployment is too high and must be lowered.

Inflation—A strong anti-inflation program has been initiated and pursued aggressively, to deal both with the short-term inflation problem and with the long-term causes of inflation. The effects of the short-term effort are now evident: inflation is beginning to come down. Although some interest rates remain high, they are falling at record rates. This progress will continue as short-term actions continue to work and long-term initiatives begin to take hold.

Economic Growth—Despite the economic declines of the past few months, for the first three years of the Carter Administration our economy was strong. For the 1977-1979 period:

—Gross National Product increased by 11.8 percent in real terms.

—Real after-tax income per person increased by 10.3 percent.

—Industrial production increased by 14.8 percent.

—Dividends increased by 36 percent.

—Real business fixed investment increased by 22.9 percent.

Energy—Our dependence on foreign oil has decreased—in 1977 we imported 8.8 million barrels of oil per day, and our nation is now importing approximately 6.5 million per day, a decline of 26 percent.

Solving Economic Problems

The Democratic Party commits itself to a strong economic program—one that builds on the progress we have made to date, one that corrects the very real problems we face now, one that is responsible, one that offers realistic hope, and one that can unify our Party. Such a Democratic program would contrast dramatically with the simplistic rhetoric and the traditional economic policies of the Republican Party.

Full Employment—We specifically reaffirm our commitment to achieve all the goals of the Humphrey-Hawkins Full Employment Act within the currently prescribed dates in the Act, especially those relating to a joint reduction in unemployment and inflation. Full employment is important to the achievement of a rising standard of living, to the pursuit of sound justice, and to the strength and vitality of America.

Anti-Recession Assistance—Immediately, we must undertake a short-term anti-recession program to reverse the tide of deepening recession and rising unemployment. Each percentage point increase in the unemployment rate adds $25 billion to the federal deficit.

A Democratic anti-recession program must recognize that Blacks, Hispanics, other minorities, women and older workers bear the brunt of recession. We pledge a $12 billion anti-recession jobs program, providing at least 800,000 additional jobs, including full funding of the counter-cyclical assistance program for the cities, a major expansion of the youth employment and training program to give young people in our inner cities new hope, expanded training programs for women and displaced homemakers to give these workers a fair chance in the workplace, and new opportunities for the elderly to contribute their talents and skills.

Coupling our need to rehabilitate our railroads with the need to create new job opportunities, we must commit ourselves to a $1 billion railroad renewal program which can employ 20,000 workers.

We must take steps to restore the housing industry, including effective implementation of the Brooke-Cranston program, and the addition of 200,000 new units a year for low and moderate income families.

National Accord—The National Accord with labor must be strengthened and continued. This enhances the unique opportunity afforded by a Democratic Administration for government, labor and business to work together to solve our inflationary and other economic problems.

Tax Reductions—We commit ourselves to targeted tax reductions designed to stimulate production and combat recession as soon as it appears so that tax reductions will not have a disproportionately inflationary effect. We must avoid untargeted tax cuts which would increase inflation. Any tax reduction must, if it is to help solve pressing economic problems, follow certain guiding principles:

—The inflationary impact must be minimized;

—Reductions provided to individuals must be weighted to help low and middle income individuals and families, to improve consumer purchasing power, and to enhance a growing economy while maintaining and strengthening the overall progressive nature of the tax code;

—Productivity, investment, capital formation, as well as incentives, must be encouraged, particularly in distressed areas and industries;

— The effect on our economy must be one which encourages job formation and business growth.

Federal Spending — Spending restraint must be sensitive to those who look to the federal government for aid and assistance, especially to our nation's workers in times of high unemployment. At the same time, as long as inflationary pressures remain strong, fiscal prudence is essential to avoid destroying the progress made to date in reducing the inflation rate.

Fiscal policy must remain a flexible economic tool. We oppose a Constitutional amendment requiring a balanced budget.

Interest Rates — The Democratic Party has historically been committed to policies that result in low interest rates in order to help our nation's workers, small businesses, farmers and homeowners. Therefore, we must continue to pursue a tough anti-inflationary policy which will lead to an across-the-board reduction in interest rates on loans.

In using monetary policy to fight inflation, the government should be sensitive to the special needs of areas of our economy most affected by high interest rates. The Federal Reserve shall use the tool of reserve requirements creatively in its effort to fight inflation. The Federal Reserve should also take particular care to make certain that it is aware of the concerns of labor, agriculture, housing, consumers and small business in its decision-making process. Finally, its Open Market Committee should continue to provide regular information to the public about its activities.

Regulatory Reform — Consistent with our basic health, safety, and environmental goals, we must continue to deregulate over-regulated industries and to remove other unnecessary regulatory burdens on state and local governments and on the private sector, particularly those which inhibit competition.

Targeting and Regional Balance — From the time of Franklin Roosevelt, the Democratic Party has dedicated itself to the principle that the federal government has a duty to ensure that all regions, states and localities share in the benefits of national economic prosperity and that none bears more than its share of economic adversity.

Our 1976 platform stated: *Even during periods of normal economic growth there are communities and regions of the country — particularly central cities and urban areas — that do not fully participate in national economic prosperity. The Democratic Party has supported national economic policies which have conscientiously sought to aid regions in the nation which have been afflicted with poverty, or newer regions which have needed resources for development. These policies were soundly conceived and have been successful. Today, we have different areas and regions in economic decline and once again face a problem of balanced economic growth. To restore balance, national economic policy should be designed to target federal resources in areas of greatest need.*

A Democratic Administration has welcomed and encouraged the sustained growth of the West and Southwest in recent years. Policies now in place ensure that this growth will continue and bring the greatest benefits to the nation as a whole.

At the same time, a Democratic Administration will be committed to the economic growth and prosperity of the other regions of the nation. The era of federal policies directed exclusively to the development of one region or another should be succeeded by government-wide policies designed to bring about balanced and shared growth in all regions.

To restore balance, we must continue to improve the targeting of federal programs in order to maximize their benefit to those most in need. To involve the private sector in solving our economic problems, and to reduce the burden on government, we must leverage federal dollars with funds from the private sector.

Rebuilding American Industry by Increasing Economic Productivity and Competitiveness — The Democratic Party has a long tradition of innovation, foresight, and flexibility in creating policies to solve the nation's most urgent economic needs. We now stand at another watershed in our economic history which demands our Party's full attention, creative powers, resources, and skills. To revive productivity and revitalize our economy, we need a national effort to strengthen the American economy. It must include new tax depreciation rules to stimulate selective capital investment; a simplified tax code to assist business planning; removal of governmental regulations which are unnecessary and stifle business initiative; effective incentives for saving that do not discriminate against low and middle income taxpayers; reform in patent rules and new incentives for research and development, especially by small business; cooperative efforts with labor and management to retool the steel, auto and shipbuilding industries; and strengthened worker training programs to improve job opportunities and working skills.

Encouraging investment, innovation, efficiency and downward pressure on prices also requires new measures to increase competition in our economy. In regulated sectors of our economy, government serves too often to entrench high price levels and stifle competition. Regulations must balance protective benefits against potentially adverse effects on competitiveness. Necessary regulations should be achieved at minimum cost and at reduced burden to industry. In unregulated sectors of the economy, we must increase antitrust enforcement; greatly improve the speed and efficiency of antitrust litigation; and renew efforts to prevent the concentration of economic power—both in specific industries and across the economy as a whole—which operate to stifle growth and to fuel inflation.

United States non-farm exports have risen 50 percent in real terms in the last three years. A Democratic President and a Democratic Congress have recognized and strengthened the export trade functions of the federal government. To create new markets for American products and strengthen the dollar, we must seek out new opportunities for American exports; help establish stable, long-term commercial relationships between nations; offer technical assistance to firms competing in world markets; promote reciprocal trading terms for nations doing business here; and help ensure that America's domestic retooling is consistent with new opportunities in foreign trade.

One of our main goals in this effort will be to enable American industry to compete more effectively with foreign products. We must intensify our efforts to promote American exports and to ensure that our domestic industries and workers are not affected adversely by unfair trade practices, such as dumping. We must make international trade a major focus of our domestic and international policy. We will continue to support the development of trading companies which will compete more effectively in world markets. We must ensure that our efforts to lower tariff barriers are reciprocated by our trading partners. We recognize the superior productivity of American agriculture and the importance of agricultural exports to the balance of trade. We support continuing efforts to promote agricultural exports.

ENSURING ECONOMIC EQUITY

Budget

The budget policy that has been put forth by the Democratic Party traditionally has been based on providing adequate federal resources to meet our nation's urgent needs. The current Democratic Partnership has continued that tradition while restraining the growth of the federal budget.

We have increased support for vital domestic programs. We have increased funding for education by 75 percent over the Ford budget. We have increased Head Start by 73 percent, basic skills programs by 233 percent, bilingual education by 113 percent, Native American education by 124 percent, summer jobs by 66 percent, Job Corps by 157 percent, employment and training programs by 115 percent, Medicare by 54 percent, National Health Service Corps by 179 percent, Child Nutrition by 43 percent, and Women, Infants and Children (WIC) Program by 300 percent.

We have been able to do this, while restraining the growth in federal spending, because the country has had a growing economy; tax cuts have been moderate; waste and fraud have been reduced; and aid has been targeted to those most in need.

International events have required increased defense spending. The Soviet challenge cannot be ignored. We have had to reverse the steady decline in defense spending that occurred under the Republican Administration. A Democratic Administration and a Democratic Congress have done this; real defense spending has increased, in part through the elimination of waste and the emphasis on increased efficiency.

In the eight years preceding the first Carter budget, real federal spending had been growing at an average rate of 3 percent each year. By contrast, between FY 1978 and 1981, real federal spending will have declined at an average annual rate of 0.6 percent.

The federal budget has not been and must not be permitted to be an inflationary nor a recessionary force in our economy, but it also must not be permitted to ignore pressing human needs.

We support the discipline of attempting to live within the limits of our anticipated revenues. Government must set the example of fiscal responsibility for all our citizens who are helping in the fight against inflation. Spending discipline allows us to concentrate our resources to meet our most pressing human needs.

We as Democrats will continue our policy of opposing drastic cuts in social programs which impose unfair burdens on the poor and the aged, on women, on children and on minorities. We have always opposed and will continue to oppose imposition of ever greater burdens on the poor, who can least afford them.

We also recommit ourselves to operating our government more efficiently, and concentrating our efforts on eliminating waste, fraud, and abuse in government programs to make our tax dollars go further.

Worker Protection

The Democratic Administration has worked with Congress to take actions which protect our nation's workers from declining incomes, unsafe working conditions, and threats to their basic rights. The Democratic Party will not pursue a policy of high interest rates and unemployment as the means to fight inflation. We will take no action whose effect will be a significant increase in unemployment, no fiscal action, no monetary action, no budgetary action. The Democratic Party remains committed to policies that will not produce high interest rates or high unemployment.

But much more needs to be done to protect our nation's workers. The Democratic Party has a long and proud tradition in this area and we must pledge to continue our efforts over the next four years.

Over a generation ago this nation established a labor policy whose purpose is to encourage the practice and procedure of collective bargaining and the right of workers to organize to obtain this goal. The Democratic Party is committed to extending the benefit of this policy to all workers and to removing the barriers to its administration.

In the future the Democratic Party will concentrate on the following areas.

Our labor laws should be reformed to permit better administration and enforcement, and particularly to prevent the inordinate delays and *outright defiance* by some employers of our labor laws. We can no longer tolerate the fact that certain employers are willing to bear the cost of sanctions which are in our current laws in order to violate the rights of those attempting to organize.

OSHA protections should be properly administered, with the concern of the worker being the highest priority; legislative or administrative efforts to weaken OSHA's basic worker protection responsibilities are unacceptable. OSHA has significantly reduced workplace accidents and fatalities. We will not limit its scope for any reason, including the size of business, since all workers face significant workplace dangers. The Democratic Party strongly opposes and urges all actions to defeat legislation which weakens OSHA's critical protections.

Hatch Act reforms should be enacted to give federal workers their basic First Amendment rights. We must protect federal workers from interruptions in their pay due to delays in the federal appropriations process and must seek ways to assure the comparability of pay scales between the federal and private sectors.

We support the right of public employees and agricultural workers to organize and bargain collectively. We urge the adoption of appropriate federal legislation to ensure this goal.

Legislation must be enacted to allow building trades workers the same peaceful picketing rights currently afforded industrial workers.

All fair labor standards acts, such as the minimum wage and Davis-Bacon protections, must continue to be effectively enforced against employers seeking to circumvent their worker protections.

Section 14-b of the Taft-Hartley Act should be repealed.

Special assistance should be made available for unemployed workers in a distressed industry, such as the automobile, steel, and shipbuilding industries.

We must improve and strengthen our trade adjustment assistance programs.

We support federal legislation designed to give protection and human rights to those workers affected by plant closings.

Just as we must protect workers in their workplace, so must we protect them when they are disabled by accidents or sicknesses resulting from their work. The Democratic Party supports federal legislation to assure adequate minimum benefit levels to those who are unemployed, including expansion of coverage to all wage and salary workers and extended benefits for the long-term unemployed. It must not artificially disregard those who have already been unemployed for a long time.

We will continue to oppose a sub-minimum wage for youth and other workers and to support increases in the minimum wage so as to ensure an adequate income for all workers.

Small Business

The prosperity of small business is an important national priority. Over half of the major innovations in the past twenty years have come from firms with less than 1,000 employees, and technological innovation has accounted for nearly half of America's economic growth. Small firms have a cost-per-scientist or engineer half that of larger firms. Ninety-six percent of the six million jobs created in the private sector between 1968 and 1976 came from small businesses—primarily firms in business less than four years, employing less than 20 workers. In contrast, the biggest 500 manufacturing companies—accounting for 80 percent of national output—employed precisely the same number of workers in 1968 as they did in 1976.

Of course, larger firms may offer other economic benefits to society, but the contribution of small business is vital and unique, and no overall program for economic recovery will succeed unless it relies heavily on small businesses. For this reason, the Democratic Party commits itself to the first comprehensive program for small business in American history. That program will include the following measures.

A prompt review and response for the recommendations of the White House Conference on Small Business.

Legislation to transfer from the SBA to the Farmers Home Administration responsibility for providing loans to farmers in financial need.

Allocation of a fair percentage of federal research funds to small business.

Protection of small and independent businesses against takeover by giant conglomerates.

Continued efforts to end federal regulations which reinforce barriers to entry by new and small firms, and which thereby entrench the dominance of market leaders.

A review of regulations and requirements which impose unnecessary burdens upon smaller firms. Results should provide relief for smaller firms which now pay $12.7 billion a year to fill 850 million pages of government paperwork. We will adopt regulatory requirements to meet the needs of smaller firms, where such action will not interfere with the objectives of the regulation.

Minority Business

A Democratic Congress and a Democratic Administration have worked together to increase opportunities for minority businesses, which have suffered from inadequate capitalization. Enormous progress has been made in the last four years.

Federal procurement from minority-owned firms has increased by nearly two and a half times.

Federal deposits in minority-owned banks have already doubled.

Minority ownership of radio and television stations has increased by 65 percent.

Almost 15 percent of the funds spent under the Local Public Works Act went to minority-owned firms.

The Section 8(a) program operated by the Small Business Administration has been reformed and strengthened.

The Democratic Party pledges itself to advance minority businesses, including Black, Hispanic, Asian/Pacific Americans, Native Americans and other minorities to:

— Increase the overall level of support and the overall level of federal procurement so that minority groups will receive additional benefits and opportunities.

— Triple the 1980 level of federal procurement from minority-owned firms as we have tripled the 1977 levels in the past three years.

— Increase substantially the targeting of Small Business Administration loans to minority-owned businesses.

— Increase ownership of small businesses by minorities, especially in those areas which have traditionally been closed to minorities, such as communications and newspapers.

— Expand management, technical, and training assistance for minority firms, and strengthen minority capital development under the SBA's Minority Enterprise Small Business Investment Company (MESBIC) program.

— Establish a Minority Business Development Agency in the Department of Commerce under statutory mandate.

— Implement vigorously all set-aside provisions for minority businesses.

Women in Business

The Democrats have exercised effective leadership in the field of support to women-owned businesses. A national policy was developed to support women's business enterprises, and SBA created the first program to help women entrepreneurs. President Carter has issued an Executive Order creating a national women's business enterprise policy and prescribing arrangements for developing, coordinating, and implementing a national program for women's business enterprise.

Support of this program must be expanded through effective implementation of the Executive Order to ensure an equitable distribution of government prime and subcontracts to women business owners. Cabinet Secretaries and agency heads, working with the Office of Federal Procurement Policy, must monitor realistic goals established for the award of government business and financial support to women-owned businesses.

As the key office within the federal government for these programs, the Office of Women's Business Enterprise in SBA must be strengthened through adequate staffing and funding, and should receive continued emphasis by key White House and Office of Management and Budget personnel.

Women and The Economy

We pledge to secure the rights of working women, homemakers, minority women and elderly women to a fair share of our economy. A sound economy in the next four years is of vital importance to women, who are often at the bottom of the economic ladder. But if our economy is to be truly fair, additional steps are required to address the inequities that women now face.

Special attention must be paid to the employment needs of women. Today, women who can find work earn, on average, only fifty-nine cents for every dollar earned by men.

The Democratic Party, therefore, commits itself to strong steps to close the wage gap between men and women, to expand child care opportunities for families with working parents, to end the tax discrimination that penalizes married working couples, and to ensure that women can retire in dignity.

We will strictly enforce existing anti-discrimination laws with respect to hiring, pay and promotions. We will adopt a full employment policy, with increased possibilities for part-time work. Vocational programs for young women in our high schools and colleges will be equalized and expanded. Fields traditionally reserved for men . . . from construction to engineering

. . . must be opened to women, a goal which must be promoted through government incentives and federally sponsored training programs.

Perhaps most important, the Democratic Party is committed to the principle of equal pay for work of comparable value. Through new job classification studies by the Department of Labor, job reclassification by the Office of Personnel Management and new legislation from Congress if necessary, we will ensure that women in both the public and private sectors are not only paid equally for work which is identical to that performed by men, but are also paid equally for work which is of comparable value to that performed by men.

The Democratic Party must lead the way in ensuring that women and minorities are afforded real equality in the workforce, neither displacing the other. As the nation's single largest employer, the hiring and promotion practices of the federal government must set an example. Every branch of government will be mandated not only to hire qualified women and minorities, but also affirmatively to seek out able minorities and women within the government for training and promotion. Opportunities for part-time work will be expanded and pay equalized to reflect the value of the work which is done.

Economic Inequities Facing Minorities

We must expand jobs and job training including apprenticeship training programs for those who have special problems — groups such as the young, veterans, older workers, minorities, those with limited fluency in English, and the handicapped. The Democratic Party pledges that anyone who wants to learn the skills necessary to secure a job will be able to do so.

We also must improve the quality of the programs designed to help the structurally unemployed. We must give trainees a better sense of what work will be like, assure a higher level of training, and undertake greater efforts to place people in jobs and help them adjust to the world of work. We should explore several methods for making such improvements, including performance funding. More money should go to those training programs which prove most successful. Particular emphasis should be given to training programs run by community-based organizations which have a superior record of success.

Where public agencies have trouble reaching those who seem unemployable, and where the training they provide is not effective, we should assist business to provide that training. We should ensure that business is not paid merely for hiring those that would be hired anyway, and that federal subsidies are truly training subsidies and not disguised wage subsidies.

A major effort must be undertaken to address youth employment. Half the unemployed are under twenty-five. Teenage inner city unemployment is at disastrous levels of 50 percent or higher. The problem is one of both employment and employability — a lack of jobs and a lack of skills.

We need new combinations of work experience and training for young people, new links between schools and the workplace, new ways to reach out to those who are out of school and out of work, but who have special need for skill development and job experience.

Consumer Protection

Since the first administration of Franklin Roosevelt, the Democratic Party has stood as the Party which championed consumer rights. It is our tradition to support and enact policies which guarantee that the consumer is sovereign in the market place. It is our history to institute necessary government programs to protect the health, safety and economic well-being of the American consumer. And it is our way of governing to ensure that consumers have full opportunity to participate in the decision-making processes of government.

Working together, the Democratic Administration and Congress have maintained that tradition. Prominent consumer advocates have been appointed to key government positions. A new National Consumer Cooperative Bank has been created, and a Fair Debt Collection Practices Act has been enacted. Each federal agency has been directed to establish procedures so that consumer needs and interests are adequately considered and addressed on a continual basis. The basic consumer protection authorities of the Federal Trade Commission have been preserved.

Over the next four years, we must continue to guarantee and enhance the basic consumer rights to safety, to information, to choice and to a fair hearing.

Government must continue its efforts to create a strong independent voice to ensure that the consumer's interest is considered in government proceedings. We pledge continued support for an independent consumer protection agency to protect the rights and interests of consumers. Until one is created, we must ensure that each department and agency of the government has established and adequately funded a consumer program which complies with the requirements of Executive Order 12160. Each agency must provide ample opportunity for public involvement in its proceedings and should strive to adopt a program to provide funds for consumers and small businesses to participate in those proceedings.

We must continue our support of basic health, safety, environmental and consumer protection regulatory programs and must undertake the following new initiatives to provide additional basic protections to consumers:

—Comprehensive review of food safety and drug statutes, with particular emphasis on food labeling which discloses product ingredients.

—Requirements for full warranties for new automobiles.

—Class action reform to remove unnecessarily burdensome and expensive procedures.

—Reform of requirements for legal standing to seek judicial redress.

—Protection for consumers against dangerous products, including standards for automobile safety, clothing flammability, new drugs and chemicals, and food and children's products.

—Vigorous enforcement of truth-in-lending, anti-redlining, and fair credit reporting laws.

—Curtailment of abuses in sale of credit life insurance.

While consumer regulatory programs are necessary to achieve social goals, we recognize that an effective competition policy frees the market place from regulation. Therefore, we support vigorous enforcement and strengthening of the antitrust laws. Legislation should be enacted to overturn the *Illinois Brick* case and allow consumers who are injured as a result of a violation of the antitrust laws to seek redress, whether or not they have dealt directly with the violator.

We are committed to ensuring that America's poor do not suffer from lack of food. To this end, we support continued funding of the Food Stamp Program and expansion of the Women, Infant and Children (WIC) program.

We support the efforts of the National Consumer Cooperative Bank to assist grassroots consumer organizations to undertake self-help programs.

We support a nationwide program of consumer education to enable citizens to fully understand their rights in the market place, to be informed of the opportunities for participation in government decision-making, and to be equipped to make intelligent, rational consumer decisions.

Antitrust Enforcement

America must commit itself to a free, open and competitive economy. We pledge vigorous antitrust enforcement in those areas of the economy which are not regulated by government and in those which are, we pledge an agency-by-agency review to prevent regulation from frustrating competition.

To accomplish these goals, we must:

—Enact the *Illinois Brick* legislation.

—Permit consumers and other interested parties to seek enforcement of consent decrees issued in antitrust cases brought by government.

—Prevent anti-competitive pricing by firms in concentrated industries, and combat price signalling and other forms of anti-competitive conduct which do not fall into the current legal categories of either monopoly or collusion.

—Control conglomerate mergers, when such mergers undermine important economic, social and political values without offsetting economic benefits.

—Reform antitrust procedures to speed up cases and deter dilatory conduct by any party.

—Provide strong support for antitrust enforcement by the federal enforcement agencies.

—Provide technical and financial support for the antitrust enforcement efforts of the state attorneys-general and other state antitrust agencies.

—Develop a "single stop" clearance procedure to allow exporters to determine whether specific export agreements are permissible under the antitrust law.

CHAPTER II: GOVERNMENT AND HUMAN NEEDS

The Democratic Party has properly been known as the Party of the people. We Democrats believe in making government responsive to the needs of the people . . . making it *work* for the people. We do not claim that government has all the answers to our problems, but we do believe that government has a legitimate role to play in searching for those answers and in applying those answers.

The Democratic Party has a proud record of responding to the human needs of our citizens. After eight years of Republican government and systematic Republican efforts to dismantle all of the hard-won New Frontier and Great Society social programs, the Carter Administration and the Democratic Congress have resurrected, preserved and strengthened those programs which have proven effective.

In the areas of health care, housing, education, welfare and social services, civil rights, and care for the disabled, elderly and veterans, a Democratic President and a Democratic Congress have put the federal government back in the business of serving our people.

Our progress has been significant, and in many areas unprecedented. In 1980, the people must decide whether our country will continue that progress, or whether we will allow the federal government to revert to four years of Republicanism—which means neglect of the poor and disadvantaged, disdain for working men and women, and compassion only for the rich and the privileged.

We will not allow this to happen. We pledge to build on the Democratic record of the past four years—to continue the process we have begun.

While we recognize the need for fiscal restraint — and have proposed specific steps toward that goal — we pledge as Democrats that for the sole and primary purpose of fiscal restraint alone, we will *not* support reductions in the funding of any program whose purpose is to serve the basic human needs of the most needy in our society — programs such as unemployment, income maintenance, food stamps, and efforts to enhance the educational, nutritional or health needs of children.

Health

The Carter Administration and the Congress have worked closely together to improve the health care provided to all Americans. In many vital areas, there has been clear progress.

The United States spent over $200 billion for health care in 1979. Despite these high expenditures and although we possess some of the finest hospitals and health professionals in the world, millions of Americans have little or no access to health care services. Incredibly, costs are predicted to soar to $400 billion by 1984, without improvement in either access to care or coverage of costs. Health care costs already consume ten cents of every dollar spent for goods and services.

The answer to runaway medical costs is not, as Republicans propose, to pour money into a wasteful and inefficient system. The answer is not to cut back on benefits for the elderly and eligibility for the poor. The answer is to enact a comprehensive, universal national health insurance plan.

To meet the goals of a program that will control costs and provide health coverage to every American, the Democratic Party pledges to seek a national health insurance program with the following features:

— Universal coverage, without regard to place of employment, sex, age, marital status, or any other factor;

— Comprehensive medical benefits, including preventive, diagnostic, therapeutic, health maintenance and rehabilitation services, and complete coverage of the costs of catastrophic illness or injury;

— Aggressive cost containment provisions along with provisions to strengthen competitive forces in the market place;

— Enhancement of the quality of care;

— An end to the widespread use of exclusions that disadvantage women and that charge proportionately higher premiums to women;

— Reform of the health care system, including encouragement of health maintenance organizations and other alternative delivery systems;

— Building on the private health care delivery sector and preservation of the physician-patient relationship;

— Provision for maximum individual choice of physician, other provider, and insurer;

— Maintenance of the private insurance industry with appropriate public regulation;

— Significant administrative and organizational roles for state and local government in setting policy and in resource planning;

— Redistribution of services to ensure access to health care in underserved areas;

— Improvement of non-institutional health services so that elderly, disabled, and other patients may remain in their homes and out of institutions; and

Child Health Assurance Program — We must continue to emphasize preventive health care for all citizens. As part of this commitment, we call for the enactment of legislation during the 96th Congress to expand the current Medicaid program and make an additional 5 million low-income children eligible for Medicaid benefits and an additional 200,000 low-income pregnant women eligible for prenatal and postnatal care.

Mental Health Systems Act — We must enact legislation to help the mentally ill, based on the recommendations of the President's Commission on Mental Health. The legislation should focus on de-institutionalization of the chronically mentally ill, increased program flexibility at the local level, prevention, and the development of community-based mental health services. It is imperative that there be ongoing federal funding for the community-based mental health centers established under the 1963 Mental Health Act and that sufficient federal funding be provided for adequate staffing. We also endorse increased federal funding for ongoing training of mental health personnel in public facilities.

In the 1980s we must move beyond these existing health care initiatives and tackle other problems as well.

Long-Term Care — We must develop a new policy on long-term care for our elderly and disabled populations that controls the cost explosion and at the same time provides more humane care. We must establish alternatives to the present provisions for long-term care, including adequate support systems and physical and occupational therapy in the home and the community, to make it unnecessary to institutionalize people who could lead productive lives at home.

We must support legislation to expand home health care services under Medicare and other health programs. Visits from doctors, nurses and other health personnel are a cost-effective and necessary program for the elderly who often cannot travel to medical facilities. Without home health services, many elderly citizens would be forced to give up their homes and shift their lives to institutions.

Multilingual Needs — We must support the utilization of bilingual interpreters in English-Spanish and other appropriate languages at federal and state-supported health care facilities. In addition, we support broader, more comprehensive health care for migrants.

Health Care Personnel — This nation must maintain an adequate supply of health professionals and personnel. Particular emphasis should be given to programs which educate nurses and other health professionals and related personnel, especially for the traditionally underserved rural and inner city areas.

The rising cost of education in health fields bars many who wish to enter these fields from doing so. In order to expand representation in the health professions of traditionally underrepresented groups, we support programs of financial assistance such as capitation grants. These programs must increase the presence of men and minorities in nursing, and must be targeted toward women and minorities in other health professions.

Minority and Women Health Care Professionals — We recognize the need for a significant increase in the number of minority and women health care professionals. We are committed to placing greater emphasis on enrollment and retention of minorities and women in medical schools and related health education professional programs.

We are also committed to placing a greater emphasis on medical research and services to meet the needs of minorities, women and children.

Reproductive Rights — We fully recognize the religious and ethical concerns which many Americans have about abortion. We also recognize the belief of many Americans that a woman has a right to choose whether and when to have a child.

The Democratic Party supports the 1973 Supreme Court decision on abortion rights as the law of the land and opposes any constitutional amendment to restrict or overturn that decision.

Furthermore, we pledge to support the right to be free of environmental and worksite hazards to reproductive health of women and men.

We further pledge to work for programs to improve the health and safety of pregnancy and childbirth, including adequate prenatal care, family planning, counseling, and services with special care to the needs of the poor, the isolated, the rural, and the young.

Financially Distressed Public Hospitals — Frequently, the only source of medical care for much of the inner city population is the public general hospital. The ever-increasing costs of providing high quality hospital services and the lack of insurance coverage for many of the patients served have jeopardized the financial stability of these institutions. Immediate support is required for financially distressed public hospitals that provide a major community service in urban and rural areas.

In underserved areas where public hospitals have already been closed because of financial difficulty, we must explore methods for returning the needed hospitals to active service.

We must develop financial stability for these hospitals. Our approach should stress system reforms to assure that more primary medical care is provided in free-standing community centers, while the hospital is used for referral services and hospitalization.

Medicaid Reimbursement — The Democratic Party supports programs to make the Medicaid reimbursement formulae more equitable.

Unnecessary Prescriptions — We must reduce unnecessary prescribing of drugs and guarantee the quality and safety of products that reach the market through improved approval procedures.

Substance Abuse

Alcoholism and drug abuse are unique illnesses which not only impair the health of those who abuse those products, but impose costs on society as a whole — in production losses, in crimes to supply habits, and in fatalities on the highway.

The Democratic Partnership has worked to reduce the serious national problem of substance abuse, and progress has been made.

As a result, in part, of a major adolescent drug abuse prevention campaign, levels of drug abuse among adolescents have begun to decline. However, as long as abuse still exists, we consider it a major problem requiring our attention.

Because of a coordinated, concerted attack on drug trafficking, heroin availability in the U.S. over the past four years has decreased by 44 percent; heroin-related injuries have declined by 50 percent.

Progress made since 1977 must be continued.

We must continue to focus on preventing substance abuse in the early years of adolescence by working with grassroots organizations and parent groups throughout the country.

Special efforts must be made to strengthen prevention and rehabilitation resources in the major urban areas that are so acutely affected by drug and alcohol abuse problems because of the cumulative effect of joblessness, poor housing conditions and other factors.

We must provide adequate funding for alcohol and drug abuse research and treatment centers designed to meet the special needs of women, and end the currently widespread discrimination, based on sex, age, race, and ethnicity, in alcohol and drug abuse programs.

We must treat addiction as a health problem and seek flexibility in administering Medicare and Medicaid for substance abuse treatment, especially alcohol and drug services.

We must reduce the availability of heroin and other illicit narcotics in this country and in the source countries.

We must conduct investigations leading to the prosecution and conviction of drug traffickers and to the forfeiture of financial and other assets acquired by their organizations.

Older Americans

In other sections of this platform (for example, health and the extensive section on Social Security), we have listed programs and commitments for improving the status of older Americans. As a Party, we are aware of the demographic and biomedical developments that call for a high priority approach to the issues of retirement, work, and income maintenance for the growing number of older citizens.

The Democratic Party stands for the achievement and maintenance of the quality of life for Americans in their later years. We speak for our future selves, as well as for the elderly of today.

There has been substantial progress, but much remains to be done. Too many senior citizens (especially among minority groups) live close to or below the poverty line, in isolated conditions, and without access to needed services.

The Democratic Party pledges to continue to improve the policies and programs which ensure a high quality of life for older Americans. This includes the following measures.

All Americans, regardless of age, must be afforded an opportunity to participate in the mainstream of society, and in activities at local and national levels, as useful citizens. The 1967 Age Discrimination in Employment Act, and the milestone amendments to that Act in 1978, are concrete examples of this principle. So are programs such as senior centers, nutrition services, and home attendants, as well as those programs under ACTION, the Administration on Aging, and the Community Services Administration.

Such programs have helped to diminish the conditions of dependency, isolation, and unnecessary institutionalization. We propose to continue and expand these programs to reach underserved areas and all segments of the elderly.

The Democratic Party is proud of the passage of legislation to protect and improve private pensions through the Employees Retirement Income Security Act (ERISA), as well as current proposals to extend such protection to larger numbers of workers. No worker, after long years of employment, should lose his or her pension rights because of mobility, poor management, or economic reasons.

Other priorities include working with the private sector to assure maintenance and expansion of employer-employee pension systems and continuing support of the federal-state partnership in SSI (Supplemental Security Income) for the least fortunate.

A comprehensive program of long-term care services is a goal of the Democratic Party. The fastest growing segment of our population is the "very old" and the "frail elderly." The Democratic Party will continue to be concerned with the provision of services for these groups, increasingly composed of women without access to family care. This will include home attendant care, day centers, and quality institutional care for those elderly with functional disabilities who cannot rely on non-institutional alternatives.

For many older citizens, continuing participation in the mainstream means continuing employment, or a return to the labor force as a result of widowhood or the "empty nest." In addition to increasing employment opportunities by raising the allowable mandatory retirement age, we must continue existing, and create new, programs for the retention and re-entry of adult and older Americans in our labor force, including the private and community service sectors.

The Democratic Party will encourage the development of services by the public and private sectors to provide meals-on-wheels for those who need them; senior day centers; friendly visiting services; and similar supportive, educational-recreational, and outreach services.

We pledge to make the elderly secure in the necessities of life. The Democratic Party pledges that it will seek to increase the number of meals served under Title III of the Older Americans Act until it covers at least a quarter of all older people at or near the poverty level while at least maintaining current services for those who are not in poverty. The Democratic Party will seek expanded funding provided for the Section 202 housing program for the elderly.

Social Security

No group in our society deserves the commitment and respect of the Democratic Party more than the elderly. They have built the factories and mills of the nation. They have fought to defend our country. They have paid taxes to finance the growth of our cities and towns. They have worked and sacrificed for a lifetime to give their children a better chance to achieve their dreams. They have a continuing reservoir of talent, skill and experience to contribute to our future.

The basic program and guarantee for older citizens is Social Security. It is the single most successful social program ever undertaken by the federal government. Ninety-five percent of those reaching 65 are eligible for this program; without it, 60 percent of the elderly would have incomes below the poverty level.

The Democratic Party will oppose any effort to tamper with the Social Security system by cutting or taxing benefits as a violation of the contract the American government has made with its people. We hereby make a covenant with the elderly of America that as we have kept the Social Security trust fund sound and solvent in the past, we shall keep it sound and solvent in the years ahead.

In 1977, the Social Security system faced bankruptcy. The Carter Administration and the Congress enacted legislation ensuring the Social Security system's financial stability and making certain that each of the 35 million recipients received his or her monthly check without interruption. They also worked together to strengthen the benefits provided to Social Security recipients. As a result of our actions:

—Workers have been protected against inflation;

—Minimum benefit payments have been reformed to protect low-paid, long-time participants;

—A 3 percent increase in primary benefit amounts has been added;

—The retirement test has been liberalized.

Despite our efforts, much remains to be done if the elderly are to receive the respect and dignity they have earned. Elderly households have only half the income of younger households. For women, the annual median income of those over 65 is only $2,800. One out of seven persons over 65 lives in poverty. Three-quarters of all elderly unmarried, widowed, or divorced women live in poverty. Millions of elderly persons live in special fear of crime. Health care costs for the elderly are now three and a half times the level for younger people. Actual out-of-pocket health expenditures for the elderly today are greater in real dollars than when Medicare was enacted.

In the 1980s we must continue to work for a financially strong Social Security system. The levels and types of benefits, as well as rates and systems of financing, must be continually reviewed in light of current circumstances. Decisions affecting Social Security benefits should be measured by the standards of Social Security's goals, not by the program's impact on the federal budget.

The Democratic Party is responsible for the adjustments of Social Security benefits to keep pace with increases in the cost of living. We remain committed to ensuring that these adjustments continue. We oppose any caps on Social Security benefits. No change in the index which determines cost of living adjustments should be made for the purpose of achieving smaller adjustments than those granted under the current index.

We oppose efforts to raise the age at which Social Security benefits will be provided. Our Party seeks to protect and assist those most in need. We continue to be sensitive to the economic and physical plight of the older worker and the elderly. We therefore stand unalterably opposed to the taxation of any portion of Social Security benefits. Taxing Social Security benefits would mean real hardship for millions of retired Americans. If government needs to expand the tax base, additional taxation should be borne by those most able to pay.

While these steps are critically important, they will not, standing alone, secure adequate income for the elderly women of this nation. To reach this goal, we must also move immediately to eliminate all the gender-based classifications in the Social Security system. We must consider the special needs of elderly women in future benefit increases. We must end the unfairness in the current system that penalizes two-worker families. We must devise a practical way for the Social Security system to recognize the contributions of homemakers, and thus ensure the resources they need to live in dignity in old age.

Finally, the Democratic Party vehemently opposes all forms of age discrimination and commits itself to eliminating mandatory retirement. With the surety of a guillotine, mandatory retirement severs productive persons from their livelihood, shears their sense of self-worth, and squanders their talents.

Pensions

Our nation's complex and uneven pension system is a continuing source of concern. To help address this important problem, President Carter created a Presidential Commission on Pension Policy, charged with developing recommendations to improve public and private, federal, state and local pension systems. We applaud this initiative. We must achieve an equitable pension system with improved benefit safeguards and adequate benefit levels.

We urge the Commission to give special attention to recommendations which address the discrimination and hardships imposed on women in pension plans. Problem areas include pension rights in divorce proceedings, lack of pension benefits for survivors when a worker dies before retirement age, the rules for establishing Individual Retirement Accounts, the vesting rules and participation in pension plans.

We support strong programs of portability in teacher and other public employee retirement programs and private pension plans in order to offer employees involved in geographic employment moves the opportunity to continue retirement security.

Welfare Reform

The nation's welfare system continues to be inequitable and archaic. The existing organization of our delivery system is chaotic. The roles of the federal, state, and local governments, and of the courts are scrambled, with each vying for power and control over delivery. This confusion lends credence to public outrage.

States and cities which make an honest effort to meet the welfare crisis find themselves in deepening fiscal difficulty. In the past few years, the federal share of welfare costs in many of these states has actually declined.

The fiscal crisis of welfare recipients has also deepened, since states and localities are unable or unwilling to adjust benefits to prevent inflation from robbing them of their worth.

The fiscal crisis for taxpayers continues, as states have little ability or incentive to reduce welfare error rates.

Incentives continue that cause families to break apart and fathers to leave home so that children may survive. Disincentives continue for welfare families to seek work on their own; no regular method links welfare recipients to the work force.

We are at a crossroad in the delivery of welfare. Serious reform is necessary if the inequities are to be remedied and administration improved.

The various components must be reorganized and simplified, with each level of government performing those services most suited to its organizational structure, taking advantage of economies allowed by large-scale delivery where appropriate, and of customized services where they are required, always treating each person with fairness and equity.

The components of an effective human service delivery system are these.

Employment — We must require work or necessary training leading to work of every capable person, except for the elderly and those responsible for the care of small children. However, we cannot make this requirement effective unless we can assure employment first through the private sector and, if that is insufficient, through public employment. We must provide an income floor both for the working poor and the poor not in the labor market. We must adopt a simple schedule of work incentives that guarantees equitable levels of assistance to the working poor.

The training and job program must emphasize supported work programs, in which welfare recipients receive intensive training, personnel counseling and help in the job search. Such services can lead to large increases in job placement, lower government expenditures and more productive workers.

Income Transfer — For those persons who cannot work and who have no independent means of support, we must provide assistance in an integrated, humane, dignified, and simple manner. These problems are national in scope and require a unified, national response.

Social Services — As society becomes more complex and faster paced, people such as senior citizens, handicapped, children, families, and those who need protection are under greater pressure and find it more difficult to find the help they need. As these issues vary among communities, communities should take the lead in design and provision of these services.

Social services must continue to be developed and operated at the local level, close to the users, with knowledge of and sensitivity to both the particular problems of each case and the community's unique infrastructure, resources, and support networks.

We must develop a community-level system for coordinating existing public and voluntary programs that support the family and individual initiative, and develop programs to fill existing gaps in order to provide the variety and extent of social services appropriate for each locality.

Food Stamps — Hunger is one of the most debilitating and urgently felt human needs. A government pledged to a fairer distribution of wealth, income, and power, and to holding as a guiding concern the needs and aspirations of all, must also be a government which seeks to alleviate the hunger that results from economic conditions or personal circumstances. Over the years, the Food Stamp Program, expanded and made more responsive by a Democratic Congress and Administration, has become the bulwark of this nation's efforts to relieve hunger among its citizens.

The only form of assistance which is available to all those in financial need — food stamps — provides an important cushion for poor people, including those whose incomes are temporarily disrupted by layoffs or regional unemployment, or whose age or physical handicap leaves them unable to work.

As state and local governments modify other benefit programs on which low-income people depend, the Food Stamp Program becomes increasingly important. We will continue to work toward full employment in recognition of the importance of self-support. Until that goal can be attained, and for those who cannot be self-supporting, we remain committed to our current policy of full funding for the Food Stamp Program.

Medical Care — Provision of medical care for the

poor remains essential. This is a critical part of the national health debate, and should be handled as such.

These reforms may require an additional investment, but they offer the prospect of stabilization of welfare costs over the long run, and the assurance that the objective of this expenditure will be accomplished.

Toward these goals, President Carter proposed welfare reform to the Congress in the form of the Work and Training Opportunities Act and the Social Welfare Reform Amendments Act. These two Acts would lift over two million people out of poverty by providing assistance to individuals and families to enable them to meet minimum income standards and by providing employment to those able to work. We must continue to work to ensure the passage of these two very important acts.

As a means of providing immediate federal fiscal relief to state and local governments, the federal government will assume the local government's burden of welfare costs. Further, there should be a phased reduction in the states' share of welfare costs in the immediate future.

The Democratic Party pledges in the immediate future to introduce legislation to accomplish these purposes in the next year.

Welfare policies significantly affect families. Most persons receiving Aid to Families with Dependent Children, for example, are children or the mothers of young children. Many of these young mothers want to work. So, too, many others receiving welfare are well-suited to work and want to work. A companion to any effective welfare reform must be provision for adequate and available child care, so that parents can participate in training programs and in the work force.

Government should not encourage the break-up of intact families. On the contrary, we must provide the help a family needs to survive a crisis together. In 1962, America took an action which has been one of the greatest contributors to family stability in the history of federal policy. For the first time, states were permitted to provide assistance to families with both parents, and still be eligible for federal reimbursement. We reaffirm our support for the 1962 action and urge that states not providing assistance to unified families begin to do so. We must treat stable and broken families equally.

The thirty-day waiting period for placement on the welfare rolls poses serious problems for individuals and families in dire need of assistance. We support efforts to streamline processing of new welfare recipients which also attempt to address the problem of administrative errors. Simplified rules and better administrative machinery would significantly improve the operation of the welfare system.

We strongly reject the Republican Platform proposal to transfer the responsibility for funding welfare costs entirely to the states. Such a proposal would not only worsen the fiscal situation of state and local governments, but would also lead to reduced benefits and services to those dependent on welfare programs. The Democratic policy is exactly the opposite — to provide greater assistance to state and local governments for their welfare costs and to improve benefits and services for those dependent on welfare.

Low Income Energy Assistance

Our citizens see their family budgets stretched to the breaking point by an explosion of energy costs, while the profits of oil companies multiply to record levels. Last year's 120 percent increase in energy prices by OPEC led to a drastic decrease in the ability of needy families to pay for other necessities of life. The recently enacted low income energy assistance legislation is helping, but it is providing only $1 of help for every $4 in increased costs that have been imposed upon the poor. Significant expansion in this program is urgently needed, and we support such action as a major priority of our Party.

Veterans

This Administration has worked to strengthen the federal government's commitment to our nation's veterans. The Veterans Administration has been given Cabinet-level participation. There have been three consecutive annual increases in VA compensation. The Veterans' and Survivors' Pension Improvement Act has assured veterans of an adequate minimum income. A treatment and rehabilitation program has been established for veterans with alcohol and drug-dependency disabilities. G.I. educational benefits have been considerably expanded. Unemployment among Vietnam veterans has been reduced. Veterans' health care has been improved. A process has been initiated for veterans to upgrade less than honorable discharges from the Vietnam War era.

During the 1980s, we must commit ourselves to:

— Equal opportunity and full voluntary participation in the military regardless of sex. We oppose quotas and/or percentages, rules, policies and practices which restrict or bar women from equal access to educational training and employment benefits which accrue during and after military service.

— Continue improving education and training benefits and opportunities for veterans, especially those who are economically or educationally disadvantaged and those who are disabled.

— Initiate and complete comprehensive epidemiological studies on veterans exposed to certain defoliants used during the Vietnam War as well as on veterans or civilians exposed to above-ground nuclear explosion. We then must establish appropriate and sensitive VA health care programs for those determined to have suffered from such exposure or service.

— Complete promptly the current Cabinet-level study on Agent Orange.

— Strive to maintain and improve quality health care in an independent VA health care system.

— Continue priority care to veterans with service-connected disabilities and seek ways of improving and developing special treatment for the ever-increasing aging veterans population, including burial benefit programs sensitive to the needs of veterans and their families in rural areas.

— Provide authority for the construction of a memorial in the nation's capital to those who died in service to their country in Southeast Asia.

Education

Perhaps the single most important factor in spurring productivity in our society is a skilled work force. We must begin to think of federal expenditures as capital investments, favoring those which are productive and which reduce future costs. In this context, education must be one of our highest priorities. Education is also the indispensable prerequisite for effective democracy. As Daniel Webster said, "On the diffusion of education among people rests the preservation and perpetuation of free institutions."

The Democratic Party is strongly committed to education as the best hope for America's future. We applaud the leadership taken by a Democratic President and a Democratic Congress in strengthening federal programs for education.

In the past four years:

— Federal aid to education has increased by 73 percent — the greatest income increase in such a short period in our history.

— Strong financial and administrative support has been provided for programs that enhance educational opportunities for women, minorities, American Indians and other native Americans, the handicapped, and students with limited English-speaking ability and other special needs;

— The Middle Income Student Assistance Act was adopted, expanding eligibility for need-based student financial aid to approximately one-third of the students enrolled in post-secondary education;

— A number of legislative, regulatory, and other administrative actions were taken to enhance benefits received by private school children from federal education programs; and

— A new Department of Education was created to give education a stronger, more direct voice at the federal level, while at the same time reserving control over educational policymaking and operations to states, localities, and public and private institutions.

Over the next four years, we pledge to continue our strong commitment to education. We will continue to support the Department of Education and assist in its all-important educational enterprise that involves three out of ten Americans.

In this regard, we endorse the language of the legislation which emphasized the intent of Congress "to protect the rights of state and local governments and public and private institutions in the areas of educational policies and administration of programs. . . ."

It is now a decade and a half since the passage — by a Democratic Congress at the behest of a Democratic Administration — of the landmark Elementary and Secondary Education Act of 1965. At the time, there were sound and compelling reasons to undergird all federal aid to education with specific purposes. The specific purposes remain compelling and the specific programs addressed to them must be maintained.

Federal aid to education plays a significant role in guaranteeing that jurisdictions of differing financial capacity can spend equal amounts on schooling. We favor a steady increase in federal support with an emphasis on reducing inter- and intra-state disparities in ability to support quality education. The federal government and the states should be encouraged to equalize or take over educational expenses, relieving the overburdened property taxpayer.

The Democratic Party renews its commitment to eliminating discrimination in education because of sex and demands full and expeditious enforcement of Title IX of the 1972 education amendments.

The Democratic Party strongly urges that the federal government be sensitive to mandating state and local programs without adequate provision for funding. Such mandates force the state and/or local governments to increase taxes to fund such required programs.

Equal educational opportunity is at the heart of the Democratic program for education. Equality of opportunity must sometimes translate to compensatory efforts. For the disadvantaged, the handicapped, those with limited English language skills, American Indians/Alaska Natives, Native Hawaiians, and other minorities, compensatory programs require concentrated federal spending.

The Democratic Administration and Congress have supported a comprehensive program of compensatory education and have expanded it to include secondary education. We will continue to target categorical assistance to low income and low achieving students.

We reaffirm our strong support for Title I concentration grants for remedial instruction for low income students. The Democratic Party pledges to achieve full funding of concentration grants under Title I and to expand the Headstart and Follow-through programs.

The Democratic Party will continue to advocate quality education in the Bureau of Indian Affairs and in tribally contracted schools to meet American Indian educational needs. The Democratic Party opposes the closing of schools serving American Indians and Alaska Natives without consultation with the tribes involved.

The Democratic Party recognizes the need to maintain quality education for children in school districts affected by federal activities and installations. We therefore will continue to be sensitive to the financial problems of these school districts.

School desegregation is an important tool in the effort to give all children equal educational opportunity. The Democratic Party continues to support programs aimed at achieving communities integrated both in terms of race and economic class through constitutional means. We encourage redrawing of attendance lines, pairing of schools, utilizing the "magnet school concept" as much as possible, and enforcing fair housing standards. Mandatory transportation of students beyond their neighborhoods for the purpose of desegregation remains a judicial tool of last resort.

We call for strict compliance with civil rights requirements in hiring and promotion in school systems.

We support an effective bilingual program to reach all limited–English-proficiency people who need such assistance.

The Democratic Party supports efforts to broaden students' knowledge and appreciation of other cultures, languages and countries.

We also support vocational and technical education through increased support for teacher training, personnel development, and upgrading and modernizing equipment and facilities to provide the skill and technical training to meet the workforce needs for business, industry, and government services. Increased emphasis on basic skills is essential to the success of vocational and technical training. Vocational and technical education is a viable tool for establishing people in their own business through entrepreneurship programs. Vocational and technical education contributes to the economic development and productivity of our nation by offering every person an opportunity to develop a marketable skill.

The Party reaffirms its support of public school education and would not support any program or legislation that would create or promote economic, socio-logical or racial segregation. Our primary purpose in assisting elementary and secondary education must be to assure a quality public school system for all students.

Private schools, particularly parochial schools, are also an important part of our diverse educational system. The Party accepts its commitment to the support of a constitutionally acceptable method of providing tax aid for the education of all pupils in schools which do not racially discriminate, and excluding so-called segregation academies. Specifically, the Party will continue to advocate constitutionally permissible federal education legislation which provides for the equitable participation in federal programs of all low and moderate income pupils.

The Democratic Party reaffirms its commitment to the concept and promise that every handicapped child should have a full and appropriate public education in the least restrictive environment. To assure the best placement and program for handicapped students, we support maximum involvement of the regular classroom teacher in placement planning for handicapped students with assurance of barrier-free access. We further support increasing the federal share of the costs of education for the handicapped.

We applaud the actions taken by the government in strengthening federal programs for higher education. The nation must continue to ensure that our colleges and universities can provide quality higher education in the coming period of declining enrollment and rising operating costs.

We are especially interested in extending post-secondary opportunities to students from low and middle income families, older students, and minorities. We believe that no able student should be denied a college education for reasons of cost.

The Democratic Party is committed to a federal scholarship program adequate to meet the needs of all the underprivileged who could benefit from a college education. When those who are qualified for post-secondary education cannot afford to enter college, the nation ignores talent we cannot afford to lose. Basic Education Opportunity Grants, which offer both access to a college education and the choice of a college, must continue to be strengthened and should be funded at full payment schedule.

Likewise, campus-based programs of aid must be supported. With a coordinated and reliable system of grants, loans and work study, we can relieve the crisis in costs that could close all but the affluent colleges and universities.

Since entry to institutions of higher learning is dependent upon a student's score on a standardized test, we support testing legislation which will assure that students will receive sufficient information relative to their performance on the test to determine their strengths and weaknesses on the tests.

Our institutions of higher education deserve both public and private backing. The Party supports the continuation of tax deductions for charitable gifts, recognizing that such gifts represent the margin of excellence in higher education and foster scholarly independence within our institutions of higher learning.

The Democratic Party commits itself to the strengthening of graduate education and the support of basic and applied research. Graduate education, scholarship and research are of immense importance to the nation's economic and cultural development. Universities conduct most of the nation's basic research. Their graduate and research programs are the training grounds for the research personnel and professionals who discover knowledge and translate that knowledge into action.

The federal role is critical to the quality of these endeavors. We reaffirm the federal responsibility for stable support of knowledge production and development of highly trained personnel in all areas of fundamental scientific and intellectual knowledge to meet social needs.

High priority should be assigned to strengthening the national structure for graduate education, scholarship and research and ensuring that the most talented students, especially women and minorities, can gain access to these programs.

Historically Black colleges and universities have played a pivotal role in educating minority students. The Democratic Party affirms its commitment to ensuring the financial viability and independence of these worthy institutions and supports expanded funding for Black institutions. The Democratic Party pledges to work vigorously for significant increases in programs which have traditionally provided funding for historically Black colleges and universities. Particular attention should be given to substantially increasing the share of funding Black colleges receive. We will substantially increase the level of participation of Black colleges in all federal programs for which they are eligible. In addition, we urge the establishment of an office within the Office of the Secretary of Education to ensure full executive implementation of the President's Black college directive. Similarly, colleges serving Hispanic, American Indian/Alaska Native, and Asian/Pacific Islander students should receive equal consideration in federal policies affecting their survival.

Finally, educational quality should be strengthened through adequate support for libraries, federal leadership in educational research and development, and improved teacher training.

The Democratic Party further urges the federal government to take into account the geographical barriers to access to educational and library materials which particularly affect the non-contiguous territories of the United States. A study should be conducted to review the possibility of sending airmail, at surface mail rates, said materials to and from the mainland U.S. and the non-contiguous territories of the U.S.

The Party believes that improved teacher in-service training, building upon the successful "Teacher Center Model" implemented under this Administration, could contribute substantially to educational quality. We support the establishment of federally funded teacher centers in every state and will work toward a steady increase in the number of teachers served. Teacher centers should address such issues as bilingual, multicultural, non-racist, and non-sexist curricula.

The Party continues to support adult education and training to upgrade basic skills.

We propose federally financed family-centered developmental and educational child care programs available to all who need and desire them.

We support efforts to provide for the basic nutritional needs of students. We support the availability of nutritious school breakfast, milk and lunch programs. Students who are hungry or malnourished can experience serious learning difficulties. The Democratic Party affirms its commitment to restore fair eligibility requirements for this program and to set fees at a level which does not unfairly deny students the ability to participate.

The Democratic Party recognizes the importance of family and community involvement in public schools, and the impact their involvement can have on the quality of a child's educational environment. We support initiatives that will encourage parents and all members of the community to take an active interest in the educational future of our children.

Child Care

While the American family structure has changed radically in recent years, the family remains the key unit of our society. When the needs of families and children are ignored, the nation as a whole ultimately suffers. It is not only morally right, but also far less expensive, for government to assist children in growing up whole, strong and able, than to pay the bill later for children and adults with health, social and educational problems. Government cannot and should not attempt to displace the responsibilities of the family; to the contrary, the challenge is to formulate policies which will strengthen the family.

The Democratic Party shall seek vigorously to enact

an adequately funded, comprehensive quality child-care program based upon a national commitment to meet the health, safety, and educational needs of *all* children. Such a program shall provide for alternative low-cost child care arrangements so that parents may decide what is in the best interests of their children. To ensure the availability of choices, the Child Care Tax Credit shall be revised to benefit low and moderate income families. National policies shall ensure the availability of child care services for all parents. Our programs shall also address themselves vigorously to the issues of flex-time work programs, job sharing, and incentives for child care in private industry, in recognition of the social responsibilities of all citizens to children and their parents as the guardians of our future.

Juvenile Justice

Juvenile delinquency and other problems of young people, like truancy and running away, are often manifestations of serious problems in other areas—family, school, employment, or emotional disturbance. We are committed to maintaining and strengthening the Juvenile Justice and Delinquency Prevention Act of 1974 and the Runaway Youth Act to help deal with these problems. In particular, we reaffirm our commitment to ending unnecessary institutionalization of young people who have not committed serious crimes and strengthening preventive efforts and other services at the community level to help young people and their families in the sometimes difficult transition to adulthood. Equally important, we are committed to continuing reform in the juvenile courts to assure right of due process and adequate counsel to young people who become enmeshed in the juvenile justice system.

We must continue and strengthen efforts at prison reform to upgrade the safety of our penal institutions. Our penal institutions enhance rehabilitation to offenders, and lower the recidivism level.

Families

The Democratic Party supports efforts to make federal programs more sensitive to the needs of the family, in all its diverse forms.

Housing

Since 1976, the Administration's efforts in the area of housing have concentrated on achieving an adequate housing supply. From 1977-1979, housing starts increased substantially over the level of the prior Republican Administration. Additionally, increased emphasis has been placed on saving our existing housing stock through rehabilitation.

But the momentum to increase the housing supply for the 1980s has been threatened by the high rate of inflation. The downturn in economic activity during the first half of 1980 has created a period of severe difficulty for the housing industry and for those Americans in need of housing. These circumstances make it imperative that the Democratic Party redouble its efforts to meet the goal of a decent home in a suitable environment for every citizen. It is essential that we expand the construction and availability of affordable housing in order to match the growing needs of Americans during the 1980s and to help stabilize housing costs.

Housing shortages and deterioration, and the need for economic development, are among the most critical problems facing local government today.

Through a patchwork of programs and tax incentives developed over the past fifty years, this nation is now spending between $25 and $30 billion each year on housing and economic development. These funds must be redirected in a cogent manner, to provide a comprehensive response to the housing problem. This effort should be pressed forward with the same national will that put a man on the moon, and will be a major step toward the revitalization of our local economies.

During the 1980s, we must work to meet the nation's need for available, affordable housing by:

—Achieving steady, high levels of production;

—Continuing progress toward a non-inflationary environment with lower interest rates;

—Pursuing monetary and credit policies which are especially sensitive to the needs of the housing and construction industries in order to help provide jobs;

—Continuing progress toward eliminating substandard housing and meeting the housing needs of this nation's low and moderate income families, the elderly, and the handicapped, including a substantial increase in the authorization for public housing and Section 8 rental housing assistance;

—Expanding the coverage of the Fair Housing laws to prohibit discrimination against single parents or single persons;

—Ensuring that federal housing projects meet the needs of single-parent families;

—Strengthening our efforts to provide higher levels of multi-family housing production to meet the rental housing needs of the postwar generation in the 1980s;

—Continuing the development and expansion of new financial instruments designed to attract increased capital to the housing sector throughout the interest rate cycle;

—Continuing to improve the efficiency and management of our housing programs;

—Continuing support for efforts to improve our housing codes;

—Expanding urban homestead and rehabilitation programs which will preserve neighborhoods in our cities for the people who live there;

—Financing moderate income housing at below-market interest rates;

—Adopting condominium conversion policies which protect tenants, particularly the elderly, against unfair and unreasonable conversion practices; and

—Assisting cities, counties, and states which have effective programs to combat the growing and dangerous problem of housing abandonment.

Transportation

Since 1977, the Carter Administration has worked closely with the Congress to improve all the transportation modes so essential to our nation. These efforts have resulted in the elimination of unnecessary regulations, the expansion of the federal commitment to mass transit, and the savings of billions of dollars for consumers. In the 1980s we must continue our efforts in the same direction.

The Democratic Party commits itself to a balanced, competitive transportation system for the efficient movement of people and goods.

The trucking industry must be deregulated, and legislation to do that is now in place. This legislation would open entry to new truckers, lift restrictions on the goods truckers may haul and the routes they may use, promote vigorous price competition, reduce regulatory delays and improve road safety.

To improve their long-term viability, we must give railroads more flexibility in setting rates, without burdening excessively shippers dependent on rail service. Congress is now progressing on comprehensive legislation in this area. We expect regulatory reform of the railroad industry to speed the elimination of wasteful regulations and improve the facilities and equipment of railroads.

Coal is a centerpiece of our nation's energy policy. We are concerned about the cost of transporting coal to its markets, particularly the cost of rail transportation. Within the context of regulatory reform, we must therefore be especially sensitive to the effects of railroad rates on coal. A healthy rail industry is of critical importance to our economy and our society.

We must ensure, through such efforts as completion of high-speed rail passenger service in the Northeast Corridor, that railroads are an efficient means for personal travel. The decline in the nation's railroad system must be reversed. Tracks must be rehabilitated, equipment modernized and maintenance improved if the nation is to have a rail system that adequately meets the needs of passengers and shippers. We must ensure that flexibility in setting rates does not become a license either for anti-competitive pricing at the expense of consumers, or for anti-competitive mergers that create or maintain inordinate market power at the expense of consumers.

The vital artery of urban America is mass transit. It saves energy by providing fuel-efficient alternatives to the automobile. For the poor, the elderly, the disabled, and many other city dwellers, there is no other transportation. If they are to travel at all, to go to work or to shop, they must rely on mass transit. Mass transit serves them, as well as the employers for whom they work and the businesses where they shop. It aids all of us, by unclogging our cities, cleansing our air, and increasing the economic health of our urban areas.

The Democratic Party pledges to strengthen the nation's mass transit systems. Federal funds must be provided for maintenance and repair of deteriorating systems, and for new equipment purchases for growing systems. Federal aid formulae should be amended to give greater weight to ridership in the allocation of dollars. Reasonable operating subsidies must be provided to help subsidize rider fares.

Mass transit is a high priority in our national transportation policy. We pledge support for significant increases in capital and operating subsidies for mass transit to enhance the reliability, safety, and affordability of existing and expanding systems.

The auto industry and its workers must be assisted during this difficult time. We are committed to an intensive review of the automobile industry's fundamental problems, and to prompt, effective action to help ameliorate those problems. We are also committed to a strong trade adjustment program to help currently unemployed auto workers.

To meet the needs of international commerce and national security, this nation must have a strong, competitive and efficient American-flag ocean transportation system. In recent years, there has been a significant reduction in the ability of our merchant marine to compete for the carriage of world commerce because of economic policies pursued by other nations. Action must be taken to revitalize our merchant marine.

To achieve this objective, we must develop a coherent, consistent, and responsive maritime policy which will encourage the development and maintenance of an American-flag ocean transportation system, staffed with trained and efficient American personnel, and capable of carrying a substantial portion of our international trade in a competitive and efficient manner. Our maritime policy must also lead to the development and maintenance of a domestic shipbuilding and ship repair mobilization base adequate to satisfy the commercial and national security requirements of the United States. Furthermore, we pledge continued commitment to the Merchant Marine Act of 1970 and greater utilization of the private merchant marine by the Navy for its support functions.

Urban Policy

During the campaign of 1975-1976, our nation's great cities and urban counties were mired in a depression. Unemployment was well above 10 percent in many cities and counties; private sector investment and jobs were leaving the great urban centers; poverty and other serious social problems were left unattended; a severe budget squeeze was causing layoffs and cutbacks in essential city services; and the public works of our cities had been allowed to decay. The nation's mayors spent a portion of the year urging Congress to override the Republican Administration's veto of vitally important anti-recession programs. Most seriously, the leadership and citizens of our great urban centers had lost the hope that the future would be better.

Upon taking office, the Democratic Administration responded to these conditions immediately with an $11 billion anti-recession package and, one year later, with the nation's first comprehensive urban policy. The urban policy was the product of a unique effort which actively involved the elected officials of state and local government, representatives of labor, neighborhood organizations, civil rights groups and the members of Congress.

These deliberations produced a blueprint to guide federal action toward cities. The Democratic Administration, in partnership with the Democratic Congress, has moved aggressively to implement parts of the urban policy. Some of these programs have already begun to contribute to the revitalization of the nation's older cities and to assure the continued health of the nation's growing cities. For example, the urban policy has:

—Created the Urban Development Action Grant (UDAG) Program to encourage private investment and jobs to locate or remain in our nation's major cities. UDAG, which is funded at $675 million annually, has already leveraged more than $7 billion of private investment and created more than 200,000 permanent jobs;

—Targeted federal government procurement, facilities and jobs to the high unemployment central cities;

—Increased funding for the Community Development Block Grant program by more than 30 percent and proposed a formula change that provides substantial new aid to the older, more distressed cities and urban counties; and

—Proposed a massive increase in the urban development programs of the Economic Development Administration.

Although many gains have been made, we recognize that a great deal more remains to be done. This is especially true in those cities which have borne the brunt of the current recession. We recognize that no urban policy can completely succeed in a period of high inflation and deepening recession.

In this platform, the Democratic Party dedicates itself to the strength and survival of urban America. We are committed to developing imaginative, compassionate steps to deal with the causes and effects of rising unemployment, to make our cities fiscally strong, to provide jobs and economic growth, to preserve neighborhoods and communities and to meet the basic human needs of urban residents.

Our policies must include the following features:

—A strong jobs policy which supports productive employment of people in the public sector and encourages employment in the private sector by attracting and strengthening business in the cities.

This jobs policy—and the need to guarantee a job for every American who is able to work—is our single highest domestic priority, and will take precedence over all other domestic priorities.

—Public works programs which help rebuild our cities' infrastructure and which provide the unemployed with the opportunity to rebuild their own neighborhoods;

—Incentives for energy conservation by residents, business and industry in urban areas including incentives to convert oil facilities to coal and the construction of new coal-fired replacement plants;

—Increased education and training programs with special attention to employment of youth, women, and minorities and to training people for private sector jobs;

—National economic policies intended to maintain growth in our economy and reduce the inflation rate, thereby easing the fiscal burden on cities and their residents;

—Prompt enactment of the Carter Administration's proposal to expand the economic development initiative programs of the Department of Commerce. When fully implemented, this initiative will provide more than $1 billion in new loan guarantees to our urban centers and will double the amount of economic development grants available;

—Prompt enactment of the Administration's five-year extension of the local government revenue sharing program, including a $500 million transitional aid program for the areas most in need;

— A serious examination of the urban impact of the federal tax code, to ensure that businesses have substantial incentives to invest in our nation's neediest locales; and

— Renewed efforts to consolidate existing grants-in-aid programs in order to provide state and local governments with the flexibility to use these programs efficiently.

In the last analysis, we must recognize that America's cities are centers of people with needs . . . needs for jobs, decent housing and health care, affordable mass transit, quality education and streets where they can walk in safety. Each is a crucial part of any effective urban program. The Democratic Party is committed to placing the highest priority in our budgets and our programs on meeting these needs of city-dwellers.

Neighborhoods

From the beginning of the Carter Administration, the government has worked to revitalize neighborhoods and to make them a central component of urban life. As a result of these efforts, the federal government now has a strong neighborhoods policy.

During the 1980s we must continue to strengthen neighborhoods by:

— Making neighborhood organizations partners with government and private sectors in neighborhood revitalization projects;

— Continuing to make neighborhood concerns a major element of our urban policy;

— Developing urban revitalization programs that can be achieved without displacing neighborhood residents; and

— Continuing to reduce discriminatory redlining practices in the mortgage and insurance industries.

Small Community and Rural Development

This Democratic Administration instituted the nation's first comprehensive small community and rural development policy. This policy establishes specific goals, directs numerous organizational and management changes, and initiates an extensive program of action to improve the quality of life for all rural Americans including American Indians/Alaska Natives, rural Hispanics, rural Blacks, and other minorities. Its principles emphasize the need for a strong partnership between the public and private sectors and among all levels of government. Recognizing rural America's great diversity and the limits of the federal

role, the Administration's policy invites the nation's governors to establish rural affairs councils to define state rural development strategies and to advance federal-state coordination in addressing priority needs.

Since assuming office in 1977, the Democratic Administration has acted to increase rural access to credit and capital, expand job opportunities, alleviate persistent rural poverty, rehabilitate substandard housing, address the shortage of health professionals in rural areas, improve the mobility of the rural transportation disadvantaged, and enhance educational and training opportunities for disadvantaged rural youth. For example, we have:

— Addressed the problem of substandard housing through substantial increases in rural housing and community development assistance, and through revisions in minimum property standards to permit housing construction which is less expensive and better suited to rural conditions.

— Improved rural access to credit and capital by tripling the economic development resources of the Farmers Home Administration.

— Alleviated rural unemployment by doubling Department of Labor employment and training assistance to rural areas.

— Addressed the shortage of doctors and other health professionals in rural areas through the Rural Health Clinic Services Act and a special initiative to construct 300 rural primary care health clinics by the end of 1981 in medically underserved areas.

For the future, we must move aggressively to address longstanding rural problems and to implement fully the Administration's small community and rural development policy, with emphasis on:

— Synthesizing efforts to improve the quality of life for American Indians/Alaska Natives. We must provide incentives for the development of an economic base that will improve the quality of life on reservations;

— Ensuring that federal programs are administered in ways which encourage local solutions to local problems; target assistance to communities and individuals most in need; make federal investments in ways that leverage private sector investments and complement local and tribal investments; and make federal programs more accessible to rural jurisdictions, better adapted to rural circumstances and needs, and better coordinated in their administration and delivery;

— Promoting rural energy self-sufficiency through improved rural transit and the application of alternative energy technologies on farms and in our rural homes and communities;

— Passing satisfactory welfare reform legislation, with special attention to the needs of the rural disadvantaged;

—Protecting prime agricultural land as rural populations and the rural economy continue to grow;

—Continuing to upgrade substandard rural housing to make it safe, decent, and sanitary;

—Giving full attention to the health, education, and other basic needs of rural citizens, especially the young, the old, and the poor; and

—Providing low cost electric and telephone services to rural areas through the Rural Electrification Administration and the hundreds of rural cooperatives that provide these services.

Science and Technology

The Nixon-Ford Administration permitted serious decline in the state of science and technology in our country.

There had been a decade of erosion of federal support of research and development. The funding of basic research in particular was far below its peak level of the mid-1960s.

Science and technology advice had been seriously downgraded and removed from the White House, until pressures from the science and engineering community had it restored through an act of Congress.

The previous decline in support had affected opportunities in science and engineering. It had resulted in the inadequate replacement of facilities and instrumentation and their growing obsolescence in the face of new scientific advances and needs.

Not only the work of our academic research centers, but also our technological innovation and economic competitiveness were impaired by this erosion of federal support.

To counter these conditions and help revitalize the country's science and technology, the Carter Administration, working with Congress, has taken a number of steps. The Office of Science and Technology Policy has been strengthened and upgraded. Growth has been restored in the budgets for federal research and development activities. Basic biomedical research has been strengthened to increase our fundamental knowledge of health and disease.

These are just a few of the innovations that have been made. Our scientific and technological agenda remains unfinished. The 1980s offer great promise. During the next four years, we will work to:

—Continue to strengthen our science and technology and provide for continuity and stability of support to research and development;

—Continue to monitor the flow of talent into science and engineering and provide the appropriate training and opportunities to ensure an adequate number of well-trained scientists and engineers in the

coming years, with particular emphasis on women and minorities;

—Pay continued attention to the support of research facilities to make certain they remain among the best in the world;

—Successfully launch the Space Shuttle, take advantage of the many opportunities it offers to make space activities more economic and productive, and release new resources for the future scientific exploration of space; and

—Expand our programs of cooperation in science and technology with all nations who seek development and a stable, peaceful world.

In sum, we must continue to expand our scientific and technological capabilities and apply them to the needs of people everywhere.

The Arts and the Humanities

The arts and humanities are a precious national resource.

Federal commitment to the arts and humanities has been strengthened since 1977 by expanding government funding and services to arts institutions, individual artists, scholars, and teachers. The budgets for the National Endowment for the Arts and the National Endowment for the Humanities have increased substantially. The Federal Council on the Arts and Humanities has been reactivated. Policies of the Carter Administration have fostered high standards of creativity across our nation. The Administration has encouraged the arts and humanities through appropriate federal programs for the citizens of our smallest communities, as well as those of our largest cities. During the 1980s, the Party is committed to:

—Continuing federal encouragement and support for institutions relating to the arts and to learning in the humanities;

—Encouraging business participation in a comprehensive effort to achieve a truly mixed economy of support for the arts and humanities by individuals, foundations, corporations and governments at every level;

—Exploring a variety of mechanisms to nurture the creative talent of our citizens and build audiences for their work;

—Supporting strong, active National Endowments both for the Arts and the Humanities, and strengthening the Public Broadcasting System; and

—Seeking greater recognition for the rich cultural tradition of the nation's minorities. We will work to meet the cultural needs of minorities, encourage their greater participation in the performing arts on a national level, and provide grants for the arts in low-income neighborhoods.

ENSURING BASIC RIGHTS AND LIBERTIES

Equal Rights Amendment

The Democratic Party recognizes that every issue of importance to this nation and its future concerns women as well as men. As workers and consumers, as parents and heads of households, women are vitally concerned with the economy, energy, foreign policy, and every other issue addressed in this platform. The concerns of women cannot be limited to a portion of the platform; they must be reflected in every section of our Party's policy.

There is, however, a particular concern of women which deserves special emphasis — their entitlement to full equality in our society.

Women are a majority of the population. Yet their equality is not recognized in the Constitution or enforced as the law of the land. The choices faced by women — such as whether to seek employment or work at home, what career or profession to enter, and how to combine employment and family responsibilities — continue to be circumscribed by stereotypes and prejudices. Minority women face the dual discrimination of racism and sexism.

In the 1980s, the Democratic Party commits itself to a Constitution, economy, and society open to women on an equal basis with men.

The primary route to that new horizon is ratification of the Equal Rights Amendment. A Democratic Congress, working with women's leaders, labor, civil and religious organizations, first enacted ERA in Congress and later extended the deadline for ratification. Now, the Democratic Party must ensure that ERA at last becomes the 27th Amendment to the Constitution. We oppose efforts to rescind ERA in states which have already ratified the amendment, and we shall insist that past rescissions are invalid.

In view of the high priority which the Democratic Party places on ratification of the ERA, the Democratic National Committee renews its commitment not to hold national or multi-state meetings, conferences, or conventions in states which have not yet ratified the ERA. The Democratic Party shall withhold financial support and technical campaign assistance from candidates who do not support the ERA. The Democratic Party further urges all national organizations to support the boycott of the unratified states by not holding national meetings, conferences, or conventions in those states.

Furthermore, the Democratic Party shall seek to eliminate sex-based discrimination and inequities from all aspects of our society.

Civil Rights

The Democratic Party firmly commits itself to protect the civil rights of every citizen and to pursue justice and equal treatment under the law for all citizens.

In the 1960s, enormous progress was made in authorizing civil rights for all our citizens. In many areas, the promises of the civil rights efforts of the 1960s have been met, but much more remains to be done.

An effective affirmative action program is an essential component of our commitment to expanding civil rights protections. The federal government must be a model for private employers, making special efforts in recruitment, training, and promotion to aid minority Americans in overcoming both the historic patterns and the historic burdens of discrimination.

We call on the public and private sectors to live up to and enforce all civil rights laws and regulations, i.e., Equal Employment Opportunity Programs, Title VI and Title VII of the Civil Rights Act, the Fair Housing Laws, and affirmative action requirements.

We advocate strengthening the Office of Civil Rights in the Department of Education and in the Department of Health and Human Resources.

We oppose efforts to undermine the Supreme Court's historic mandate of school desegregation, and we support affirmative action goals to overturn patterns of discrimination in education and employment.

Ethnic, racial and other minorities continue to be victims of police abuse, persistent harassment and excessive use of force. In 1979, the Community Relations Service of the Department of Justice noted that "alleged use of deadly force by police and the reaction of minorities was a major force of racial unrest in the nation in 1978." In response to this finding:

—We call for the Department of Justice's Civil Rights Division to develop uniform federal guidelines and penalties for the use of undue force by local law enforcement agencies;

—We call for the Department of Justice's Civil Rights Division to establish civil rights units at appropriate U.S. Attorneys' offices; and

—We call on the Department of Justice to move concurrently with federal prosecutors so that if a failure to obtain conviction takes place at the state or local level, federal prosecution can occur swiftly.

The Democratic Party strongly condemns the Ku Klux Klan and the American Nazi Party. We pledge vigorous federal prosecution of actions by the Klan and American Nazi Party that violate federal law, including the creation of such laws in jurisdictions where they do not exist. We further condemn those acts, symbols, and rituals, including cross-burnings, associated with anti-civil rights activities. We urge every state and local government to pursue vigorous prosecution of actions by the Klan and Nazi party that violate state or local law.

The Democratic Party asserts that the Immigration and Naturalization Service, in enforcing the immigration laws, must recognize its obligation to respect fully the human and constitutional rights of all within our borders. Such respect must include an end to practices affecting Hispanic, Caribbean, and Asian/Pacific American communities such as "neighborhood sweeps" and stop and search procedures which are discriminatory or without probable cause.

Our commitment to civil rights embraces not only a commitment to legal equality, but a commitment to economic justice as well. It embraces a recognition of the right of every citizen — Black and Hispanic, American Indian and Alaska Native, Asian/Pacific Americans, and the majority who are women — to a fair share in our economy. When that opportunity is denied, and the promise of social justice is unfulfilled, the risks of tension and disorder in our cities are increased. The Democratic Party condemns violence and civil disorder wherever they occur. But, we also pledge to attack the underlying injustices that contribute to such violence so that no person need feel condemned to a life of poverty and despair.

The Democratic record provides a solid basis for future progress. There should be little doubt that virtually no progress would occur under a Republican Administration. Over the next four years, our Party must strengthen and improve what has already been accomplished.

Both the ERA and District of Columbia Voting Rights Amendments to the Constitution must be ratified and our full commitment must be given to those efforts.

The Fair Housing Act must be amended to give the Department of Housing and Urban Development greater enforcement ability, including cease and desist authority.

The Equal Pay and the Age Discrimination Acts must be strongly and effectively enforced by the Equal Employment Opportunity Commission.

To end discrimination against language minorities, we must enforce vigorously the amendments to the Voting Rights Act of 1975 to assist Hispanic citizens. We must recognize the value of cultural diversity in education, expand bilingual facilities, and guarantee full protection of the civil and human rights of all workers.

We must affirm the dignity of all people and the right of each individual to have equal access to and participation in the institutions and services of our society. All groups must be protected from discrimination based on race, color, religion, national origin, language, age, sex or sexual orientation. This includes specifically the right of foreign citizens to enter this country. Appropriate legislative and administrative actions to achieve these goals should be undertaken.

We are concerned about the opportunity for minorities to be adequately represented on trial juries if the trend toward smaller juries continues. Efforts must be initiated to correct this possible underrepresentation.

Civil Liberties

The Democratic Party has been actively committed to protecting fundamental civil liberties. Toward that end, over the past four years, the Carter Administration and the Democratic Congress have enacted legislation to control the use of wiretaps by the government in the pursuit of foreign intelligence; developed the government's first comprehensive program to protect privacy; and worked to enact a criminal code which scrupulously protects civil liberties.

As we enter the 1980s, we must enact grand jury reform; revise the Uniform Code of Military Justice; enact charters for the FBI and the intelligence agencies which recognize vital civil liberty concerns while enabling those agencies to perform their important national security tasks; shape legislation to overturn the Supreme Court *Stanford Daily* decision; and enact a criminal code which meets the very real concerns about protecting civil liberties, and which does not interfere with existing workers' rights.

We call for passage of legislation to charter the purposes, prerogatives, and restraints on the Federal Bureau of Investigation, the Central Intelligence Agency, and other intelligence agencies of government with full protection for the civil rights and liberties of American citizens living at home or abroad. Under no circumstances should American citizens be investigated because of their beliefs.

We support the concept that no employee should be discharged without just cause.

Privacy

Social and technological changes are threatening our citizens' privacy. To meet this challenge, the Carter Administration has developed the first comprehensive privacy policy. Under this policy, administrative action has been taken to cut the number of federal files on individuals and legislation has been passed to protect the privacy of telephone conversations and bank accounts.

In the 1980s we must complete this privacy agenda. Broad legislation must be enacted to protect financial, insurance, medical, and research records. We must have these safeguards to preserve a healthy balance between efficiency and privacy.

The Democratic Party recognizes reproductive freedom as a fundamental human right. We therefore oppose government interference in the reproductive decisions of Americans, especially those government programs or legislative restrictions that deny poor Americans their right to privacy by funding or advocating one or a limited number of reproductive choices only.

Specifically, the Democratic Party opposes involuntary or uninformed sterilization for women and men, and opposes restrictions on funding for health services for the poor that deny poor women especially the right to exercise a constitutionally-guaranteed right to privacy.

Federal legislation is also necessary to protect workers from the abuse of their rights and invasion of their privacy resulting from increased employer use of polygraphs and other so-called "truth test" devices. Workers should have the right to review all records retained by their employers relating to medical and employment information.

Appointments

One of President Carter's highest priorities has been to increase significantly the number of women, Blacks, Hispanics and other minorities in the federal government. That has been done.

More women, Blacks and Hispanics have been appointed to senior government positions than during any other Administration in history.

Of the six women who have served in Cabinet positions, three have been Carter appointees.

More women, Blacks and Hispanics have been appointed to federal judgeships during the Carter Administration than during all previous Administrations in history.

Of the 39 women federal judges, 35 have been Carter appointees; of the 38 Black federal judges, 19 have been Carter appointees; of the 14 Hispanic judges, 5 have been Carter appointees.

This record must be continued. The Democratic Party is committed to continue and strengthen the policy of appointing more women and minorities to federal positions at all levels including the Supreme Court.

Handicapped

Great strides have been made toward ending discrimination against the handicapped, through increased employment and education opportunities and greater access to public facilities and services.

In the 1980s, we must continue to work towards the goals of eliminating discrimination and opening opportunities.

All federal agencies must complete their Section 504 regulations and implement them effectively.

We must continue to expand opportunities for independent living.

The Fair Housing Act and Title VI of the Civil Rights Act must be amended to include the handicapped.

We must face the task of making federal facilities and modes of transportation fully accessible.

Job opportunities and job training for the handicapped, including apprenticeship training programs, must be expanded.

We must make the most basic American civil right—the right to vote—fully available to the handicapped.

Dr. Martin Luther King Jr.

Dr. Martin Luther King Jr. led this nation's effort to provide all of its citizens with civil rights and equal opportunities. His commitment to human rights, peace and non-violence stands as a monument to humanity and courage. To honor this outstanding national leader, we must enact legislation that will commemorate his birthday as a national holiday.

Domestic Violence

Each year, 3 to 6 million Americans are injured in acts of domestic violence. To combat this violence the Carter Administration has initiated a government-wide effort to assist and educate victims and rehabilitate victimizers, including:

—The formation of a new Office of Domestic Violence in the Department of Health and Human Services; and

—Amendments to the Child Abuse Prevention and Treatment Act which provides funds to state and community groups.

The President has signed the Protection of Children Against Sexual Exploitation Act; HUD has developed demonstration projects for shelters for battered women; the Community Services Administration has established a pilot Family Crisis Center Program to assist low-income battered women and children; and the U.S. Commission on Civil Rights held a Consultation on Battered Women in 1978.

Existing federal programs have been coordinated through the Interdepartmental Committee on Domestic Violence, chaired by the Secretary of Health and Human Services. The Democratic Administration must continue to support the passage of the legislation before the Congress, HR 2977, which would provide direct, immediate assistance to victims effectively and sensitively.

Insular Areas

We must be firmly committed to self-determination for the Virgin Islands, Guam, American Samoa and the Northern Mariana Islands, and vigorously support the realization of whatever political status aspirations are democratically chosen by their peoples. The unique cultures, fragile economies, and locations of our Caribbean and Pacific Islands are distinct assets to the United States which require the sensitive application of policy. We are committed to pursuing initiatives we have begun to stimulate insular economic development, enhance treatment under federal programs, provide vitally needed special assistance and coordinate and rationalize policies. These measures will result in greater self-sufficiency and balanced growth.

Puerto Rico

We are committed to Puerto Rico's right to enjoy full self-determination and a relationship that can evolve in ways that will most benefit U.S. citizens in Puerto Rico. The Democratic Party respects and supports the desire of the people of Puerto Rico to associate, by their own will freely expressed in a peaceful and democratic process, in permanent union with the United States either as a commonwealth or as a state, or to become an independent nation. We are also committed to respect the cultural heritage of the people of Puerto Rico and to the elimination of discriminatory or unfair treatment of Puerto Ricans, as American citizens under federal programs.

American Indians

The Carter Administration has upheld and defended the historic special relationship between the federal government and Indian tribes. In addition, it has strongly supported the policy of self-determination and the right to practice the ancestral religions that are important to many tribal members. More than $24 million over the next ten years has been committed to assist Indian tribes with energy resources in making decisions about the development and protection of these resources. The Administration has firmly reiterated its fundamental opposition to the policy of termination which was so detrimental to Indians and their relationship with the federal government.

These policies must continue as the federal government finds better means of dealing effectively and compassionately with Indian tribes and individuals. The federal government must honor its treaty commitments. The federal government must redouble its efforts to improve the housing, health care, education and general welfare of Indians. Finally, the federal government must work as an equal partner with tribes as they decide for themselves the best means of managing their substantial energy resources.

Ethnic America

President Carter has stated that the composition of American society is analogous to a beautiful mosaic. Each separate part retains its own integrity and identity while adding to and being part of the whole.

America is a pluralistic society. Each of us must learn to live, communicate, and cooperate with persons of other cultures. Our public policies and programs must reflect this pluralism. Immigrants from every nation and their descendants have made numerous contributions to this country, economically, politically and socially. They have traditionally been the backbone of the labor movement and an integral part of the Democratic Party.

Ethnic Americans share the concerns of all Americans. They too are concerned about decent housing, health care, equal employment opportunities, care of the elderly, and education. In addition, ethnic Americans have some concerns of their own. They want to preserve the culture and language of their former homeland. They want to be integrated into the political, social and economic mainstream of American society, but at the same time they are concerned about the foreign policy issues that affect their native countries. We as a nation must be sensitive to their concerns.

President Carter established the Office of Ethnic Affairs and charged it with a broad and diverse mission. The predominant functions of the office are to link the Administration and its ethnic constituents, to foster the concept of pluralism, and to enable all Americans to partake equally in the American way of life.

Americans Living Abroad

Almost 3 million American citizens live overseas, both as government employees and private citizens. We know only too well the dangers and sacrifices some of these government officials face in serving their country. With the threat of terrorism and political unrest always present, we are committed to improving the security of our embassies and missions abroad. Our government must work with other governments to ensure that Americans are protected while performing their vital duties in the interest of the United States.

We also recognize the contributions of private citizens living overseas in bringing American ideals and culture to other lands and in helping the U.S. economy by promoting exports and increased trade with other countries.

The President's Export Council has recommended that in order to encourage American exports and redress trade imbalances, the United States should conform with the practices of other major trading nations. Existing disincentives should be removed, so that Americans working abroad can compete more equitably and effectively with citizens from other nations.

The Administration must continue to support changes in the law which make it simpler for American parents to ensure that their children born overseas are not denied U.S. citizenship.

We also believe that Medicare should be made available to Americans abroad who are eligible for Social Security.

CHAPTER III: GOVERNMENT OPERATION AND REFORM

MAKING GOVERNMENT EFFECTIVE AND EFFICIENT

The Democratic Party has long stood for an active, responsive, vigorous government. Democrats of our generation have a special obligation to ensure that government is also efficient and well managed.

We understand full well the importance of this obligation. We realize that even the most brilliantly conceived federal programs are doomed to failure if they are not intelligently and efficiently managed.

The kind of government we Democrats stand for is a government that *cares* and knows how to translate that caring into effective action; a government whose heart and head are working in concert.

Over the last four years the Democratic Administration and the Democratic Congress have built a dramatic government reform record. In the years ahead we must carefully implement the changes we have made, and we must pursue additional measures to provide the efficient government the people have a right to expect.

Regulatory Reform

Federal regulations are needed to protect consumers and providers in the areas of health, safety, and the environment. Four years ago, however, the overall regulatory machine desperately needed an overhaul. Some rules served only to protect favored industries against competition, at the public's expense. Others imposed conflicting or needlessly costly requirements.

For decades, the economy has been hamstrung by anticompetitive regulations. A Democratic Administration and a Democratic Congress are completing the most sweeping deregulation in history. Actions already taken and bills currently pending are revamping the rules governing airlines, banking, trucking, railroads, and telecommunications. Airline deregulation in its first year of operation alone has saved passengers over 2.5 billion dollars.

For the regulatory programs our country does need, the Administration has established a new management system. Under Executive Order 12044, agencies are reviewing and eliminating outdated rules and analyzing the full impact of new rules before they are issued. They are developing alternative regulatory approaches which can reduce compliance costs without sacrificing goals. They are increasing public participation in the regulatory process. The Regulatory Council is publishing the first government-wide list of upcoming rules, the Regulatory Calendar, and is using it to eliminate conflict and duplication.

The challenges of the eighties will place great demands on our regulatory system. The reforms we have put in place are building machinery that can meet those challenges. However, much work lies ahead to implement the steps we have taken and go further.

We must continue to conduct an agency-by-agency review to make regulation less intrusive and more effective.

We must find and remove barriers that prevent steady progress toward competition in each industry.

On the management side, we must increase the use of cost-effective regulatory techniques, without adversely affecting worker health or safety.

We must strengthen our research programs to ensure that we set sensible priorities for regulatory action.

We must eliminate those delays, layers of review, and litigation that unduly tie up the process.

We must make the regulatory process accessible to all members of the public who are affected.

We must oppose special interest efforts to undermine the ability of federal agencies to protect consumers, the environment, or public health and safety; and efforts to enable federal agencies to override or exempt state or federal protections of the environment or public health and safety.

Tax Reform

In 1976, this Party pledged to seek fundamental tax reform, for we believed that our tax system had lost much of its needed fairness and equity. President Carter honored that pledge by proposing to Congress the most comprehensive and far-reaching set of tax reform proposals ever made by any Administration. That proposal would have closed over $9 billion worth of tax loopholes, simplified our tax laws, and provided funds for substantial tax reduction for low and middle income taxpayers.

Once again, we call on Congress to legislate meaningful tax reform. We cannot any longer allow the special interests to preserve their particular benefits and loopholes at the expense of the average taxpayers. The fight for tax reform must go forward, and the Party pledges to be a part of that important effort. Therefore, we pledge to seek tax reforms which:

—Encourage savings by low and middle income taxpayers;

—Close tax loopholes which benefit only special interests at the expense of the average taxpayer and use the proceeds to bring relief to low and middle income Americans;

—Simplify the tax code and ease the burden on taxpayers in the preparation of their tax returns;

—Encourage capital formation, innovation and new production in the United States;

—Curb tax deductions, like those for three-martini lunches, conventions, first class travel, and other expense account deductions, which encourage consumption, discourage saving, and thus impede productivity;

—End tax discrimination that penalizes married working couples; and

—End abuses in the tax treatment of foreign sources, such as special tax treatment and incentives for multi-national corporations that drain jobs and capital from the American economy.

Capital formation is essential both to control inflation and to encourage growth. New tax reform efforts are needed to increase savings and investment, promote the principle of progressive taxation, close loopholes, and maintain adequate levels of federal revenue.

Management

The need to restrain federal spending means that every dollar of the budget must be spent in the most efficient way possible. To achieve this, the Democratic Partnership has been working to streamline the man-

agement of the federal government and eliminate waste and fraud from federal programs. Real progress has been made in these important areas.

While these reforms have produced substantial savings for the taxpayers, they must be sustained in the coming years to realize their full potential.

The Civil Service Reform Act can be used to encourage improved productivity of the federal government.

More business-like control of our assets, placing the government's operations on a sound financial basis, must be used to produce real savings.

Special investigations and improved accounting systems must be used to attack fraud, abuse and wasteful practices.

Efforts must be continued to improve the delivery of services to citizens through greater accountability, consolidation and coordination in program administration, and elimination of unnecessary red tape and duplication.

GOVERNMENT OPENNESS AND INTEGRITY

Under the Nixon-Ford Administration the federal government was closed to all but a privileged few and the public had lost faith in the integrity of its public servants.

The Democratic Party takes pride in its long and outstanding record of leadership in opening up the processes of government to genuine participation by the people, and in making government truly responsive to the basic needs of all the American people.

For the last four years, the Carter Administration and the Democratic Congress have devoted a great deal of time and resources to opening government processes and ensuring the integrity of government officials.

The Ethics in Government Act now requires all senior government officials to make a full financial disclosure and severely limits the "revolving door" practice that has developed among former federal employees of representing private parties before the federal agencies in which they recently held significant positions.

A statutory provision has now been made for the appointment of a special prosecutor in cases of alleged wrong-doing by senior government officials.

"Whistle-blowers" in the federal government (those who report waste and illegalities) have now been given special statutory protection to prevent possible retribution.

An Executive Order has been issued significantly reducing the amount of classified information, and increasing the amount of classified material to be released over the next decade by about 250 million pages.

As a result of actions such as these, trust and confidence in government officials have been restored. In the coming years, we must ensure full implementation of these initiatives. We must also work toward lobby law reform which is needed to ensure full disclosure of Congressional and executive lobbying activities.

Law Enforcement

Numerous changes were necessary when the Democrats took office in 1976. The essential trust between police officers and the public they protect had deteriorated. Funds committed by Congress had been terribly misspent during the eight Republican years.

The Carter Administration has taken solid steps toward correcting this serious problem. It has formalized the relationship between federal and state law enforcement officials to ensure maximum cooperation between federal and state agencies. It has taken long strides toward creating and implementing uniform national guidelines for federal prisons and encouraging state penal institutions to use the same guidelines.

The Democratic Party supports the enactment of a revised federal criminal code which simplifies the currently complex federal criminal law in order to make our federal criminal justice efforts more effective, and repeals antiquated laws while fully protecting all civil liberties. As that effort proceeds, we must ensure that the rights of workers to engage in peaceful picketing during labor disputes are fully protected.

The Democratic Party affirms the right of sportsmen to possess guns for purely hunting and target-shooting purposes. However, handguns simplify and intensify violent crime. Ways must be found to curtail the availability of these weapons. The Democratic Party supports enactment of federal legislation to strengthen the presently inadequate regulations over the manufacture, assembly, distribution, and possession of handguns and to ban "Saturday night specials."

Most important, the government has used its own resources to resolve satisfactorily concerns over the use of deadly force. The Administration has made progress toward the preparation of uniform guidelines for all police departments. They have also utilized the conciliation services available through the Community Relations Service to establish closer working ties among the police and community organizations.

The Democratic Party is pledged to continuing its strong record of providing needed assistance to local law enforcement. The new Law Enforcement Assistance Act, enacted by a Democratic Administration

and a Democratic Congress, provides an important framework for this purpose. We are committed to using this framework effectively, in close cooperation with state and local law enforcement authorities.

We reaffirm our support for the Juvenile Justice and Delinquency Act and the Runaway Youth Act as responses to the serious challenge of youth crime.

We must continue and strengthen efforts at prison reform, to upgrade the safety of our penal institutions, to enhance rehabilitation of offenders, and to lower the recidivism level.

We support federal assistance to the victims of crime, including special programs to assist the elderly and to aid the victims of rape and domestic violence. Further efforts should be made to demonstrate the feasibility of restitution by the perpetrators of crime.

As we work toward improved law enforcement, we must not permit or sanction excessive or illegal police force.

Minorities in some areas have been discriminated against by such police actions, and we must take every action at the federal, state, and local level to prevent that from happening in the future, including a renewed commitment to affirmative action in the hiring of law enforcement personnel, establishment of civil rights units at appropriate U.S. Attorneys' offices, and swift investigation and prosecution of suspected civil rights violations.

Paperwork Reduction

Over the years the federal government has imposed more and more paperwork on the private sector. The Carter Administration has stopped that trend and worked to cut the paperwork burden. We have eliminated unnecessary forms, simplified and consolidated needed forms, and discouraged creation of new paperwork requirements. As a result, the federal paperwork burden has been cut 15 percent, or 127 million man-hours.

The Administration is currently putting into place the tools we will need to continue and expand this program. In November 1979, President Carter signed an Executive Order that created the first "paperwork budget." This program will limit the reporting time each agency can impose on the public. In addition, the President has ordered agencies to tailor their forms to reduce the burden on individuals and small business.

We need further legislation. We urge a continuation of the effort to reduce government documents to simple English, easily understandable by all. The Administration is working with Congress to pass a Paperwork Reduction Act, which will close wide loopholes in the current oversight process.

Election Reform

Recent reforms in the election process have aided immeasurably in opening the process to more people and have begun to reduce the influence of special interests. The limitations on campaign contributions and the public financing of Presidential elections are two reforms which have worked very well. Business political action committees continue to spend excessively, however. Further reform in this area is essential. In the 1980s we need to enact reforms which will:

—Provide for public financing of Congressional campaigns;

—Lower contribution limits for political action committees;

—Close the loophole that allows private spending in Presidential elections contrary to the intent of the election law reforms;

—Encourage voter participation in elections through use of simplified procedures for registration in states that lack mail or election day registration procedures, and by resisting efforts to reduce access to bilingual ballots; and

—Increase opportunities for full participation in all areas of party and government affairs by the low and moderate income majority of Americans.

Postal Service

The private expression statutes guarantee the protection and security of the mail for all Americans. They are essential to the maintenance of a national postal system, which will require an adequate public service subsidy to assure the delivery of mail to all Americans.

Chapter IV: Energy, Natural Resources, Environment and Agriculture

ENERGY

For the past four years, the Democratic Party's highest legislative priority has been the development of our nation's first comprehensive energy policy. Our actions were necessitated by the Republican Administration's policy that fostered dependence on foreign oil. This Republican legacy led to America's petroleum paralysis, which weakened our security, undermined our strength abroad, threatened our environment and endangered our economic health.

In perhaps no other domestic area did we inherit such a dangerous situation:

—Domestic production of oil and natural gas was steadily declining, with price controls discouraging exploration and production;

—Natural gas shortages were regularly plaguing parts of our country;

—Our dependence on foreign oil was increasing every year;

—Wasteful energy practices existed in our industries, homes and transportation;

—Solar and other renewable energy resources were being almost completely ignored;

—Synthetic fuel production had been stalled;

—The federal government was not promoting energy conservation;

—Our allies were unwilling to make adequate efforts to reduce their energy consumption; and

—Our energy policy was being made by nearly a dozen different agencies and bureaus throughout the federal government.

The struggle to develop an energy policy was difficult and time-consuming. Tough decisions, especially in the area of oil price decontrol, were necessary to reduce our dependence of foreign oil.

Not all of our energy problems have been solved. Yet the achievements of the past four years leave little doubt that we are finally serious about the problems caused by our excessive reliance on foreign oil. As a result of our national energy policy, oil imports will be cut in half by the end of this decade, saving our nation hundreds of billions of dollars. A framework is now in place that will permit further progress in the 1980s. Our economic security demands that we drastically reduce the massive flow of dollars into the OPEC treasuries and oil company bank accounts at the expense of American consumers and business.

Our progress on energy has been realized because we have achieved four principal goals:

—Incentives have been provided for the production of new energy sources;

—Incentives for new oil production have been added, together with a windfall profits tax, which will fund low income energy assistance and energy research and development;

—Incentives have been provided to encourage conservation of our existing energy resources; and

—Improved international energy cooperation has reduced our dependence on OPEC.

These actions have produced enormous energy benefits to our nation:

—We are importing one million barrels of oil a day less than last year;

—Domestic natural gas exploration and production are at record-high levels;

Domestic oil exploration is at a 20-year high, and the decline in domestic production has been averted;

—Per capita energy consumption is decreasing;

—Use of solar energy has increased considerably,

and gasohol production has increased by 600 percent;

—Coal production has increased, and foreign markets for our coal have been developed;

—Gasoline consumption is 8 percent less than last year.

In the 1980s, this program can be improved, as the framework laid in the last four years is used to ensure our energy security for all time.

America's energy future requires a continued strong national policy based on two fundamental principles: efficient use of energy that will conserve our resources, preserve our economy and create jobs for Americans; and development of secure, environmentally safe and reasonably priced energy sources.

It is—and must be—the goal of the Democratic Party to mobilize this nation to use energy efficiently without asking Americans to suffer the loss of our strong economy and hard-earned standard of living. Energy efficiency, especially in buildings, transportation, and industrial production, must be made this nation's top priority.

The following specific actions must be taken.

We must make energy conservation our highest priority, not only to reduce our dependence on foreign oil, but also to guarantee that our children and grandchildren have an adequate supply of energy. If we can convince one of every four drivers exceeding the 55 mile per hour speed limit to reduce their speed, we can save 100,000 barrels a day. Conservation is the cheapest form of energy production.

We must establish a massive residential energy conservation grant program. We must provide subsidized loans, direct financial assistance, and other substantial incentives to make all residences in the United States energy efficient, through upgraded insulation, heating, cooling and waterheating. Special incentives should be afforded for the use of renewable energy resources such as passive and active solar energy systems. Our goal should be to ensure that all economically justified energy efficiency investments are made by 1990.

We should use our energy programs to aid in rebuilding the industrial heartland. Industry must be given financial incentives to improve the energy efficiency of industrial processes and to build substantial amounts of generating capacity through co-generation.

We must implement mandatory Building Energy Performance Standards (BEPS) to encourage the design and construction of energy efficient buildings. Energy efficiency standards should apply to *all* new construction. Implementation of energy efficiency standards should begin with federal government buildings. In addition, the federal government should lead the way in implementing solar and energy efficiency improvements programs through its loan and insurance agencies by requiring energy conservation standards for federally assisted properties.

In recognition of the potential for substantial energy savings if our most efficient methods of transportation are utilized, we must provide direct economic assistance where private capital is unavailable to improve those means of transport.

Major new efforts must be launched to develop synthetic and alternative renewable energy sources. In pursuing a strong program of synthetic fuel plants we must also be sensitive to environmental and water concerns. The federal government must help eliminate red tape involved in the construction of vital energy facilities. The Energy Mobilization Board, an essential mechanism to speed the construction of vital energy facilities, should be able to override state and local substantive law only with the consent of Congress and the President.

The Democratic Party regards coal as our nation's greatest energy resource. It must play a decisive role in America's energy future. We must increase our use of coal. To accomplish this, we must see that shippers are not overburdened with excessive rates for transportation. Severance taxes levied for depletion of natural resources should be equitable. We must make clean coal conversion a reality. To this end, we will assist utilities that are large enough to permit coal conversion while maintaining or improving air quality. We must also provide incentives for industrial boiler coal conversion. Coal conversion can and must be accomplished in a manner that protects public health, nationally, regionally and locally. It can and must increase the use of coal, reduce the demand for oil, and provide employment where jobs are needed the most.

The federal government should accept its responsibility as trustee for the American Indian and Alaska Native tribes to ensure that tribal resources develop at a pace that preserves the existing life-style and that the tribes participate in the contracting process for resource development with full knowledge of the environmental tradeoffs. The federal government must continue to cooperate with tribal governments in such matters as changes in the use of sacred and religious areas. The Democratic Party believes that American Indian and Alaska Native reservations should remain the permanent homeland for these peoples.

We recognize that Hawaii, U.S. territories and Trust territories in the Pacific Basin are particularly vulnerable because of their total dependence on imported oil for meeting their energy needs. These insular areas do not have access to the alternative sources of energy that are available elsewhere. Consequently, the Democratic Party recommends that these areas, where feasible, be chosen as sites for demonstration and/or pilot alternative energy projects, especially ocean thermal energy conversion, solar and wind.

We must lead the Western World in developing a program for increased use of coal in Europe, Japan, and the developing nations.

Oil exploration on federal lands must be accelerated, consistent with environmental protections.

Offshore energy leasing and development should be conditioned on full protection of the environment and marine resources. Lease sales should proceed only after appropriate safeguards necessary to preserve and protect vital natural resources are put in place. The determination of what safeguards are needed must be based on a complete assessment of the effects of offshore activity on the marine and coastal environment, and must be made in conjunction with the Environmental Protection Agency and the National Oceanic and Atmospheric Agency, the federal agencies charged with protecting our nation's fisheries and other environmental resources.

Solar energy use must be increased, and strong efforts, including continued financial support, must be undertaken to make certain that we achieve the goal of having solar energy account for 20 percent of our total energy by the year 2000.

To ensure that we reach the 20 percent goal, the Democratic Party commits itself to a federal program for solar or other renewable resources that exceeds the federal commitment to synthetic fuels. A greater share of federal funds should be committed to basic research and must be devoted to the development of renewable energy resources and fusion research and development. Moreover, we support the commercialization of solar, wind, low-head hydro, biomass and other renewable resources as quickly as possible through direct assistance, investment and loan guarantees in addition to monies available from the solar bank. The Democratic Party vigorously supports substantial funding for the construction of an engineering test facility for fusion technology. Fusion energy is a safe, clean alternative source of energy which can be used to generate electricity efficiently.

We must encourage research and development of hydrogen or electric powered vehicles. We must fully commit ourselves to an alcohol fuel program. The federal government should expand its use of alcohol fuels in government and military vehicles. This will help reduce surplus feed grain and help to stabilize prices. The Democratic Party pledges that production of fuel-grade alcohol will be increased until at least a target of 500 million barrels of ethanol by 1981 is achieved.

A stand-by gasoline rationing plan must be adopted for use in the event of a serious energy supply interruption. In times of supply interruption, rationing is essential for equitable and prompt distribution of gas to the public. The Strategic Petroleum Reserve should be filled as market conditions permit, consistent with the requirements of existing law.

We must impose a moratorium on the acquisition of competing coal companies and solar energy companies by major oil companies.

Legislation must be enacted to prohibit purchases by oil companies of energy or non-energy companies unless the purchase would enhance competition.

The major oil companies must be responsible and accountable in their production, importation and distribution of fossil fuels. Oil is as basic to our economy, defense, and general welfare as electric power and money. Consequently, the oil companies must be invested with public purpose. To accomplish this objective, we support strengthened leasing regulations, reporting requirements and monitoring by the departments of Energy and Justice.

Thorough investigations of the compliance of the oil companies with energy price laws and regulations must be continued, and tough penalties imposed in the event of non-compliance. The Department of Energy, consistent with the law, should share its energy data with the Department of Justice and the Federal Trade Commission.

We must make conservation and renewable energy our nation's energy priorities for the future. Through the federal government's commitment to renewable energy sources and energy efficiency, and as alternative fuels become available in the future, we will retire nuclear power plants in an orderly manner.

We must give the highest priority to dealing with the nuclear waste disposal problem. Current efforts to develop a safe, environmentally sound nuclear waste disposal plan must be continued and intensified.

The NRC shall issue no licenses or permits for new nuclear plants until the Kemeny Commission recommendations are fully implemented.

Existing plants must be required to meet the safety recommendations of the Kemeny Commission. The Democratic Party supports prompt implementation of their recommendations. No plant unable to meet these standards can be allowed to operate.

Safe permanent disposal of all high-level radioactive waste and transuranic waste should be the primary responsibility of the federal government, in consultation and concurrence with state, local, tribal, and territorial governments throughout the entire decision-making process, including the actual siting and operation of repositories. Neither the federal government nor the state or tribal or territorial governments should be permitted to act in a manner that forces an unsafe resolution of this problem or prevents a safe resolution from being accomplished. It is, therefore, essential that state and tribal governments, acting according to their constitutional processes, have the power to reject unsafe sites within their borders. Clear standards should be developed so that the courts may determine whether the federal government or a state or tribe is acting in an arbitrary manner. Every state should be responsible for the management and disposal of all low-level waste generated by non-defense sources within its boundaries. Where appropriate, this responsibility should be exercised through state regional compacts. There should be more federal funding for research and development of safer, more efficient methods of radioactive waste disposal.

Funds generated by the Windfall Profits Tax must be used to expand mass transit. Federal assistance should be provided for construction and operation costs.

ENVIRONMENT

We are charged with the stewardship of an irreplaceable environment. The Democratic Party must continue to be as environmentally progressive in the future as it has been in the past. Progress in environmental quality — a major achievement of the 1970s — must continue in the 1980s. The environmental problems we face today are, if anything, more challenging and urgent than those of ten years ago.

The great strides we have taken during the past few years are the best evidence of our commitment to resource conservation and environmental restoration. We have compiled a proud record.

During the next four years, we must carry forward vigorously with these important policies, and move to address a series of new challenges.

We must move decisively to protect our countryside and our coastline from overdevelopment and mismanagement. Major efforts are now underway to solve such problems as disappearing farmland and development on our barrier islands. These efforts should help forge a strong national consensus behind the realization that protection must be balanced with the need to properly manage and utilize our land resources during the 1980s.

We must develop new and improved working relationships among federal, state, local, tribal, and territorial governments and private interests, to manage effectively our programs for increased domestic energy production and their impact on people, water, air, and the environment in general. All of our energy development efforts should be carried out without sacrificing environmental quality.

We must continue on the path to a sustainable energy future — a future based increasingly on renewable resources and energy conservation. Our national goal of having 20 percent of our energy from renewable resources in the year 2000 must become a working target, not a forgotten slogan. Conservation must remain the cornerstone of our national energy supply.

New efforts at home and abroad will be required in the early 1980s to face squarely such global problems as the destruction of forests, the loss of countless irreplaceable species, growing world population, acid rain, and carbon dioxide buildup.

Passage by Congress of the hazardous waste cleanup proposal will provide the basis for a major effort beginning in 1981 to clean up the thousands of hazardous waste dump sites across the country. Toxic chemicals are a serious threat to the health of our people. We must continue our programs to improve agency performance in many areas, such as protection of groundwaters, in order to better protect the public.

We must strive to ensure that environmental regulations cost no more than necessary and are streamlined to eliminate waste, duplication and delay. We must not lose sight of the fact that the benefits of these regulations far outweigh their costs. We must work to reform legislation without deforming it.

We support the allocation of resources to the Environmental Protection Agency and other environmental agencies sufficient to carry out their mandates.

We support strict adherence to automobile pollution standards.

We will support policies to eliminate acid rain pollution from power plant emissions.

We will commit ourselves to efficient transportation alternatives, including mass transit, car pooling, van pooling, employer based commuter plans, and hydrogen and electric commuter vehicles.

We will continue to fight noise pollution in our urban centers and job sites.

We will encourage the recycling of municipal solid waste.

We will seek a strong "super-fund" law financed by government and industry.

We must continue to pursue offshore energy leasing to stimulate our domestic oil and gas production and reduce our dependence on foreign oil consistent with environmental and marine concerns.

We will fund adequately the Land and Water Conservation Fund to protect our national park system.

We will implement vigorously the Toxic Substances Control Act.

Often, actions by one nation affect the economic growth and the quality of life in other nations. Such actions can be influenced by international agreement and incentives.

To defend against environmental risks that cross national frontiers, international cooperation must be extended to new areas, such as acid rain, deforestation and desertification, buildup of carbon dioxide in the atmosphere, thinning of the ozone shield, air and water pollution, oil spills, chemicals in the environment, and disposal of radioactive waste.

Water

Water is a necessity to all, and represents life itself to much of the American Union. We recognize especially the singular dependence of the Western states on scarce water supplies. The development of navigation, irrigation, flood control, and hydroelectric projects is vital to the economic health of the West, and correspondingly to the entire nation.

Working with Congress, the Democratic Administration will implement a national water policy which recognizes the special needs of the West. Toward this end, we support the modern standards and valid cost-benefit analysis suggested by the Federal Water Resources Council. We support a federal study, in partnership with the affected states, to explore possibilities and recommend alternatives relative to importation of water into arid and semi-arid states. We also support state, local, and tribal participation in all phases of water programs within their respective jurisdictions.

Recently, water programs across the nation have become enmeshed in controversy and conflicting values. It is not unusual for a federal water project to take a generation from the time it is authorized to the time construction actually begins.

Yet the national need for expanded and accelerated investment in water development grows ever more pressing, and is increasingly acknowledged. If, as but one example, we are to develop our unequaled coal resources as a substitute for imported oil, we will require expansion of water transportation and improvement of seaports beyond the imagination of even those early Americans who sensed the path to empire in our inland waterways. The development of synthetic fuels, which must of necessity be concentrated in states with sparse water supplies, is an enormous challenge to engineering and science.

Similarly, the task of reindustrialization requires that we recognize the water development needs of all sections of the nation.

Water to supply steel mills and automobile factories, to provide for the needs of commercial cities and associated suburbs, makes a legitimate and pressing claim on national priorities.

We recognize the need to develop a truly national water program which responds to the needs of each region of our country in an active and effective manner and which recognizes the social effects of water projects.

The Democratic Party strongly supports the desalinization of sea water and the development of water resources in those areas of the country where water is scarce.

AGRICULTURE

America's farmers are among the most vital economic forces of the nation. Because of their extraordinary productivity, Americas farm workers provide more food and fiber per person at a lower cost than their counterparts in any other country. American consumers have a more certain food supply than consumers in any other nation, even though a third of our farm production is sold abroad each year.

In 1977, the Democratic Administration inherited a farm economy marked by serious over-production and badly outdated price support programs. Farm prices and incomes were plummeting, partly in response to misguided attempts at price controls. The livestock sector was in its third straight year of loss, and a herd liquidation of unprecedented scale was under way.

Because of actions taken by the Democratic Administration and Democratic Congress, this situation was turned around in 1978 and 1979. U.S. agriculture was put back on a track of steady, sustained growth and improvement. The sharp decline of farm prices and farm incomes was reversed. An aggressive program of export promotion resulted in record high agricultural exports in each of the past three years.

Recently, however, the nation's farm economy has been hurt by reduced prices; high costs of production, including energy, inflation, equipment, and high interest rates. As a result, our nation's farmers are facing a time of hardship.

Agricultural policy in the 1980s must strengthen the forces which made American farmers the most productive in the world and American agriculture the hope of hungry people everywhere. In this way, we can ensure a decade of prosperity for farmers and of agricultural abundance for America's consumers.

The Democratic Party pledges itself to the following goals.

Continued attention to expanding farm exports — American agriculture's long-run interests remain firmly tied to the sale of U.S. farm products abroad. Despite the significant progress made to date, it is important that we continue to work at breaking down barriers to trade and capitalizing on our nation's enormous advantage in the production of food and fiber.

If food is to be used as an instrument of foreign policy, it is imperative that farm income be protected. Farmers must have access to free markets.

Recognizing the patriotic sacrifices made by the American farmer during the agricultural embargo protesting the invasion of Afghanistan, we commend the agricultural community's contribution in the field of foreign affairs. Except in time of war or grave threats to national security, the federal government should impose no future embargoes on agricultural products.

Protecting farm prices and farm income — Rapidly rising costs of production, especially energy costs, make it imperative that we increase the level of support for farm prices and income by increasing target prices to cover the cost of production. For those farm products not covered by target prices, such as soybeans, cattle, hogs, poultry, sugar cane, and sugar beets, we pledge support programs that will maintain viable domestic production. Low cost farm credit should be extended with the least possible delay in times of stress from decreased farm income or disasters.

It is in the nation's long-run interest that returns to farmers keep pace with rising costs to ensure a fair return on investment.

Measures to protect and further enhance agricultural productivity — Although agricultural productivity remains high in comparison with productivity in the non-farm sector, its rate of increase has slowed over the past two or three decades. This trend must be reversed through greater attention to the effects of regulatory actions, increased support for agricultural research, and intensified efforts to conserve our vital land and water resources.

Rebuilding our agricultural transportation system — The transportation system which moves our agricultural products to their final markets, including ports for export shipment, has been strained to the limit. While needed improvements have begun, through such measures as trucking and rail deregulation and the expansion of Lock and Dam 26 (on the Mississippi River at Alton, Illinois), more intensive efforts will be required in the future. In the case of railroads, a rebuilding effort will be required.

Protecting our soil resource — American agriculture is critically dependent on the productivity of its soil. Without careful and consistent stewardship of this important resource, it can become depleted. An assessment of our nation's conservation needs is now underway. We must be prepared to act on the findings of this assessment. Emergency procedures should be enacted to increase soil conservation incentives for construction of watersheds, tile intake terraces, and other soil saving practices.

Protecting family farms — The real genius of American agriculture is the role and prominence of the farm family. It is this form of organization that provides agriculture with its vitality, independent spirit, and progressiveness. We must protect farmers from land speculators, giant farm combinations, and foreign buyers. We support laws requiring disclosure of all foreign ownership of farmland and we will continue to monitor such ownership to determine its impact on our farms.

While we recognize the need to modernize the 1902 Reclamation Act, we reaffirm our support for its intent — to assure that the federal subsidy program assists only family farmers.

We support reforms in the estate tax to strengthen the stability of family farms.

Farmer involvement — There is a continuing need to devise better ways of involving people in the decisions of their government, particularly in those decisions that have direct and important effects on their lives. We realize the need for a strong cattle industry and for ranchers' involvement in the development of farm programs. Considerable progress has been made in this regard, but more is required.

Capper-Volstead Act — We reaffirm our strong support for agricultural cooperatives and bargaining associations to engage in vigorous programs to pack, process and market their members' crops as provided for in the Capper-Volstead Act.

Farm labor — We must vigorously enforce existing laws relating to farm labor organization and recognize the right of farm workers to bargain collectively, while ensuring the legal rights of farmers.

Farm mechanization — We support retraining programs for farm workers displaced by mechanized farming.

Forestry

America's national forests contain a national treasure that provides recreation, wilderness, fish and wildlife, and timber products.

We reaffirm the Democratic Party's traditional support for multiple-use management to ensure the survival of these precious resources for this generation and generations to come.

We call for the speedy resolution by Congress of the Roadless Area Review and Evaluation, stimulated by this Administration, to determine which areas are best suited for wilderness and which should be released for timber harvest and multiple-use management.

We support continued assistance to private, nonindustrial forest owners to increase their management potential.

On federal lands identified as part of our timber resource, we support:

— Management policies which, consistent with sound, complete land management plans, will result in the highest timber yields, when trees are mature, and which can be sustained over the long term;

— Concentration of timber sales on areas of greatest potential;

—Management of these irreplaceable and environmentally unique areas to maintain perpetually their value; and

—Provision of adequate access facilities for all of these uses.

We shall insist that administration of public lands by the Department of Interior be fair and equitable. The interest of the state within which such public lands lie must be of paramount importance in the decision-making process. We encourage all federal agencies to consult with the states on such matters.

Fisheries

Under the Democratic Administration the U.S. fishing industry has made substantial progress, as evidenced by the following:

—Commercial landings of fish in 1979 were up 45 percent in value and 21 percent in quantity compared with 1977;

—The U.S. share of the catch in our 200-mile fisheries conservation zone increased from 27 percent in 1978 to 33 percent in 1979;

—Over the same period, the foreign catch of fish in the U.S. 200-mile zone dropped 6 percent, and 29 percent from the average for the five preceding years;

—The U.S. has moved from fifth in the world in 1977 to fourth in 1978 in total commercial fish landings; and

—Exports of U.S. edible fishery products in 1979 were up 116 percent in value and 67 percent in quantity compared with 1977.

While such trends are encouraging, there remains a tremendous potential for growth. By volume, 67 percent, and by value, 34 percent, of the harvest in the fishery conservation zone is still taken by foreign vessels. The value of the catch to foreign fishermen was $470 million in 1979.

The need for more rapid growth of the U.S. fishing industry is illustrated by the fact that imports of fisheries' products outweighed exports by $1.7 billion last year. With full development of our industry, this deficit could be erased. Moreover, 43,000 new jobs could be created.

One-fifth of the world's fish are found in waters off the United States. We pledge to continue the development of our fishing industry so that the U.S. achieves self-sufficiency in this sector and fully utilizes the valuable and abundant fisheries resources off our shores. To this end, continuing effort in the following areas is needed:

—Develop a balanced U.S. harvesting, processing and marketing capability on a geographical and fishery-by-fishery basis;

—Continue to phase out foreign fishing within our 200-mile zone;

—Target efforts to stimulate and expand those fisheries that are presently unutilized and underutilized;

—Increase research and development through cooperative federal-private efforts with emphasis on industry initiatives;

—Encourage the availability of capital in sectors where it is particularly needed;

—Promote market development, and to that end, continue to allocate surplus fishery resources of the U.S. 200-mile zone to foreign nations in order to stimulate improved access to their markets for our fish products;

—Enhance conservation and management of U.S. fishery resources and in that effort, increase observer coverage of foreign fishing operations in the 200-mile zone;

—Work toward ensuring that a fair share of the costs of conservation, management, research and enforcement in the 200-mile zone is borne by foreign fishermen who enjoy access to our surplus fishery resources;

—Assist the U.S. distant-water fleets through international agreements;

—Support an international ocean regime for fisheries management through successful completion of Law-of-the-Sea negotiations;

—Encourage development of a diversified U.S. aquaculture industry;

—Protect, restore and enhance fish habitats;

—Continue support for research, propagation and management of our anadromous fish resource; and

—In recognition of its economic and recreational importance, accord a high priority to maintaining and improving marine sports fishing.

CHAPTER V: FOREIGN POLICY

Introduction

When the Democratic Party came into office almost four years ago, the most dangerous threat to America's position in the world was the profound disillusionment and mistrust which the American people felt for their own government. This had reached the point where the very term "national security" had become synonymous with the abuse of power, deceit and violation of public trust. It undermined our capacity to defend our interests and to play our proper role in the world at a time when Soviet power was continuing to grow.

The hallmark of the previous eight years of Republican Administration had been to emphasize the primacy of power politics irrespective of compatibility with American values and with the increasing power of the Soviet Union. The result was disrespect abroad and discontent at home.

The Democratic Party was determined to make our values a central factor in shaping American foreign policy. The one-sided emphasis of the previous Republican Administration had led many Americans to a suspicion of power, and in some respects, even to rejection of military strength. The American people longed to see their country once again identified with widespread human aspirations. The Democratic Party understood, if the Republicans did not, that this is essential to preserve our long-term interest in the world.

The Democratic Administration sought to reconcile these two requirements of American foreign policy — principle and strength. Both are required to maintain a constructive and secure relationship between America and the rest of the world. We have tried to make clear the continuing importance of American strength in a world of change. Without such strength, there is a genuine risk that global change will deteriorate into anarchy to be exploited by our adversaries' military power. Thus, the revival of American strength has been a central preoccupation of the Democratic Administration.

The use of American power is necessary as a means of shaping not only a more secure, but also a more decent world. To shape a decent world, we must pursue objectives that are moral, that make clear our support for the aspirations of mankind and that are rooted in the ideals of the American people.

That is why the Democrats have stressed human rights. That is why America once again has supported the aspirations of the vast majority of the world's population for greater human justice and freedom. As we continue to strive to solve our own internal problems, we are proud of the values for which the United States has always stood. We should continue to be a beacon of liberty around the world and to effectively and positively state America's case for freedom to the world through various governmental and nongovernmental channels.

A foreign policy which seeks to blend our ideals and our strength does not easily reduce itself to simple statements.

First, we must consistently strengthen our relations with likeminded industrial democracies. In meeting the dangers of the coming decade the United States will consult closely with our Allies to advance common security and political goals. As a result of annual summit meetings, coordinated economic policies and effective programs of international energy conservation have been fashioned. With the cooperation of rich and poor nations alike, a new international trade agreement has been reached which safeguards our free enterprise system from protectionism and gives us greater economic opportunity in the world, while it gives the developing world a stake in the stability of the world's economy.

Second, we must continue to improve our relations with the Third World by being sensitive to their legitimate aspirations. The United States should be a positive force for peaceful change in responding to ferment in the Third World. Today, thanks to a number of steps that have been taken — strengthening the international aid institutions, the Panama Canal treaties, the Zimbabwe settlement, the normalization of relations with China — the United States has a healthier and more productive relationship with these countries.

Our third objective must be peace in the Middle East. The Carter Administration has pursued this objective with determination and together with the leaders of Israel and Egypt, has overcome great obstacles in the last three years. America made this commitment for two fundamental reasons — morality and national security.

Our nation feels a profound moral obligation to sustain and assure the security of Israel. That is why our relationship with Israel is, in most respects, a unique one. Israel is the single democracy, the most stable government, the most strategic asset and our closest ally in the region.

To fulfill this imperative, we must move towards peace in the Middle East. Without peace, there is a growing prospect, indeed inevitability, that this region will become radicalized, susceptible to foreign intrusion, and possibly involved in another war. Thus, peace in the Middle East also is vital for our national security interests.

The strength of these two impulses — our moral commitment and national security — has sustained the Democratic Administration in many difficult trials. The result has been the first peace ever between Israel and an Arab country, as well as the eventual prospect of a wider comprehensive agreement which will assure peace and security to all parties concerned. Our goal is to make the Middle East an area of stability and progress in which the United States can play a full and constructive role.

Our fourth major objective is to strengthen the military security of the United States and our Allies at a time when trends in the military balance have become increasingly adverse. America is now, and will continue to be, the strongest power on earth. It was the Democratic Party's greatest hope that we could, in fact, reduce our military effort. But realities of the world situation, including the unremitting buildup of Soviet military forces, required that we begin early to reverse the decade-long decline in American defense efforts.

In 1977, the United States joined with NATO to develop, for the first time in the history of the Alliance, a long-term defense program calling for 3 percent annual real growth in our collective defense efforts. This is being fulfilled. In the first year, the Democratic Administration decided that the U.S. needed an enhanced strategic posture and policy to deal with the increased first strike capability of the Soviet Union. To this end basic commitments were made regarding U.S. strategic capabilities for the late 1980s, in particular, the MX land-based mobile ICBM deterrent. Finally, development is now underway of a rapid deployment force capable of defending our interests and protecting our friends in those parts of the world where American military forces are not regularly present.

At the same time, the Democratic Administration has determined to cut waste in defense spending. The B–1 bomber was cancelled because it was technologically obsolete. A defense bill containing unnecessary expenditures for a new nuclear carrier, while neglecting the readiness of our day-to-day forces, was vetoed and the veto was sustained. These decisions involved difficult choices, but the result is a leaner, stronger American military posture.

As a fifth objective the Democrats have been and remain committed to arms control, especially to strategic arms limitations, and to maintain a firm and balanced relationship with the Soviet Union. Our resolve to pursue this goal remains as strong as ever.

To avoid the danger to all mankind from an intensification of the strategic arms competition, and to curb a possible acceleration of the nuclear arms race while awaiting the ratification of the SALT II Treaty, we endorse the policy of continuing to take no action which would be inconsistent with its object and purpose, so long as the Soviet Union does likewise.

Arms control and strategic arms limitation are of crucial importance to us and to all other people. The Salt II Agreement is a major accomplishment of the Democratic Administration. It contributes directly to our national security, and we will seek its ratification at the earliest feasible time.

Defense

America's military strength is and must be unsurpassed. The Democratic Administration has moved to reverse the threatened decline in America's world position. While claiming concern for our nation's defense preparedness, the Nixon-Ford Administration presided over a steady decline of 33 percent in real U.S. military spending between 1968 and 1976.

As a result of the joint efforts of the Democratic Administration and Congress, there has been a real increase in our defense spending every year since 1976.

This increase is necessary in order to compensate for the decline in U.S. military strength over the previous eight years and to assure a high quality of military personnel, an effective nuclear deterrent capability, a capable conventional fighting force and an improved intelligence capability. We will act to further improve intelligence gathering and analysis.

We must be careful that our defense dollars are spent wisely. We must make sure that we develop and deploy practical weapons and that we have the resources to ensure that the men and women who must operate these weapons have the skill to do so.

The serious question of manpower shortages must be addressed promptly. In order to prevent the necessity of a peacetime draft, the all-volunteer force must have wage standards which will retain experienced personnel or recruit new personnel upon whom an increasingly sophisticated military heavily depends.

We will upgrade the combat readiness of our armed forces. We will give the highest priority to combat training, to an effective Reserve and Guard force, and to sufficient supplies, spare parts, fuel and ammunition. Registration of 18-year-olds is intended to enable the United States to mobilize more rapidly in the event of an emergency, which is the only time it should be used. We do not favor a peacetime draft or the exclusion of women from registration. We will seek ways to expand voluntary service in both the armed forces and non-military programs such as VISTA, the Young Adult Conservation Corps, and the Peace Corps.

We need to go forward to protect our retaliatory capabilities in the face of continuing Soviet advances in their strategic forces.

The nation has moved to modernize its strategic deterrent through the MX, Trident, and cruise missile systems. The MX missile deployment will enhance the survivability of our land-based intercontinental ballistic missile force. Cruise missiles will modernize our strategic air deterrent, and the new Trident submarine, with a missile range of over 4,000 miles, will both improve and help guarantee the invulnerability of our nuclear deterrent.

The United States has acted to correct the dangerous military imbalance which had developed in Europe, by initiating and obtaining Allied support for a long overdue NATO long-term defense program and proceeding toward the deployment in Europe of long-range theater nuclear deterrents to counter the Soviet buildup of such weaponry in Europe. Our commitment to increase defense spending by at least 3 percent per year is crucial to the maintenance of Allied consensus and confidence in this regard. We need to modernize our conventional military capabilities so that we can better protect American lives and American interests abroad.

The Democratic Administration has acted to improve our ability to make rapid responses to contingencies by organizing and supporting rapid deployment forces capable of responding to military problems in any part of the world where our vital interests are threatened. To that end, we favor the development and production of a new fleet of cargo aircraft with intercontinental range, the design and procurement of a force of Maritime Prepositioning ships that will carry heavy equipment and supplies for three Marine Corps brigades, and an increase in regional military exercises, in cooperation with friendly states. We have given particular attention to developing the facilities and capabilities to further support the policy of the United States with regard to the Persian Gulf enunciated by President Carter in the State of the Union address on January 23, 1980: "Let our position be absolutely clear: an attempt by any outside force to gain control of the Persian Gulf region will be regarded as an assault on the vital interests of the United States of America and such an assault will be repelled by any means necessary, including military force."

We are confident that the negotiation of American overseas military facilities in support of this effort as well as in other areas of the world will be conducted with respect for the independence, integrity and cultural values of the host countries.

The Democratic Party recognizes the strategic value of Israel and that peace in the Middle East requires a militarily secure Israel. Because Middle East nations that have not joined the peace process have been able to purchase the latest sophisticated Soviet and other weaponry, the technological advantage which Israel holds over its adversaries has been jeopardized. The progress of the peace talks means that Israel has gained considerable security advantages from peace with Egypt. At the same time, Israel will lose some of the tactical advantages previously provided by territory occupied in 1967. Any further war Israel fights could take place close to its population centers. Therefore, we pledge a continued high level of U.S. military support for Israel.

U.S.-Soviet Relations

A strong, consistent, and principled policy toward the Soviet Union is a vital element of our foreign policy everywhere. The Democratic Administration will use all its resources — including both firm diplomacy and military power — to deter adventurism and to make restraint the only acceptable course available to our adversaries.

We stand ready to pursue good faith negotiations with the Soviet Union at every opportunity on a wide range of issues including strategic arms, forces in the European theater, and other matters which would contribute to peace and a more genuine and reciprocal detente.

At the heart of our policy toward the Soviet Union must be a clear recognition of the reality of Soviet power. We must reject the easy mythology that the Soviets see the world as we do. A long-term strategy for the 1980s requires a clear view of the Soviet Union, a view without illusion that our adversary is either benign or omnipotent.

The Soviet attack on Afghanistan, the murder of its leaders, and the ruthless effort to exterminate those resisting the Soviet invasion have violated all norms of international law and practice and have been thoroughly condemned by the international community.

This attempt to subjugate an independent, non-aligned Islamic people is a callous violation of international law, the United Nations Charter, and the principle of restraint which underlies detente.

This invasion places the Soviet armed forces within fighter aircraft range of the Straits of Hormuz, the lifeline of the bulk of the world's exportable oil.

It creates fear and instability among our friends in the region who are already buffeted by the disintegration of Iran as a stabilizing force.

More broadly, the success or failure of Soviet military aggression will affect present and future Soviet leaders' readiness to use force to gain their ends.

Hence, it is a threat not only to our strategic interests in the region but to world peace.

A strong American response to the illegal and brutal invasion of Afghanistan serves our nation's security interests. It must and will be sustained, as long as Soviet troops remain there.

In response to the Soviet invasion, the United States has cut grain exports, curbed high technology trade and interrupted scientific and cultural relations.

The United States has also committed itself to a boycott of Moscow as the site of the Olympic Games. To attend while the Soviet armed might brutally seeks to crush the national liberation movement in Afghanistan would be a travesty of the Olympic spirit.

We must continue to support U.S. actions such as the Olympic boycott and trade restrictions in order to show determined opposition to Soviet aggression. We insist on immediate Soviet withdrawal from Afghanistan and the reestablishment of a non-aligned, independent government which is supported by the people of Afghanistan. The Soviet invasion of Afghanistan makes it extremely important that the United States be ready to aid those in the Third World resisting Soviet, Cuban, and East German domination.

While the invasion of Afghanistan has sidetracked our pursuit of a productive relationship with the Soviet Union, the Democratic Party supports efforts to strengthen ties to the nations of Eastern Europe. Treating each of those nations with sensitivity to its individual situation, the U.S. has steadily improved relations with the people of Hungary, Poland, and Romania. While Soviet conduct has profoundly damaged East-West relations, the U.S. should continue to draw distinctions, to the extent possible, between the sanctions it imposes on economic dealings with Moscow and similar relations with some other members of the Warsaw Pact, as long as they are not diverting that trade, in grain or items under export control, to the use of the Soviet Union and as long as they are willing to maintain a constructive dialogue on issues of concern and significance to the United States.

Through the measures now being taken, including both denial of economic benefits and the Olympic boycott, as well as our efforts to enhance the security of the region more directly affected, the objective should be to make the Soviets pay a price for their act of international aggression. We should continue to do so along with efforts to strengthen our national defense. We cannot permit this attack across an international border, with the threat it poses to the region and thus to the strategic balance, to go unanswered. Only firmness now can prevent new adventures later.

The Democratic Administration will also seek to reverse the recent sharp downturn in Soviet Jewish emigration and to obtain the release of dissidents now detained in the Soviet Union, including 41 members of the Helsinki Watch Groups who are in Soviet prisons, labor camps and banishment for their human rights activity. We will pursue our human rights concerns as a necessary part of overall progress on the range of political, military and economic issues between the United States and the Soviet Union—including the possibility of improved, mutually beneficial economic relations between our two countries.

Consideration of human rights should be a permanent feature of U.S.-Soviet relations. We salute those Soviet citizens active in the Moscow, Ukrainian, Lithuanian, Armenian, and Georgian Helsinki Monitoring Groups, assert our support of the courageous human rights advocate, Nobel Peace Prize Winner, Dr. Andrei Sakharov, and call for Dr. Sakharov's release from forced exile as well as the release of all political prisoners in the U.S.S.R.

We pledge that a Democratic Administration will raise the question of the Soviet violation of human rights at all appropriate international forums.

Arms Control

The SALT II Treaty also serves our security interests. It is a vital step in an arms control process that can begin to lift from humanity the shadow of nuclear war. That process, also, must be sustained.

Soviet aggression against Afghanistan has delayed the course of ratification of the SALT II Treaty, but we must continue to pursue both security priorities: deterrence of Soviet aggression and balanced arms control agreements. Both the response to Afghanistan and the SALT II Treaty serve this purpose.

The SALT Treaty is in the U.S. interest because it is an important way of restraining Soviet behavior.

Without SALT II, the Soviets could have hundreds more missiles and thousands more nuclear warheads than the Treaty permits. Under the Treaty, they would have to eliminate many nuclear weapons they already have.

The Treaty helps sustain a strong American position in the world. Our Allies and other nations around the world know the SALT II Treaty serves their security interests as well as ours. American support for arms control is important to our standing in the international community, the same community that has rebuked the Soviets for their attempted suppression of Afghanistan. It is also important to our efforts to organize an enduring response to the growing threat to Europe of the Soviet SS-20 nuclear missiles and to Soviet aggression in Afghanistan.

Along with support for SALT, we seek to maintain a stable conventional and theater nuclear balance in Europe. We will support modernization programs in which European countries bear their fair share of the cost and other burdens. At the same time, we will ensure that no possibility for effective limits on theater nuclear weapons is left unexplored. The Democratic Administration will join with our NATO allies in making far-reaching, equitable, and verifiable proposals for nuclear and conventional arms control in Europe.

The Democratic Party wants an arms control process to continue, just as it wants to sustain strong policies against Soviet aggression in Afghanistan. We understand that both build peace and make our nation more secure. Accordingly, we must persist in a strong policy regarding the Soviet aggression, and we must seek ratification of SALT as soon as it is feasible.

A Democratic Administration will not accept an indefinite deferral of strategic arms control. On the basis of review and planning of U.S. security requirements in the coming decade, we are determined to pursue negotiations with the Soviet Union, aimed at the achievement of strategic stability and, for the first time, of major reductions and qualitative limits on strategic systems. The American SALT proposals in March 1977 were the first effort to seek such reductions, which remain the goal and justification of arms control. A Democratic Administration will treat the Soviet government's readiness to negotiate verifiable, substantial and significant reductions and qualitative limits as a test of its seriousness about arms control and the compatibility of its approach to arms control with that of the United States.

We will pursue other arms control opportunities that can enhance both our national security and the prospects of peace. In particular, the Democratic Administration will pursue a Comprehensive Nuclear Test Ban Treaty. Such a treaty is vital to our hopes to control the proliferation of nuclear weapons. Following the 1980 Review Conference on the Nuclear Non-Proliferation Treaty, we will step up our efforts to expand adherence to the treaty, to strengthen international safeguards and controls over nuclear materials, equipment and technology, and to forestall the spread of nuclear explosive capabilities. In any peaceful nuclear supply, we will continue to seek the full application of international safeguards and undertakings not to explode nuclear devices.

We have placed significant limits on our conventional arms transfers and will vigorously press other arms suppliers and recipients to accept mutual restraints.

The Democratic Administration has increased our capacity to counter national terrorism, both on a national basis and in coordination with other governments, and to deal with acts of terrorism including hostage-taking committed either by individuals or by governments. We will strengthen multilateral arrangements for contingency planning, information sharing, military coordination, and the isolation of countries that harbor terrorists.

Human Rights

In the area of international affairs, the Democratic Administration has placed America's power in the service of a more decent world by once again living up to our own values and working in a formal, deliberate way to foster the principles set out in the Universal Declaration of Human Rights.

This has been accomplished through a strong commitment to human rights, which must be seen not only as a moral imperative but as the only secure and enduring basis upon which a truly stable world order can be fashioned. There have been successes in Asia, Latin America, and elsewhere in the world. We must be undaunted by the increasing repression in the Soviet Union. We support measures designed to restrict trade with the Soviet Union until such time as Soviet emigration policy is made fair and non-restrictive.

We must be vigilant about human rights violations in any country in which they occur including South Africa. We note in particular that many of the Communist-dominated countries are persistent violators of the most basic human freedoms—the right to free speech, the right to religious freedom, the right to travel and emigrate, and the right to be free from arbitrary harassment.

We support Senate ratification of the Genocide Convention and the International Covenants on Human Rights as soon as possible.

We support continuation of the leadership role taken by the United States in the area of human rights and urge that the Democratic Administration continue to speak out openly and forcefully on human rights violations whenever and wherever they occur.

We will fulfill the letter and the spirit of current law by denying assistance to governments that violate fundamental human rights, except for that aid which is clearly humanitarian. We also recognize the exception for assistance that is required for overriding security purposes, but that exception should not be used as an excuse for ignoring abuses of human rights.

We will provide additional assistance and support, as needed, to governments that strive successfully for greater political liberty and protection of human rights.

Refugees and Migration

America's roots are found in the immigrants and refugees who have come to our shores to build new lives in a new world. The Democratic Party pledges to honor our historic commitment to this heritage.

The first comprehensive reform of this nation's refugee policies in over 25 years was completed with the signing in March 1980 of the Refugee Act of 1980, based on legislation submitted to Congress by the Carter Administration in March 1979.

This act offers a comprehensive alternative to the chaotic movement and the inefficient and inequitable administration of past refugee programs in the United States. We favor the full use of refugee legislation now to cope with the flow of Cuban and Haitian refugees, and to help the states, local communities and voluntary agencies resettle them across our land. We urge that monies be distributed to voluntary agencies fairly so that aid is distributed to all refugees without discrimination.

The Administration also established the first refugee coordination office in the Department of State under the leadership of a special ambassador and coordinator for refugee affairs and programs.

The new legislation and the coordinator's office will bring common sense and consolidation to our nation's previously fragmented, inconsistent, and, in many ways, outdated refugee and immigration policies.

A Select Commission on Immigration and Refugee Policy is now at work to further reform the system. We pledge our support to the goals and purposes of the

Commission, and we urge the Administration to move aggressively in this area once the Commission submits its report.

Once that report has been completed, we must work to resolve the issue of undocumented residents in a fair and humane way. We will oppose any legislation designed to allow workers into the country to undercut U.S. wages and working conditions, and which would re-establish the bracero program of the past.

World population projections, as well as international economic indicators—especially in the Third World—forewarn us that migration pressures will mount rapidly in many areas of the world in the decade ahead. Our own situation of undocumented workers underscores how difficult it is to deal with economic and employment forces that are beyond any nation's immediate control. Most of Europe, and many parts of Latin America and Asia, face similar dilemmas. For example, Mexico faces the pressure of migration from Central America.

We will work with other nations to develop international policies to regularize population movement and to protect the human rights of migrants even as we protect the jobs of American workers and the economic interest of the United States. In this hemisphere, such a policy will require close cooperation with our neighbors, especially Mexico and Canada.

We must also work to resolve the difficult problems presented by the immigration from Haiti and from the more recent immigration from Cuba. In doing so, we must ensure that there is no discrimination in the treatment afforded to the Cubans or Haitians. We must also work to ensure that future Cuban immigration is handled in an orderly way, consistent with our laws. To ameliorate the impact on state and local communities and school districts of the influx of new immigrants from Cuba and Haiti, we must provide the affected areas with special fiscal assistance.

We support continued financial backing of international relief programs such as those financed by the United States, the International Red Cross, UNICEF and the private, non-profit organizations to aid the starving people of Kampuchea. We also endorse such support for the Cambodian refugees and encourage participation in the campaign of the National Cambodian Crisis Committee.

We support, through U.S. contributions to the UN High Commissioner for Refugees and other means, aid for the mounting Afghan refugee population in Pakistan and other desperate refugee situations.

The Middle East

When the Democratic Administration began in 1977, the prospects for peace in the Middle East were bleak. Despite efforts over thirty years, Israel still faced an Arab world that was totally hostile to it; it was still denied any movement towards its dream of living at peace with its neighbors, behind secure and recognized frontiers.

Almost immediately after his inauguration, President Carter undertook to move the peace process forward. Following the historic visit of President Sadat to Jerusalem, the Administration's efforts led to Camp David, where the two presidents and Prime Minister Begin in thirteen days created the Camp David Accords—the most promising effort in three decades for creating a genuine and lasting peace in the Middle East.

Following President Carter's trip to the Middle East in March 1979, Prime Minister Begin and President Sadat signed the Israel-Egypt peace treaty at the White House. A year later, that treaty has led to the transfer of two-thirds of the Sinai to Egypt—along with the Sinai oil fields; ambassadors have been exchanged; borders have been opened; and normalization of relations is well underway. Israel has finally gained peace with its largest Arab neighbor. In sum, this Democratic Administration has done more to achieve Israel's dream of peace than any other Administration in thirty years.

Negotiations are continuing under the Camp David framework on full autonomy for the inhabitants of the West Bank and Gaza, in order to preserve fully Israel's security while permitting the Palestinians living in the territories to participate in determining their own future. The United States is a full partner in negotiations between Israel and Egypt to provide for a five-year transitional regime in the West Bank and Gaza.

It is recognized that the Democratic Administration has to proceed with special care and sensitivity resulting from its deep engagement in the delicate process of promoting a wider peace for Israel.

At the same time, the United States' commitment to the independence, security, and future of Israel has been strengthened. Nearly half of all U.S. aid to Israel since its creation as a sovereign state—more than $10 billion—has been requested during the last three and a half years. We provide Israel with modern military equipment and we fully support Israel's efforts to create a just and lasting peace with all of its Arab neighbors.

U.S. policy is—and should continue to be—guided also by the following principles.

UN Security council Resolution 242, unchanged, and the Camp David Accords are the basis for peace in the Middle East.

We support Israel's security, and will continue to provide generous military and economic aid to that end.

We pledge not to provide Israel's potential enemies with sophisticated offensive equipment that could endanger the security of Israel.

Jerusalem should remain forever undivided, with free access to the holy places for people of all faiths.

We oppose creation of an independent Palestinian state.

We will not negotiate with or recognize the Palestinian Liberation Organization, unless and until it accepts Israel's right to exist and UN Security Council Resolutions 242 and 338. It is also long past time for an end to all terrorism and other acts of violence against Israel.

We have not and will not use our aid to Israel as a bargaining tool; and we will never permit oil policies to influence our policy toward peace or our support for Israel.

As stated in the 1976 platform, the Democratic Party recognizes and supports "the established status of Jerusalem as the capital of Israel, with free access to all its holy places provided to all faiths. As a symbol of this stand, the U.S. Embassy should be moved from Tel Aviv to Jerusalem."

Elsewhere in the Middle East, we support the improvement of relations with moderate Arab states. We support the independence, sovereignty, and integrity of Lebanon. We call upon all states in the region to support the historic efforts of Israel and Egypt to build a comprehensive peace.

We believe a cooperative effort among the nations of the Middle East and the United States can help provide needed assistance to Israel and her Middle East neighbors engaging in the peace process with Israel in the vital areas of refugee resettlement, agricultural development, water development, health and medical facilities, and productivity and trade. A planning group should be created to pursue an effort to provide this type of assistance.

The Democratic Administration will also take needed measures to protect American interests in the Persian Gulf, including energy security, regional stability, and national independence. This will require sophisticated diplomacy as well as military capability. We will seek both to counter external threats and to encourage necessary political and economic development. In the end, our allies have an equal or greater interest than we in the security of oil supply and regional stability, and the Democratic Administration will continue to cooperate with them in a common strategy and to share common burdens.

We condemn the government of Iran for its outrageous conduct in the taking of our diplomatic personnel as hostages. We insist upon respect for the principle—as repeatedly enunciated by the UN Security Council and the International Court of Justice—of the inviolability for diplomatic personnel. We call upon all governments to abide by and uphold this basic tenet of civilized international conduct.

In the region as a whole, we must end our dangerous dependence on foreign oil. Only in this way can our foreign policy counter effectively the pressures of OPEC and of Soviet power poised above the Persian Gulf in Afghanistan. The Democratic Administration will fulfill its commitments to the Strategic Petroleum Reserve to protect America against an oil embargo. As we reduce oil consumption and dependence on OPEC, we will be able to bargain on equal terms with the OPEC states for an assurance of more certain supplies of oil at more stable prices.

Europe and Japan

America and her allies must continue the mutual confidence and commitment, the sense of common purpose, that marked our relations for decades. The problems we face are global in scope. We cannot begin to solve them if each of us goes a separate way. We must learn to work in partnership, on an increasing range of problems, in areas such as Africa and the Persian Gulf, and on worldwide economic and security issues.

The Democratic Administration will be committed to a strong NATO and a stable military balance in Europe. We will pursue both modernization of NATO conventional and nuclear forces and equitable limitations between NATO and the Warsaw Pact.

The Democratic Administration will seek collective solutions to the common economic problems of inflation, unemployment, energy, trade and monetary relations which confront us and our allies. This will require increased cooperation and coordination among all OECD countries.

The Democratic Administration will continue to support the growth and cohesion of the European community, and will increase our support for Greece, Spain and Portugal, which have rejoined the ranks of democracy.

We have been particularly concerned about the need to maintain strategic stability in the eastern Mediterranean. To this end, we have worked with Congress toward the resolution of differences between Greece and Turkey over Cyprus and other divisive issues. We have worked toward a balanced treatment of both countries in our assistance programs.

We will give priority to the reintegration of Greece into NATO's military structure and to the strengthening of NATO's southern flank, including the economic progress of each of our allies in southern Europe.

We have worked towards a fair settlement of the Cyprus issue by giving our support to the United Nations efforts to encourage intercommunal talks. We agree with Secretary General Waldheim's opinion that such talks, if properly used, represent the best possible solution to a just and lasting political settlement of the Cyprus problem based on the legitimate rights of the two communities.

We must do all that is possible, consistent with our interest in a strong NATO in southern Europe and stability in the eastern Mediterranean, to encourage a fair settlement of the Cyprus issue, which has caused so much suffering in that area.

We will press strongly for the full implementation of UN Resolution 3212 in order to bring about an agreed resolution to the tragic conflict in Cyprus; including the withdrawal of all Turkish military forces from Cyprus, the safe return of all refugees to their homes, full cooperation of all parties with a negotiated solution and a full peace and respect for human rights in Cyprus.

Consistent with our traditional concern for peace and human rights, the next Democratic Administration will play a positive role in seeking peace in Northern Ireland. We condemn the violence on all sides. We will encourage progress toward a long-term solution based upon consent of all parties to the conflict, based on the principle of Irish unity. We take note of the Saint Patrick's Day statement ". . . that the solution offering the greatest promise of permanent peace is to end the division of the Irish people" and its urging of ". . . the British Government to express its interest in the unity of Ireland and to join with the government of Ireland in working to achieve peace and reconciliation." New political structures which are created should protect human rights, and should be acceptable to both Great Britain and Ireland and to both parts of the community of Northern Ireland.

Our relations with Japan have moved to a new level of maturity and cooperation. The United States is able to deal with patience and understanding on a wide range of difficult and contentious economic issues. In the foreign policy and security area, Japan's record in support of U.S. foreign policy objectives is second to none. We will continue to nurture this relationship.

The International Economy

A vigorous American foreign policy and a sustained defense effort depend on the strength of the U.S. economy and its ability to compete in the international marketplace.

Through annual economic summits in London, Bonn, Tokyo, and Venice, we have established a sound basis for economic progress in the 1980s by improving the coordination of our economic policies. We have sought to strengthen international institutions to deal with our common problems; to reduce worldwide inflation, which undermines Western security and prosperity; to encourage investment and innovation to increase productivity; and simultaneously to find ways to reduce unemployment, especially among our youth. We have made substantial progress, but the battle continues.

The Democratic Administration, which has wrestled with these issues over the past three and a half years, pledges a renewed effort to revitalize the world economy and to maintain our position as the leader of the free world's economic forces.

Trade

In 1976, we called for trade policies that would benefit economic growth. Trade promotes new jobs for American workers, new markets for farmers and businessmen, and lower prices for consumers. But trade can also cause dislocations within the economy, and we have sought — and will continue to seek — ways to ease the burden of adjustment to foreign competition without impeding the process of structural change so vital to our economic health. We favor a free international trading system, but that system must also be fair. We will not allow our workers and industries to be displaced by unfair import competition. We have entered orderly marketing agreements and other arrangements in areas such as color television, footwear and textiles, to help promote the competitive position of American industry. Others may be necessary.

Last year, we successfully concluded the Multilateral Trade Negotiations, an ambitious set of negotiations designed to reduce barriers to international trade. Before the Democratic Administration took office, these negotiations had proceeded at a snail's pace, and there had been a growing risk of failure which could have sparked a trade war damaging to our interests. It was the imaginative leadership of this Administration which breathed new life into an otherwise somnolent negotiation.

To strengthen the U.S. economy and improve our competitive position in the world economy, U.S. export-import policy must be based on the principle of fair trade that will enhance our exports while safeguarding domestic industry from unfair trade practices. In assuring orderly foreign trade, the U.S. must require observance of our trade laws, as well as cooperation with our trade policies if economic disruption is to be avoided. This will require:

—Encouragement of export expansion through vigorous negotiations to open foreign markets and enforce U.S. rights;

—The government to take swift, effective antidumping actions and enforce all U.S. trade laws to assure an end to unfair trade practices that lead to the export of American jobs;

—Regulations of imports of textiles and apparel in accordance with current laws and agreements;

—Enforcement of customs laws through the assessment of appropriate penalties. Imports, exports, technology transfers, money flows and investments must be reported in accordance with current laws, monitored and regulated to protect U.S. interests; and

—Implementation of the government procurement code only as negotiated and on a truly reciprocal basis.

We bargained long and hard to obtain concessions which would benefit Americans and open new markets to U.S. producers of both agricultural and industrial goods. The agreements, which won the overwhelming support of the U.S. Congress, achieved that objective. They represent a sensible balance of benefits. At the same time, they will ensure a liberal, but fair, international trading environment for the 1980s.

Monetary Affairs

We will continue to take whatever actions are necessary to maintain a sound and stable dollar. We will cooperate with other nations to minimize exchange rate disturbances. We fully support efforts underway to strengthen the ability of international financial institutions to adapt to changing needs and to facilitate the recycling of funds from the surplus oil-producing nations to those countries facing large, oil-induced deficits. We will urge OPEC countries to participate constructively in this process.

International Energy Cooperation

We have cooperated with other industrial countries, at summit meetings and in the International Energy Agency, in developing joint programs to conserve oil and increase production of alternative energy sources. Only through a truly global effort can the present imbalance between energy supply and demand be redressed. We will continue to support such efforts, showing our leadership by continuing the actions that have reduced oil consumption and imports by a greater proportion in the U.S. than in any other industrial country in the last year. We will work with our partners abroad to elicit increased effort by them, even as we seek increased U.S. effort at home, to the same ends.

The Developing World

Under the previous Republican Administration, the nations of the Third World viewed the United States as uninterested in or hostile to the need to treat the North-South economic issues which are of greatest importance to developing countries. Since then, the United States has adopted a range of economic policies on trade (MTN, Generalized System of Preferences expansion), commodities (Common Fund, sugar, coffee, tin), aid (International Financial Institutions replenishments) which have demonstrated that the Carter administration is responsive to the aspirations of peoples in developing countries.

But this task is only begun. We share the globe with more than 4 billion people, more than three-quarters of whom live in developing nations, most of them poor. By the end of this century, the population of developing countries will grow by about 1.7 billion people. Their prospects for jobs, food, and peace will increasingly affect our own prospects. These nations can be the fastest growing market for our exports, as they are today, or they can become sources for new immigration and hostility toward the industrial democracies.

Thus, America's defense, energy, and economic security depend on stability and growth not only among our allies, but among our friends in the Third World. It is unacceptable that the United States ranks 13th among 17 major industrial powers in percentage of GNP devoted to development assistance.

The Democratic Administration will work with the Congress to develop and sustain policies and programs of economic cooperation with the developing nations, guided by the test of mutual interest. We will approach the global negotiations next year on economic relations between the industrial North and developing South in this positive spirit. We will contribute the United States' fair share to the capital of the multilateral development banks and agencies, and we will continue substantial and innovative U.S. programs of direct development assistance to low-income countries.

These policies will be reflected in further concentration of U.S. development assistance in countries that make good use of aid and on programs that address the basic needs of poor people, especially food, health, and voluntary family planning services. We will increase U.S. and multilateral technical and financial assistance to oil-importing nations for the development of their energy resources. The participation of U.S. private enterprises in the economic growth of developing nations will be selectively encouraged, with due regard for our own employment objectives.

We are deeply concerned about the growing problem of world hunger as reported by the President's Commission on World Hunger. We are determined to increase our resources, and to seek a similar increase on the part of other nations, with a view toward solving this problem by the end of the century.

Together with our allies, the Democratic Administration will challenge OPEC and the Communist nations to reach a new collective worldwide commitment to economic development. All sides must increase their contributions for this development, so that the world may escape the spectre of international bankruptcy from rising energy costs and rising burdens of debt. Development in the Third World is vital to international political and economic stability and therefore to our own national security.

In all of our relations with developing nations, we will actively promote the cause of human rights and express America's abhorrence of the denial of freedom.

Our security depends critically on events in the Middle East, Asia, Latin America, and Africa, events marked by either the pursuit of goals common to or conflicting with our interests. We will continue to cooperate with key friendly developing nations in security relations and in economic measures ensuring our mutual security. Great care will be exercised in our security assistance activities to avoid stimulating regional arms races or needlessly diverting resources from development to armament.

The Third World

Under the previous Republican Administration relations with the Third World were at their nadir. The United States appeared hostile and indifferent to the developing world's aspirations for greater justice, respect, and dignity. All this has changed.

Latin America and the Caribbean

In stark contrast to the policies of previous Republican Administrations, this Democratic Administration has begun to forge a new, collaborative relationship with nations of Latin America and the Caribbean; one resting on a firm commitment to human rights, democratization, increased economic and industrial development, and non-intervention.

We must now move innovatively to strengthen our ties with our neighbors in the Western Hemisphere, first to obviate any vacuum for outside intervention and second to promote bilateral approaches for social progress and economic development including energy resources.

Through systematic and structural high level attention to the problems of the Western Hemisphere we will mobilize the resources of our government to achieve this end. One such possibility to be considered is to appoint an Under Secretary of State for the Western Hemisphere. This would encourage both economic and political freedom throughout the Hemisphere.

We have given particular attention to developing a more balanced relationship with Mexico, a country with which we share so many important interests and also problems.

The successful negotiation of the Panama Canal Treaties — after fourteen fruitless years of effort — was seen as an indication of our willingness to treat Latin America on the basis of mutual respect. With those treaties ratified, the United States in 1980 is not only identified with the cause of human rights and democracy, but also we have opened a new chapter in our relations with the nations of this Hemisphere. Moreover, through regular multilateral consultations at all levels, more balanced relationships with the nations in the region have been forged.

The United States has worked hard to encourage the expansion of democracy in Latin America, respect for human rights, and the preservation of national independence and integrity from the threat of Soviet and Cuban intervention.

For the first time, an approach has been developed and tailored to the unique needs and aspirations of the Caribbean area. The Administration has supported change within a Democratic framework; more than doubled aid programs; and worked with twenty-nine other nations and fifteen international institutions to establish the Caribbean Group for Cooperation in Economic Development, which has quadrupled external aid to the region.

Through strengthened relations with the Caribbean Community and the Andean Pact, the Administration has worked to enhance subregional cooperation as well.

President Carter has worked for peace in the region. By signing Protocol I of the Treaty of Tlatelolco, President Carter has demonstrated his support for nonproliferation objectives in the Hemisphere. We support its ratification. By supporting regional efforts at arms restraints, the United States has taken the lead in trying to reduce the possibilities for conflict in the region.

We reaffirm our commitment to the protection of universally recognized and fundamental human rights throughout the Americas by urging that the Senate ratify the American Convention on Human Rights, which was signed by President Carter in June 1977.

We will join with other like-minded states in pursuing human rights, democracy, and economic development throughout the region. We will uphold our own law and terminate all aid except for clearly humanitarian purposes to human rights violators. In our relationships with Argentina, Chile, El Salvador, Guatemala, Haiti and others throughout the Hemisphere we will press further for respect for human rights and political liberalization. In Central America especially, we will align ourselves with those who are trying to build a better future out of the aftermath of tyranny, corruption and civil war.

We will oppose a spiral of confrontation with Cuba, for its own sake, but we will not evade the real issues between that country and the United States. Under no condition will we accept a Soviet military offensive capability based in Cuba or anywhere else in the Hemisphere.

In order to permit the pursuit of normal relations between our countries, Cuba should stop its disorderly movement of those seeking to leave; it should cooperate with the international community to develop a fair and orderly emigration program; it must withdraw its armed forces from Africa; it must cease subversive activities throughout the Hemisphere; and it should follow the principles of the American Convention on Human Rights.

Asia

The establishment of normal diplomatic and economic relations with China is an historic foreign policy achievement.

Progress in U.S.-China relations was stalled in 1977, but with patience, political courage and historic vision, the deadlock was broken by this Democratic Administration.

In the fifteen months since normalization, the benefits of normalization have already become clear: trade, travel, cultural exchange, and, most important of all, the security and stability of the Pacific region is greater now than in any time in this century.

The Democratic Party commits itself to a broadening and deepening of our relationship with China in a way that will benefit both our peoples and the peace and security of the world. We will continue to seek new areas where the United States and China can cooperate in support of common interests. We have not and will not play "China cards" or other dangerous games; nor will we allow our relationship with any other country to impede our efforts to continue the process of normalization of relations with China.

In 1976, the so-called Koreagate affair had badly hurt our ties to Korea. A friendly and increasingly frank dialogue with the Korean government has been promoted. We will continue not only to fulfill our commitment to security, but equally to the promotion of a more democratic government. North and South Korea have renewed their dialogue and made a difficult but hopeful start down a long, uncertain road. In our relationships with the Philippines, Taiwan and others in the region, we will also press for political liberalization and human rights.

With ASEAN, the Democratic Administration has developed a coherent and supportive approach, encouraging the cohesion of those five nations just at the time when their unity was being tested by the Vietnamese aggression in Kampuchea. ASEAN now stands as one of the most viable regional organizations in the world. The Democratic Party recognizes the important role the U.S. territories and other emerging island states in the Pacific Basin play in the solidification of defense and economic ties with the ASEAN nations. The Democratic Party commits itself to humanitarian aid to the people of East Timor.

Africa

Africa will be of central importance to American foreign policy in the 1980s. By the end of the previous Republican Administration in 1977, the United States had little credibility in Black Africa for they had made little or no attempt to see African problems from an African perspective. Our policy had no clearly defined goals. As a consequence, our attempts to bring an end to the war in Southern Africa were ineffective. We were becoming, in African eyes, irrelevant — even antagonistic — to African aspirations.

The Democratic Administration developed a long-term African policy — a policy that is viable on its own merits and does not treat Africa as an appendage to great power competition. It recognized the need for a new approach to the Continent, an approach based on mutual respect, fundamental concern for human rights and the necessity for economic justice.

Considerable success has been achieved, perhaps most notably in Southern Africa. Our diplomatic efforts there have been instrumental in helping to bring about a peaceful settlement in Rhodesia — now Zimbabwe — while lessening Soviet/Cuban influence in the area. We will continue to assist in the reconstruction and development of an independent Zimbabwe, as a means of promoting stability in the region.

Much remains to be done. Many of the fifty African nations are politically unstable and economically weak — partially as a result of their colonial heritage, but increasingly due to endemic drought and the economic dislocation resulting from ever-rising energy costs.

The Democratic Party pledges itself to continue efforts to improve U.S. relations with all African nations, on the basis of mutual respect and a mutual commitment to enhance economic justice and human dignity everywhere, with particular emphasis on the recurrent problem of drought and starvation. U.S. aid in the form of grain and foodstuffs must be continued but, in addition, we must seek with African governments ways of removing famine permanently from the African Continent.

The Democratic Party pledges itself to the process of economic reconstruction in Zimbabwe within the context of a coherent multi-donor development plan for all the cooperating nations of the Southern African region.

The Democratic Party pledges active support for self-determination in Namibia, and for full social and economic justice for all the peoples of Southern Africa.

The Democratic Administration will press for the withdrawal of Soviet and Cuban troops.

In Southern Africa, we will exert our influence to promote progress toward majority rule and to end the racist system of apartheid. We condemn the brutal suppression of Black Native African people in Soweto and Capetown by the South African regime and support increased political and economic pressure on this oppressive regime, through legal sanctions.

We support increased pressure through legal diplomatic sanctions on the oppressive South African regime. Initially we will divest, under legal procedures, South African holdings of all public institutions and deploy full legal economic sanctions until that government abandons its undemocratic apartheid system.

Following the removal of Cuban troops from Angola, we will seek to normalize relations with Angola. We will strengthen relations with nations committed to the objectives of economic development, respect for human rights and political liberalization. In the western Sahara we will support a negotiated settlement to the conflict.

The United Nations and International Agencies

In each of the regions of the globe, international organizations and agencies will be tested in the coming decade and will play an increasingly crucial role. The United Nations remains the only forum where rich and poor, East and West, and neutral nations can come together to air their grievances, participate in respected forums of world opinion, and find mechanisms to resolve disputes without resort to force. In particular, in recent months the UN has been a forum for expressing the world's condemnation and rejection of both the hostage-taking in Iran and the Soviet invasion of Afghanistan.

The United Nations is also vital in other ways — through its international refugee efforts, coordination of development assistance, support for agricultural research, and worldwide eradication of disease.

In the next decade, international monetary and development institutions will also be under increasing pressure. Their efforts must be expanded to meet more fully the urgent needs of the two-thirds of the world's population which suffers the damaging and depressing effects of underdevelopment.

The United Nations and these agencies perform a vital role in the search for peace. They deserve America's continuing support — and they will receive it from the Democratic Administration. We support the U.S. position on freedom of the press to be voted again in Belgrade during the 1980 UNESCO meeting.

We support the call in Section 503 of the Foreign Relations Authorization Act of 1978, for the United States to make "a major effort toward reforming and restructuring the United Nations system."

We also endorse that portion of the President's report to Congress in March, 1978 on UN reform and restructuring which calls for the Senate "to re-examine the Connally reservation," "the creation of a U.N. Peacekeeping Reserve composed of national contingents trained in peacekeeping functions," the establishment of "a new UN senior post as High Commissioner of Human Rights," and the development of autonomous sources of income for the international community.

We will work toward new structures which will enhance the UN in the fields of economic development, including international trade organizations, higher education, volunteer service, mediation and conciliation, international disarmament, implementation of the Law of the Sea Agreement, and controlling international terrorism.

Into the 1980s

As we look to the 1980s, we have a full and challenging agenda.

With our Allies, we face the challenge of building greater unity of action while preserving the diversity of our democracies. Europe is increasingly united and is finding its own identity and voice. We must forge new links of consultation and revive the political process within the North Atlantic Alliance so that Europe remains America's partner in meeting the challenges to our common security and economic interests. We must find ways to include Japan in this process, broadening the mechanisms for cooperation which exist in current international forums, such as the Seven-Nation Summit.

With the Third World countries, we must continue to do our part in the realization of their aspirations for justice, respect, and freedom. We must continue to work for full political participation by all in South Africa, including independence and majority rule in Namibia. We must work to strengthen democracy in the Caribbean and Central America in the face of efforts by the Cubans to export their failed revolution. Throughout Latin America, we must continue to cooperate for the realization of greater human rights and the fulfillment of basic human needs. In Asia, we must continue to strengthen our relationships with our friends and Allies as they confront the twin dangers flowing from the Soviet invasion of Afghanistan and the Soviet-backed invasion of Cambodia.

We must persevere with the Middle East peace process. There is no viable alternative. We can welcome initiatives from other countries so long as they contribute to the Camp David process that is leading toward a comprehensive peace in that region. But we will oppose efforts that undermine Camp David while offering no viable alternative. Our goal is to see the achievement of a comprehensive peace for all parties.

With our defenses, we will continue to meet the requirements of the Administration's five-year defense program, including the deployment of the MX missile, cruise missiles, the Trident submarine, and long-range theater nuclear forces in Europe. At the same time, we intend to increase readiness and strengthen the All-Volunteer Force with a standby system of draft registration. We will continue with our Allies to meet the commitments of the long-term NATO defense program and, as we strengthen our military capabilities and presence in Southwest Asia and the region of the Persian Gulf, we will look to our Allies to assume more of the burden for the defense and security of Europe. Finally, we must recognize that development assistance represents a crucial part of our national security. As such, we may have to make a greater contribution of resources to these programs.

In the field of arms control, in addition to ratification of SALT II, we must proceed to more comprehensive and drastic reductions and qualitative limitations on strategic nuclear forces. SALT III must also include effective limitations and reductions in long-range theater nuclear forces based on the principle of equality. We must pursue to a conclusion a comprehensive test ban, effective curbs in the international traffic of conventional arms and a more rigorously effective international regime to prevent the spread of nuclear weapons and weapons technology. We must bring to at least an initial conclusion the negotiations for mutual and balanced force reductions in Europe. The decade of the 1980s is not to become the decade of violence. We must make renewed efforts to stabilize the arms competition and widen the scope of arms control arrangements.

As we look to the future, we hope the progress in arms control and the strength and determination we shall demonstrate in the face of Soviet aggression in Afghanistan will soon result in the fashioning of a stronger, more productive relationship with the Soviet Union. We favor a genuine detente—one with equivalent benefits to ourselves and the Soviets, one that is based on genuine restraint, one that benefits all mankind by harnessing the enormous potential of our two societies for cooperation rather than competition and confrontation. This will take patience, but we shall persevere for the prize is peace.

By reaffirming America's values as the centerpiece of our foreign policy and by pursuing realistically the requirements of military strength, the Democratic Party is forging a new and broader consensus among the American people in support of our foreign policy. We are turning the tide against the paralysis of despair that came from a tragic war in Asia and political scandal at home. We are restoring America to its rightful place, not only as the strongest nation in the world, but as the nation which is the champion of human justice and freedom.

Libertarian Platform 1980

STATEMENT OF PRINCIPLES

We, the members of the Libertarian Party, challenge the cult of the omnipotent state and defend the rights of the individual.

We hold that all individuals have the right to exercise sole dominion over their own lives, and have the right to live in whatever manner they choose, so long as they do not forcibly interfere with the equal right of others to live in whatever manner they choose.

Governments throughout history have regularly operated on the opposite principle, that the State has the right to dispose of the lives of individuals and the fruits of their labor. Even within the United States, all political parties other than our own grant to government the right to regulate the lives of individuals and seize the fruits of their labor without their consent.

We, on the contrary, deny the right of any government to do these things, and hold that where governments exist, they must not violate the rights of any individual: namely, (1) the right to life—accordingly we support prohibition of the initiation of physical force against others; (2) the right to liberty of speech and action—accordingly we oppose all attempts by government to abridge the freedom of speech and press, as well as government censorship in any form;

and (3) the right to property — accordingly we oppose all government interference with private property, such as confiscation, nationalization, and eminent domain, and support the prohibition of robbery, trespass, fraud, and misrepresentation.

Since governments, when instituted, must not violate individual rights, we oppose all interference by government in the areas of voluntary and contractual relations among individuals. People should not be forced to sacrifice their lives and property for the benefit of others. They should be left free by government to deal with one another as free traders; and the resultant economic system, the only one compatible with the protection of individual rights, is the free market.

INDIVIDUAL RIGHTS AND CIVIL ORDER

No conflict exists between civil order and individual rights. Both concepts are based on the same fundamental principle: that no individual, group, or government may initiate force against any other individual, group or government.

1. *Freedom and Responsibility*

Members of the Libertarian Party do not necessarily advocate or condone any of the practices our policies would make legal. Our exclusion of moral approval and disapproval is deliberate: people's rights must be recognized; the wisdom of any course of peaceful action is a matter for the acting individual(s) to decide. Personal responsibility is discouraged by society routinely denying people the opportunity to exercise it. Libertarian policies will create a society where people are free to make and learn from their own decisions.

2. *Crime*

The continuing increase in violent crime threatens the lives, happiness, and belongings of Americans. At the same time, governmental violations of rights undermine the people's sense of justice with regard to crime. Impartial and consistent law enforcement protecting individual rights, and repeal of victimless crime laws, which themselves breed crimes with victims, are the appropriate ways to suppress crime.

3. *Victimless Crimes*

Because only actions which infringe the rights of others can properly be termed crimes, we favor the repeal of all federal, state, and local laws creating "crimes" without victims. In particular, we advocate:

a. The repeal of all laws prohibiting the production, sale, possession, or use of drugs, and of all medical prescription requirements for the purchase of vitamins, drugs and similar substances;

b. The repeal of all laws regarding consensual sexual relations, including prostitution and solicitation, and the cessation of state oppression and harassment of homosexual men and women, that they, at last, be accorded their full rights as individuals;

c. The repeal of all laws regulating or prohibiting gambling;

d. The repeal of all laws interfering with the right to commit suicide as infringements of the ultimate right of an individual to his or her own life; and

e. The use of executive pardon to free all those presently incarcerated for the commission of these "crimes."

4. *Safeguards for the Criminally Accused*

Until such time as persons are proved guilty of crimes, they should be accorded full respect for their individual rights. We are thus opposed to reduction of present safeguards of the rights of the criminally accused.

Specifically, we are opposed to preventive detention, so-called "no-knock laws," and all other measures which threaten individual rights.

We advocate the repeal of all laws establishing any category of crimes applicable to minors for which adults would not be similarly answerable, and an end to the practice in many states of jailing children accused of no crime.

We support full restitution for all loss suffered by persons arrested, indicted, tried, imprisoned, or otherwise injured in the course of criminal proceedings against them which do not result in their conviction. When they are responsible, government police employees or agents should be liable for this restitution.

We call for a reform of the judicial system allowing criminal defendants and civil parties to a court action a reasonable number of peremptory challenges to proposed judges, similar to their right under the present system to challenge a proposed juror.

5. *Justice for the Individual*

The present system of criminal law is based on punishment with little concern for the victim. We support restitution for the victim to the fullest degree possible at the expense of the criminal or wrongdoer.

We accordingly oppose all "no-fault" insurance laws which deprive the victim of the right to recover damages from those responsible in case of injury. We also support the right of the victim to pardon the criminal or wrongdoer, barring threats to the victim for this purpose.

6. Sovereign Immunity

We favor an immediate end to the doctrine of "Sovereign Immunity" which implies that the State can do no wrong and holds that the State, contrary to the tradition of redress of grievances, may not be sued without its permission or held accountable for its actions under civil law.

7. Government and "Mental Health"

We oppose the involuntary commitment of any person to a mental institution. To incarcerate an individual not convicted of any crime, but merely asserted to be incompetent, is a violation of the individual's rights. We further advocate:

a. The repeal of all laws permitting involuntary psychiatric treatment of any person, including children, and those incarcerated in prisons or mental institutions;

b. An immediate end to the spending of tax money for any program of psychiatric or psychological research or treatment;

c. An end to all involuntary treatments of prisoners by such means as psycho-surgery, drug therapy, and aversion therapy;

d. An end to tax-supported "mental health" propaganda campaigns and community "mental health" centers and programs; and

e. An end to criminal defenses based on "insanity" or "diminished capacity" which absolve the guilty of their responsibility.

8. Freedom of Speech and the Press

We oppose all forms of government censorship, including anti-pornography laws, whatever the medium involved. We oppose the burgeoning practice of the government's invading newsrooms or the premises of any other innocent third parties in the name of law enforcement. We also condemn court orders gagging press coverage of criminal proceedings — the right to publish must not be abridged merely for the convenience of the judicial system.

Events have demonstrated that the already precarious First Amendment rights of the broadcast industry are becoming still more precarious. Regulation of broadcasting including the "fairness doctrine" and "equal-time" provisions, cannot be tolerated. We support legislation to repeal the Federal Communications Act, and to provide for private ownership of broadcasting rights, thus giving broadcasting First Amendment parity with other communications media. The removal of these regulations and privileges would open the way for greater diversity in the broadcast

media. We deplore any efforts to impose thought control on the media by the use of anti-trust laws and other government action in the name of stopping "bias." We specifically oppose such government efforts to control broadcast content as banning advertising for cigarettes and sugar-coated breakfast foods or regulating depiction of sex or violence.

Government ownership or subsidy of broadcast band radio and television stations and networks — in particular, the tax funding of the Corporation for Public Broadcasting — must end. We oppose government restriction and regulation of "pay TV" and cable facilities.

9. Freedom of Religion

We defend the rights of individuals to engage in (or abstain from) any religious activities which do not violate the rights of others. In order to defend religious freedom, we advocate a strict separation of church and state. We oppose government actions which either aid or attack any religion. We oppose taxation of church property for the same reason that we oppose all taxation.

We condemn the attempts by parents or any others — via kidnappings, conservatorships, or instruction under confinement — to force children to conform to their parents' or any others' religious views. Government harassment or obstruction of unconventional religious groups for their beliefs or nonviolent activities must end.

10. The Right to Property

There is no conflict between property rights and human rights. Indeed, property rights are the rights of humans with respect to property and, as such, are entitled to the same respect and protection as all other human rights.

We further hold that the owners of property have the full right to control, use, dispose of, or in any manner enjoy their property without interference, until and unless the exercise of their control infringes the valid rights of others. We specifically condemn current government efforts to regulate or ban the use of property in the name of aesthetic values, riskiness, moral standards, cost-benefit estimates, or the promotion or restriction of economic growth.

We demand an end to the taxation of privately owned real property, which actually makes the State the owner of all lands and forces individuals to rent their homes and places of business from the State.

Where property, including land, has been taken from its rightful owners by government or private action in violation of individual rights, we favor restitution to the rightful owners.

11. Protection of Privacy

The individual's privacy, property, and right to speak or not to speak should not be infringed by the government. The government should not use electronic or other means of covert surveillance of an individual's actions or private property without the consent of the owner or occupant. Correspondence, bank and other financial transactions and records, doctors' and lawyers' communications, employment records, and the like should not be open to review by government without the consent of all parties involved in those actions. So long as the National Census and all federal, state, and other government agencies' compilations of data on an individual continue to exist, they should be conducted only with the consent of the persons from whom the data are sought.

We oppose the issuance by the government of an identity card, to be required for any purpose, such as for employment, voting, or border crossings.

12. Government Secrecy

We condemn the government's use of secret classifications to keep from the public information which it should have. We favor substituting a system in which no individual may be convicted for violating government secrecy classifications unless the government discharges its burden of proving that the publication:

a. Violated the right of privacy of those who have been coerced into revealing confidential or proprietary information to government agents, or

b. Disclosed defensive military plans so as to materially impair the capability to respond to attack.

It should always be a defense to such prosecution that information divulged shows that the government has violated the law.

13. Internal Security and Civil Liberties

We call for the abolition of all federal secret police agencies. In particular, we seek the abolition of the Central Intelligence Agency and the Federal Bureau of Investigation, and we call for a return to the American tradition of local law enforcement. We support Congressional investigation of criminal activities of the CIA and of wrongdoing by other government agencies.

We support the abolition of the subpoena power as used by Congressional committees against individuals or firms. We hail the abolition of the House Internal Security Committee and call for the destruction of its files on private individuals and groups. We also call for the abolition of the Senate Subcommittee on Internal Security.

14. The Right to Keep and Bear Arms

Maintaining our belief in the inviolability of the right to keep and bear arms, we oppose all laws at any level of government restricting the ownership, manufacture, transfer or sale of firearms or ammunition. We oppose all laws requiring registration of firearms or ammunition. We also oppose any government efforts to ban or restrict the use of tear gas, "mace," or other non-firearm protective devices. We further oppose all attempts to ban weapons or ammunition on the grounds that they are risky or unsafe.

We support repeal of the National Firearms Act of 1935 and the Federal Gun Control Act of 1968 and demand the immediate abolition of the Bureau of Alcohol, Tobacco, and Firearms.

We favor the repeal of laws banning the concealment of weapons or prohibiting pocket weapons. We also oppose the banning of inexpensive handguns ("Saturday night specials").

15. The Draft, National Service, and the Military

Recognizing that registration is the first step toward full conscription, we oppose all attempts at compulsory registration of any person and all schemes for automatic registration through government invasions of the privacy of school, motor vehicle, or other records. We call for the abolition of the still-functioning elements of the Selective Service System, believing that impressment of individuals into the armed forces is involuntary servitude. We also oppose any form of national service, such as a compulsory youth labor program. For this reason, we oppose the Youth Conservation Corps, which is designed as a pilot program for national service.

We support the immediate and unconditional exoneration of all who have been accused or convicted of draft evasion, desertion from the military, and other acts of resistance to such transgressions as imperialistic wars and aggressive acts of the military. Members of the military should have the same right to quit their jobs as other persons.

We call for the end of the Defense Department practice of discharging armed forces personnel for homosexual conduct when such conduct does not interfere with their assigned duties. We further call for retraction of all less-than-honorable discharges previously assigned for such reasons and deletion of such information from military personnel files.

We recommend the repeal of the Uniform Code of Military Justice and the recognition and equal protection of the rights of the armed forces in order to promote thereby the morale, dignity, and sense of justice within the military.

16. Unions and Collective Bargaining

We support the right of free persons to voluntarily establish, associate in, or not associate in, labor unions. An employer should have the right to recognize, or refuse to recognize, a union as the collective bargaining agent of some or all of his or her employees.

We oppose government interference in bargaining, such as compulsory arbitration or imposing an obligation to bargain. Therefore we urge repeal of the National Labor Relations Act, and all state Right to Work Laws, which prohibit employers from making voluntary contracts with unions. We oppose all government back-to-work orders as imposing a form of forced labor.

Workers and employers should have the right to organize secondary boycotts if they so choose. Nevertheless, boycotts or strikes do not justify the initiation of violence against other workers, employers, strikebreakers, and innocent bystanders.

17. Immigration

We hold that human rights should not be denied or abridged on the basis of nationality. We condemn massive roundups of Hispanic-Americans and others by the federal government in its hunt for individuals not possessing required government documents. Undocumented non-citizens should not be denied the fundamental freedom to labor and to move about unmolested. Furthermore, immigration must not be restricted for reasons of race, religious or political creed, or sexual preference.

We therefore call for the elimination of all restrictions on immigration, the abolition of the Immigration and Naturalization Service and the Border Patrol, and a declaration of full amnesty for those people who have entered the country illegally. We oppose government welfare payments to non-citizens just as we oppose government welfare payments to all other persons.

We welcome Indochinese and other refugees to our shores, and condemn the efforts of U.S. government officials to induce Indochinese governments to create a new "Berlin wall" that would keep them captive.

18. Discrimination

No individual rights should be denied or abridged by the laws of the United States or any state or locality on account of sex, race, color, creed, age, national origin, or sexual preference. Protective labor laws, Selective Service laws, and other laws which violate rights selectively should be repealed entirely rather than being extended to all groups.

Discrimination imposed by the government has brought disruption in normal relationships of peoples, set neighbor against neighbor, created gross injustices, and diminished human potential. Anti-discrimination enforced by the government is the reverse side of the coin and will for the same reasons create the same problems. Consequently, we oppose any governmental attempts to regulate private discrimination, including discrimination in employment, housing, and privately owned so-called public accommodations. The right to trade includes the right not to trade — for any reasons whatsoever.

19. Secession

We support recognition of the right to political secession. Exercise of this right, like the exercise of all other rights, does not remove legal and moral obligations not to violate the rights of others.

20. Children's Rights

We believe that "children" are human beings and, as such, have the same rights as any other human beings. Any reference in this Platform to the rights of human beings includes children.

TRADE AND THE ECONOMY

Because each person has the right to offer goods and services to others on the free market, and because government interference can only harm such free activity, we oppose all intervention by government into the area of economics. The only proper role of existing governments in the economic realm is to protect property rights, adjudicate disputes, and provide a legal framework in which voluntary trade is protected.

Efforts to forcibly redistribute wealth or forcibly manage trade are intolerable. Government manipulation of the economy creates an entrenched privileged class — those with access to tax money — and an exploited class — those who are net taxpayers.

1. The Economy

Government intervention in the economy imperils both the personal freedom and the material prosperity of every American. We therefore support the following specific immediate reforms:

    a. drastic reduction of both taxes and government spending;

    b. an end to deficit budgets;

    c. a halt to inflationary monetary policies;

    d. the removal of all governmental impediments to free trade; and

    e. the repeal of all controls on wages, prices, rents, profits, production, and interest rates.

2. Taxation

Since we believe that all persons are entitled to keep the fruits of their labor, we oppose all government activity which consists of the forcible collection of money or goods from individuals in violation of their individual rights. Specifically, we:

    a. recognize the right of any individual to challenge the payment of taxes on moral, religious, legal or constitutional grounds;

    b. oppose all personal and corporate income taxation, including capital gains taxes;

    c. support repeal of the Sixteenth Amendment, and oppose any increase in existing tax rates and the imposition of any new taxes;

    d. support the eventual repeal of all taxation; and

    e. support a declaration of unconditional amnesty for all those who have been convicted of, or who now stand accused to tax resistance.

As an interim measure, all criminal and civil sanctions against tax evasion should be terminated immediately.

We oppose as involuntary servitude any legal requirements forcing employers or business owners to serve as tax collectors for federal, state, or local tax agencies.

In the current fiscal crisis of states and localities, default is preferable to raising taxes or perpetual refinancing of growing public debt.

3. Inflation and Recession

We recognize that government control over money and banking is the cause of inflation, depression and distortion of relative prices and production. Individuals engaged in voluntary exchange should be free to use as money any commodity or item that is mutually agreeable. We therefore call for the repeal of all legal tender laws and of all compulsory governmental units of account. We support the right to private ownership of and contracts for gold. We favor the elimination of all government fiat money and all government minted coins. All restrictions upon the private minting of coins should be abolished so that minting will be open to the competition of the free market. We favor the use of a free market commodity standard, such as gold coin denominated by units of weight.

We favor free market banking. We call for the abolition of the Federal Reserve System, the Federal Deposit Insurance Corporation, the National Banking System, and all similar state and federal agencies. Such governmentally sponsored credit agencies as the Federal Home Loan Banks, the Federal National Mortgage Association, the Student Loan Marketing Association, and the various institutions supervised by the Farm Credit Administration must either be abolished or totally privatized.

To complete the separation of bank and state, we favor the Jacksonian independent treasury system, in which all government funds are held by the government itself and not deposited in any private banks. The only further necessary check upon monetary inflation is the consistent application of the general protection against fraud to the minting and banking industries.

Pending its abolition, the Federal Reserve System, in order to halt rampant inflation, must immediately cease its expansion of the quantity of money. As interim measures, we further support:

    a. the lifting of all restrictions on branch banking;

    b. the repeal of all state usury laws;

    c. the removal of the prohibition of interest for demand deposits;

    d. the abolition of Federal Reserve control over the interest paid on time deposits;

    e. the elimination of margin requirements on stock purchases; and

    f. the revocation of all other selective credit controls.

4. Monopolies

We condemn all coercive monopolies. We recognize that government is the source of monopoly, through its grants of legal privilege to special interests in the economy. In order to abolish monopolies, we advocate a strict separation of business and state.

"Anti-trust" laws do not prevent monopoly, but foster it by limiting competition. We therefore call for the repeal of all "anti-trust" laws, including the Robinson-Patman Act which restricts price discounts, the Sherman Anti-Trust Act, and the Clayton Anti-Trust Act. We further call for the abolition of the Federal Trade Commission and the anti-trust division of the Department of Justice.

We defend the right of individuals to form corporations, cooperatives, and other types of companies based on voluntary association. Laws of incorporation should not include grants of monopoly privilege. In particular, we oppose special limits on the liability of corporations for damages caused in noncontractual transactions. We also oppose state or federal limits on the size of private companies and on the right of companies to merge. We further oppose efforts, in the name of social responsibility or any other reason, to expand federal chartering of corporations into a pretext for government control of business.

5. Subsidies

In order to achieve a free economy in which government victimizes no one for the benefit of anyone else, we oppose all government subsidies to business, labor, education, agriculture, science, broadcasting, the arts, sports, and any other special interest. Relief or exemption from involuntary taxation should not be considered a subsidy. We oppose any resumption of the Reconstruction Finance Corporation, or any similar plan which would force the taxpayer to subsidize and sustain uneconomic business enterprises.

6. Tariffs and Quotas

Like subsidies, tariffs and quotas serve only to give special treatment to favored interests and to diminish the welfare of other individuals. These measures also reduce the scope of contracts and understanding among different peoples. We therefore support abolition of all tariffs and quotas as well as the Tariff Commission and the Customs Court.

7. Public Utilities

We advocate the termination of government-created franchise privileges and governmental monopolies for such services as garbage collection, fire protection, electricity, natural gas, telephone, or water supplies. Furthermore, all rate regulation in these industries should be abolished. The right to offer such services on the market should not be curtailed by law.

Domestic Ills

Current problems in such areas as energy, pollution, health care delivery, decaying cities, and poverty are not solved, but are primarily caused, by government. The welfare state, supposedly designed to aid the poor, is in reality a growing and parasitic burden on all productive people, and injures, rather than benefits, the poor themselves.

1. Energy

We recognize the great mischief that a host of government interferences have caused in the energy industry, and the even greater mischief — amounting to a total regimentation of the American economy and society — that is threatened by recent and proposed interventions.

We oppose all government control of energy pricing, allocation, and production, such as that imposed by the Federal Power Commission, the Department of Energy, state public utility commissions, and state pro-rationing agencies. Thus, we advocate decontrol of the prices of oil, petroleum products, and natural gas. We call for the immediate decontrol of gasoline prices, and elimination of the federal allocation program for crude oil and gasoline. We condemn the proposed "windfall profits tax" which is really a graduated excise tax on the production of crude oil, and which would cripple the discovery and production of oil. We oppose all government subsidies for energy research, development, and operation. We oppose a subsidized Federal Energy Security Corporation, which would develop synthetic fuels. We also oppose its financing via the issue of small denomination bonds, which would rapidly tend to lose their value in an era of inflation. We further oppose government subsidies to a solar development bank for solar energy.

We oppose all direct and indirect government participation in the nuclear energy industry, including subsidies, research and development funds, guaranteed loans, waste disposal subsidies and federal uranium enrichment facilities. The Nuclear Regulatory Commission should be abolished; the imposition of full liability — not government agencies — should regulate nuclear power. The Price-Anderson Act, through which the government limits liability for nuclear accidents and furnishes partial payment at taxpayer expense, should be repealed. Nuclear energy should be denationalized and the industry's assets transferred to the private sector. Any nuclear power industry must meet the test of a free market.

We support abolition of the Department of Energy. We oppose the proposed federal Energy Mobilization Board, which would wield dictatorial powers in order to override normal legal processes. We oppose all government conservation schemes through the use of taxes, subsidies and regulations, as well as the dictated conversion of utilities and other industries to coal. We denounce all temperature level regulations as despotic and oppressive. We oppose any attempt to give the federal government a monopoly over the importation of oil, or to develop a subsidized government energy corporation whose privileged status would be used as a yardstick for condemning private enterprise. We oppose the "strategic storage" program, any attempts to compel national self-sufficiency in oil, any extension of the cargo preference law to imports, and any attempts to raise oil tariffs or impose oil import quotas. We oppose all efforts to nationalize energy companies or break up vertically and horizontally integrated energy companies or force them to divest their pipelines.

We consider all attempts to impose an operating or standby program of gasoline rationing as unworkable, unnecessary, and tyrannical.

We favor the creation of a free market in oil by instituting a system of full property rights in underground oil and by repeal of all federal and state controls over price and output in the petroleum industry. All government-owned energy resources should be turned over to private ownership.

2. Pollution

We support the development of an objective system defining individual property rights to air and water. We hold that ambiguities in the area of these rights (e.g., the concept of "public property") are a primary cause of our deteriorating environment. Present legal principles which allow the violation of individual rights by polluters must be reversed. The laws of nuisance and negligence should be modified to cover damage done by air, water, and noise pollution. While we maintain that no one has the right to violate the legitimate property rights of others by polluting, we strenuously oppose all attempts to transform the defense of such rights into any restriction of the efforts of individuals to advance technology, to expand production, or to use their property peacefully. We therefore support the abolition of the Environmental Protection Agency.

3. Consumer Protection

We support strong and effective laws against fraud and misrepresentation. However, we oppose paternalistic regulations which dictate to consumers, impose prices, define standards for products, or otherwise restrict risk-taking and free choice. We oppose governmental promotion or imposition of the metric system.

We oppose all so-called "consumer protection" legislation which infringes upon voluntary trade, and call for the abolition of the Consumer Product Safety Commission. We advocate the repeal of all laws banning or restricting the advertising of prices, products, or services. We specifically oppose laws requiring an individual to buy or use so-called "self-protection" equipment such as safety belts, air bags, or crash helmets.

We advocate the abolition of the Federal Aviation Administration, which has jeopardized airline safety by arrogating to itself a monopoly of safety regulation and enforcement.

We advocate the abolition of the Food and Drug Administration and particularly its policies of man-

dating specific nutritional requirements, and denying the right of manufacturers to make non-fraudulent claims concerning their products. We advocate an end to compulsory fluoridation of water supplies. We specifically oppose government regulation of the price, potency, or quantity able to be produced or purchased of drugs or other consumer goods. There should be no laws regarding what substances (nicotine, alcohol, hallucinogens, narcotics, laetrile, artificial sweeteners, vitamin supplements, or other "drugs") a person may ingest or otherwise use.

4. Education

We advocate the complete separation of education and State. Government schools lead to the indoctrination of children and interfere with the free choice of individuals. Government ownership, operation, regulation, and subsidy of schools and colleges should be ended.

As an interim measure to encourage the growth of private schools and variety in education, we support tax-credits for tuition and for other expenditures related to an individual's education. We support the repeal of all taxes on the income or property of private schools, whether profit or non-profit.

We condemn compulsory education laws, which spawn prison-like schools with many of the problems associated with prisons, and we call for the immediate repeal of such laws.

Until government involvement in education is ended, we support elimination within the governmental school system, of forced busing and corporal punishment. We further support immediate reduction of tax support for schools, and removal of the burden of school taxes from those not responsible for the education of children.

5. Population

We support an end to all subsidies for childbearing built into our present laws, including all welfare plans and the provision of tax-supported services for children. We further support the repeal of all laws restricting voluntary birth control or the right of the woman to make a personal moral choice regarding the termination of pregnancy. We call for the elimination of special tax burdens on single people and couples with few or no children. We shall oppose all coercive measures to control population growth.

6. Transportation

Government interference in transportation is characterized by monopolistic restriction, corruption, and gross inefficiency. We therefore call for the dissolution of all government agencies concerned with transportation, including the Department of Transportation, the Interstate Commerce Commission, the Civil Aeronautics Board, the Federal Maritime Commission, Conrail and Amtrak. We demand the return of America's railroad system to private ownership. We call for the privatization of the public roads and national highway system.

As interim measures, we advocate an immediate end to government regulation of private transit organizations and to government favors to the transportation industry. In particular, we support the immediate repeal of all laws restricting transit competition, such as the granting of taxicab and bus monopolies and the prohibition of private jitney services. We urge immediate deregulation of the trucking industry. Likewise, we advocate the immediate repeal of the federally imposed 55 mph speed limit.

7. Poverty and Unemployment

Government fiscal and monetary measures that artificially foster business expansion guarantee an eventual increase in unemployment rather than curtailing it. We call for the immediate cessation of such policies as well as any governmental attempts to affect employment levels.

We support repeal of all laws which impede the ability of any person to find employment, such as minimum wage laws, so-called "protective" labor legislation for women and children, governmental restrictions on the establishment of private day-care centers, and the National Labor Relations Act. We deplore government-fostered forced retirement, which robs the elderly of the right to work.

We seek the elimination of occupational licensure, which prevents human beings from working in whatever trade they wish. We call for the abolition of all federal, state, and local government agencies which restrict entry into any profession, such as education and law, or regulate its practice. No worker should be legally penalized for lack of certification, and no consumer should be legally restrained from hiring unlicensed individuals.

We oppose all government welfare, relief projects, and "aid to the poor" programs. All these government programs are privacy-invading, paternalistic, demeaning, and inefficient. The proper source of help for such persons is the voluntary efforts of private groups and individuals.

To speed the time when governmental programs are replaced by effective private institutions, we advocate dollar-for-dollar tax credits for all charitable contributions.

8. Health Care

We support the right of individuals to contract freely with practitioners of their choice, whether licensed by the government or not, for all health services. We oppose any compulsory insurance or tax-supported plan to provide health services, including those which finance abortion services. We favor the abolition of Medicare and Medicaid programs. We further oppose governmental infringement of the health care practitioner-patient relationship through regulatory agencies such as the Professional Standards Review Organization. We oppose any state or federal area planning boards whose stated purpose is to consolidate health services or avoid their duplication. We oppose laws limiting the liability of health care professionals for negligence, and those regulating the supply of legal aid on a contingency fee basis. We oppose laws which invalidate settlements of malpractice suits through the use of private arbitration services. We also favor the deregulation of the medical insurance industry.

We condemn attempts at the federal, state, or local level to cripple the advance of science by governmental restrictions on research. In particular, we oppose government attempts to suppress recombinant DNA research, which has opened the way for increased supply of medically useful human proteins, such as insulin, and shows promise of revealing the nature of hereditary diseases, the structure of bacteria and viruses, and the nature of the immune response. We oppose any laws which limit liability for injuries arising from recombinant DNA research.

We call for the repeal of laws compelling individuals to submit to medical treatment, testing, or to the administration of drugs or other substances.

9. Resource Use

The role of planning is properly the responsibility and right of the owners of the land, water, or other natural resources. We therefore urge an end to governmental control of land use through such methods as urban renewal, zoning laws, building codes, eminent domain, regional planning, or purchase of development rights with tax money, which not only violate property rights, but discriminate against minorities and tend to cause higher rents and housing shortages. We are further opposed to the use of tax funds for the acquisition or maintenance of land or other real property. We recognize the legitimacy of private, voluntary land use covenants.

We call for the privatization of the inland waterways, and of the distribution system that brings water to industry, agriculture and households. We oppose all government controls over, or rationing of, water; these despotic measures can only aggravate a water shortage. We oppose the construction of government dams. We favor the privatization of presently government-occupied dam sites. We also favor the abolition of the Bureau of Reclamation and the Army Corps of Engineers.

Instances of government recognition of homesteading in which the government reserves surface mining rights to itself are invalid and forced surface-mining of such lands is a violation of the rights of the present land holders. We call for the immediate abolition of the Bureau of Land Management and the transfer to private ownership of federally held so-called public lands, which constitute more than 80 percent of certain states. Further, we oppose any use of executive orders invoking the Antiquities Act to set aside public lands in Alaska and elsewhere.

10. Occupational Safety and Health Act (OSHA)

We call for the repeal of the Occupational Safety and Health Act. This law denies the right to liberty and property to both employer and employee, and it interferes in their private contractual relations. OSHA's arbitrary and high-handed actions invade property rights, raise costs, and are an injustice imposed on business.

11. Social Security

We favor the repeal of the fraudulent, virtually bankrupt, and increasingly oppressive Social Security system. Pending that repeal, participation in Social Security should be made voluntary. Victims of the Social Security tax should have a claim against government property. We note that federal, state and local government employees, members of the U.S. Congress, and members of the armed forces, have been accorded the privilege of non-participation, one which is not accorded the working men and women of America.

12. Postal Service

We propose the abolition of the governmental Postal Service. The present system, in addition to being inefficient, encourages governmental surveillance of private correspondence. Pending abolition, we call for an end to the monopoly system and for allowing free competition in all aspects of postal service.

13. Civil Service

We call for the abolition of the Civil Service system, which entrenches a permanent and growing bureaucracy upon the land. We recognize that the Civil Service is inherently a system of concealed patronage. We therefore recommend return to the Jeffersonian principle of rotation in office.

14. Campaign Finance Laws

We urge the repeal of federal campaign finance laws, and the immediate abolition of the despotic Federal Election Commission, which suppress the voluntary support of candidates and parties, compel taxpayers to subsidize politicians and political views they do not wish to support, invade the privacy of American citizens, and entrench the Republican and Democratic parties. Such laws are particularly dangerous as they enable the government to control the elections of its own administrators and beneficiaries, thereby removing it even further from public accountability. We call for the repeal of restrictive state laws that effectively prevent new parties and independent candidates from being on the ballot.

15. None of the Above

In order to expand the range of choice in federal, state and local elections of government officials, we propose the addition of the alternative "None of the above is acceptable" to all ballots. In the event that "none of the above" wins a plurality of votes, the elective office for that term will remain unfilled and unfunded.

FOREIGN POLICY

American foreign policy should seek an America at peace with the world and the defense — against attack from abroad — of the lives, liberty and property of the American people. Provision of such defense must respect the individual rights of people everywhere.

The principle of non-intervention should guide relationships between governments. We should return to the historic libertarian tradition of avoiding entangling alliances, abstaining totally from foreign quarrels and imperialist adventures, and recognizing the right to unrestricted trade, travel, and immigration.

ECONOMIC

1. Foreign Aid

We support the elimination of tax-supported military, economic, technical and scientific aid to foreign governments or other organizations. We support the abolition of government underwriting of arms sales.

We further support abolition of federal agencies which make American taxpayers guarantors of export-related loans, such as the Export-Import Bank and the Commodity Credit Corporation. We also oppose the participation of the U.S. Government in international commodity cartels which restrict production, limit technological innovation, and raise prices.

We call for the repeal of all prohibitions on individuals or firms contributing or selling goods and services to any foreign country or organization.

2. Unclaimed Property

We oppose recognition of claims by fiat, whether made by nations or international bodies, to presently unclaimed property such as the ocean floors, broadcast bands, and planetary bodies. We urge the development of objective standards for recognizing claims of private ownership of such property, including transportation lanes, shell-fish beds, mineral rights, and fishing rights, based on homesteading concepts.

3. International Money

We favor the withdrawal of the United States from all international paper money and other inflationary credit schemes. We favor withdrawal from the World Bank and the International Monetary Fund.

MILITARY

1. Military Policy

We recognize the necessity for maintaining a sufficient military force to defend the United States against aggression. We should reduce the overall cost and size of our total governmental defense establishment.

We call for the withdrawal of all American troops from bases abroad. In particular, we call for the removal of the U.S. Air Force as well as ground troops from the Korean peninsula.

We call for withdrawal from multilateral and bilateral commitments to military intervention (such as to NATO and to South Korea) and for abandonment of interventionist doctrines (such as the Monroe Doctrine).

We view the mass destruction potential of modern warfare as the greatest threat to the lives and liberties of the American people and all the people of the globe. We favor international negotiations toward general and complete disarmament down to police levels, provided every necessary precaution is taken to effectively protect the lives and the rights of the American people.

Particularly important is the mutual disarmament of nuclear weapons and missiles, and other instruments of indiscriminate mass destruction of civilians.

2. Presidential War Powers

We call for the reform of the Presidential War Powers Act to end the President's power to initiate military action, and for the abrogation of all Presidential declarations of "states of emergency." There must be no further secret commitments and unilateral acts of military intervention by the Executive Branch.

We favor a Constitutional amendment limiting the presidential role as Commander-in-Chief to its original meaning, namely that of head of the armed forces in wartime. The Commander-in-Chief role, correctly understood, confers no additional authority on the President.

DIPLOMATIC

1. Negotiations

The important principle in foreign policy should be the elimination of intervention by the United States government in the affairs of other nations. We would negotiate with any foreign government without necessarily conceding moral legitimacy to that government. We favor a drastic reduction in cost and size of our total diplomatic establishment. In addition, we favor the repeal of the Logan Act, which prohibits private American citizens from engaging in diplomatic negotiations with foreign governments.

2. The United Nations

We support immediate withdrawal of the United States from, and an end of its financial support for, the United Nations. We also call for the United Nations to withdraw itself from the United States. We oppose any treaty that the United States may enter into or any existing treaty under which individual rights would be violated.

3. Human Rights

We condemn the violations of human rights in all nations around the world. Today, no government is innocent of such violations, and none can approach the issue of human rights and liberties with clean hands. Therefore, in keeping with our primary goal of peaceful international relations, we call upon the U.S. government to cease its hypocrisy and its sullying of the good name of human rights. Only private individuals and organizations have any place speaking out on this issue.

In keeping with our principles prohibiting the initiation of force to achieve political and social goals, we specifically condemn the use of terror tactics against innocent persons, whether the terrorist acts are initiated by government or by political or criminal groups. At the same time, we recognize the right of all persons to resist tyranny and defend themselves and their rights. We call also for an end to the use of torture as an instrument of interrogation.

4. The Middle East

We call upon the United States government to cease all interventions in the Middle East, including military and economic aid, guarantees, and diplomatic meddling, and to cease its prohibition of private foreign aid, both military and economic. Voluntary cooperation with any economic boycott should not be treated as a crime.

5. Southern Africa

We call upon the United States to cease all interventions in Southern Africa, including military and economic aid, guarantees, and backing of political groups, and to refrain from restricting American trade and investment in the region.

6. China

We condemn the growing alliance between the United States government and the People's Republic of China, just as we condemn the previous alliance with the Republic of China on Taiwan. China should not be considered as part of America's defense perimeter, nor should the United States government pursue joint military or diplomatic policies with China in Southeast Asia or Africa.

7. Colonialism

United States colonialism has left a legacy of property confiscation, economic manipulation, and overextended defense boundaries. We favor immediate independence for all colonial dependencies, such as Samoa, Guam, Micronesia, the Virgin Islands, and Puerto Rico, both to free these lands from United States dominance, and to free the United States from massive subsidization of them at taxpayer's expense. Land seized by the U.S. government should be returned to its rightful owners.

The United States should liquidate its government-run canal operation in Panama and withdraw all U.S. troops from the Canal Zone.

OMISSIONS

Our silence about any other particular government law, regulation, ordinance, directive, edict, control, regulatory agency, activity, or machination should not be construed to imply approval.

National Statesman Platform 1980

We, the representatives of the National Statesman Party, assembled in National Convention at Birmingham, Alabama, June 18-19, 1979, recognizing Almighty God as the Source of all just government and with faith in the teachings of the Lord Jesus Christ, promise that, if our party is chosen to administer the affairs of our nation, we will, with earnest dedication to the principles of righteousness, seek to serve the needs and to preserve the rights, the prerogatives, and the basic freedoms of the people of the United States of America. For the realization of these ends, we propose the following program of government:

CONSTITUTIONAL GOVERNMENT

We affirm our loyalty to the Constitution of the United States of America. We will resist all attempts to violate it by legislation, by means of evasion or through judicial interpretation. We support our system of representative government with this plan of checks and balances. We support Constitutional means to end the present situation in which the judicial branch is usurping legislative and executive authority.

COMMUNISM — TOTALITARIANISM

Communism seeks to overthrow our present form of government by means of subversion and violence. We oppose Communism and all other totalitarian economic and political systems.

GOVERNMENTAL ECONOMY AND TAXATION

America today faces mounting unemployment, runaway inflation and a tax system which takes about

45 percent of our earnings to operate our government. Unwise fiscal policies of our government are the chief cause of our economic plight.

We favor a return to the gold standard to halt the dangerous erosion of the value of the American dollar. We also favor amending the Constitution to provide that, except in case of a war declared by Congress, there shall be:

1. A balanced budget.
2. A limit on the taxing and spending powers of Congress.
3. The sale of all government-owned businesses competing with tax-paying enterprises.
4. A systematic reduction of the national debt.

FOREIGN AFFAIRS

We favor a foreign policy whose chief objectives are the preservation of American liberty and independence and the promotion of justice and freedom throughout the world. We believe foreign aid should usually be in the form of loans at commercial rates of interest and should be extended only to those nations who are friendly to the United States and share our devotion to freedom. We condemn the give-away of the Panama Canal and the sellout of Nationalist China, both actions being in contradiction to treaty commitments.

A FREE ECONOMY

We believe free enterprise is threatened by: (1) excessive government regulation, (2) growth of public or private monopoly, and (3) unethical practices of both management and labor. We will act to prevent both monopoly and excessive regulation and to protect the consuming public from irresponsible or deceptive business practices.

LABOR AND MANAGEMENT

Management and labor must be held accountable for their economic behavior. Neither must dominate at the expense of the other or of the common good. Antitrust laws must be applied to both business and labor. We will end governmental discrimination in favor of union members in the awarding of contracts. We will vigorously enforce laws against strikes by federal employees.

A person's right to work for an employer willing to hire him and his right to join or not to join a labor union without affecting his employment must be protected. Governmental interference in collective bargaining and violence or coercion by either management or labor must be prohibited.

STATES RIGHTS

Our Founding Fathers stressed both individual and states rights by adopting the Bill of Rights. For many years the Federal Government has been usurping many of the states' Constitutional Rights. The states which created the Federal Government are now often dominated by their creature. We will take whatever action is needed to preserve and, where necessary restore, states' Constitutional Rights. We reject "regional government" or un-elected layers of government between the states and the federal government and between the states and county and local governmental units. Un-elected governments are unresponsive to the will of the electorate.

INDIVIDUAL RIGHTS

All Americans, regardless of race, sex, religion or national origin are guaranteed equality of treatment before the law by our Constitution. We condemn violent, anarchistic behavior or arbitrary pressure tactics as means of resolving differences among our citizens. We oppose all discriminatory measures such as quotas in employment, education and housing whether such discrimination is directed against a minority or the majority.

As the first American political party to support equal rights for women we oppose the so-called Equal Rights Amendment. E.R.A. would grant women no new rights and would strip them of many protections they now enjoy, such as exemption from fighting in the armed forces in time of war. We deplore the violation of our Constitution by a majority of the Democrats and Republicans in Congress in unfairly granting an extension of time for the advocates of E.R.A. to try to secure passage of this mis-named proposed amendment.

PUBLIC MORALITY

We deplore the low level of morality culminating in recent shocking revelations of crime and of political and economic corruption. We will strengthen and enforce laws against gambling, narcotics and commercialized vice and seek to provide the moral leadership so sadly lacking in both the Democratic and Republican parties today. We oppose the promotion of unnatural life styles.

RIGHT TO LIFE

The God-given Right to Life is being denied by governmental action which permits the massive destruction of unborn infants. Most who support this morally indefensible crime of abortion also advocate euthanasia (so-called mercy killing) for many of our handicapped and senior citizens. We favor a Constitutional Amendment to protect all human life from the moment of conception until the time of natural death. Our courts and legislatures have proven they cannot be trusted to protect the gift of Life. Only by enshrining this principle in our Constitution can we avoid a continuing American holocaust.

MILITARY PREPAREDNESS

Since eternal vigilance is the price of liberty we favor a sound program of military preparedness. We pray for peace but we cannot ignore potential threats to our nation. We still strongly support a peacetime voluntary armed force which was first advocated by our party.

NATIONAL SOVEREIGNTY

We believe in national sovereignty and oppose full or partial surrender of this sovereignty to any international organization.

WELFARE

Our party has pioneered in social reform and favors assistance to the handicapped, the aged, the chronically ill and families without a breadwinner. However, action must be taken to remove the undeserving now on our welfare rolls and to encourage more recipients to become self-supporting. Unless the crushing tax burden is eased soon a taxpayers revolt may doom the whole welfare program.

We oppose a guaranteed annual income as a plan which would further swell the welfare ranks and stifle initiative. We will end the government program which encourages immorality by dispensing birth-control devices to minors without parental consent or knowledge.

MARRIAGE AND DIVORCE

Ordained of God, the family is a sacred institution and the basic unit on which our society is built. To protect and preserve that institution we favor: (1) more stringent uniform marriage and divorce laws; (2) an end to all present tax structures which discriminate against married people; and (3) a deliberate governmental policy which disallows any legal benefits of marriage to persons living together in an unmarried state. We oppose any laws or governmental regulations which conflict with traditional parental authority and cohesion of the family unit.

CHURCH AND STATE

We support the separation of Church and State. We favor tax exemptions for non-profit religious institutions, including church publishing houses and religious schools. We favor taxation of all income received by any tax exempt group from business operations which compete with tax-paying businesses. We oppose the appropriation of tax money for private religious or sectarian purposes.

We deplore the effort to re-interpret the principle of Separation of Church and State into a belief in a militantly secular state. The same Founding Fathers who set forth this principle showed by word and deed that they did NOT mean separation of God and Biblical principles from the operation of government. We share their conviction that the Bible is a volume of universal appeal and application which is woven into our history, our laws and our culture. We favor Constitutional action to restore our traditional rights to have Bible reading and voluntary prayer in all public institutions including our schools.

RELIGIOUS LIBERTY

We believe in the freedom of the individual to believe, fellowship, worship, evangelize, educate and establish educational institutions in accordance with his beliefs. Christian schools, broadcasters and other religious groups and individuals have suffered religious discrimination at the hands of the Internal Revenue Service, the Federal Communications Commission and other federal, state and local agencies and officials. We pledge to end this activity and to safeguard the precious right of religious liberty.

BALLOT LAW REFORM

In most states Republicans and Democrats have enacted laws which deny other political parties fair access to the ballot. We will pass laws to end this unConstitutional two-party monopoly and restore to all legitimate political parties and to Independents their Constitutional Rights. Ballot status should not be accorded any person or group which advocates the violent overthrow of our government.

EDUCATION

Under the Tenth Amendment, public education is clearly under the jurisdiction of the states and the people. We will end all direct federal aid to and control over education. We protest the efforts of I.R.S. and other state and federal officials to interfere with the operation of private Christian schools. These privately financed institutions are not and should not be subject to governmental interference. Their tax-free status is a matter of right under our law and not a gift which can be removed by arbitrary governmental action.

SOCIAL SECURITY

The present Social Security system is discriminatory, actuarially unsound and destructive of individual initiative. We will reform the system by: (1) allowing workers the option of enrolling in private insurance and retirement plans in lieu of Social Security, and (2) placing the system of taxes and payments on a sound actuarial basis which is fair to payers and to recipients.

AGRICULTURE

Those engaged in agricultural pursuits should be free from authoritarian control and coercion by the government. Consumers should not pay artificially contrived higher food prices. We therefore propose a return to the free market and the elimination of all governmental controls and subsidies.

PUBLIC HEALTH AND OUR ENVIRONMENT

We favor legal bans against harmful drugs such as marijuana, L.S.D., heroin, cocaine etc. Since tobacco is the prime cause of lung cancer and many other health problems we oppose promotional advertising and governmental subsidies for tobacco products. We favor laws by the state and federal governments to protect the right of non-smokers to breathe air which is uncontaminated by poisonous tobacco smoke.

We will protect citizens against unjust incarceration in mental institutions and compulsory participation in those programs of mass medication which violate individual rights. We oppose socialized medicine and federal interference in the operation of hospitals, nursing homes and other health care facilities.

MIS-USE OF FIRE-ARMS

We favor the imposition of long-term prison sentences for those convicted of using fire-arms in the commission of a crime.

ILLEGAL IMMIGRATION

Massive illegal immigration, tolerated by both Republican and Democrat parties and our federal government, is causing severe economic, political and social problems for our nation and her people. We favor strict enforcement of present immigration laws and the prompt deportation of all illegal aliens now residing in the United States. Repeat offenders should be given non-parolable jail sentences to deter future illegal entry.

THE ALCOHOL PROBLEM

Beverage alcohol is the chief cause of poverty, broken homes, juvenile delinquency, vice, crime, political corruption, wasted manpower and highway accidents in America. By very conservative estimates some 24,000,000 Americans are now alcoholics or problem drinkers. The liquor traffic admits that bootlegging is today a big business estimated by that traffic to be producing one-third of all alcoholic beverages consumed in America today. An estimated 500,000 Americans die yearly because of highway deaths, homicides and health problems which can be traced directly to beverage alcohol. Included in this estimate are the many who die prematurely because alcohol has damaged or destroyed vital organs such as the liver.

The liquor traffic is linked with and supports a nationwide network of gambling, vice and crime. It also dominates the Republican and Democrat parties and much of the governmental life of our nation. We therefore favor the prohibition of the manufacture, distribution and sale of all alcoholic beverages.

Our party alone offers a program of publicity, education, legislation and administration leading to the elimination of the liquor traffic. We hold that if it is right and logical to ban the production, distribution and sale of heroin which has killed thousands, it is even more needful to do so with beverage alcohol which has claimed millions of American lives.

CHALLENGE

Voters concerned about the wide-spread corruption and erosion of our freedoms and the low level of morality in government should cease supporting the two political parties which created these problems. Our party, with a clean record of over one hundred and ten years of service to America, invites the support of all citizens who believe in our program of good government.

National Unity Campaign Platform 1980

I. INTRODUCTION

Nearly thirty years ago, at the beginning of his campaign for the Presidency, Adlai Stevenson declared:

"Let's talk sense to the American people. Let's tell them the truth, that there are no gains without pains."

This courageous warning is as necessary now as it was in 1952. We cannot expect that the 1980's will be an easy decade. Our nation faces its gravest challenge since the Second World War. We cannot expect that our problems will solve themselves. They are not going to go away like some bad dream. We must make changes, and in the short run they will be painful. We can rebuild our economy and regain control of our national destiny, but we will have to pay a price for our recovery.

To cure our nation's ills, we must begin by understanding them.

In the century after the Civil War, we Americans built the greatest economy and society the world has ever seen. We planned for the future, and we invested in it. We built railroads and dams and factories and cities. We invented the telephone and mass-produced automobiles at prices most people could afford. We created an unsurpassed system of public education and universities. We invested in systems of security for the ill, the aged, and the unemployed. Our nation worked, and other countries admired our efficient, undogmatic common sense. When the world asked: What is the future? the answer always was: Look at America.

But in the past twenty years our political leaders and political parties have failed the nation. We gradually abandoned the practices that made us great. We stopped planning, we stopped saving, and we stopped investing. We ignored the needs of tomorrow. We failed to take care of what we had built. And we lived beyond our means.

Nations, like families, cannot postpone their bills indefinitely. And our nation's bills have now come due.

Our economy is locked in a cycle of inflation, recession, and high interest rates.

Our factories are outdated and uncompetitive in world markets.

The foundations of our older cities—the bridges, the streets, the water mains—are crumbling.

Our system of public education is no longer teaching many of our children the skills they need to get jobs and survive in our society.

We have neglected our military equipment and our military personnel.

Worst of all, we have lost control over our economy, our foreign policy, indeed our very destiny, because we have lacked the will to declare our independence from foreign oil.

A generation of political leaders has told us that we could run bigger and bigger budget deficits without raising inflation and interest rates. A generation of political leaders has told us that we could concentrate on the interests of particular groups in our society and that the general interest of the nation would somehow take care of itself. A generation of political leaders has told us that we could get something for nothing.

We were told that we could fight a war without paying for it.

We were told that we could clean up the environment without paying for it.

We were told that we could increase pensions and social services without paying for them.

We were told that we could increase our consumption of ever-costlier foreign oil, without paying for it.

It has been a time of deception and illusion. And it must end now. Let us never again be told that we can get something for nothing. And let us never again be told that we can govern ourselves without making hard choices.

Turning this country around won't be easy. Our political system is now dominated by a jumble of special interest groups locked in a heedless struggle for private gain, ignoring the greater good of a healthier and more just society. We are close to becoming a stalemated society, locked into a politics of paralysis, where each interest group blocks any policy, no matter how wise and how necessary, if its own interests are threatened.

But our difficulties go even deeper than political illusion and political stalemate. We are also suffering from the manifest exhaustion of our political ideas.

Nearly half a century ago, Franklin Roosevelt took office amidst a national crisis and set in motion the policies that we have come to call the New Deal. These policies were designed to solve specific problems and to confront the devastation of the Great Depression. They were appropriate to the times, and they contributed to the relief of human misery and to the national recovery.

The Democratic party still clings to the policies of the New Deal. But today our circumstances are very different. The policies that once battled deflation now spur inflation. The policies that stimulated production now diminish productivity. The policies that attacked unemployment now actually contribute to it. The policies that once ministered to human misery now perpetuate it.

The Republican party has responded to the exhaustion of the New Deal approach in two contradictory, and equally erroneous, ways: it has embraced New Deal economics while it seeks to repeal New Deal social policy.

The Republicans tell us that we should cut personal income taxes across the board, by one-third. If we follow this advice, we will not save and invest more, we will spend and consume more. We will have sky-rocketing interest rates that will choke off economic recovery, further stifle our automobile and housing industries, and plunge us into an even deeper recession. We will have record budget deficits and, to finance them, we will have an explosive growth in the money supply that will produce a record inflation. This is not a program for national recovery; it is a formula for national bankruptcy.

At the same time, Republicans advocate massive cutbacks in social programs. Their platform talks incessantly about freedom, but hardly ever about justice. It talks of liberating individuals from big government, but it would only liberate those least in need of assistance from their responsibilities to the nation.

This outdated quarrel between the old liberalism and an even older conservatism, which the two major parties are about to resume, has ceased to illuminate our most pressing public problems. Far away from the discord and rancour of party strife, the American people have reflected on the experience of this century, and we now agree on some basic truths.

We are all liberals, we are all conservatives. We all believe that prosperity without justice is unacceptable, and that justice without prosperity is unattainable. We all know that government must be bold and purposeful, but that it cannot do for us what we can only do for ourselves. We all believe that individuals are responsible for their acts, but not for the conditions within which they act. We all believe that life without liberty is intolerable, but that liberty without order is self-defeating. And we all know that this consensus must guide us as we seek solutions to our problems.

The Anderson campaign is based on a new public philosophy — one that neither repeats nor repeals the past, but rather builds upon it. Its principles are clear and simple. America is in peril because her foundations have been neglected in the past generation. We must plan for the future, we must save for the future, and we must invest in it. We must rebuild America. For the most part, government cannot do this directly. Rather, it must act boldly to create a new climate, and a new framework of incentives, that encourage individuals and businesses to get to work at the task of rebuilding. All Americans must contribute to, and help pay for, our national recovery, but the burdens must be allocated in proportion to the ability of individuals and groups to bear them. The rebuilding of America cannot succeed unless we move toward the future united; but we cannot remain united unless we persevere in our efforts to establish justice for all Americans.

To rebuild America, we must begin by restoring our economic vitality. To do this, an Anderson Administration will move forward on three fronts.

First, we will use the tax code to limit consumption, and increase savings and capital formation.

Second, we will use fiscal policy to bring inflation under control and to restore a stable, predictable environment for long-term planning and investment. We cannot halt inflation until we stop printing money faster than we produce goods and services. But we can only slow the creation of money if we restore the balance of our federal budget, not in every year necessarily, but rather over the course of each business cycle. This will require moderation, discipline, and the willingness to make hard, explicit choices.

Third, an Anderson Administration will move aggressively to keep American capital at home to be used for American purposes, by sharply reducing our dependence on imported oil. We will tax gasoline to reduce consumption, and we will set in motion programs to save energy in transportation, in our homes, and indeed in every aspect of our lives.

These measures will generate a substantial pool of investment capital. An Anderson Administration will use these funds to put Americans back to work rebuilding America by creating new arenas for their energy and inventiveness.

We will put Americans back to work retooling our aging factories. We will not allow the Detroits and the Youngstowns of this nation to die. And as we retool our factories, we will preserve the kinds of jobs American workers want and deserve — permanent, productive jobs with prospects for advancement, not temporary, make-work, dead-end jobs.

We will assist the smaller businesses that have always produced most of the new ideas and new jobs for America and will do so again, if only we lift the burden of taxation and regulation from their backs.

We will stimulate technological innovation by providing new tax incentives to industry for research and development, and by increasing federal support for basic scientific research and for our space program.

We will put Americans back to work rebuilding the streets, the bridges, and the water mains of our crumbling cities with a $4 billion annual Urban Reinvestment Trust Fund. We will put our unemployed construction workers back to work building housing for America with cost-effective mortgage subsidies, and tax-exempt mortgage savings accounts for young couples. And we will use tax incentives and direct subsidies to neighborhood organizations to put Americans to work renovating the dwellings and rebuilding the economic base of the decaying neighborhoods of our inner cities.

We will put Americans back to work building public transportation for the 1980's with a $4 billion annual Community Transportation Trust Fund. At the same time, we will move toward the transportation system our economy needs, by rebuilding the railroads, the highways, and the ports of this country.

We will rebuild our system of public education. We will make public education an attractive career once again for our ablest college graduates, and we will vigorously employ the new Department of Education to promote quality basic education for all our children.

We will keep Americans at work in our most basic industry, agriculture, by taking steps to preserve the family farm. We will treat farmers as small businessmen, and give them tax breaks for investment in machinery and buildings. We will change the tax code to recognize the contribution of farm women and to reduce obstacles to the transmission of family farms from parents to children.

An Anderson Administration will rebuild American military strength. We will pay the men and women in our volunteer armed forces what they need and richly deserve. We will rehabilitate our military equipment, so that it is really ready for use in emergencies. And we will restore the military balance with efficient and reliable new weapons systems, but not with costly boondoggles like the MX missile that will not increase our security but will only take away scarce resources from the weapons we really need.

As we move toward energy self-reliance, and as we rebuild our economy and our military strength, we will once again be able to deal consistently with friends and foe alike.

An Anderson Administration will follow the prudent policy of rebuilding America's alliances with the nations that most closely share our interests and our values, by treating them as equal partners. We will never act in matters of joint concern without consulting them and we will never expect them to follow us blindly.

To our adversaries, an Anderson Administration will always offer opportunities for negotiation, for the reduction of arms, and for the easing of tensions. We will press for the ratification of SALT II and for the next stage in arms control negotiations—a real reduction, not just limitation, of strategic weapons. At the same time, we will allow no one to mistake moderation for weakness. We will make it clear to our adversaries that we will resist to the utmost any attempt at subversion and conquest. And we will never fear to aid those who are truly fighting for freedom.

As we rebuild America, at home and abroad, we will hold fast to our vision of a just America.

An Anderson Administration will work for the even-handed application of our statutes to all citizens, and we will strongly support the efforts of the United States Commission on Civil Rights to impose reasonable, uniform standards on police use of deadly force.

An Anderson Administration will work for fair housing laws with teeth in them.

An Anderson Administration will carefully review the report of the Select Commission on Immigration, with the goal of devising a truly color-blind immigration policy.

An Anderson Administration will use its resources of persuasion to obtain enactment of the Equal Rights Amendment and to block adoption of statutory and Constitutional restrictions on every woman's freedom of choice in matters of reproduction.

An Anderson Administration will strive to promote economic justice. We will work for a more equitable system of taxation, and we will resist tax cuts, such as the Reagan-Kemp-Roth proposal, that give a bonanza to the rich, crumbs to the middle class, and nothing at all to the poor. As we reduce unemployment, we will seek to reduce disparities in the rate of unemployment among different groups in our population. We will not continue to tolerate unemployment rates above 40 percent in our inner cities. And we will not use unemployment as a weapon in the fight against inflation.

These measures are all part of a larger whole—the American vision of a society in which all enjoy genuinely equal opportunity to develop their gifts and to go as far as their talents and energies will allow. This is the justice the Preamble of our Constitution requires us to establish.

The struggle to rebuild America and to establish justice will be long and arduous. But we can do the job. The American people do not suffer from any mysterious malaise. They are weary of bad government, to be sure. But they are bursting with ideas, with energy, and with the desire for a better future. They are willing to sacrifice to gain that future. All they want is a government that presents them with a clear, believable program for the future, that enables them to save and to plan with confidence, that encourages innovation and risk-taking, that reduces regulation and liberates their energies. This is the kind of government an Anderson Administration will give them.

With sensible policies, we cannot fail to surmount our current problems. We are rich in natural resources, and in human skill and energy. We have stable and flexible political institutions. We hold fast to a vision of human freedom that brings streams of refugees to our shores each year.

So let us take heart as we recall our strengths. We

must make sacrifices, to be sure. We must allocate them openly and honestly. We must protect those who cannot easily bear additional burdens. Those of us who have prospered in America must contribute generously to the task of rebuilding the nation. And we must move toward the future resolutely united, as one nation, indivisible. For, as Theodore Roosevelt once reminded us, "The fundamental rule in our national life — the rule which underlies all others — is that in the long run, we shall go up or down together."

II. THE ECONOMY

Something has gone wrong. A nation whose productive capacity made it the arsenal of democracy and the envy of the world today finds itself plagued by a shrinking capacity to produce and a growing inability to compete in the world marketplace.

Once the world's leading producer of steel, we now find our output surpassed by both the Soviet Union and Japan. A year ago, the United States was the leading manufacturer of automobiles. Today, we are second. Even in high technology markets, once the near-exclusive reserve of American business, we find ourselves increasingly unable to compete.

Something indeed is wrong.

The nation's productive capacity has suffered from a decade of neglect. The "guns and butter" policies of the late 1960's led to a level of public and private consumption that ignored the critical investment needs of the economy. During the course of the past decade, the rate of personal savings has declined sharply, and government borrowing has dramatically increased. As a result, our rate of capital investment, which long ago fell behind the efforts of our chief foreign competitors, has declined further still. Our continuing failure to save and invest imperils our economic vitality and mortgages our hopes for a better and more prosperous tomorrow.

We can no longer afford to live off our past labors, manufacturing in obsolete plants with outmoded technology. There is an urgent need to rebuild our productive capacity to create jobs for the unemployed and to lessen inflationary pressures. The continuing failure of the Carter Administration to take necessary actions threatens to generate yet another decade of economic stagnation with a resulting loss of purchasing power and employment opportunities.

Our tax laws penalize thrift. A penny saved is no longer a penny earned. Although inflation erodes the value of personal savings, the federal government still taxes the nominal interest received. As a consequence, the personal savings rate has declined steadily in recent years. In January of this year, the personal savings rate fell to a 29-year low.

Our tax laws have discouraged investment in capital plant and equipment. Between 1962 and 1968, real business investment expanded at an annual rate of 7 percent. During the past six years, however, real business investment has expanded at an annual average of only 2 percent.

A nation once famed for its entrepreneurial spirit is in danger of losing its competitive vitality. Small businesses, burdened by excessive taxation and regulation and saddled by high interest rates, have failed in recent years to generate the necessary jobs and technology. Large businesses, hampered by inadequate depreciation allowances, have failed to undertake the necessary retooling — resulting in an erosion of our industrial base.

Throughout most of the 1950's and 1960's, productivity grew at an annual rate of nearly 3 percent. Growth slowed to less than 2 percent in the 1970's. And in the first half of 1980, after 18 months of near constant decline, productivity has fallen to 1977 levels.

As individuals, as businesses, and as a nation, we have lost our ability to plan for the future. We have become a society that lives for today and ignores the needs of tomorrow.

The job of restoring our economic vitality requires a broad-based attack on the root causes of our economic decline. Nothing less than a comprehensive approach will suffice.

Our task is the rebuilding of America.

IMMEDIATE PROBLEMS

The 1980 Recession

The disastrous rise in interest rates to record peaks in the first half of 1980 precipitated one of the worst, if not the worst, recession in the post-war era. Auto sales in May fell 42 percent below the previous year's level. Housing starts declined from an annual rate of 1.8 million earlier in the year to less than 1.0 million new starts in May.

Today, over 250,000 auto workers are on indefinite layoffs with 50,000 more on temporary layoffs. Over 2 million Americans have been added to the unemployment rolls in the past four months. While there are preliminary indications that the housing and auto sectors of the economy are beginning to recover, unemployment is expected to rise still higher in the months ahead.

We cannot remain indifferent to the hardship of those who have lost their jobs, nor to the threat of future layoffs. We must expand the eligibility for extended unemployment compensation and adopt a countercyclical revenue sharing program providing $500 million in relief for hard-pressed communities in fiscal year 1981 and $1 billion for fiscal year 1982. We must ensure adequate funding of summer youth jobs programs and other youth employment initiatives. We must also seek effective implementation of the Brooke-Cranston program to revive the housing market if present conditions persist.

Most important, however, we must resist appeals for either large-scale spending increases or massive tax cuts that would serve to further exacerbate the $30 billion deficit anticipated for fiscal year 1981. A larger deficit at this juncture would mean increased government borrowing and higher interest rates. The resulting credit squeeze would further retard the recovery of the interest-sensitive sectors of the economy, including the auto, housing, and the capital goods industries. This danger requires a very cautious and selective approach to all fiscal policy choices.

Inflation

Although inflation, as measured by the consumer price index, has receded from the 18 percent rate recorded in the first quarter of 1980, the underlying inflation rate remains at historically high levels. A central focus of national economic policy must be a progressive, year-by-year reduction in the inflation rate until reasonable price stability is achieved.

While fiscal and monetary restraint is essential to the achievement of price stability, we must also endeavor to reach a broader national accord on appropriate wage and price increases. Upon taking office, we will construct a Wage-Price Incentives Program. An Anderson Administration will seek to call labor and management leaders together to agree upon fair and realistic wage and price guidelines and to determine an appropriate means of encouraging compliance with those standards through tax-based incentives.

In the absence of sharp and prolonged increases in the rate of inflation, the Anderson Administration will oppose any mandatory wage and price standards. Experience has demonstrated that such controls are difficult to administer and result in a misallocation of economic resources.

Full Employment

A sound economic policy must incorporate a commitment to full employment. We reaffirm the goals of the Humphrey-Hawkins Act and condemn the President for his failure to consult with Congress this past January before altering the timetables set forth in that Act. The establishment and attainment of national economic objectives is the joint responsibility of the President and Congress.

While the central focus of America's full employ-ment policy must be on the creation and preservation of productive, private sector jobs, there will be a continuing need for creative and complementary federal employment programs to reach areas of unmet needs.

Existing federal employment programs — administered under the Comprehensive Employment and Training Act (CETA) — place an undue reliance on public service employment and other jobs programs that do not significantly upgrade the labor skills or the employment prospects of program participants. While recent program initiatives, such as Title VII of CETA, have sought to expand the role of the private sector, such efforts have been underfunded and underutilized. We propose to expand the role and funding of the Private Industry Councils under Title VII and to otherwise enlarge the role of private employers in federally sponsored job training efforts.

State unemployment compensation programs, for the most part, are not linked to the retraining needs of displaced workers. As a result, those who exhaust their unemployment benefits frequently lack the necessary skills for gainful employment. We propose establishing federally funded pilot projects integrating State unemployment benefits with retraining benefits for those with long records of unemployment.

The Congress, in 1977 and again in 1978, approved an employment tax credit of 50 percent of the first $6,000 in wages of qualified new employees hired by small businesses. Many small businesses, however, have not taken advantage of the tax credit because they have no tax liability against which to apply the credit. An Anderson Administration will initiate an inter-department study on the advisability of making the tax credit refundable on a one-year trial basis.

Special attention must be devoted to the problem of youth unemployment, particularly minority youth unemployment. Nationwide, the unemployment rate for black and other minority youth is nearly 40 percent, and in many urban areas it exceeds 50 percent! To deal with this critical social problem an Anderson Administration will propose a number of youth employment initiatives:

Enactment of the proposed Youth Act of 1980 that will provide over $2 billion a year for job training and state and local educational programs designed to improve the employability of disadvantaged and out-of-school youth;

Increased funding for youth career intern programs;

A youth opportunity wage incentive that would exempt eligible youths and their employers from social security taxes during the first six months of employment; and

A Youth Energy Projects Act that would provide up to $1 billion a year (by fiscal year 1983) for multiyear,

large-scale energy and energy conservation projects—
including mass transit—offering career opportunities
for economically disadvantaged youth between the
ages of eighteen and twenty-four.

STRUCTURAL INITIATIVES

If we are to rebuild the American economy, we cannot be content with short-term measures employed
first to stimulate and then to dampen the swings of the
business cycle. We must address the basic long-term
problems of job creation, inflation, productivity, economic growth, and the quality of life.

To solve these long-term problems, we must avoid
stop-and-go economic measures. We cannot fight
higher prices with higher unemployment and we cannot combat the decline of purchasing power with inflationary, across-the-board, consumption-oriented tax
cuts like the Reagan-Kemp-Roth proposal.

We believe that America needs a coherent program
for long-term economic recovery and growth. This
program must be designed to stimulate investment and
to hold back consumption in a fair and equitable way
so that we can rebuild and renew our capital plant—
industrial, commercial, and public.

We believe that basic industry must be given the opportunity to rebuild and restore its competitive edge
by creating a new climate for investment and entrepreneurship. It is not our intention to use protection or
direct subsidies to achieve this end. Nor is it our intention to imitate the Japanese experience by putting the
government into the business of picking the winners
and losers of industrial competition. Such policies may
be relevant to the requirements of those nations, but
they are not relevant to a country that expects to be at
the cutting edge of economic innovation and growth.
Instead, we will create the conditions within which
enterprises can flourish, provided they are well
managed by forward-looking entrepreneurs.

Although we will make every effort to facilitate the
growth of major industry, and although we hope that
major industry will expand strongly during the next
decade, we believe that the major engine for American
economic growth during the 1980's will come from
small- and medium-sized businesses as they grow into
large businesses. Therefore, we will also seek to encourage their formation and expansion in recognition
of their role as the principal providers of new jobs and
technologies in our economy.

To create a climate for economic recovery, rebuilding, and growth for businesses of all sizes, we will
seek to enact five major structural initiatives:

First: We will use a prudent, restrained fiscal and
monetary policy to dampen inflation, lower interest

rates, and foster a stable economic environment for
long-range planning by investors and government
alike.

Second: We will use the tax code to encourage
greater personal savings and capital formation.

Third: We will use tax incentives and direct federal
assistance to stimulate research and development and
to spur productivity.

Fourth: We will use legislation and executive authority to review and to prune regulations that waste
capital and do not adequately promote valid regulatory objectives.

Fifth: We will use a tough, conservation-oriented
energy program to curtail the rapid flow of American
capital overseas to pay for imported oil.

Without these measures, we cannot hope to offset
our economic decline. With them, we can produce a
climate within which investment will be possible and
attractive. It will then be the task of our managers and
entrepreneurs to make use of the opportunities our policies will create. If they do—and we believe they
will—our economy will once again generate a wealth
of new jobs and rising real incomes.

Monetary and Fiscal Stability

We need to create a stable economic climate conducive to industrial development and the full employment of our human resources. Efforts in recent years to
"fine tune" the economy have served to accentuate,
rather than moderate, cyclical economic swings. The
resulting economic dislocation has damaged our
productive capacity. The record jump in interest rates
experienced this past spring brought the corporate
bond market near collapse, forced thousands of small
businesses into bankruptcy and pushed the consumer
price index to a post-war high.

An Anderson Administration will seek to avoid "stop
and go" economic policies and will work to achieve a
better balancing of monetary and fiscal policies: we
should not rely upon a monetary tourniquet to stop the
hemorrhage of inflation.

In ordinary times, federal expenditures should not
exceed revenues. Thus, while declining tax revenues
and increasing transfer payments can be expected to
unbalance the budget during times of economic difficulty, the budget should be in balance, or in surplus,
during times of economic expansion.

It should be understood that fiscal stringency requires an element of sacrifice on the part of all Americans. Fairness dictates, however, that no segment of
our society should be asked to bear a disproportionate
share of the burden. Moreover, all federal expenditures—whether for defense or nondefense-related pur-

poses—should be rigorously examined to determine whether they are cost-effective means of achieving national objectives.

Once balance in the federal budget has been achieved, the Anderson Administration will propose legislation "indexing" the personal income tax brackets to prevent taxpayer incomes from being pushed into higher tax brackets by inflation. To the extent that further economies are made in federal spending, we will propose tax cuts that go beyond the tax relief afforded by indexing.

The Anderson Administration, however, will not propose tax cuts that run counter to the goal of balancing federal revenues and expenditures. Proposals to cut personal income tax rates by one-third are fiscally irresponsible. A tax cut of that size would widen the deficit, increase government borrowing, hike interest rates, and accelerate inflationary expectations and underlying inflationary pressures. Rather than spurring new investments and savings, the plan would choke off recovery of the capital goods sector and lower the personal savings rate.

The goal of fiscal and monetary stability taken in the context of a fight against inflation will provide a climate of greater economic certainty in which investment decisions—large and small—can be made more rationally. Without such a climate of realizable expectations an investment oriented rational recovery program will be extremely difficult to implement.

The independence of the Federal Reserve, which has come under increasing attack in recent years, must be protected. While it is critically important for the Federal Reserve Board to observe its responsibility to report to the Congress and the President on the growth targets for the monetary aggregates, it is equally important that the Federal Reserve be free from undue political pressures. An Anderson Administration will respect the traditional independence of the Federal Reserve.

While mindful of the need for fiscal discipline and economic predictability, an Anderson Administration will oppose any new Constitutional limitation on the spending and taxing powers of Congress. Necessary budget reforms, including the tying of government spending to an appropriate percentage of GNP, should be enacted in the form of amendments to the Congressional Budget Act in a manner that will reserve to Congress and the President the power to adapt fiscal policies to changing circumstances.

America's Capital Needs

Sustained economic recovery requires an adequate pool of savings and capital. As individuals and as a nation, we need to save and invest more. Current federal tax laws—and in some instances regulations—have served to foster debt and penalize thrift.

An Anderson Administration will commit itself to working with Congress toward the formulation of a comprehensive program designed to meet America's capital needs in the decade ahead.

The personal savings rate should be increased. Individuals need to save, not only for retirement purposes, but also to guard against unforeseen financial troubles. Personal savings are also an important component of economic growth, providing the resources with which to finance new housing and capital expansion.

We must make it both possible and desirable for the average American to save again. Lowering the inflation rate will be a powerful stimulus to savings. The phasing out of interest rate restrictions on savings accounts, recently approved by Congress, will also be an important stimulant. More remains to be done, however, to remove the disincentives to savings and investment currently in our tax code. We propose the following initiatives:

Expanding the existing interest and dividend income exclusion (now $200 for individuals and $400 for married couples filing jointly) to $750 for individuals, $1500 for married couples filing jointly, by 1986;

Liberalizing the eligibility and income requirements for Individual Retirement Accounts, particularly for homemakers; and

Instituting a further review of capital gains tax treatment.

Our existing capital cost recovery system operates as a strong deterrent to capital expansion of plant and equipment. The historic cost method of calculating depreciation allowances vastly understates actual depreciation, effectively boosting business tax liabilities and discouraging the purchase of the capital equipment needed to improve worker productivity. Capital cost recovery problems are particularly acute for small businesses that do not take advantage of the liberalized depreciation allowances afforded by the asset depreciation range because of the complexity of the schedules.

We propose a comprehensive reform of the capital cost recovery system that would:

Establish a Simplified Cost Recovery System (SCR) for investments in capital equipment and machinery. Equipment should be assigned to one of four recovery accounts with recovery periods of 2, 4, 7 or 10 years depending upon its nature and normal useful life. Equipment and machinery can be depreciated an average of 40 percent faster than under existing law, and depreciation deductions should be computed by use of the "open-ended account" system currently in use in Canada.

Reduce the current useful life depreciation of structures to a standard twenty-year straight line depreciation with Section 1250 recapture provisions. The new depreciation guidelines would apply to all industrial and commercial structures and qualified low-income rental housing.

Provide a special 25 percent investment tax credit (in lieu of the existing 10 percent investment tax credit) for the rehabilitation of commercial and industrial structures.

Allow small businesses to expense (write off in one year) the first $50,000 in annual expenditures for equipment and machinery.

The current state of the economy and of our most basic industries, including the auto and steel industries, requires the adoption of added capital cost recovery measures designed to insure that troubled companies and industries will not suffer from a competitive tax disadvantage in undertaking the necessary capital expansion and improvements in the forthcoming economic recovery.

The 10 percent investment tax credit, now permanent, allows businesses to offset the credit against 80 percent of tax liabilities in 1981 and 90 percent in 1982. Any part of the credit which cannot be applied against current tax year tax liability may be carried back three years and forward seven years. Restricting the credit to offsets against federal tax liabilities effectively denies the full benefit of the credit to businesses not currently showing a profit (and hence having no tax liabilities). This inequity can be resolved by making the investment tax credit refundable. While Congress has been understandably reluctant to approve the refundability of tax credits, the current state of many of our most basic industries and businesses requires a reevaluation of this policy as it relates to the investment tax credit.

To encourage unprofitable companies to modernize their plants and equipment, an Anderson Administration will propose amendments to the existing investment tax credit provisions to accelerate the time for applying the 90 percent limit based on tax liability and to provide for the prospective refundability of currently earned investment tax credits after the close of the year in which they are earned. To insure that Congress will have adequate opportunity to review and reconsider this measure, we propose to "sunset" the refundability provision three years after its enactment.

We believe that these measures will provide a strong stimulus to re-investment in America. An Anderson Administration will, however, be prepared to go even further in the direction of investment-oriented incentives should that be necessary to complete the job of re-

tooling our basic industries and to create a climate of rapid replacement for capital equipment so that our threatened firms can become internationally competitive once again.

Research and Development

Thirty years ago, three American scientists working for Bell Laboratories invented the transistor. As a technological breakthrough, it transformed communications, computing, education, entertainment and weaponry. In the early 1960's, scientists at Hughes Aircraft invented the laser, a breakthrough for which the full potential is still to be realized. Between 1950 and 1970, American scientists constructed the great accelerators which opened up vast new areas of human knowledge and technology.

These fundamental advances were the products of a nation that recognized the importance of scientific achievements and the role that science plays in our everyday lives. Total U.S. research and development spending as a percent of the gross national product, however, has fallen by nearly 50 percent in the past fifteen years. We are in danger of losing our technological edge.

Declining technological growth has real consequences for all Americans. Technological improvements account for 40 to 70 percent of productivity growth. We all benefit from rising productivity in the form of increased purchasing power and higher real incomes. It is more than coincidence that our declining rate of productivity growth was preceded by an equally serious decline in our research and development effort.

To revive our flagging R&D effort, we propose a number of new initiatives and program improvements. An Anderson Administration will seek to:

Reverse the decline in the real dollar level of federal funding for research and development;

Provide a 10 percent investment tax credit for qualifying research and development expenditures;

Establish a federal program to re-equip the laboratories of our universities, our nonprofit research centers, and our government facilities;

Redefine the working relationship between government and universities so as to avoid the substitution of paperwork for genuine creativity;

Provide fixed objectives and more predictable project funding for scientists and engineers on the cutting edge of technology;

Establish regional technology centers under the aegis of the National Science Foundation and NASA to lower the costs of selling and licensing new technologies to private business;

Establish a more uniform patent policy for all federal agencies;

Require federal agencies to determine in an expeditious manner whether they will retain the patent on inventions developed by private contractors with federal monies;

Reorganize and increase the funding of the Patent and Trademark Office to improve its operations and handling of patent requests;

Explore the possibility of creating a separate patent court to reduce the time needed to establish the validity of a patent.

Regulation

Federal regulations are required to protect workers and consumers in such vital areas as health, safety, the environment, and maintenance of competition. Attempts to reform the regulatory process must recognize the contribution that appropriate regulations can make to a safer and more prosperous economy.

The pledge of the Carter Administration notwithstanding, the vast bulk of the federal regulatory machinery has not been properly streamlined and scrutinized. If we are to realize the widely-shared objective of reducing the estimated $100 billion in regulatory compliance costs, we must establish a comprehensive timetable for the review of the entire regulatory framework, instead of relying upon piecemeal review.

We will seek the passage of legislation that would:

Set forth an eight-year timetable for thorough Congressional review of regulatory agencies;

Require the President by May 1st of the first session of each new Congress to submit a regulatory reform plan for each of the regulatory agencies scheduled for review in that Congress;

Require Congress to act on the regulatory reform plan by August 1st of the second session;

Provide "action-forcing" means of assuring Congressional action, including denying the affected agency the power to promulgate new rules and regulations until Congress has acted.

An Anderson Administration will be firmly committed to the growth and maintenance of competition in our modern economy. We support recent efforts toward deregulation of the transportation industry, and we will support thorough review of other federal laws affecting competition including our antitrust laws.

Energy

The availability and cost of energy have been among the most important structural factors in the American economy during the decade of the 1970's. Our increased dependence upon overseas oil has been responsible for a massive capital outflow. The rise in OPEC prices has fueled our inflation and precipitated two major recessions. Ownership of American industry, land, and structures is being transferred overseas to pay for our oil bill. It is not an overstatement to say that our ability to rebuild America will depend in large part upon our ability to reduce our dependence on foreign oil.

Six years have passed since the Arab oil embargo made energy a major issue in U.S. domestic and foreign policy. Despite his proclamation characterizing the energy problem as the "moral equivalent of war," President Carter has not succeeded in producing an effective comprehensive energy policy for the nation. The present situation is dangerous not only for the U.S. but also for world stability. It is time for us to move forward with consistent short-term and long-term policies designed to protect our economic vitality, security, and environmental health. This requires a new context for energy — a new way of viewing the energy opportunities before us, backed up by a set of policies to take advantage of those opportunities.

A healthy economy and a high standard of living for all citizens are not dependent on a given quantity of energy consumed but on maximizing the services or benefits derived from consumption. The goal of the Anderson energy program is to design policies aimed at providing individual and industrial consumers with all the heat, light, and mechanical power they require at the least cost. Our policies must encourage competition among various fuels and numerous technologies for using energy more efficiently.

To create an economic environment which enhances competition, energy supplies must be priced to reflect their real economic value. The incentive provided by correct energy pricing will hasten the transition away from scarce and expensive energy sources to economical renewable resources and more efficient ways of using finite supplies. Because these technologies have been at a competitive disadvantage in the past (due to price controls on oil and gas) they lack the capital investment needed to exploit their full potential. The Anderson energy program encourages economic investments in conservation technologies, new sources of oil and gas supplies, coal consumption technologies, and solar applications. In addition, policies are required to reduce our vulnerability to oil import disruptions and, for the longer term, to explore new technologies not now economical or fully developed.

While conservation is often thought of as simply doing without, conservation policies included in this program emphasize increasing the energy efficiency of housing, transportation, and industrial equipment that is needed to sustain our economy. Since the goods and services required by society can be produced by using various combinations of energy, capital, and labor, a least-cost strategy can be followed by encouraging technologies which require less energy to supply the same level of services. Application of economic conservation technologies to improve energy productivity now costs less than developing new energy supplies and so reduces the total cost of providing energy services to consumers.

These concerns are addressed by the programs covered in the following sections.

Conservation Policy — Energy conservation deserves the highest priority in U.S. energy planning because it is the least expensive way to provide energy services for homes, transportation, and industry. Conservation must be viewed as an additional option for providing energy benefits in the same way oil, gas, coal, and other technologies do. The energy services provided by conservation have distinct advantages over those provided by conventional fuels: they are cleaner, they are safe, they do not rely on foreign sources, and most important they are less costly.

A recent study by the National Academy of Sciences concluded that "throughout the economy, it is now a better investment to save a BTU than to produce an additional one." Conservation can be the most important method of providing the energy benefits we need over the next decade. The problem is that investments of major proportions are needed in conservation. Several studies indicate that $400–$500 billion in capital could be invested in retrofitting homes, improving auto efficiency, and increasing energy productivity in industry with economically attractive returns. Unfortunately, those sectors of the economy most in need of improved energy efficiency are also those least able to generate the necessary capital. We need to shift capital into energy-efficiency improvements, remove institutional barriers to such investments, and provide technical assistance and educational programs to motivate consumers to adopt energy-savings measures. To realize these goals, we should:

(Pricing Reform) Firmly support continued decontrol of domestic oil and gas prices. Letting prices rise is the most efficient way to exploit our conservation potential. When consumers face the full economic value of the energy they use (prices which reflect more expensive domestic production costs, the insecurity of import dependence, and environmental risks) they will respond by substituting conservation technology to provide the energy services required.

Urge further reform of utility pricing to better reflect the varying costs of providing electricity service, thereby giving accurate cost signals to consumers. Since generating costs are higher during peak demand periods, consumption will shift to off-peak hours when power will be supplied by more efficient baseload equipment. The federal government should support local experiments around the country to demonstrate the cost effectiveness of this pricing strategy.

(Residential/Commercial Buildings) Encourage utility companies to experiment with new ways to deliver and finance building retrofits. For example, interest-free loans could be offered to consumers for weatherproofing or solar water heating investments, with the costs of the program added into the rate base rate of the utility. The federal government should fund short-term demonstration programs to help utilities start up such programs and then disseminate the results to public utility commissions.

Develop a residential energy performance rating system to reflect the relative energy efficiency of a dwelling for a given geographic location and size. FHA and VA appraisers should include such an evaluation in their housing assessments. Preferential treatment for conservation investments should be built into federal lending practices by requiring lower down payments for mortgage loans on homes with high energy performance ratings.

Use local community action groups to educate consumers on energy conservation opportunities and their costs and benefits. Since effective conservation is the result of many individual decisions, we must establish informational and technical assistance programs directed to the individual consumer. Community block grant programs should expand funding for home audits, direct retrofit assistance, promotion of "life cycle" costing and other measures to help consumers make more economical choices and reduce their energy consumption.

Promote a strategy for retrofitting existing buildings to reduce energy costs and provide new employment. Financing is generally a more difficult problem for retrofits than for new construction, especially for inner-city multi-family rental dwellings. To remove such barriers, the federal government should substantially increase the investment tax credit for building rehabilitation. (See the program section on America's capital needs.)

(Conservation in Transportation) Substantially increase the federal tax on motor fuels and use the proceeds to lower payroll taxes and increase social security benefits. A 50 cent per gallon tax would achieve a reduction in gas consumption of as much as 700,000 barrels per day in the short-run and over one million barrels per day in the longer term. It would also generate over $50 billion per year in net revenues to be returned to consumers through offsetting tax relief.

Seek Congressional approval of an auto fuel economy standard of 40 miles per gallon by 1995. Enhanced fuel economy would save one million barrels per day over the level of consumption anticipated if the 1985 standard of 27.5 mpg is not raised. In addition, a special fuel economy minimum should be established for light trucks weighing 3 to 5 tons (a rapidly increasing share of the personal transportation market). By exempting these trucks from such standards, much of the conservation benefit of higher auto efficiency levels is being negated.

Enforce strict adherence to the 55-mile per hour speed limit on all major highways. It has been estimated by the Department of Transportation that this restriction on excessive speed cuts U.S. gasoline consumption by 3.4 billion gallons annually. Even more convincing, however, is that since its introduction in 1974, this law has saved 37,500 lives and prevented untold numbers of accidents on our roads.

Improve and expand mass transit to supplement the use of private vehicles. Short-haul public transportation designed to meet local commuter needs will reduce street congestion and air pollution as well as energy consumption. A much greater federal investment in a variety of public modes is required. (See the Community Transportation Program.)

(Conservation in Industry) Promote industrial cogeneration by increasing DOE funding for demonstration projects and by providing technical assistance to industries and utilities. Because cogeneration is a highly efficient use of oil and gas, cogenerators should not be restricted in the use of these fuels by the Fuel Use Act and Windfall Profits Tax Act. Removal of these barriers would stimulate the operation of economic, decentralized systems to provide energy services.

Provide incentives to investment in energy productivity improvements including new conservation technologies. Adoption of accelerated depreciation allowances would stimulate general productivity increases as well as promote the purchase of energy-saving equipment. Also, consideration should be given to increasing the tax credits for industrial conservation measures, after careful evaluation of the response to existing incentives.

(Conservation in Government) Set high energy efficiency standards in federal, state, and local government activities. Emphasizing conservation in the acquisition and operation of buildings and motor vehicle fleets demonstrates both the seriousness of our energy problems and the cost-effectiveness of our solutions.

Provide a market for energy-saving technology. The government should act as a proving ground for new conservation ideas directly through its procurement practices and should widely publicize those that are most successful.

(Low-Income Energy Assistance) Continue federal financial aid to help pay residential energy costs incurred by the poor. Higher prices which result from oil and gas price decontrol will most adversely affect low-

income families because they are most limited in what they can do to reduce their home heating bills and electricity demand.

Continue federally funded weatherization services to low income families, those least able to invest in energy-saving measures. The recent changes in the Weatherization Assistance Program to expand the labor component and improve the selection of qualified local agencies should help insure a more timely and efficient program.

Petroleum Policy — Federal petroleum policy must address two major problems. The first is the inability of the domestic resources base to supply the huge volumes of oil and gas required by the economy. Proven domestic reserves of these fuels declined by about 30 percent in the last decade because production levels far exceeded new discoveries. With each increase in demand, the balance of the nation's oil requirements was met by foreign imports. The second problem is the vulnerability created by a dependence on imports. Aside from the continuing problems of inflation and balance of payments deficits, the U.S. could suffer enormous economic damage if a sudden and severe disruption in supplies were to occur. Our oil dependence, particularly during periods of economic growth, contributes to instability in the world market by gradually reducing the market's flexibility which in turn leads to further large OPEC price increases. Both components of the problem have been aggravated by past policies that restricted the full development of domestic resources and subsidized greater imports.

The rate of decline in domestic reserves needs to be reduced by policies that encourage enhanced recovery from existing sources, increase — subject to environmental priorities — the amount of federal land and offshore tracts available for exploration, and make greater use of previously marginal resources of oil shales, heavy oil deposits, gas trapped in tight sand formations, and similar unconventional deposits. Since these sources will not be adequate in themselves, it is also necessary to produce synthetic oil and gas using abundant coal reserves. Regulatory and pricing policies must be changed to discourage imports and promote competition among all sectors of the energy industry.

Problems caused by the extent of our dependence on foreign oil cannot be solved immediately, but our vulnerability can be reduced by the storage of a greater volume of emergency supplies and effective advance preparation to handle the effects of supply disruptions. It should also be recognized that major price increases might be reduced in the future by implementing supply and demand management programs well before world market conditions become dangerously strained. To make larger and more secure petroleum supplies available in the future, we should:

(Developing New Supplies) Continue federal support for research and development programs on enhanced oil recovery from existing reserves, production from oil shale, tight sands, and heavy oil deposits.

Expand the off-shore tracts and federal land made available for petroleum exploration provided the best available and safest technology is used, cost effectiveness is demonstrated and environmental impacts are acceptable.

Diversify the sources of foreign supply by establishing a supply development function — an Agency for International Energy Development — within the International Energy Agency, by providing additional financial assistance to existing World Bank and Agency for International Development programs, and by increasing technical assistance to developing countries that are not currently net oil exporters.

Continue start-up funding for projects to develop synthetic gas and oil supplies using feedstocks. Support for production beyond present targets will depend on whether environmental problems are solved, whether technical feasibility is clearly demonstrated, and, most important, whether synthetics are more economic than other energy sources.

Increase federal support for efforts to define the availability and characteristics of new gas resources from geopressurized methane, devonian shales, and tight sand formations.

Restrict federal approval for new LNG projects until safety, siting, and security of supply issues have been resolved. This policy would not affect imports of gas by pipeline from either Mexico or Canada.

(Contingency Planning) Complete and fill the Strategic Petroleum Reserve. At least one billion barrels should be in storage in order to provide significant protection from possible supply disruptions. A regional reserve for the Northeast, an area particularly dependent on imported oil, should be constructed.

Modify the current policy regarding use of oil in storage to permit withdrawal whenever world market conditions become overly rigid. In the past, accelerating demand for world oil supplies in the latter stages of the recovery cycle has strained the market to the point where a small disruption of supply causes disproportionately large increases in the world price. Use of the Strategic Petroleum Reserve to alleviate these conditions should require simultaneous economic measures to reduce overall demand.

Cooperate with other members of the International Energy Agency to arrange for mandatory restrictions on unusually large purchases in periods of tight supply. Often in the past, petroleum companies, anticipating a major OPEC price increase, have contributed to its magnitude by increasing inventories for short-term benefits.

Prepare several stand-by emergency conservation plans to promote fuel switching, electric power transfers, and reduced gasoline consumption in the event of an oil embargo.

Revise the present emergency rationing plan to reduce the length of time needed to put it into operation. A plan that takes longer than three months to be implemented has limited usefulness.

(Pricing and Regulatory Policy) Continue the phasing out of price controls on oil and gas under the schedules provided in current legislation. The Windfall Profits Tax is necessary to meet national standards of equity.

Since the elimination of well head price controls will give all refiners comparable costs, end the Entitlement Program. Emergency allocation authorities should be retained for use in a major supply disruption.

Have the Energy Information Administration monitor transfer pricing practices by integrated petroleum companies to determine whether independent refiners are placed at an unfair competitive disadvantage by subsidies to the refining segment of integrated firms. Similarly, competitive conditions in the coal industry will be monitored to determine whether the use of profits from oil and gas operations give an excessive competitive advantage to the coal mining subsidies of oil companies in relation to independent coal companies.

Coal — This nation has the resources for coal to assume a much larger share of our energy supply mix. In conjunction with conservation, it offers an important alternative supply to reduce our dependence on imported oil. Coal also can serve to improve substantially our balance of payments through exports to other industrialized countries. Despite these opportunities, the demand for this fuel has not kept pace with the capability of coal industry miners and operators to produce it. Greater coal production and use will depend on resolving environmental and health problems and on rectifying constraints in coal transportation.

The combustion of coal is a major source of several major air pollutants. There is evidence that large quantities of sulfur oxides and nitrogen oxides emitted into the atmosphere from midwest power plants are contributing significantly to acid rainfall in New England and Canada. Such precipitation is believed to account for declines in certain species of fish and to have adversely affected crops and forests. In addition, there is growing speculation that large increases of carbon dioxide in the atmosphere will produce significant adverse changes in climate around the world.

While carbon dioxide presents no direct threat to health or welfare at present levels, scientists are concerned that greater coal use will create a "greenhouse" effect, trapping heat that normally radiates away from the earth, thereby raising global temperatures.

Another environmental problem associated with coal is land degradation. Much of the expansion in output over the next few decades will require strip mining, a method of production which causes extensive land disruption and water problems if not properly controlled. Standards must be maintained to assure that land is returned to its original contour.

The expansion of coal output for both domestic and foreign markets is hindered by bottlenecks in our transportation system. Increased coal shipments, especially from Western states, would strain rail and port facilities. The ability of railroads to move coal on a timely and efficient basis requires increasing mainline trackage and supplying rolling stock. At East Coast ports, the capacity for storing and handling coal is inadequate, causing high demurrage charges.

To improve the competitiveness of coal while limiting adverse environmental impacts, we should:

(Increase the Demand for Coal) Expedite the conversion of oil-fired electric power plants to coal beginning with the eighty plants targeted in the Senate oil backout bill. The government should provide financial assistance in the form of grants or loans to be repaid out of the fuel savings subsequently realized. All conversions must meet current air quality standards.

Encourage industrial use of coal by offering tax incentives to firms that convert from oil. The government has yet to implement regulations for the investment tax credit for coal-fired industrial boilers authorized in 1978.

(Mitigate Environmental Impacts) Reduce acid rainfall by requiring electric power pools to use available plant capacity on a least emissions rather than least cost basis. Mandatory pre-combustion coal "washing" may also be a cost-effective way of curbing area-wide sulfur dioxide emissions.

Accelerate research and development of fluidized bed combustion and direct limestone injection processes to reduce air pollution. Adapting these technologies for new power plants offers a promising alternative to current expensive scrubber systems.

Increase funding to established independent agencies for research on the possible climatic effects of carbon dioxide emissions. Since the problem is a global one, parallel efforts need to be undertaken on an international level.

Support existing legislation to insure that states adequately regulate mining practices. Surface mining should not be allowed where land cannot be restored to the level of productive use which existed before strip mining.

(Improve Coal Transportation) Facilitate the movement of coal to domestic markets by reducing railroad regulation while providing protection for "captive" coal shippers. Rates set by the ICC must compensate railroad companies for building, maintaining, and equipping an adequate transportation system.

Propose the establishment of a Coal Export Authority to review the need for expanded port facilities to accommodate coal for export and coastal movements. Where appropriate, this authority should undertake to aid in the funding of new coal terminals on both the East and West coasts. (See the Transportation Program.)

(Reform the Regulatory Process) Improve the stability and predictability of environmental regulations and occupational health and safety standards. All rule-making should be conducted openly and policies should be consistent over time. It is possible to eliminate costly and unnecessary delays in the regulatory process while maintaining strict operating standards.

Resume the leasing of public land for coal production. Federal leasing policy should be designed to make low-cost coal available in efficient mining blocks, at a fair return to the public treasury, while insuring sound environmental practices.

Nuclear Power — Escalating problems with the cost and safety of nuclear power have raised serious questions regarding its role in America's energy future. The expansion of nuclear power, which presently accounts for 10 percent of the nation's electrical generating capacity, must be linked to the resolution of the nuclear waste and reactor safety problems, along with a reassessment of both the full costs of nuclear power and the anticipated demand for electrical generating capacity in the 1980's and 1990's. If the safety and nuclear waste questions cannot be satisfactorily resolved, we must halt the further expansion of nuclear power and phase out existing plants. If those questions can be satisfactorily answered, the future of nuclear power will be contingent on competitive cost factors, as well as the need for additional electrical generating capacity.

The Kemeny and Rogovin reports found major deficiencies in the management and practices of the Nuclear Regulatory Commission (NRC) and the industry itself. Both studies recommended substantial changes affecting the organization of the NRC, the operation and design of nuclear plants, evacuation plans, and the training of plant operating personnel. Prudence requires that we respond fully to their recommendations. The NRC should be barred from issuing new operating licenses unless the Commission certifies that the stringent safeguards adopted since Three Mile Island have been incorporated into the plant's design, operating procedures and emergency plans, and that all other safety issues pertinent to the plant and its design have been resolved.

We propose a moratorium on new construction permits, beyond those now being processed, until work has commenced on a permanent geologic disposal site. We have postponed the nuclear waste question for too long. If no suitable means of permanent disposal is available or technically feasible, then it would be irresponsible to put more nuclear power plants on the drawing board. If, on the other hand, a suitably safe means exists, we should begin a demonstration project at the earliest appropriate time.

While safe, permanent disposal of all high-level radioactive and transuranic waste must be the principal responsibility of the federal government, all levels of government—including state, local, and tribal—must be allowed to participate in the entire decision-making process.

While every state must be responsible for the management and disposal of all civilian low-level nuclear wastes generated within its boundaries, disposal should proceed on an acceptable regional basis. Regionalization is favored by cost, transportation risk, geologic and other circumstances which make some states unsuitable as sites. We endorse the Task Force Report on Low Level Radioactive Waste Disposal of the National Governors' Association, which recommends that Congress authorize states to enter into compacts to select disposal sites.

Our commitment to nuclear power must be no greater than our commitment to the safety of nuclear reactors and the safe disposal of nuclear wastes. For twenty years now we have allowed our thirst for a cheap and reliable source of energy to outstrip the safeguards and other steps that should have accompanied the development of nuclear power.

It is important to remember that what happened at Three Mile Island was not merely a "loss of coolant"; there was also a "loss-of-confidence": public confidence. Just as a "loss-of-coolant" can lead to the shutdown of a nuclear reactor, so too can a "loss-of-confidence" lead to a shutdown of the entire nuclear industry. We must restore public confidence in nuclear power; but we must restore it by the force of our actions, rather than by the volume of our rhetoric.

In the meantime, we must begin in earnest to reduce our demand for electricity through conservation and enhanced energy efficiency, and to speed the development of renewable energy sources, and other alternatives to nuclear power.

Direct Solar Energy—Harnessing the sun's energy in active and passive solar applications should be one of our most important energy sources. However, the breakthrough required to have the potential offered by the various solar technologies realized has yet to occur in practice. In part, this has been due to the competitive advantage traditional fuels have enjoyed because of controlled prices and also because the federal program in solar energy has failed to offer sustained and adequate support for the most promising technologies. In the future, higher oil, gas, and electricity prices will sharply increase demand for the already cost-effective technologies and will provide necessary impetus for photovoltaic systems. The federal government, however, should undertake a much larger effort to promote research and development, improve consumer confidence in solar technologies, remove institutional barriers, and make a substantial commitment in solar energy for its own use. To attain the goal of meeting 20 percent of our energy needs from renewable resources by the year 2000, we should:

Develop uniform performance standards for active solar systems. This would significantly reduce consumer uncertainty about the prospective performance of solar devices by using standard performance criteria to facilitate comparisons between competing systems.

Encourage public utilities to establish special lending arrangements to help finance the purchase or lease of economical solar devices. Utility customers could then be supplied with a number of energy services at least cost.

Reduce the cost of photovoltaic systems by authorizing a larger federal procurement program. Significant federal purchases of these systems would encourage mass production by assuring manufacturers of an adequate intermediate market, lower unit production costs, and generate useful performance data. In addition, this program would serve as a training ground for building trades workers and increase consumer confidence in solar energy.

Focus federal research and development programs on identifying the basic reasons for the present high capital or operating costs of solar systems and on ways to reduce them. New construction materials and methods and energy storage devices should be explored seriously so that many options for using solar energy will be available.

Monitor the activities of the Solar Energy and Energy Conservation Bank to determine whether the $525 million authorized by Congress to subsidize solar energy for the next three years will be sufficient to maximize the long-term effectiveness of the program.

Other Energy Sources—In addition to the renewable and non-renewable energy resources discussed so far, significant contributions to meeting our energy needs can come from alternative energy sources. It is in our nation's best interests to make substantial investments in a wide range of promising technologies to determine which can provide energy services at least cost. Because our financial resources are limited, we must distinguish between those options which will deliver within the next twenty years and those which offer promise on a 30- to 50-year horizon. In the near term, there are several technologies, including wind and biomass energy systems, which require no major technical breakthroughs for their introduction. In the longer run, large quantities of energy from ocean power, geothermal resources, and nuclear fusion may be forthcoming, provided technical and economic hurdles can be overcome.

While greater reliance on these alternatives will occur eventually, critical decisions should be made now to speed the timing and reduce the costs of this transition. New incentives are needed to encourage more rapid implementation of these technologies beyond the demonstration stage. While current federal programs provide some experience in establishing financial incentives, development of a comprehensive and balanced approach to alternative energy commercialization remains a crucial problem.

Although many of the institutional and technical barriers to development have been resolved, incentives to invest in "new" energy sources have been limited in comparison with conventional sources of supply. This has been due, in part, to domestic price controls which maintain market prices below true replacement costs. By giving investors a false sense of the value of alternative sources, the market has biased decisions away from more energy efficient, economical, and environmentally benign systems. A second barrier to full commercialization of alternative technologies is the high cost and limited availability of capital. Projects which are cost effective still have difficulty competing for financing in a tight capital market with high interest rates. Another difficulty is that private investors have been reluctant to commit funds to innovative projects where the returns are perceived to be uncertain. This has resulted in a cautious, wait-and-see attitude on the part of many potential users.

Recent federal actions to deal with some of these problems have included the passage of the Crude Oil Windfall Profits Tax Act and the Energy Security Act. To further stimulate the timely development and commercialization of alternative energy sources, we will:

Expand DOE funding for nonhardware activities. For small-scale decentralized systems, greater attention should be paid to increasing user awareness and acceptability, reducing utility interface problems, and developing competitive systems' manufacturing capability.

Direct DOE to demonstrate the reliability of wind energy equipment. Operating experience, power production and maintenance will instill consumer confidence by providing valuable information on machine designs and economics.

Emphasize smaller scale biomass conversion facilities to maximize its potential at least cost. Also, near term technologies, such as the production of methanol from wood, should be included in programs to commercialize biomass energy systems.

Prepare a comprehensive plan for the development of ocean thermal energy conversion (OTEC) in order to estimate its total cost and the federal involvement required to bring it to commercialization. DOE should complete a detailed resource assessment of the potential for OTEC to determine where it is likely to be the least-cost alternative.

Support accelerated funding of fusion energy research, contingent upon continued progress toward the demonstration of technical feasibility.

TARGETED MEASURES

As we create a new climate that promotes economic stability, long-range planning, capital formation, investment, innovation, and risk-taking, we will lay a foundation for a resumption of steady growth, rising productivity, lowered inflation, and high employment.

In addition, however, we need specific initiatives to enable the various sectors of our economy to build on this foundation.

We need an industrial policy sensitive to the special problems of our basic industries.

We need to restore small business to its traditional role as a generator of new ideas and new jobs.

We need to ensure that our transportation system can meet the demands of an economy changing in light of changing energy usage practices.

We need to seek new solutions to the traditional problems of the farm economy.

We need to revitalize our space program, another important source of innovation.

We need to remove existing barriers to exports and to work aggressively to increase them.

We need to protect our trade and our currency through increased international economic cooperation.

Finally, we must preserve and extend the gains our working men and women have achieved in nearly a century of organization and struggle.

Industrial Policy

Once the Colossus of international trade and industry, America is now losing its ability to compete in the world marketplace. In 1968, U.S. manufacturing exports accounted for 24 percent of world exports. Last year, however, America's share of world manufactured exports was only 17 percent.

Our inability to compete in the world marketplace not only aggravates the balance of trade, it also erodes confidence in the dollar overseas, and leads to a loss of jobs and purchasing power here at home.

If we are to avoid yet another decade of economic stagnation, we must rebuild our declining industrial base. The rebuilding process must begin with a new industrial policy. By industrial policy, we mean the sum of government policies affecting industrial growth. Nothing less than a comprehensive review of those policies will do.

Industrial policy, however, should not be a subterfuge for the selective bailout of troubled companies or the artificial propping up of failing industries. Rather, our task is to promote a climate conducive to the recovery of troubled industries, the advancement of growing industries and the creation of new ones.

Neither should industrial policy be used as a vehicle for the elimination of necessary environmental and safety and health regulation. While regulatory objectives can sometimes be achieved by less burdensome and costly means of compliance, our environmental, safety, and health laws serve real public needs.

The principal focus of industrial policy must be on the five structural initiatives discussed above which we believe will spur industrial growth and innovation. Other important program initiatives include transportation and trade initiatives discussed below. There are, however, a number of other tasks that must be undertaken which are peculiar to the requirements of industry.

A decade of lagging research and development has led to a dangerous erosion of the competitiveness of some of our most basic industries, including the auto and steel industries. Many of those companies now lack the ability to attract the capital needed to finance the development of cost-saving innovations.

To assist in the recovery of established, but troubled, industries, an Industrial Development Administration should be established in the Department of Commerce. Like the existing Economic Development Administration (also in the Commerce Department), the Industrial Development Administration (IDA) should be authorized to give loan guarantees for selected projects. Unlike EDA, however, the new agency should be directed to assist in the financing of projects involving the development of new technologies and cost-saving techniques for industries as a whole.

IDA's assistance should be targeted at troubled industries; the agency should not be authorized to support projects in new or expanding industries.

It should encompass a cooperative government-industry program of directed basic research in automobile and steel technologies. IDA's support in this and other areas, however, should be limited to basic research and cost-saving production techniques.

Since IDA's limited objective is to assist in the remodernization of America's basic industries in the difficult decade ahead, authority to issue loan guarantees should expire December 31, 1989. On that date, IDA's financial obligations and responsibilities should be assumed by the Economic Development Administration or a related Commerce Department authority.

A commitment to the revitalization of American industry requires a White House staff structure that ensures proper attention to matters affecting the health of vital industries and the well-being of the American worker. To achieve this end, we propose to create, through legislative initiative, an Industrial Development Council modeled in part on the National Security Council.

The council should be chaired by the President and have as members relevant Cabinet officers, other executive branch officials, and selected business and labor leaders. The Council should also have an adequate staff, headed by a Presidential advisor for Industrial Development to be appointed by the President, subject to Senate confirmation.

The Council should be charged with the responsibility of coordinating and reviewing those government policies which touch on industrial matters, fostering closer relations between leaders of management and labor, and encouraging American industry to adapt to the rapidly changing developments in international economics, technology, and consumer preferences.

Of particular importance is the need to open a closer dialogue between management, labor, and government leaders. When industries of major significance are in trouble, business, labor, and government all have a common interest in a remedy. The success of earlier labor-management committee experiments in the United States suggests these cooperative efforts should be conducted on a broader and more formal scale. The formation of a limited number of national, industry-wide labor-management committees should serve as useful adjuncts to the work of the proposed Industrial Development Council by providing a vehicle for direct input from the private sector.

The Auto Industry — The domestic auto industry is in trouble. Foreign imports in May of this year accounted for 28 percent of auto sales in this country. Domestic sales for May were 42 percent below last year's level, resulting in the lowest sales rate since the early 1960's. This summer, 250,000 auto workers have been on indefinite layoff and thousands more on temporary layoff.

While there has been a summer rebound, auto sales remain sluggish and the outlook clouded. Short-term prospects for the industry will be determined by the availability of consumer credit and the competitiveness and attractiveness of the newer, more fuel efficient models due to be marketed this fall and next spring. The long-term future of the industry will be determined by the resourcefulness of management, the cooperation of labor, the availability of capital and consumer credit, the level of import competition, and the tax and regulatory policies of the federal government.

The policies of an Anderson Administration will serve to assist the automotive industry's recovery:

Lower interest rates will enable more people to finance the purchase of automobiles.

The liberalized depreciation allowances will be specifically applicable to the special capital needs of the auto industry.

The refundability of the investment tax credit will serve to lower the effective costs of capital expansion and will be of special relevance to companies operating at a loss, as the auto industry now is.

The 10 percent investment tax credit for qualifying research and development will help spur innovation in an industry where demands for more fuel-efficient products are great and where product redesign is fundamental.

The Industrial Development Administration will help, through loan guarantees and other assistance, to establish a cooperative government-industry program of directed basic research in automotive technology.

The Industrial Development Council, through its industry-wide labor management committees, will provide a vehicle for cooperation between industry, labor, and government to coordinate a concerted attack on industry problems.

Finally, an Anderson Administration will consult with foreign automotive producers in an effort to avoid arbitrary trade restrictions by persuading them to observe voluntary restraint during times of sharply slumping domestic sales.

The Steel Industry — Once the world's leading producer of steel, U.S. steel production recently fell into third place, behind both the Soviet Union and Japan. Steel shipments for 1980 are estimated at 80–88 million tons, compared to 100 million tons in 1979.

While U.S. steel shipments can be expected to rebound as the economy recovers from the 1980 recession, the steel industry faces serious long-term difficulties. A recent Office of Technology Assessment report concluded that "continued low profitability and some

Federal Government policies, such as long depreciation time for new facilities, will cause the domestic steel industry to contract substantially."

From the standpoint of jobs and national security we must make every reasonable effort to revive the steel industry. OTA's report concluded that the "U.S. steel industry can be revitalized through increased investment in research and development (R&D) and the adoption of new technology." It is anticipated, however, that steelmakers will have to expand their capital spending by 50 percent (to approximately $3 billion per year) in order to make the necessary modernizations in plant and equipment.

The policies of the Anderson Administration will help rescue the steel industry as long as that industry is willing to make a commitment to its own future. The structural initiatives set forth above will be important factors in the steel industry's recovery — especially the liberalized depreciation allowances, the refundability of the investment tax credit, and the R&D investment tax credit. The institutional initiatives of the IDA and the IDC will also play important roles. Efforts to revive the auto industry will, quite rationally, also assist the steel industry. Furthermore, the heavy emphasis on capital expenditures for industry, as set forth above, and for basic urban and transportation needs, as set forth below, will provide a strong and predictable domestic market for steel manufacturers during the decade.

As with autos, an Anderson Administration will consult with foreign steel producers in an effort to avoid arbitrary trade restrictions by persuading them to observe voluntary restraint during times of sharply slumping domestic sales.

Small Business

The strength and vitality of the American economy is dependent on the health and competitiveness of small businesses. Twelve million small businesses today account for nearly one-half of the gross national product and employ more than one-half of the work force.

Small businesses make up the cutting edge of our economy. They are responsible for a majority of the nation's technological innovations and create over 80 percent of all new jobs.

Despite their economic importance, short-sighted government policies have over-regulated and over-taxed small businesses. Between 1960 and 1976, the share of total corporate after-tax profits earned by small and medium-sized companies fell from 41 percent to 27 percent.

To reduce the excessive taxation of small business enterprises, we propose to:

Allow small businesses to elect to write-off in the first year the first $50,000 in investments in equipment and machinery each year, as described above;

Provide simplified and liberalized depreciation allowances for capital equipment and structures;

Provide an investment tax credit for qualifying research and development expenditures;

Defer capital gains tax on the sale of a small business if the proceeds are reinvested in another qualified small business within six months;

Expand the eligibility for Subchapter S status by expanding the maximum number of allowable investors;

Initiate a further review of capital gains treatment; and

Reduce corporate tax rates by two percentage points across-the-board by 1986.

The regulatory problems affecting small business deserve special consideration. Small businesses are often less suited or equipped to deal with federal regulatory requirements. Legislation should be enacted that would require federal regulatory agencies to consider the feasibility of enacting less burdensome regulatory requirements for small businesses, providing the new regulations do not jeopardize important safety and health objectives.

Transportation Policy

In a national program to rebuild our industrial base, save energy, and meet special requirements such as the export of coal and wheat, the quality of our transportation network assumes a fundamental importance.

Much of America's transportation infrastructure was designed at a time of declining fuel prices. That infrastructure must now be adapted to meet the nation's needs during a time of growing energy scarcity and rising prices. In transportation, as in other areas of the economy, there are unmet capital needs. Many of the nation's railbeds are in a state of serious disrepair. Highway maintenance costs are escalating. Our port facilities must be upgraded to meet rising and changing demands. Our traffic control systems need to be updated. We ignore these problems at our peril.

Rail Policy — For ninety years, the railroad industry has taken signals from government rather than from a free market. The government has used the railroad industry to promote economic and social goals, often forcing shippers on profitable, heavily travelled routes to cross-subsidize shippers on less remunerative lines. Competition from other modes superimposed on this regulatory regime has fashioned a financially troubled industry. Not only has the railroad industry been unable to provide shippers with quality service at reasonable rates, it has also failed to exploit the fuel efficiency advantages it enjoys over the trucking industry.

We must revitalize our nation's rail system. Railroads must be freed from the anachronistic regulation which now encumbers many aspects of the industry. Government must shift its focus from preserving unprofitable portions of the system to preservation of the system itself. An Anderson Administration will:

Give railroads more flexibility to determine their pricing and operating policies. In many parts of the country, however, shippers of bulk commodities over long distances remain captive to rail carriage. For reasons of both equity and, in the case of coal, national security, an Anderson Administration will guarantee rate protection to such shippers.

Abolish procedures that allow railroads collectively to set general rates. We applaud the recent ICC decision to withdraw antitrust immunity from rate bureaus setting general rates.

Continue those provisions of the 4-R Act that provide matching funds to States for the purchase of abandoned lines to ease the impact of abandonments on State and local economies.

Make the investment tax credit refundable to provide additional investment incentives, particularly for railbed investment. This proposal will be helpful to the weaker, marginally profitable and unprofitable roads in their efforts to maintain and modernize.

Encourage the future formation of several long-haul rail lines to maximize the efficiency of uninterrupted rail movement.

Support Conrail at least until the United States Rail Association, Conrail's oversight body, completes its study and makes its recommendations to Congress this coming December.

Continue financial support for Amtrak. Amtrak should be provided with the funds necessary to meet its operating costs and to aid in roadbed improvements. Emphasis must be placed on rapid line corridor service through such programs as the Northeast Corridor Improvement Program.

Port Policy — In the 1980's America must stop exporting its dollars and start exporting its industrial produce. Our ports handle more than 95 percent of the tonnage moving in U.S. overseas foreign trade. Foreign trade currently accounts for 20 percent of our nation's GNP. That figure will grow throughout the decade, and with it will grow the demands placed upon our ports. We must take action to ensure that our ports will be able to bear the responsibilities placed upon them.

Oil price increases have opened up prospects for dramatic increases in U.S. coal exports. These exports could engineer a major turnaround in this nation's balance of payments. Yet a number of obstacles could delay or prevent the growth of this valuable trade. Harbor channels must be dredged to accommodate the deep-drafted vessels necessary to transport coal shipments economically. Processing time for dredging permits must be shortened and delays by environmental agencies and the Army Corps of Engineers minimized. The environmental problems raised by port expansion must be solved, including the development of an adequate method for the disposal of contaminated spoil.

An Anderson Administration will establish a Coal Export Authority within the Department of Commerce to accelerate the revitalization of our nation's ports. The Authority will:

Explore the need for expanded and improved port facilities to accommodate coal for export and coastal movements.

Aid, where appropriate, in the funding of coal terminals on both the East and West coasts.

Reduce processing time for dredging permits. Specific criteria would be established for approving time extensions, highlighting the Corps' and the federal agencies' performance in meeting time frames through periodic reports, and more clearly delineating specific areas of review for each agency.

Urgently work toward solving the problem of disposal of contaminated spoil from dredging operations. This will also reduce delays caused by the three environmental agencies.

Highway Rehabilitation — In 1956, President Eisenhower launched the most successful transportation program in the nation's history — the Interstate Highway Program. Today, however, the highways are deteriorating at an alarming rate.

The Highway Trust fund was established by Congress to provide a stable source of revenue to finance construction of the Interstate system. It provides the funds necessary for much of the rehabilitation work on both Interstate and non-Interstate roads as well as for the costs of new construction. But over the past two years expenditures have exceeded revenues. Revenues coming into the Trust Fund have declined while the costs of completion of the Interstate system and rehabilitation of federal-aid highways have skyrocketed. If conditions remain unchanged, the current Trust Fund balance of $12.6 billion could be depleted in a matter of years.

We must make a strong commitment to maintain our nation's highways. An Anderson Administration will:

Complete the few segments of our Interstate system which are deemed necessary in an energy-conscious and environment-conscious era.

Rehabilitate those federal highways which have deteriorated to the point of eroding their serviceability.

Make a strong commitment to increasing revenues for the Highway Trust Fund, recognizing that the fund may face lower revenues as fuel costs rise. We will

review the federal highway program's revenue policy in order to develop additional sources adequate to meet the nation's highway needs. This will probably mean increased taxes no later than the mid 1980's.

Aviation Safety — Throughout its history the aviation industry has maintained a commendable safety record. But that record could be jeopardized without the implementation of major improvements. Outdated air traffic control equipment, and a steady increase in the number of flights, has endangered scores of passengers in recent months.

An Anderson Administration will recognize the need to revamp existing procedures and equipment to permit safe air travel by our nation's air commuters. Our proposals are not large budget items but will contribute significantly to aviation safety. Specifically, an Anderson Administration will recommend:

Replacement or upgrading of outdated traffic control equipment.

Installation of effective new control systems at airports of all sizes. New systems at small airports will allow small aircraft to land in bad weather, reducing congestion at the larger airports handling commercial aircraft.

Improvements, where necessary, in the certification, inspection and maintenance procedures utilized by the Federal Aviation Administration.

Study of the feasibility of improving the post-crash safety of planes. Prevention of the fires and noxious fumes which cause the majority of air crash fatalities would be addressed.

Redesign of regulations to improve the safety and licensing requirements of commuter airlines and private planes. Most aviation fatalities occur as a result of accidents involving these types of aircraft.

Agriculture

Agriculture is America's most basic industry. The American farmer, however, is in trouble. Net farm income in the second quarter of this year fell by an estimated 40 percent over the prior year's level. Squeezed by low grain and livestock prices, high interest rates, and escalating farm production costs, net farm income for all of 1980 is projected to fall an estimated 29 percent below last year's level.

For farmers in many parts of this country, the news has turned from bad to worse. A severe drought has crippled farm production in several important agricultural states, resulting in both higher prices for consumers and financial hardship or ruin for many farmers.

Agricultural policy in the 1980's must restore the fundamental strength of American agriculture. To achieve that goal, we must expand farm exports, assure adequate farm prices, restrain rising farm production costs, strengthen the family farm, provide ample farm credit, preserve agricultural land, and stabilize farm incomes.

Farm Exports — Agricultural products are the mainstay of U.S. exports. Farm exports this year will total an estimated $40 billion. World trade in farm commodities is heavily encumbered by import restrictions and other barriers to fair competition.

An Anderson Administration will work to liberalize world trade and expand U.S. exports. We propose to:

Negotiate aggressively to reduce protectionist barriers overseas and to increase farm exports;

Provide for the maintenance of realistic inventories of basic farm commodities, principally in farmer-held reserves, sufficient to insure adequate and secure supplies at reasonably stable prices in the event of production shortfalls;

Expand export markets for American food products through continued support of economic development programs in the developing countries and to develop longer-range patterns of bilateral trade with those nations; and

Provide generous relief programs for the emergency feeding of refugees and the victims of famine or natural disaster.

Farm Prices — The collapse of farm incomes this year points to a continuing need to maintain adequate farm prices. Neither consumers nor producers are well served by the boom and bust cycle of farm prices. It is in the best interests of both parties to maintain full and ample farm production at fair and stable prices.

Many government actions have powerful effects upon the prices American farmers receive, some actions by limiting commodity price decreases and others by restricting price increases contrary to actual supply and demand conditions. Such actions have been taken during recent years without any recognized test of whether the resulting prices are fair. Both the recent Republican and Democratic Administrations have repudiated the parity formula established by law for that purpose. Government action which interferes with market forces in the establishment of commodity prices should be reduced to a minimum, but when it becomes necessary, the government should insure that the price consequences of its action will be fair. The current restriction on sales of grain to the Soviet Union is a case in point.

The Anderson Administration will re-examine the parity formula and other proposals for measuring the equitability of farm commodity prices. Such a review should call for the views of both farmers and consumers in an effort to determine fair and equitable returns for farmers.

We propose also to improve and administer farm price supports and other commodity programs so as to make them less cumbersome and their effects more predictable and stable.

Recent drought conditions have dramatized the continuing need to expand the eligibility of coverage of federal crop insurance programs to better protect farmers from the financial devastation of drought and other natural disasters, while also providing adequate emergency farm credit.

We also reaffirm our support for the Capper-Volstead Act, the basic charter under which agricultural producers are empowered to organize for group action in pricing and marketing their products.

Farm Costs — Net farm incomes in recent years have been sharply affected by the rising costs of fuel, petroleum-based fertilizers and pesticides, transportation, and farm equipment. Restraining those costs and lowering interest rates can further boost America's already high agricultural productivity and raise net farm incomes.

We propose to:

Reduce the cost of energy for farmers by encouraging efficient programs to convert farm and forestry products into alcohol and other forms of energy, and promoting and facilitating increased use of solar, wind, and water energy resources;

Continue efforts to free farmers from excessive federal regulation by requiring federal regulators to assess the special impacts of their rule-making on small businesses;

Assure consideration in rail deregulation legislation of the needs of captive rail shippers for access to their markets and distribution systems at reasonable costs;

Insure priority allocation of fuel for agricultural use in the event of supply shortages;

Insure farmers fair and adequate access to farm credit; and

Reduce farm costs overall by instituting sound federal fiscal policies designed to reduce government borrowing, lower interest rates, and curb inflation.

The Family Farm — The real strength of American agriculture is the family farm. If we are to preserve this institution, however, we must adopt new measures designed to insure the continuity of family farm ownership and eliminate those aspects of current law that discriminate against the family farmer.

An Anderson Administration will:

Support further reform of estate and inheritance tax policies to permit opportunities for successor generations to assume ownership and management of farm enterprises without incurring crippling tax burdens;

Insure smaller farmers fair and equal access to federal credit programs;

Expand current, long-term low-equity financing programs to better enable young farm families to begin full-time farming enterprises while guarding against abuse of the program by speculators;

Recognize the vital role of women in the farm enterprise and work to repeal the application of the estate tax to the transfer of family farms between spouses — the so-called "widows tax"; and

Reform the tax laws to discourage the purchase of farm land for tax loss farming purposes.

The Farm and Rural Women — The Anderson Administration will strive to gain legal recognition for the role of farm and rural women as full partners with their husbands or brothers, sons or daughters. Farm women contribute their time, their labor and in many instances their money to the farming enterprise. They work in the fields and barns, they keep farm accounts and they participate in making farm business decisions.

Yet, today, because of high inflation and declining farm income, many farm and rural women find they cannot participate as they choose. Low farm returns force many to seek additional employment and another income off their farms, frequently to the detriment of their health and emotional well being. We will support programs that assure recognition of their contributions to the farming enterprise and a sound economic policy that will allow farmers to maintain a decent standard of living for their families.

Agricultural Lands — The U.S. loses an estimated 20,000 acres of its best farmland each week to other uses. Much of it is irretrievably lost due to the enormous costs of reclamation. Preliminary statistics compiled by the National Agricultural Lands Study, now being conducted by the U.S. Department of Agriculture and the Council on Environmental Quality, suggests that the nation may lose as much as 22.4 million acres (7 percent) of its prime farmland by the year 2000. An Anderson Administration will encourage state and local units of government to develop programs to protect vital agricultural lands and seek to bring federal actions into better conformity with state and local plans for agricultural land use.

Soil and Water Conservation — Conservation of our increasingly valuable soil and water resources is vital to America's future and to its future generations. America grew up on its farms. However, the pressures of rising population, economic growth and world food requirements have subjected these resources to steadily intensified competition and conflict among potential users.

Almost one-third of our total harvested acreage — 109 million acres of cropland — is being subjected to erosion each year at a rate the USDA deems to be over "permissable erosion rates." If this continues, it would eventually destroy these lands' utility as cropland.

We must institute a closer, on-going review of soil and water depletion rates, while seeking to increase the delivery of technical and educational services. At the same time, however, we must recognize the very difficult decisions that will have to be made in these areas.

There are no easy solutions to the growing erosion, salinization and water scarcity problems. The Anderson Administration will seek to frame these choices in the frankest manner possible and strive for an equitable resolution of conflicting needs and claims.

Agricultural Policy and Consumers — Although the food distribution process begins on the farm, food often goes through a complex chain of distributors before it reaches the consumer. This process adds two-thirds or more to the consumer's food bill. It is in the processing, distribution and advertising costs of food that the greatest potential for economies exists.

An Anderson Administration will shift the federal government's research efforts on food processing and marketing towards reducing non-farm-added costs of food. Review should include new food forms and more efficient marketing practices and systems.

We also pledge to support and strengthen the food assistance programs, including the food stamp and school lunch programs, to better meet the nutritional needs of the truly needy.

The U.S. Space Program

Since its inception over twenty years ago, the U.S. space program has yielded an impressive array of technological and economic benefits. But after achieving the Kennedy Administration's goal of putting a man on the moon by 1970, America's space effort has faltered. While the U.S. has made impressive strides with the development of the space shuttle, the overall level of dollar commitment has declined in real terms.

We believe an invigorated space program can play an important role in raising productivity and revitalizing our economy since the space program funds basic research in a wide range of fields such as photography, communications, metallurgy, life-support systems, and many other areas of science and engineering.

An expanded space program based generally on NASA's current five-year plan should be established. The objectives of that plan should be:

To fill the transportation and orbital needs of space missions in an economical and effective manner;

To improve our ability to apply space technology in areas that promise immediate or potential benefits to humanity, including remote sensing, communication and materials processing;

To improve our ability to acquire, transmit, and process data;

To increase our knowledge about the history of the cosmos and expand our understanding of the evolutionary process involved; and

To advance our fundamental knowledge of how energy is transported from the sun and through the intergalactic medium and what effects that energy has on Earth's environment.

NASA's current five-year plan does not include funding for several vital programs needed for the development of space science, technology, and industrialization. Many of these programs, included in earlier plans and cut from the current proposal by the Carter Administration, should be reinstated. They include:

An intensified effort to achieve routine operational use of the space shuttle, with improvements in lift and on-board power capabilities, that will enable it to realize its full potential.

Establishment of an operational Landsat-type system for Earth resources surveys, as repeatedly urged on a bipartisan basis in Congress, in lieu of the hesitant, half-hearted motions of the Carter Administration in this direction.

Proper support of a long-term program to explore the solar system with unmanned space probes, avoiding the costly starts and stops we have experienced under the Carter Administration. The Galileo mission to Jupiter, the Venus Orbiting Imaging Radar and Halley's Comet Flyby missions are important steps in this program.

Full support for scientific study of the universe through completion and operation of the large optical space telescope and other specialized scientific satellites.

Eventual establishment of a permanent U.S. presence in space through planning and design of a general purpose orbiting space station to work with and be serviced by the space shuttle, thereby regaining the economically important lead in space research which the Soviet Union now enjoys as a result of its ongoing space operations.

Continuation and amplification of satellite power system evaluation (including the possible manufacture from nonterrestrial materials) in order to determine the practical desirability of collecting solar energy in space and safely transmitting it to Earth.

Active research on large space structures, expanded space power generation, and the other technological advances needed to form a sound basis for developing a substantial national space industrialization capability within the foreseeable future.

Export Promotion

A nation once famed for its "Yankee traders" now finds itself out-traded and out-maneuvered in the world market place. If America is to prosper domestically, it must compete more effectively.

A nation, such as ours, which pays nearly $100 billion a year for foreign oil must export aggressively if it is to survive the decade ahead with its economy and currency intact. Viewed in that light, our export policy must be immediately invigorated. The policy of "benign neglect" that has characterized export administration in recent years cannot continue.

We propose a revitalized export promotion program, including the following new initiatives:

Expanded, competitive U.S. Export-Import Bank financing of U.S. exports;

Reduced taxation of American nationals living abroad and engaging in export activities;

Provision for duty-free entry of machinery and materials for use in export manufacture in foreign trade zones;

Amendments to the Webb-Pomerene law to permit business associations engaged in export activities to obtain pre-clearance anti-trust immunity for certified activities;

Measures designed to encourage the formation of export trading companies to assist small and medium sized firms in entering export markets;

Amendments to the Commodity Credit Corporation Charter Act creating an Agricultural Export Credit Revolving Fund to assure adequate financing of agriculture exports; and

Renewed efforts at obtaining international agreement on foreign business practices.

International Economic Relations

The present weakness of the U.S. economy reflects not only our own lack of capital investment and productivity improvements in recent years but also the larger fragility of the international economy due to the massive shifts of wealth from the oil-consuming nations to the oil-producing nations. It is anticipated that the current accounts surplus of the OPEC nations will reach $131 billion this year—a 15-fold increase over the 1979 surplus of $8.8 billion. By year's end, it is also expected that the industrialized countries will show an aggregate current account deficit of $49 billion, as compared to a 1978 surplus of $131 billion.

As severe as the oil-price pressures are to the industrialized West, they are even more severe for the non-oil exporting developing countries. Their deficit in 1980 is expected to reach nearly $70 billion, as compared to a $37.5 billion deficit in 1978. The combined debts of these countries has increased from $70 billion at the end of 1970 to approximately $300 billion by the end of 1979.

The continuing imbalance in world trade will put an enormous strain on world financial markets and test the limits of our international monetary system. Now more than ever, there is a need for closer international consultation and cooperation on international trade and monetary affairs. We cannot permit our shared problems to rupture either international trade or the international monetary order.

To meet the recurring challenges to international economic stability, we pledge:

Continued cooperation with our allies in attempting to achieve the energy conservation and production targets set forth in the recent Venice Summit Agreement;

Closer cooperation among our trading partners in an effort to reduce through common agreement the frictions which, if left unattended, could lead to arbitrary trade restrictions and a resulting trade war;

More effective and timely coordination of economic and financial policy among the leading industrialized nations, including the full use of facilities provided by the International Monetary Fund (IMF) and the Organization for Economic Cooperation and Development (OECD);

Continued efforts to enhance the effectiveness of IMF exchange rate surveillance;

Expanded financial and technical assistance to non-OPEC developing countries in their efforts to explore and market new energy sources; and

Renewed efforts to establish a new stable monetary order through further refinement and extension of the Special Drawing Rights, rather than reverting to an anachronistic and rigid gold standard as proposed by the Reagan platform.

Working Men and Women

An Anderson Administration will strive to improve the purchasing power of American workers, safeguard their working conditions, and protect their bargaining rights. In working toward these goals, we pledge to consult on a regular basis with the interested party — the working man and woman of America.

Within the last year, the purchasing power of the average urban worker has declined by over 7 percent. This is the record by which the Carter Administration's labor policy must be judged; and, by any reasoned interpretation, it must be adjudged a failure.

The policies of the past four years have not served to reduce unemployment at the expense of purchasing power. They have served to aggravate both joblessness and inflation. Unemployment today is higher than when President Carter took office. The average American worker today is neither more secure in his job nor richer in his pay than when the President took office.

The collective bargaining rights of the American worker must be protected. We find unacceptable the willingness of certain employers to bear the cost of defying sanctions for unfair labor practices. The ad-ministration and enforcement of our labor laws must be strengthened through selective improvements in the National Labor Relations Act.

An Anderson Administration will support measures designed to expedite the National Labor Relations Board hearing process, adequately compensate those who are illegally dismissed by their employer for union-organizing activities, and give the Secretary of Labor discretionary authority to withhold federal contracts from employers guilty of flagrant or repeated labor law violations.

We reaffirm our support for a fair and equitable federal minimum wage. The minimum wage should bear a consistent and reasonable relation to the average manufacturing wage. Congress should exercise proper oversight of the federal minimum wage laws by periodically reviewing both the level and scope of minimum wage protection.

Upon proper review and evaluation, an Anderson Administration will submit legislation in the first session of the 97th Congress to ensure a fair and adequate minimum wage for 1982 and beyond. We will oppose, however, efforts to "index" the minimum wage to an arbitrary wage or price formula. The minimum wage should be subject to normal and periodic review by Congress.

The health and safety of working men and women deserves the highest measure of protection. We reaffirm our longstanding support for the full and effective enforcement of the Occupational Safety and Health Act of 1970. The right of every American to a safe and healthful workplace should be safeguarded by a fully funded Occupational Safety and Health Administration (OSHA).

We pledge to oppose legislation, currently before the Congress, which would effectively exempt 90 percent of all workplaces from safety inspections, including inspections triggered by employee complaints of hazardous working conditions. The proposed legislation would put undue reliance upon "voluntary compliance," jeopardizing the lives of thousands of American workers. The proper role of OSHA is accident prevention, not after-the-fact accident investigation.

In addition to fair wages and improved working conditions, our working men and women want meaningful work. They have unique knowledge of what lowers the quality and raises the cost of what they make, and they have important views on how the workplace can be organized more sensibly and humanely. Workers in many of the world's healthiest economies have won the right to cooperate with their companies to help determine the structure of production. An Anderson Administration will seek to encourage this development in the United States in a prudent manner consistent with our own traditions.

Workers on indefinite layoffs in distressed industries such as the automobile, steel, and shipbuilding industries require special assistance. We support an extension of job-retraining and relocation assistance for displaced workers and Economic Development Administration assistance to distressed communities. We support on a pilot-project basis the adoption of work-sharing programs designed to minimize plant layoffs through voluntary work-sharing agreements supported by modified unemployment compensation benefits for those working shortened hours.

We shall oppose efforts to repeal the Davis-Bacon Act of 1931. Workers on federal projects should be paid the prevailing wage of the community in which the construction takes place. We reserve judgment, however, on the advisability of extending prevailing wage protections into new areas.

III. MEETING HUMAN NEEDS

INTRODUCTION

A dynamic and growing economy is the necessary condition of social progress, of domestic harmony and equity, and of military strength and national security. And only such an economy can allow all its citizens the basic freedom to choose and to pursue their own occupations. But economic health is not an end in itself. The worth of every society is determined by what its members do — as individuals and as citizens — with the wealth they create.

We believe that a modern society must accept its responsibility to provide for basic human needs, in three ways.

First, it must act to furnish all its citizens with those public goods that cannot be attained through individual effort, but only through cooperative endeavors. It must, therefore, care for its cities, its transportation, and its community environment.

Second, a modern society must accept responsibility for those who cannot support themselves. It must provide sustenance for those who are unable to work, income for those who have reached the age of retirement from the workforce, and medical care and other services for those who cannot afford them without assistance.

Third, a modern society must create an environment within which human beings can strive to fulfill their own needs. It must encourage, not discourage, family life through tax policies and child care. It must enable its citizens to develop their abilities through systems of education and training, and through a wide variety of cultural experiences. And it must enable them to apply their abilities to their own betterment and that of their community, in productive and satisfying occupations. And it must protect the large environment in which we all must live.

An Anderson Administration will accept these three responsibilities. It will not seek to return this nation to the 1920's, as the Republicans dream of doing, but neither will it simply repeat the programs and ideas of the past, as the Democrats do. Rather, it will propose new means to attain the ends on which the overwhelming majority of Americans are in agreement: means that are as efficient, as equitable, and as humane as our ingenuity can devise.

THE FUTURE OF AMERICA'S CITIES

General Background

In the century after the Civil War, the United States underwent an economic expansion without precedent in world history. In the course of this great transformation, the United States, predominantly rural in 1865, became an urban nation. Once primarily service and trade centers, our cities became manufacturing centers as well. Massive urban capital investments were made — not only in factories but also in housing, roads, bridges, public transportation, sewers, and water systems. Population steadily shifted from farms to cities as urban employment opportunities expanded and the efficiency of the agricultural sector increased. This human tide was swollen by European immigrants and by Southern blacks.

After the Second World War, many older cities — particularly in the Northeast and Midwest — entered a period of economic decline. The proliferation of the automobile, coupled with the construction of our highway system, made it possible for members of the middle class to leave the central city for the suburbs. This trend was encouraged by the FHA, which directed capital toward single-family suburban housing construction. The newly burgeoning economies of the South and Southwest began to attract capital, skilled workers, corporate headquarters, and government contracts. Simultaneously, older cities received large numbers of new residents, from the South and from abroad, with below-average income, skill, and education but above-average requirements for public services. The net outflow of population these cities experienced slowed the growth of property values and promoted blight and crime in many neighborhoods.

These developments have had a marked effect on the composition of the inner cities. Between 1970 and 1977, the population of major American cities dropped by 4.6 percent, compared with a growth in suburban population of 12.0 percent and 10.7 percent in nonmetropolitan areas. The change has been even more pronounced in the cities of the Northeast and

Midwest as population has shifted from those regions to the South and West.

Of the total population below the government's poverty level, 38 percent were living in the major cities by 1977, compared with 34 percent in 1970. In contrast, the proportion of the poor living outside the metropolitan areas fell during the same period from 44 percent to 39 percent.

Racial and ethnic population statistics are equally dramatic and disturbing. Fifty-five percent of the nation's black population now live in the large cities, compared to 25 percent of white Americans. Growing proportions of urban residents today belong to Hispanic or female-headed households. These three groups — Blacks, Hispanics, female-headed households — suffer from severe deprivation in housing, jobs, and income.

A recently released major study demonstrates that, despite the massive government assistance cities have received in the past two decades, the older, distressed cities of our nation are in worse shape than they were in 1960. Clearly the old policy of putting cities on welfare has not dealt successfully with their real problems.

We must do better. But we must not fall into the trap of seeking a new grand design or of attempting to devise a new set of policies while ignoring what we now have. The Carter Administration has tried to do this, and it has only made matters worse.

We should not fear to innovate. But we must also be concerned with the sound administration of existing programs. Regulations must be simplified, and better linkages established among related programs. Programs that work must be identified and expanded, while those that do not should be terminated or reoriented.

Federal urban policy should be guided by appropriate general principles.

We should strive for a suitable balance between federal and local initiatives, recognizing that neither centralization nor decentralization will succeed in all circumstances. Tasks, the equitable and efficient performance of which require national coordination, should be handled at the federal level, while others are the proper function of states and localities.

We must recognize that there is no major urban problem that the federal government can solve solely through its own efforts. Federal initiatives should seek to mobilize local resources and to involve the private sector. Federal policy should try to substitute incentives for regulations and prohibitions whenever possible. The federal government should aim to create a climate within which individual initiative is encouraged and rewarded.

Some problems are best dealt with through sharply focused, categorical programs. In general, however, the federal government should employ block grants to consolidate related programs, reduce burdensome regulations, and increase flexibility and access on the state and local level. We thus strongly support the general revenue sharing program.

To advance truly national interests, the federal government should minimize the use of discretionary programs that vest excessive decision-making authority in the bureaucracy. In general, formula-based allocation stemming from explicit, public legislative decision-making is sound public policy.

The federal government must seek to identify the most urgent needs of our urban centers and to concentrate its efforts upon them. We propose that the federal involvement in urban problems be increased because of the unmet human needs in many of our nation's cities, not because cities as such deserve special attention.

The federal government should distinguish between a short-term support function and a long-term investment function in its urban policies. While we meet today's needs, we should search for ways of rebuilding the economic capacity of our cities so that they can move toward eventual revenue independence and fiscal self-sufficiency.

The Urban Reinvestment Trust Fund

Most urban experts agree that the deterioration of our massive investment in urban capital stock — housing, roads, bridges, public transportation, sewers, water systems — is the most serious problem now confronting the nation's cities. Caught between declining tax bases and escalating costs, many cities particularly the older cities of the Northeast and Midwest have been forced to defer essential maintenance to meet immediate operating needs. A recent comprehensive survey of twenty-eight major cities concluded that:

Deterioration in the capital stock of older cities has accelerated in the past five years as a consequence of fiscal stress and aging.

As repair needs mount, maintenance work forces are being cut.

In many cases, cities facing severe budgetary pressures have curtailed maintenance spending more sharply than spending for other current operations.

Similarly, capital spending has been squeezed.

Older cities, predominantly those located in the Northeast and Midwest, face investment backlogs and lack the financial capabilities to meet their needs from local resources.

To address this massive and urgent problem, an Anderson Administration will propose an Urban Reinvestment Trust Fund (URTF) to assist distressed cities in rehabilitating and replacing their capital stock.

Funding — The URTF would be funded through 45 percent of the federal alcohol and tobacco excise taxes, to be phased in over a three-year period. When fully funded, it would receive and disburse approximately $3.8 billion annually (in 1980 constant dollars).

Allocation — The URTF would be allocated to cities and metropolitan areas on the basis of a three-factor formula: pre-1939 housing stock (weighted 50 percent); population in poverty (weighted 30 percent); population loss (weighted 20 percent). This formula is the best indicator of the two most relevant dimensions of community need: degree of decay of capital stock, and ability to raise and use tax revenues for maintenance.

Disposition of Funds — The funds made available through the URTF would be used for:

The upgrading and repair of existing capital plant and equipment: streets, bridges, sidewalks, street lighting, water mains, sewers, waste processing and sanitary facilities, pollution control facilities and equipment, and related items;

The replacement or installation of such plants and equipment when current facilities are either beyond repair or altogether lacking.

Local authorities would be free to determine their own priorities and allocation procedures, subject to three constraints. Legislation would require:

That equity prevail in the use of funds within cities, with immediate emphasis on upgrading facilities in the most severely decayed areas;

That neighborhood organizations be adequately consulted in the process of determining community-wide priorities;

That URTF funds supplement, not replace, local funds currently employed for capital stock maintenance and rehabilitation.

Because the revenues from the federal excise taxes on alcohol and tobacco have been rising more slowly than the rate of inflation, at the end of the phase-in period we will consider raising current excise tax rates to meet the urgent national needs to which our Trust Fund is addressed.

Housing

The quality of life in our cities, and throughout our nation, is crucially affected by the availability of decent, affordable housing for all citizens. But the Carter policy of fighting inflation with tight money and high interest rates has had a devastating effect on this sector of the economy. Housing starts have declined to an annual rate of one million, the lowest since World War II and one million units lower than predicted last year. This level of activity will result in: the loss of 1.6 million jobs; the loss of $27.6 billion in wages; the loss of over $3.5 billion in federal tax revenues and $7.5 billion in combined federal, state, and local revenues. Moreover, this lost production will produce an even more rapid inflation in housing costs as the economy recovers from the Carter recession.

The underlying demand for housing is very strong and will grow substantially through the 1980's. During this decade, 41 million Americans will reach the prime homebuying age, compared with 31 million in the previous decade, and the rate of new household formation will be 25 percent higher. This demand cannot be satisfied even by levels of production considered high in the past. Unfortunately, the crisis in rental housing means that new rentals will not be able to meet any substantial portion of the existing demand. Recent statistics show that in the past three years, there has been an annual net loss of rental units of nearly 2 percent. High interest rates, increased operating costs, and burdensome regulations have nearly shut down the private construction of rental housing. As a result, the nationwide multi-family vacancy rate has fallen to the lowest level since this statistic was first compiled twenty years ago. In many cities there is virtually no vacant rental housing.

In the early part of the 1970's, the federal government stepped into the breach by subsidizing the construction of new rental housing. This assistance reached its peak in 1976. Since then, because of soaring unit costs and fiscal constraints, the amount of subsidized new construction has declined sharply.

If we do not undertake effective new initiatives, housing will become a major source of social conflict in the 1980's, as new families struggle with dwindling supplies and escalating costs. In the past year, the percentage of families able to afford the monthly payments on their first house has declined sharply at the same time that rental housing has become scarcer and less affordable. We run the risk of being split into two nations: those who were fortunate enough to buy while housing costs were a reasonable fraction of personal incomes, and those who were unfortunate enough to arrive on the scene too late.

To deal with our housing problems, we propose the following steps:

We must begin to attack the housing problem in this nation by stabilizing our economy. Reckless spending and huge deficits lead to inflation which in turn escalates long-term interest rates, the key determinant of housing costs. In addition, inflation produces a flight from savings and paper money into real property, reducing funds available for mortgages and further hiking housing prices. The housing industry cannot function properly until we restore a sound economic climate for planning and investment. This we pledge to do, as our first order of business.

We must work to dampen the inefficient and damaging housing cycle. We support the reactivation of a program such as that proposed by Republican Senator Edward Brooke and Democratic Senator Alan Cranston, a countercyclical mortgage-subsidy program that would be automatically triggered whenever housing starts fall below a designated level for a significant length of time. This is not a permanent subsidy, but rather a low-cost, temporary, recoverable government investment that works effectively to place a floor under housing starts.

We must embark on a comprehensive review of federal, state, and local regulations affecting housing construction and renovation which have been estimated to add up to 20 percent to the cost of each new unit. Where possible, we must simplify or eliminate this burdensome system of regulation.

We support the reauthorization of tax-exempt revenue bonds to support single and multi-family housing construction, subject to reasonable restrictions.

We support new initiatives to stimulate the private construction and operation of multi-family housing, including increased shallow interest rate subsidies and increased tax incentives, particularly accelerated depreciation, for multi-family buildings.

We support an urgent effort to increase the supply of urban housing stock to usable condition. All remaining federal restrictions on the use of HUD funds for renovation of existing housing should be eliminated. Programs, such as urban homesteading, that mobilize local renovation efforts should be encouraged. We especially support an increased partnership between the federal government and community organizations to put the people of our neighborhoods to work rebuilding their own homes.

We should explore policies that would increase the supply of urban housing by encouraging the conversion of abandoned buildings from other uses to housing. Such policies include providing technical assistance, identifying and donating surplus government buildings, and providing accelerated depreciation.

We support the extension of current programs that encourage low and moderate income urban residents to develop a stake in their community through ownership of their own residences. The federal government should assist apartment dwellers to form cooperative organizations to purchase and renovate their buildings.

To increase the supply of mortgage funds, and to assist prospective homeowners, we support the gradual expansion of the existing interest income exclusion ($200 for individuals, $400 for married cou-

ples) to $750 for individuals and $1,500 for married couples as stated elsewhere in the platform.

Neighborhoods

A healthy city is a place of ethnic and economic diversity, neither a playground for the rich, nor a dumping ground for the poor. It is an association of stable, vigorous neighborhoods, secure in their differences, linked by common interests and purposes. A liveable physical environment is only a first step.

For too long, federal policy has discouraged or neglected neighborhoods. In the past, "urban renewal" obliterated existing neighborhoods, replacing them with public housing projects, highways, and office buildings. Today, although the federal government no longer levels whole neighborhoods, it continues to sponsor initiatives that damage neighborhood interests while neglecting and underfunding programs that directly benefit neighborhoods.

The following steps are essential to remedy this situation:

The next administration must appoint a new, high-level executive task force to review and, where appropriate, to implement the recommendations of the National Commission on Neighborhoods. The Commission's report was released nearly eighteen months ago, after extensive research and numerous public hearings, but the Carter Administration has almost completely ignored its findings;

We must promote the formation and activities of neighborhood associations, through such means as:

A neighborhood improvement tax credit, providing an 80 percent credit on the first 50 dollars of each taxpayer's contribution to a neighborhood group;

The provision of federal matching money to local neighborhood improvement groups in designated distressed areas;

Increased support for such ventures as the Neighborhood Housing Service, operating under the aegis of the Neighborhood Reinvestment Corporation, which seeks to form partnerships among neighborhood associations, financial institutions, and local governments to increase the supply of affordable housing;

Adequate funding for HUD's Office of Neighborhood Development which, in spite of significant accomplishments, has been neglected by the Carter Administration.

We must promote economic development in neighborhoods through:

Directing the Small Business Administration to comply with its authorizing legislation, which mandates that SBA programs be made accessible to Community Development Corporations;

Reauthorizing the SBA's 502 direct loan program,

which is on the verge of termination in spite of its proven record of stimulating small business in declining neighborhoods;

Insuring that the Urban Development Action Grant program sponsors projects that distribute federal funds more equitably within cities and more directly benefit neighborhoods;

Offering increased tax incentives to the private sector to enter into partnerships with community development corporations and other neighborhood-based economic development groups.

We must recognize that although the increased flow of suburban dwellers back to our central cities has favorable consequences for urban tax bases and housing stock, it also generates a significant problem of dislocation, particularly among the poor and elderly. In the past, dislocation has meant declining housing quality, persistent overcrowding, increased costs, and severe psychological and social disruption for those forced to move.

Federal policy must be more responsive to the needs and legitimate claims of those presently residing in neighborhoods undergoing these changes. If some dislocation is unavoidable, the federal government must accept its fair share of the responsibility to assist displacees.

Enterprise Zones

Within our distressed older cities, there are neighborhoods that can only be called zones of devastation. Dwellings are boarded up and abandoned, or inhabited by derelicts. Businesses are failing and fleeing. Arson is rife. Gangs fight for control of the streets while ordinary citizens live in constant fear. All who are able to escape do so, leaving behind those without alternatives or hope. In the South Bronx, for example, 96 percent of the residents are now black or Hispanic, compared to 66 percent in 1970. One-quarter of the residents live in households with annual incomes under $3,000. One-third of the population is entirely dependent on welfare.

Some have suggested what amounts to urban triage—that we declare that certain areas are unsalvageable and leave them to their fate. We completely reject this proposal. It makes no economic sense to abandon our enormous investment in housing, factories, and capital stock, much of which is still usable or capable of being renovated. And it is inhumane to abandon viable neighborhoods where families have lived and worked for generations, and which still provide continuity and identity for many residents. Clearly, however, the traditional tools of federal urban and social policy have not worked, and cannot reasonably be expected to work, in these areas.

In an effort to give these devastated zones a chance to recover and thrive, Republican Congressman Jack Kemp and Democratic Congressman Robert Garcia have recently introduced a bill that would permit the designation of "enterprise zones."

The enterprise zone approach seeks to improve conditions in the most run-down urban areas by encouraging local governments to participate with the federal government in creating a climate favorable to the establishment and success of small business, by lowering existing corporate, capital gains, payroll, and property taxes and by furnishing new tax incentives. Two-thirds of all new jobs are in companies employing fewer than twenty people. Such companies are more able to develop new, profitable ideas and to utilize existing facilities. In addition, entrepreneurs with marketable skills and ideas but little capital are often willing to devote long hours in poor working conditions to build up their businesses. Moreover, although small business entrepreneurs often have little knowledge of business skills when they begin, as their businesses grow they gain management competence and are able to utilize increasing amounts of local labor. In short, the enterprise zone concept seeks to use federal legislation to mobilize already existing local resources—structurally sound buildings, surplus labor, enterpreneurial spirit—to help people in need to help themselves and to work toward pride and independence.

The Kemp-Garcia bill is still in a relatively early stage of legislative development and needs considerable refinement. Specifically, we propose that:

To be eligible to participate, local governments be required to lower sales taxes within the zones;

A residency requirement be added to ensure that a significant percentage of those hired under the payroll tax reduction provision actually live in the zones; and

Local lending institutions receive tax incentives to direct capital towards new ventures in the zones.

We believe that, appropriately amended, the enterprise zone bill will give new hope to urban areas that presently have no hope. Although it is an experiment, it will be undertaken only in areas that have little if anything to lose. We therefore support the passage and rapid implementation of well crafted enterprise zone legislation.

Community Transit

Through years of [poor?] planning, negligence, profligate consumption, and lack of federal leadership, the United States has slid into a state of dependence on foreign oil that threatens our economic viability and national security. Transportation consumes half the petroleum used in this country, and the single-passenger automobile is the largest consumer. While the automobile provides—and will continue to offer— freedom of mobility and flexibility of response, its technical performance must be improved and its efficient use encouraged. Additionally, as a nation, we must commit ourselves fully to the development of a broad range of transportation alternatives. Increasing transportation choices requires strong federal support for public mass transit and incentives to encourage the private sector provision of energy-efficient and consumer-responsive transportation service options. It further requires a dedicated and predictable federal funding source. Such a federal policy will bring enormous fuel savings as well as increased and more fuel-secure personal mobility.

An Anderson Administration will propose a plan to provide a continuing and predictable federal commitment to:

Provide long-term financial support for the capital and operating costs of mass transit systems;

Finance effective auto management plans for urban areas;

Stimulate the innovative involvement of the private sector in offering options to the solo use of the automobile; and

Respond to the increasing need of rural populations for transportation alternatives.

A major part of this commitment will be met by the establishment of a new Community Transportation Trust Fund to fund capital and maintenance costs of metropolitan and local transit systems. Operating costs and other assistance programs would continue to be funded out of general revenues.

The CTTF would be funded through 45 percent of the federal alcohol and tobacco excise taxes. Over the next five years, 15 billion dollars would be expended, $2.5 billion in fiscal year 1981 alone. The surplus—as much as an additional $1.5 billion—would be reserved as a hedge against inflation. The reserve fund would be used to provide federal loan guarantees for automobile and other manufacturing companies that produce transit vehicles. The companies could use their federally guaranteed loans for research and development into the design, safety, and energy-efficiency of transit vehicles and for capital and tooling costs in manufacturing vehicles that respond to local procurement requests.

The CTTF will provide for the maintenance and modernization of rail, light rail, and bus systems for metropolitan areas, and for the building of new cost-effective surface light rail systems that contribute to rational land use planning and development objectives in accordance with the following priorities:

Assurance that long-term federal commitments to new energy-efficient rapid transit lines are consistent

with sound urban planning objectives;

More flexible funding to modernize, upgrade, and extend older fixed-rail and light rail systems and stations;

Rigorous review of the cost- and energy-effectiveness of any new fixed guideway transit systems proposals;

Investment in new light rail systems, using existing railroad right-of-ways, highway medians, or urban streets;

Production or rehabilitation and deployment of 10,000 buses annually for the next ten years;

Employment of "track-sharing" systems where feasible, by which both commuters and freight-haulers make use of the same urban railbeds.

An Anderson Administration will also use funds from the CTTF to stimulate the revitalization of the cities. Urban areas would be encouraged to bring together civic leaders in making commitments to include: providing new jobs and training; establishing strong affirmative action goals; bringing new businesses and industries to the area; and designing new private facilities that enhance the environment.

The beneficial impact of transportation investment on urban economic development necessitates the coordination of transportation policies with other public decisions. The federal tax code, water and sewer grants, and highway programs tend to encourage scattered suburban development. An Anderson Administration will propose to realize the full economic revitalization potential of transportation by supporting transportation policy with other federal programs that influence urban development patterns. Housing, environmental, and overall urban policy will be coordinated to achieve this objective.

An Anderson Administration will prepare a twenty-year community transportation financing plan with state and community participation, to be enacted by Congress. The plan would provide both long-term funding predictability and greater local decision-making flexibility, enabling local transit agencies to plan more effectively and to allocate their resources in response to overall community needs. The long-term community transportation financing plan will have the following objectives:

Establishment of a national goal of a 10 percent annual growth rate in transit ridership and private ridesharing;

Establishment of a comprehensive bus or rail system for every urban area with a population of 200,000 or more by the end of the decade;

Establishment of effective ridesharing programs in all fifty states to provide alternatives to the automobile for urban and rural workers and others who are dependent on the automobile; and

Development of a nationwide, coordinated approach to providing transportation choices for all rural Americans.

Efficient use of federal funds to provide transportation choices requires that communities also undertake comprehensive programs to ensure the responsible use of the automobile. An Anderson Administration will use federal funding, tax incentives, and technical assistance to encourage shared ridership and effective traffic management planning. Funds should also be administered to encourage all types of public and private operators to offer specialized collective transportation services.

The dynamics of private competition must be reintroduced into collective transportation. An Anderson Administration will create opportunities for specialized profit-making transit services. These opportunities include removing legal barriers, providing tax credits, and amending the tax laws to encourage the use of alternatives to the automobile.

An Anderson Administration will encourage local alternatives to reverse the serious decline in transportation services to rural Americans. Car pooling, block grants for collective transportation, and technical assistance are vital federal options which will be utilized.

Federal support for local mass transit systems must be placed on a predictable long-term basis, enabling communities to respond to their transportation needs in the most effective manner. A creative Anderson Administration will achieve this goal by establishment of the CTTF and the twenty-year financing plan coupled with a flexible and realistic approach to transportation planning.

Health Care

The underlying strength of the health care system in the United States lies in the quality, ingenuity, and diversity that is a hallmark of a free and diverse society. Federal health care policy must build on these strengths.

We cannot afford comprehensive, nationalized health care at this time. Nor can we afford a laissez faire attitude that simply blames our problems on federal regulation. The fundamental federal objective must be to contribute toward the overall health of our society while providing for those who cannot adequately take care of their own health care needs. We need an innovative, practical federal health policy which closes the gaps in our health care system, and complements and sustains the inherent strengths of a private-based system.

Federal health care policy must address the serious problems and weakness in our system, which include:

Rampant inflation in health care costs;

Gaps in health care coverage, including the limited access of the urban and rural poor to health care;

The lack of a comprehensive, long-term care policy for the elderly; and

The disproportionate emphasis of federal programs on the treatment of disease and the under-emphasis on preventive medicine and keeping people well.

Of these problems, the most severe is rampant inflation in health care costs. The health care industry accounts for 9 percent of GNP, nearly doubling since 1960. The average cost of a day in a hospital has increased from $15 in 1950 to $225 in 1978, seven times the general rate of inflation. Some of these increases in health care costs are undoubtedly attributable to remarkable but expensive improvements in health care technology and in expanded health care technology and in expanded health care coverage for people previously underserved. But spiralling health care costs are also fueled by severe economic distortions in the health care financing systems.

Prior public policy decisions are responsible for a non-competitive health care environment. Heavy regulation of alternative delivery systems such as health maintenance organizations (HMOs) have made it nearly impossible for these systems to operate on a competitive basis. Cost-plus reimbursement under Medicaid and Medicare encourages doctors and hospitals to increase the volume and quality of hospital services without considering cost. The federal health insurance tax subsidy program, costing $13 billion annually, promotes adoption of health policies without full regard for costs. Regulatory programs such as the health system agencies (HSAs) and professional standards review organizations (PSROs), while successful in some areas, have not yet demonstrated nation-wide success in holding down health care costs.

An Anderson Administration will reform federal financing, and encourage market-oriented incentives in order to reward cost-conscious behavior, contain rising health care costs, and respond to real health needs in the most appropriate and caring manner. Specifically, an Anderson Administration will:

Phase out retroactive cost-plus reimbursement under federal programs and replace it with prospective rate or fixed-premium financing. This will eliminate much of the expensive cost accounting and cost-reporting practices now imposed on hospitals, nursing homes, home health agencies, and health maintenance organizations, giving providers the incentive to contain costs rather than rewarding excessive spending;

Amend Medicare and Medicaid to allow participants to choose among competing health care options. This will promote flexibility, by allowing participants to select according to their needs, whether that be through prospective financial arrangements with hospitals or ambulatory care facilities, or through fixed-premium financing like a health maintenance organization;

Make employer health insurance tax deductible, contingent upon the offering of several qualified competitive insurance plans to encourage private sector competition. Employers should be required to make the same dollar outlay for health benefits per employee, regardless of the plan's cost, thus encouraging employees to make cost-effective selections and insurers to monitor the cost and efficiency of health care providers. Appropriate exemptions for small businesses should be allowed; and

Eliminate unnecessary and inefficient health system regulations as the principles of completion take effect. Federal funding for the health systems agencies and professional standards review organizations programs should be maintained. These regulatory programs were established in response to the failure of marketplace mechanisms to curb rising health costs. As competition is brought back into the health system, however, these regulatory activities can be phased out.

These reforms are designed to create incentives, control costs, deliver services efficiently, and provide quality services for all participants in the health care industry. An Anderson Administration will endeavor to hold down costs and provide quality health care simultaneously.

A second major problem is the lack of health care coverage for 22 million Americans. Despite considerable investment in medical care payments for the poor, these populations still suffer from poorly coordinated and episodic health care, and decreased access to medical care services.

An Anderson Administration will propose a responsible federal health care policy to better insure access to adequate health care and protection from impoverishment. Specifically, an Anderson Administration will:

Increase the supply of medical personnel to underserved areas through increased funding of the National Health Service Corps. The NHSC has been successful in placing physicians, dentists and nurses in underserved areas where many have remained to practice.

Convert, where possible, urban hospitals with severe financial predicaments to serve, in whole or in part, as primary-care centers with federal assistance.

Stimulate demonstration projects utilizing the Independent Provider Association (IPA) model for rural area physicians, linking them to existing central urban HMOs. By facilitating the specialty services through the urban HMO, IPAs can "subcontract" the delivery of services to rural patients through existing solo practice or small-group physicians;

Expand the Medicare and Medicaid programs to include provision of mental health services; and

Expand, in gradual steps, the Medicaid program to provide adequate coverage for the poor and working poor not yet covered, including coverage of low-income intact families, childless couples, and singles, as more efficient practices free up resources for such growth in beneficiary population.

To better insure access to catastrophic coverage for working men and women, the Anderson Administration will propose legislation requiring private-sector employers to offer a catastrophic insurance option in order to qualify their health plans for federal tax deductions.

Our health care system also lacks effective, long-term care services for the elderly. Federal programs frequently foster unnecessary hospitalization, which not only has serious financial impact on the individual and the government, but also creates a class of demoralized and dependent senior citizens. We must shift our emphasis from institutionalization to home health care. Approximately 2.5 percent of the federal health care budget is spent on home health care, compared to 20 percent spent on nursing home care, yet it is estimated that many of the 1,100,000 nursing home residents could be cared for more cheaply, humanely, and appropriately by alternative health care services.

An Anderson Administration will propose a comprehensive federal policy supporting long-term care needs of older Americans that is directed toward optimal health care maintenance through prevention, care, and rehabilitation. We must provide the necessary care to allow older Americans to remain financially secure and productive participants in their community. Specifically, an Anderson Administration will:

Provide, as part of the Medicare program, a number of home health services: 1) homemaker and healthaide programs to provide such services as meal preparation, cleaning, and personal care; 2) adult day care centers for the elderly who need full supervision, but are cared for at night and weekends by relatives; 3) respite services to allow families to leave elderly members in care of competent individuals during vacations; 4) patient education to encourage the elderly toward greater self-reliance and self-sufficiency;

Allow tax credits for families caring for elderly relatives to assist them in meeting rising costs for goods and services for the elderly individual;

Extend Medicare benefits to cover services provided by alternative health care professionals, such as nurses and physician's assistants;

Extend Medicare benefits to cover eyeglasses, dentures, and hearing devices;

Promote provision of low-cost housing communities

through tax credits, low-interest loans, or direct-funding incentives; and

Expand the Institute on Aging's research budget at NIH beyond the current 2 percent level.

An Anderson Administration will propose these reforms to insure greater security and fulfillment for elderly Americans. We must begin to take a step away from viewing the elderly as a burden and back toward seeing them as sources of wisdom and guidance.

Our present health care system also places disproportionate emphasis on the treatment of illness and lacks appropriate emphasis on preventive health care and health research. This practice is cost-inefficient and discourages proper health maintenance. We must place increased emphasis on protecting the healthy populations of our country from illness and on encouraging their continued good health. Health research must be recognized as a legitimate operating cost of the health care system.

An Anderson Administration will support programs to promote and extend good health to all Americans. Specifically, an Anderson Administration will:

Continue enforcement of clean air, clean water, solid waste, and toxic substances standards;

Increase funding for prevention and treatment of drug and alcohol abuse, and mental illness;

Pursue handgun control and automotive safety initiatives to reduce the loss of life and disability resulting from handgun and car accidents;

Support a Child Health Assurance Program to extend care to low-income children and pregnant women. Preventive health care and early detection of disease for these groups would do much to eliminate birth defects and decrease the incidence of many chronic debilitating diseases;

Provide adequate funding for all forms of biomedical and health care research particularly in the area of prevention. The results of research relating health to lifestyle, diet, and the environment must be adequately disseminated to the public, so that enlightened personal decisions can be made;

Make tax moneys to professional health care education facilities that are heavily dependent upon federal financing contingent upon instruction on preventive medicine, nutrition, and epidemiology as part of their core curriculum; and

Continue support of OSHA and encouragement of innovative and economic ways of achieving safety and occupational health standards.

The measures outlined above form a health care policy that is fiscally responsible, incentive-based, and targeted on the gaps and weaknesses that currently exist in our fundamentally strong, private-sector based health care system. To curb escalating health care costs, we propose competition among health care options in the private and public sector. To reduce the gaps, we propose to extend Medicaid eligibility for the poor and support National Health Service Corps for under-served inner city and rural citizens. To care for the elderly, we extend home health care coverage and other Medicare provisions. And finally, we change the focus of health care to preventive measures like the Child Health Assurance Program. These measures stop short of comprehensive national health care, but they address the most critical needs of the American health care system in an affordable fashion.

Welfare Reform

Welfare reform remains one of the great unfulfilled promises of government. The existing patchwork of public assistance programs is fragmented, irrational, wasteful, duplicative and inefficient. Repeated efforts at comprehensive welfare reform have failed under both Democratic and Republican Administrations.

The continuing failure to enact the necessary reforms has manifested itself in several forms. State and local governments which have sought to meet legitimate public assistance needs have been burdened by escalating costs, despite honest attempts to eliminate welfare fraud. States and localities that have permitted inflation to erode benefit levels have fared better financially, but welfare recipients in those states have suffered from increasingly inadequate support levels.

In many states, Aid for Families with Dependent Children (AFDC) benefits have been limited to one-parent households, forcing the breakup of families when fathers leave home to retain benefits for the children. In nearly all states there remains substantial work disincentives with welfare recipients confronting high "effective" marginal tax rates.

Transferring all responsibility for public welfare programs back to the states is not an appropriate means of dealing with the problems. We must seek to utilize the greater administrative efficiency that can be realized by large-scale delivery programs at the federal level with the greater equity and savings that can be realized at the local level by closer supervision and oversight.

Our task is to devise a more rational public assistance delivery scheme. Experience has demonstrated that welfare reform is best addressed by a series of selective reforms, rather than by attempting to secure immediate comprehensive reform. Adoption of the Social Welfare Reform Amendments of 1979, approved by the House of Representatives last December, would be a good first step towards reform of public assistance. The bill would:

Establish a national AFDC minimum benefit level

equal to 65 percent of the poverty level for all families with children;

Raise income limits in certain states and provide a system of declining cash welfare supplements to recipients until the income ceiling is reached;

Require states to offer Aid for Families with Dependent Children (AFDC) benefits to families with two parents, one of whom is unemployed, providing the family meets an income and "unemployment test";

Decrease the non-federal funding share of AFDC benefits by 10–30 percent, depending on the nature of the benefit provided; and

Liberalize the Supplemental Security Income (SSI) program for the aged, blind and disabled, by permitting a husband and wife who separate to qualify for individual benefits earlier; and "cash out" foodstamps for certain classes of SSI recipients.

We must, however, go beyond these reforms in our efforts to provide a more responsive and cost-effective delivery system. Public assistance should be tied to both work incentives and work requirements for the able-bodied. Our principal objective must be the provision of private sector employment. While public sector employment programs will continue to play an important role in job-training and temporary employment, special attention must be directed at longer-term, private sector job opportunity.

We support an expansion of the Supportive Work Program, based on the recent successful demonstration project, in conjunction with the WIN program for AFDC recipients. We also endorse further expansion of the Earned Income Tax Credit for the working poor. These and other initiatives, including proposed changes in the benefit reduction formula, would go a long way toward increasing work incentives; but renewed emphasis must also be placed on job creation. We support retention of the Employment Tax Credit, which encourages new hiring of disadvantaged workers, and expanded reliance upon the private sector jobs initiatives under Title VII of CETA. We must recognize, however, that the greatest provider of jobs for the disadvantaged in this country has always been a growing and vibrant economy.

If welfare costs are to be contained without sacrificing benefit levels for the truly needy, we need continuing administrative improvements in welfare programs, including standard procedures for the periodic determination of income and eligibility, and expansion of electronic management information systems. We support the use of innovative new approaches, like the National Recipient Systems (NRS), to the problem of erroneous payments.

Food Stamps

Despite some of the earlier problems associated with the program, the Food Stamp Program remains a vitally important element of our public assistance delivery system. Food Stamps have provided timely and critical assistance to millions of Americans whose household budgets have been disrupted by temporary or permanent layoffs or whose incomes have suffered due to age or physical handicap. As a compassionate and humane society, we cannot ignore the legitimate nutritional needs of those who would otherwise go hungry. We shall continue to support full and adequate funding of the Food Stamp Program.

Senior Citizens

Senior citizens desire to live a useful and secure life. Yet, for many, this goal remains elusive despite new federal initiatives and expenditures which consume one-fourth of the current federal budget. An estimated nine million older Americans now live in poverty, lacking wholesome food, adequate housing, and proper health care. For those living in isolation, a sense of being unneeded and unwanted robs their later years of meaning and dignity.

An Anderson Administration would be committed to meeting the real needs of older citizens, strengthening effective programs and initiating reforms as experience dictates. Before recommending any additions, however, we would insure that ineffective programs are eliminated.

An Anderson Administration would remove the barriers discouraging productive activity by the aging by:

Liberalizing the Social Security "retirement test," which limits outside earnings from part-time and temporary employment; and

Tightening loopholes in the Age Discrimination in Employment Act and enforcing current provisions to eliminate early mandatory retirement.

In the vital area of health care for the aging, reforms in the Medicare system could both improve care and reduce cost by eliminating unnecessary institutionalization. Older persons not needing intensive care in high-cost facilities could receive appropriate personal attention from their families or neighbors assisted by local supportive services. To encourage this approach we would:

Modify provisions which tax Social Security recipients living with their families, rather than in institutions;

Propose income tax deductions for families which care for relatives in their homes; and

Provide supportive services such as geriatric day care, homemaker services, nutrition programs, and sheltered living arrangements to allow the aging to remain in their communities at reduced cost.

The Medicare program would be revised to include home health services;

Homemaker and health-aide programs to provide services such as meal preparation, cleaning and personal care;

Adult day care centers for aging persons requiring full-time supervision who receive care from relatives on nights and weekends;

Respite services to allow families to entrust aging family members to the care of competent individuals during vacations; and

Patient education to help ill persons achieve greater self-reliance and self-sufficiency.

We would also encourage the development and use of health maintenance organizations (HMOs), which offer health services for predetermined annual fees. Prospective payment encourages preventive care and discourages unnecessary medical procedures.

We would support legislation to end fraud and abuse in the sale of private health insurance purchased by many aging persons to cover the gaps in Medicare coverage.

Lack of adequate, affordable housing plagues many aging persons. We favor increased support of public housing for older persons and pledge to continue to aid the aging in coping with rising energy costs.

Social Security Financing — The Social Security system is a public trust. It must be protected and preserved. We cannot allow potential insolvency to jeopardize the benefits of those who have contributed to the system during their working years.

Despite a series of scheduled payroll tax increases approved by the Congress in 1977, it is evident that neither the short-term nor the long-term financing questions have been resolved. It is anticipated that the Old Age and Survivors Insurance Trust Fund will approach insolvency within a few years.

The recurring problems with Social Security financing require close Congressional scrutiny. The 1977 amendments corrected one flaw in the Social Security program (the method for indexing benefits), which contributed to the long-term instability of the trust funds. There are, however, other problems. One factor is the increase in the number of retirees relative to the number of contributing workers. The changing beneficiary/contributor ratio means that more benefits will have to be paid out while contributions to the trust fund decline. The second factor is inflation. Social Security benefits are indexed to inflation to maintain the value of the benefits. In recent years, however, inflation rates have exceeded wage increases, resulting in a further depletion of the funds.

The short-term financing problems of the Old Age and Survivors Insurance Trust Fund can be resolved by either reallocating a portion of the payroll tax from the disability and health insurance trust funds, or allowing the OASI Trust Fund to borrow from one of the other two funds.

The longer-term problems of the Social Security system require a more fundamental adjustment. When the "baby boom" generation reaches retirement age, the ratio of beneficiaries to contributors will rise sharply, requiring correspondingly sharp increases in payroll taxes in order to keep the Social Security system solvent. The problem can be avoided, either by substantially reducing benefits at that time or by gradually increasing the retirement age beginning in the year 2000. It would be unconscionable to postpone such a decision until that date. Individuals must be allowed to plan for their retirement future with the confidence that last minute changes in Social Security will not disrupt their plans. An Anderson Administration will urge Congress to resolve this question so as to better facilitate retirement planning by young Americans.

The problems associated with rising Social Security payroll taxes — lowered employment and higher prices — can be resolved in part by alternative financing, including the use of revenues from higher gasoline taxes. A 50 cent a gallon increase could generate enough revenues in 1980 to reduce the employee's contribution by 50 percent. Such a trade-off, if coupled with other forms of relief, could satisfy an urgent conservation need and reduce the adverse economic impacts associated with payroll taxes.

The Family

American families, while evolving in diverse ways in recent years, remain a cornerstone of American society. However, complex forces have recently confronted the American family. Spiralling inflation, discriminating tax structures, conflicting welfare policies, and declining educational experiences are indicative of the challenges confronting family life in the 1980's. The many social tensions a family must face include the problems of material health, family planning, day care, and child welfare. In addition, the malaise in single parent families living in poverty deserves special attention. This broad catalogue of problems and needs includes abortion, adolescent pregnancy, health care, protection of the elderly, housing discrimination, unemployment, alcoholism and drug abuse, domestic violence, and flexible working schedules.

Given the diverse ideological opinions held as to the meaning of a family, it is unwise for government to think in terms of a "family policy." The government, however, should recognize the impact that its laws and practices have upon our social institutions, and try wherever possible to see that these laws and practices do not actively discriminate against the initiatives of the family. An Anderson Administration will support:

The elimination during the next few years of the "marriage tax" which discriminates against working spouses whose combined incomes are taxed at a proportionately higher rate than if they were single.

Elimination of inheritance and gift taxes in transfers between spouses.

Individual retirement accounts (IRA) for homemakers.

Government assistance for displaced homemakers.

Gradual revision of the federal welfare laws to eliminate discrimination against two-parent families.

Reform of the federal health care system as set forth elsewhere in the platform.

Elimination of the existing biases against intermediate care facilities and home-care treatment in federal health care programs.

Support for added tax deductions for wage earners in families that care for relatives instead of institutionalizing them.

Support for federal funding for child care for children whose parent or parents are employed and cannot afford privately funded child care.

Support for increased child care facilities for welfare mothers who want to work or are training for work.

Recognition in our laws that the role of the homemaker is of equal value and dignity with that of the providing spouse.

Reform of child support and alimony enforcement machinery.

Elimination of discrimination against women as set forth elsewhere in the platform.

Support for Child Health Assurance Plan (CHAP) to provide preventive health care for children.

Consumer Affairs

Fundamental to the functioning of a sound and stable domestic order is the protection of the health and safety of the American consumer. The American marketplace was founded upon the premise that the consumer is sovereign — we must continue to adhere to this principle. While we must uphold essential health and safety standards, we must also recognize that the American consumer does not benefit from an excessively regulated economy. We must protect the recent gains made in protecting the basic rights of the American consumer.

We must take the following steps to ensure the basic rights of consumers:

Support the improvement of management coordina-

tion and effectiveness of agency consumer programs through the efforts of the existing Inter-Agency Consumer Affairs Council and the implementation of government-wide standards for these consumer programs;

Continue support for essential food safety and drug statutes;

Preserve product disclosure requirements;

Protect consumers against dangerous products with appropriate standards for auto safety, clothing flammability, new drugs and chemicals, and food and children's products;

Support the right of a fair hearing for consumers and public participation in government proceedings;

Enforce legislation prohibiting debt collection agencies from engaging in unfair collection practices;

Enforce truth-in-lending and fair credit reporting laws;

Support for legislation to overturn the *Illinois Brick* case to provide indirect purchasers the right to seek redress against a manufacturer;

Eliminate abuses in the sale of credit life insurance;

Eliminate fraud in sale of health policies to the elderly;

Support a nation-wide program under the Elementary and Secondary Education Act to alert consumers of their rights, enhance their ability to make rational and well informed choices, and to inform them of their opportunity for participation in government decision-making;

Enforce anti-trust laws to protect consumers and assure an efficient and productive marketplace; and

Enforce anti-redlining laws.

Veterans

Our veterans have risked their lives to defend our nation's interests, and deserve our deepest respect. We must be willing, as a nation, to show our appreciation of veterans of our foreign wars.

The Veterans Administration was established to insure that our veterans would be treated properly. Yet, despite its resources, despite its manpower, the Veterans Administration often fails to fulfill its responsibilities. Too frequently, veterans are turned away from V.A. Hospitals; they are denied the medical care they need and deserve. An outside evaluation team should make a thorough review of the Veterans Administration and recommend measures for reorganization and improvement.

One of the Veterans Administration's most glaring failures has been its response to Vietnam veterans. We recognize the unique problems facing these veterans, victims of a war that left many of them physically, psychologically, and emotionally shattered. In general, Vietnam veterans have a higher unemployment rate than non-veterans, and 20 percent earn less than $7,000 per year. It has been estimated that 25-30 percent of all Vietnam veterans suffer from high-level readjustment problems, including drug addiction, alcoholism, and chronic depression.

The most serious effects of the Vietnam War, however, may not be realized for many years. It is now known that the herbicide code-named "Agent Orange," which was used extensively in Vietnam, contains a deadly chemical which may produce cancer, anemia, and hemorrhaging in those exposed to it and birth defects in their children. Thousands of American soldiers and Vietnamese were exposed to this deadly herbicide. Today many veterans face the uncertainty of not knowing whether the delayed effects of Agent Orange will claim them or their offspring as victims.

We believe that the plight of the Vietnam veterans can no longer be ignored. We strongly support the enactment of comprehensive legislation to improve our nation's treatment of Vietnam veterans, such as the Vietnam Veteran's Act currently proposed by Senator Heinz.

An Anderson Administration will:

Extend the limitation date for Vietnam veterans' education benefits with a 10-year extension for theater veterans and a 3-year extension for era veterans. Educational benefits should be adjusted to reflect the cost of living. The limitation of state matching requirements will be eliminated;

Require the Veterans Administration to undertake a major outreach program to contact the victims of Agent Orange poisoning. This program should include evaluation, treatment, and compensation, where due, for both veterans and their children;

Authorize the Veterans Administration to pay the administrative start-up costs needed to establish state-run programs providing direct housing loans at an interest rate below the prevailing market rate;

Provide for necessary personal counseling of Vietnam veterans. There should be no fixed deadline on this counseling. Theater veterans should be able to take advantage of non-V.A. facilities, such as community health centers or private mental health services. An outreach program should be employed to contact those Vietnam era veterans who have become disenchanted with the current Veterans Administration; and

Implement programs, under the auspices of the Veterans Administration, to reimburse employers for wages and other training expenses incurred for veterans. These reimbursements would be available up to the value of the monthly educational entitlement available to the veteran.

These proposals will cost money. To neglect our veterans, however, could prove even more expensive, both to society and to the military. Our past practices have led to great attrition from our voluntary army; recruitment of qualified and competent people is becoming increasingly difficult. A major effort must be made to reverse our past decade of neglect.

Primary and Secondary Education

Public education is an investment in America's future — an investment of even greater value to the nation than our capital plant and equipment. We must upgrade our investment in our human capital, just as we seek to rebuild our physical capital.

Despite a rising federal dollar investment in primary and secondary education, there is a growing concern about the rate of return on those federal dollars. The question, "Why can't Johnny read?" is asked with concern at the third grade level. At the high school level, it is asked with dismay.

Governor Reagan proposes to abolish the Department of Education. We propose to make it work. This is no time to sound the retreat on public education.

Over the past four years, federal aid to education has increased by 73 percent. An Anderson Administration pledges to make better use of those dollars.

Education and Regulatory Reform — The federal government, in recent years, has assumed a larger and larger role in local education programs, resulting in waste and duplication of effort. Grantsmanship has replaced scholarship at the local level in the scramble for federal dollars. The Anderson Administration will work for formula federal aid to local school districts to take school boards out of educational finance and back to educational excellence.

We must work to redefine the federal role in primary and secondary education. There must, of course, be oversight of federal dollars, but such oversight should not be intrusive or destructive of local school matters. The federal government should serve as a catalyst — providing the funds which can help public school systems achieve their goals, rather than dictating those goals.

To assist in the task of redefining the federal role, we propose to appoint, with Congressional authorization, a Presidential Commission on Primary and Secondary Education. The Commission's mandate will expire 18 months after its authorization, after providing recommendations on ways to:

Reduce the federal paperwork burden on local schools;

Evaluate better the financial needs of public schools;

Restore state and local initiative;

Minimize unnecessary federal intrusion; and

Harmonize federal and state regulation.

Federal Aid to Primary and Secondary Education — The creation of the new Department of Education affords the opportunity to review the full range of federal education programs in a coherent and comprehensive fashion. The new department should review the proper role and mix of categorical and block grant programs. In a number of areas, including special education, categorical grants play an essential role in assuring federal objectives. In the absence of a compelling federal interest in program supervision, federal assistance should take the form of block grants in order to minimize paperwork and maximize local initiative.

Federal aid to education must continue to play a leading role in assuring that school districts with insufficient local resources can provide equal education opportunity. Federal assistance must put a greater emphasis on reducing the intra-state disparities that still exist.

An Anderson Administration will continue to support the Title I concentration grants for remedial instruction of low income and disadvantaged students. We also reaffirm our support for the Headstart Program and related program initiatives.

An Anderson Administration will oppose tuition tax credits for primary and secondary education. Tax expenditures of this nature would drain much needed resources from public education needs at a time when the public school system's long-standing role as the principal provider of quality education is endangered. An Anderson Administration, while recognizing the important role of private primary and secondary institutions, is committed to preserving the traditional importance of free public education.

We recognize the special education needs of the disadvantaged or the specially situated. We reaffirm our commitment to quality education for all and for federal support of special education initiatives, including targeted assistance for low income and low achieving students and bilingual education programs for those who possess limited English language skills.

Special attention must be directed at the problems associated with federally mandated education requirements. An Anderson Administration is committed to reducing federally imposed education costs by increasing the federal funding of those costs. The federal government must shoulder the fiscal responsibility for its own legislative mandates.

Education of the Handicapped — There are an estimated 8 million handicapped children under the age of twenty-one in the United States. Nearly half of them are enrolled in programs that fail to address their special problems. Many of those problems remain undiagnosed. As a consequence, many of these children are wrongfully labeled as "slow learners" or charac-terized as having "attitude problems." The Department of Education, under an Anderson Administration, will encourage more extensive testing at the pre-school or first grade level in order to better identify hidden handicaps.

We reaffirm our commitment to the Handicapped Children's Act of 1975, P.L. 94–142, which requires that handicapped children be educated with the unhandicapped. We will support additional federal funds for the supplemental training of the classroom teachers needed to meet the federal requirements.

An Anderson Administration will also focus on the transitional problems that many handicapped students meet when they seek to move from the classroom to the workplace. Better linkages are required between special education programs and private sector affirmative action employment programs.

Vocational and Technical Education — Despite an unemployment rate of nearly 8 percent, many skilled jobs in this country still go unfilled for lack of qualified employees. The paradox of high unemployment and unfilled jobs illustrates the continuing need for federal support of vocational and technical education. Vocational programs can serve not only to improve the employability of program participants, but also make education more relevant to disillusioned youth.

An Anderson Administration will encourage a vigorous vocational and technical education program, tied to comprehensive career counseling programs. We pledge continuing efforts aimed at upgrading technical equipment and facilities and encouraging private industry to establish work-study programs at the school level.

Gifted and Talented — The creativity and intelligence of American children are our most valuable natural resource. Our most promising investment in the future is in the gifted and talented children who excel through a combination of ability and perseverance, and test the limits of our traditional educational resources.

The federal government has a special responsibility to these children, and to the school systems which must continually challenge and motivate them. Ironically, these students, who have the greatest potential to benefit from education have the highest drop-out rate. Many schools lack the facilities and personnel to identify and provide for the special needs of the gifted. Currently, only 12 percent of the 2,000,000 to 2,500,000 talented children in the United States are receiving special attention, and interstate differences in participation are profound. We are mandated to reduce the inequities and to guarantee that every gifted child is inspired to actualize his or her potential.

John Anderson would direct the Department of Education to develop programs to serve gifted and talented students in every state.

Federal funding can also be used to assist in the development of cooperative programs between private and public secondary and post-secondary schools and to improve programs now established by various public institutions, such as the National Science Foundation.

The private sector can and must participate in the education of these unique students. By opening the arts, business, and industry to the inquisitive and creative minds of talented students, we can provide them with invaluable opportunities for discovery and learning.

Bilingual Education — We have an obligation to deliver a fair and equitable education to all residents of this nation. We must strengthen our commitment to bilingual education. Bilingual programs should not simply be transitions toward a single language education, but rather should be jointly designed by government and community representatives with minority participation to maintain and cultivate a student's multiple linguistic capability.

Under an Anderson Administration, the Department of Education would be required to provide appropriate guidance to state and local governments and school boards for the joint development of responsive and effective bilingual education programs. The federal government will provide funding to cover the additional costs of mandated programs.

Literacy — At present, estimates indicate that between 20 and 30 million adults lack the fundamental skills necessary to read a newspaper or fill out a job application. We believe that without the ability to read, an individual is deprived of the ability to pursue his or her basic rights. Without reading skills, an individual has little opportunity for employment. Illiteracy prevents the people who need the greatest voice in government from having much of a voice at all.

Illiteracy contributes to an increased inefficiency of the American worker. Education programs of the past have failed to address to needs of the illiterate. We need to attack the problem where it begins — in our primary and secondary schools.

Success rates in adult education have been low and only a small percentage of the illiterates in this nation have ever been reached by such programs. This nation cannot afford to hire the individual tutors that literacy training requires. It must be up to individual communities to muster the resources and manpower necessary for literacy training.

An Anderson Administration will direct the Department of Education to undertake experimentation with community-developed and community-run literacy programs. Such programs should involve all appro-

priate resources in a region: the local school system, colleges, the private sector, local government, and the community. The Department should also have the responsibility for informing the nation of the severity of the literacy problem and devising methods to convince those who are illiterate to seek aid.

Higher Education

In the 1960's and 1970's, our federal and state governments invested heavily in the expansion of higher education. They created an educational system unparalleled in human history, an asset of priceless value. Our modern institutions of higher education not only provide educational opportunity, they also are centers of scientific research, and have a major impact on economic growth in a technologically oriented society which requires the services of skilled professionals. Most important to our democratic society, institutions of higher learning are a primary mode of social and economic mobility.

In the 1980's, we enter a critical period for our higher education establishment. The expansion of the last two decades has halted. By 1983, enrollment in higher education will peak, and then decline by 15 percent by 1990. As with any sector when it enters a static period, our nation's universities and colleges face a period of disruption. These institutions must entrench, rebuild, and revitalize to help our nation face the demanding years ahead. Just as the steel and other basic industries in our country face a time of rebuilding, so too do our educational institutions.

The federal government has a crucial stake in sustaining the educational establishment. Hundreds of programs in a variety of federal agencies have invested in higher education: its academic quality and fiscal health; the vitality of its research and scholarship; and the availability of educational and self-development opportunities.

The federal government has supported our institutions of higher education by grants to students, faculty members, and to the universities themselves. As we look toward the 1980's and beyond, we must continue and strengthen all three means of support.

Federal financial aid to students in higher education is not a coherent program. It is a complicated mixture of programs reflecting different national commitments and goals developed over the past thirty-six years. Many of the programs are inadequately funded, and others are misdirected.

Our primary objective in providing grants and loans should be to increase access to higher education by lowering financial barriers to all members of society. We must encourage the provision of quality educational services, and promote traditional values which may have been ignored by efforts to rectify past inequities. There are no simple solutions to the weaknesses in the current federal financial aid programs.

We can identify problem areas but much research is necessary to develop comprehensive solutions. An Anderson Administration will make a commitment to develop these solutions, and will:

Develop a more rational, equitable, and widely available loan program to provide needed aid to middle income families. Currently, there are numerous loan programs, each with different repayment terms and degrees of availability;

Gradually increase the Basic Educational Opportunity Grants (BEOG) to reflect changes in the costs of education;

Liberalize the half-cost rule, which presently limits grant assistance to $750 annually for disadvantaged students attending a tuition free institution;

Support renewed emphasis on self-help College Work-Study Program;

Encourage and increase funding of the TRIO programs — Talent Search, Upward Bound, Special Services for Disadvantaged Students, Educational Opportunity Centers, and Educational Information Centers — that deal with special problems and difficulties of access for the educationally disadvantaged;

Develop targeted post-enrollment remedial programs for students coming from disadvantaged educational environments;

Establish both an undergraduate and graduate Merit Scholarship Program at an estimated cost of $60 million; and

Maintain real spending on Supplemental Educational Opportunity Grants (SEOG) and State Students Incentive Grants (SSIG), currently funded at $440 million annually.

In addition to student financial aid, we must recognize the importance of subsidizing basic research in our institutions of higher learning. These centers play a significant role in the research and development needed to advance the technological genius and cultural heritage of our society. Recognizing this role, an Anderson Administration will:

Maintain real levels of support for the humanities;

Modestly increase funding for foreign language and area studies programs as described below;

Increase support for engineering research;

Increase support for quality scientific equipment, instrumentation, and facilities through a four-year phase-in program;

Upgrade research laboratories and equipment at universities and colleges with a five-year program of grants;

Create a fund for competitive post doctorate and research fellowships; special attention will be given to

people out of universities for several years;

Increase support for research libraries collection development and collection preservation;

Improve the administration policies federally sponsored research to assure that regulations do not unduly restrict research programs;

Encourage both stability and predictability of resources; and

Encourage flexibility by federal regulators and auditors in the exercise of financial oversight; and recognize that efforts to document fully and precisely how every federal dollar is spent are often counterproductive.

Our nation has lead the world in the quality of our medicine and medical professionals. As we renew our emphasis in comprehensive health care, we must continue to provide quality educational and research resources. The federal government can play a crucial role in sustaining these capabilities. An Anderson Administration will:

Support House Resolution 3633 Nurse Training and Health Programs Extension Act, providing continuing capitation funding for nursing education, and increased funding for the training of nurse practitioners and nurse midwives;

Increase funding for the National Health Service Corps;

Encourage the training of more health professionals, including physicians' assistants, nurse practitioners, paramedics, physical therapists, and midwives; and

Support predictable, long-term funding for biomedical research.

Federal involvement in higher education has resulted in numerous restrictions, changes in institutional procedures, and additional costs and burdens. Indiscriminately applied federal regulations have hampered our institutions of higher learning, impeded freedom of action and restricted self-management.

More care must be taken in the application of regulations to insure they do not unfairly impinge on the role of educational institutions. An Anderson Administration will not retreat from a forceful policy of affirmative action and environmental concern. But within these constraints, we must reexamine the effect of government regulations. Specifically, an Anderson Administration will propose to:

Subsidize compliance costs with a modest grant program;

Develop a comprehensive regulatory policy;

Take greater efforts to assess the impact of grant compliance requirements before their enactment; and

Increase flexibility in fund management for research.

International studies programs in our nation's institutions of higher learning are currently in a state of decline. America's ability to understand and deal effectively with both friends and foes depends heavily on trained and educated people knowledgeable in international affairs and competent in foreign languages. But the network of institutions and programs created in the 1950's and 1960's through the combined efforts of the government, private foundations and the universities has been seriously eroded. Federally funded foreign language and area fellowships declined from a peak of 2,557 in 1969 to 828 in 1978. Federal expenditures for university-based foreign affairs research declined from $20.3 million to $8.5 million, or 58 percent in constant dollars. At a time when America's needs for competence in international studies and foreign languages is becoming increasingly complex and urgent, our ability to respond to these needs is decreasing precipitously.

In a nation as large and pluralistic as the United States, only the federal government can provide the leadership and resources essential to improve substantially our foreign language and international studies capabilities. An Anderson Administration will establish long-term, enduring policies to:

Provide financial support for existing international studies programs at our universities and colleges and encourage the creation of new centers to correspond to national needs;

Provide funding for language teaching and support research designed to discover more adequate and effective language teaching techniques at all levels of instruction;

Increase support for foreign area and global issues research; and

Strengthen and expand our various international affairs programs at the community level, especially through the resources of our vast community college system.

The diversity and special services of minority-oriented institutions of higher learning are essential to rectifying past inequities. An Anderson Administration will:

Continue to support black colleges and universities;

Fully support the maintenance and development of American Indian community colleges. We are opposed to the transferring of schools under BIA control to the Department of Education. We recognize the need for community members to become further involved in the running of their schools. Decisions on the creation or termination of schools should not be made without tribal consent.

The Arts

Our nation has always been distinguished by its rich and full artistic culture. The arts, in their popular as well as their professional forms, have played a key role in enriching the lives of all Americans. John Anderson affirms the essential role the arts play in American society.

John Anderson believes that the federal government should be a strong supporter of the arts. Yet, we must be careful in choosing the form of this support. The government should foster the development of the arts without controlling their content. Government support of the arts should consist primarily of creating an environment that, while encouraging a balanced development of all arts, allows the mechanisms of private and popular selection to play a predominant role.

John Anderson cites the following areas in which the government can assist the arts:

National Endowments — Funding for the National Endowments for the Arts and the Humanities should keep pace with inflation. The President should monitor the Endowment's operations to insure that the public has access to the Endowment's programs, and to insure that their funds are being spent wisely.

White House Conference on the Arts and Humanities — John Anderson has supported efforts to hold a White House Conference on the Arts and Humanities. He will continue to help to arrange this Conference, which would provide a needed opportunity to discuss the future of American arts.

Cultural Heritage Preservation — The federal government should take measures to assure that the nation's cultural heritage — its monuments, artifacts, works of art, languages, and cultural traditions — is protected and preserved.

Art Bank — John Anderson supports the bill to create a National Art Bank within the National Endowment for the Arts. The funds for this Art Bank would be used to purchase works of American art, which would then be leased for exhibition in government buildings, hospitals, and civil centers. The Art Bank would benefit all Americans by increasing exposure to American artists, and bringing the best of contemporary American art to all regions of the country.

Private Support — Private financial support is the element essential to the well-being of our national arts. The federal government offers a tax credit to those private individuals and corporations contributing to the arts. The Anderson Administration would encourage the private sector to take maximum advantage of this tax credit.

The challenge grant program, which provides matching funds for contributions from the private sector, has proven very successful. Anderson strongly supports this method of giving financial assistance to the arts.

A patron awards program is a third measure that could be used to foster contributions from the private sector. Individuals and corporations who provide essential support to the arts deserve to have their support publicly recognized.

Fair Compensation — John Anderson would investigate improvements in copyright and patent laws to insure that artists receive proper compensation for their work. He favors tax credits in those instances where an artist lends his or her talents to public performances.

Taxes — John Anderson supports the Artists Equity Tax Act, and endorses the clarifications of the bill's language that have been suggested by the Authors League of America. This bill would modify our tax laws to: (1) encourage donations of art into the public domain, and (2) eliminate unfair tax burdens on artists and their heirs.

While recognizing the costs of these programs to foster the arts, John Anderson believes we must remember the arts' proven role in economic renewal and development. The establishment of art centers leads to improved property values, the growth of ancillary industries, with an accompanying increase in tax revenues. The arts could prove particularly useful in urban renewal programs, as they would help to attract people back into the cities. It is clear that the arts play an essential role in the well being of our nation.

Environment

The protection and preservation of the Earth's biosphere is vital to human survival. It is therefore necessary to ensure that our environmental initiatives of the past decade are not abandoned. We need to encourage a new ethos in our society that is built upon a greater respect for the environment and a greater willingness to protect it.

The Anderson Administration will accept the challenge offered by continuing threats to the environment by ensuring strong enforcement of our present environmental laws, and by enacting additional environmental legislation when necessary.

The Anderson Administration will be willing to accept the economic costs related to the protection and preservation of our air, land, and water against pollution, exhaustion, and depletion. We will ask the same of all our citizens. Our values cannot be oriented to short-term measures taken at the expense of future generations.

The nation's environmental standards were enacted to protect the health and safety of the American people and to ensure the quality of our lives and the lives of our children. We will exert our best efforts to meet our national commitment of protecting our environment. We will not relax these standards.

The following are important issues where an Anderson Administration will take new initiatives.

Oceans and Coastal Areas — The United States continues to neglect its connections to the seas. The rapid deterioration of our nation's coastlines and water is visible in oil-stained tidal pools, quarantined shellfish beds, the depletion of shorebird populations, and the loss of 300,000 acres of wetlands and 6,000 acres of fragile barrier islands which protect the Atlantic and Gulf Coasts.

Dumping of sewage sludge, catastrophic oil spills, chronic oil spills, and development of offshore oil and gas threaten to turn portions of our seas into large polluted sinks with barren underseas plains.

Once considered useless, our coastal wetlands are now seen as invaluable endangered resources. They provide vital habitat for water fowl, other coastal wildlife, food for commercially valuable fish and shellfish, natural waste treatment for tons of sewage effluent, storage for flood waters and the recharging of groundwater supplies. These valuable wetlands are being altered, polluted, and plundered by the pressures of energy siting, escalating demand for shipping channels, commercial development and second-home development.

Fish are in great demand as a source of protein; new sources of continental shelf oil and gas are urgently required to meet energy needs; seabed nodules are about to be mined for strategic minerals; global shipping grows; ports and harbors have become busier. Along the attractive coastal rim, urban populations concentrate more heavily and seek recreational joys from both water-related sports and esthetic surroundings. Finally, well over 100 nations face the sea, and they are exploring the potential of the oceans in contributing to their future.

To protect our oceans and coastlines from rampant resource exploitation, the Anderson Administration will institute the following programs:

It will actively lobby for the passage of "Oil Spill Superfund" legislation which would provide funds for rapid clean-up and damage compensation. Under our program:

Revenue for the superfund will be obtained through the taxation of companies involved with the transport and storage of oil that could result in the pollution of our country's waters.

Administration of the superfund will be by the EPA.

Use of superfund monies will be for:

The clean-up of oil spills.

Immediate compensation for damages caused by the oil spill.

The superfund will have the ability to sue the polluter to recover funds disbursed for damages, and the tax be adjusted on a biennial basis in the light of actuarial calculations.

With increased shipping of petroleum and hazardous cargo, and with increased size and decreased maneuverability of ships, greater attention is necessary to reduce risk to the environment and to assure safety for human life.

The Anderson Administration will direct the Coast Guard to strengthen traffic management systems and to devise means to enforce safety regulations more strictly. Additionally, new incentives and penalties will be provided to the shipping industry itself, so as to facilitate its assuming greater responsibility for operations. The Anderson Administration will also ask Congress to increase Coast Guard funding to cover the costs of these new programs.

The Anderson Administration will direct the Department of Transportation to research ways and means to accommodate increased maritime traffic, while reducing risk.

Sophisticated technology required for Arctic hydrocarbon exploration has not been tested and is still only in the developmental stage. Under the Anderson Administration, leasing in the Beaufort Sea will proceed only after technological methods are proven — *and* the annual review of the leased areas is comprehensive and conclusive enough to determine whether oil and gas exploration is having a detrimental impact on species such as the endangered Bowhead and Gray whales. Exploration in other Arctic areas such as the Chukchi Sea, Norton Sound and Navarin Basin will not proceed until the effects of Beaufort leasing is known, and consideration will be given to limiting exploration only within the barrier islands.

The Anderson Administration will require the following safeguards before any drilling is allowed to occur on Georges Bank, the world's most abundant fishery:

The barging of drill muds and cuttings off-site away from spawning areas except when meteorological conditions make this more hazardous than on-site disposal. Many of these materials contain toxic substances.

The reinjection of formation waters into the drilled cavity. These are waters associated with oil and gas reservoirs which are usually separated from oil and gas, and dumped overboard. Benzene, toluene, xylene, and ethyl-benzine are some of the materials found in these waters, and they are also the most toxic to marine organisms. The dumping of those materials could have a disastrous effect on fish larvae which circulate near the surface areas of the water columns.

Improvement in the composition and authority of the Biological Task Force established to monitor the effects of oil and gas activity on biological resources.

Lessees will be required to factor costs of safeguards into their costs of production in determining the feasibility of a particular tract. If the tract is subsequently determined to be economically infeasible, the de-

veloper will not be allowed to waive the safeguards; rather, the tract will be deleted.

Existing legislative and administrative authorities under the Federal Water Pollution Control Act (Section 404) will be strictly enforced, and federal agencies will encourage and solicit local support and aid in this enforcement.

The 1972 Coastal Zone Management Act is due for Congressional reauthorization. The Anderson Administration would seek to have this Act reauthorized by Congress and strengthened with more effective management incentives and enforcement tools. The following points should be included:

The CZMA should provide stronger incentives and penalties for states to develop and adopt their own management plans.

Periodic reports should be required from state and federal governments on the coastal areas, including reviews of state management plans.

Incentives for states to identify and preserve coastal areas of national significance.

Funding for additional beach access.

An Anderson Administration would address the issue of reducing federal funding for projects in high hazard areas especially on flood plains, wetlands, and barrier islands.

An Anderson Administration would support a strong, viable Marine Sanctuary Program.

Recent proposed changes in Section 404 of the Federal Water Pollution Control Act giving the Army Corps of Engineers more authority in the permitting process would be opposed by an Anderson Administration. (We favor the present procedure in which EPA has final veto over the Corps permits in the case of fragile areas.)

An Anderson Administration will require a review of our major ports in order to establish what are our national needs for ports and how established infrastructure can meet these needs without encouraging additional construction at the expense of our wetlands.

Through the United States Law of the Sea conference, the Anderson Administration would encourage adoption of environmental standards that would better control ocean pollution, the dumping of waste and the continuing disposal of radioactive materials on an international basis.

Public Lands — To fill the resource demands of a continually growing consumer population, many people wish to exploit the vast tracts of resource rich public lands in the West, and the remote undeveloped spots in the East. We must recognize that once we begin the exploitation of our public lands, however, that we are creating irreversible change. For this reason, it is in the best interest of the American people to hold portions of our natural lands in safekeeping, forever to be free from the threat of exploitation. Other federally owned lands can provide large amounts of valuable timber, minerals, and grazing land, if they are carefully managed. The next administration will have to address the following land management and resource preservation topics:

Alaska Lands. The Udall-Anderson Alaska Lands Bill (H.R. 39) passed the House of Representatives due in large part to intensive support by its primary minority co-sponsor, John Anderson. If enacted into law, this measure will protect approximately 128 million acres of unspoiled Alaska lands; of these, 67 million acres will be given "wilderness" designation. More recently, the Senate passed its own version of the Alaska Lands Bill, proposing the protection of approximately 100 million acres, but excluding some prime regions that are protected by the House bill.

We will exert our best efforts to secure enactment of a strong Alaska Lands Bill, as introduced by John Anderson in the House of Representatives.

Sagebrush Rebellion. The Bureau of Land Management of the Department of Interior manages the nation's "unappropriated, unreserved lands." This now amounts to about one-fourth of the land area of the United States. Ninety percent of these unreserved lands are west of the Rocky Mountains. There is currently local political pressure to enable the states to assume management of these lands.

It is, however, also argued that states will find it too expensive to manage the lands and will succumb to overwhelming pressures to sell them. (It would cost Idaho $51 million to manage 20 million acres of national forest lands at the current level of management by the federal government.) With the zeal to develop these areas, environmental concerns could easily be overlooked or ignored.

The Anderson Administration will work to have federal lands remain in the possession of the federal government to ensure they are managed in the best national public interest, according to principles of conservation and multiple use of all resources.

Forestry. More and more pressure has come from the timber industry and building trades to cut more heavily in our national forests as lumber shortages increase. Yet, we currently export logs to Japan. The hard choice here is between the preservation of an important and substantial part of the environment and the accumulation of needed export revenues. In an area as important as the national forests, we must allocate our resources more wisely. We must have respect for the land that extends beyond our time. Broad interests definitely should be represented in the preservation of national forests.

The Anderson Administration will vigorously enforce the multiple use/sustained-yield policy set forth in the National Forest Management Act of 1976.

The Anderson Administration will require the Forest Service to renew its timber pricing policy to bring it in line with sound business practices, since the subsidizing of timber prices discourages private forest investment and other uses of the forests. More emphasis will be placed on private timber farms by the Forest Service to increase its cost-sharing and assistance programs.

RARE II Process. Through the RARE II (Roadless Area Review and Evaluation) process, the Forest Service has reviewed 62 million acres of roadless lands in the national forest system. The Forest Service has recommended 15.4 million acres as wilderness, 35 million acres be managed for multiple use (logging, grazing, recreation), and 10.8 million acres be studied further.

Under the Anderson Administration, wilderness designations will be increased and areas not previously studied will be reevaluated for their wilderness potential.

Urban Parks. To improve the urban environment and to assist urban areas to maintain and protect their valuable parks, an Anderson Administration will:

Encourage the National Park Service to attend to the special needs and problems of parks and public recreational areas within the urban setting.

Air and Water Quality — In recent years the energy needs of our country have been the primary issue in the minds of our government officials and the general public. Since this issue receives focused attention and efforts, other domestic programs and issues at times go lacking or are even submerged. Environmental concerns are often considered hindrances to energy development and industry is continually attempting to have standards eased. Auto manufacturers plead to have auto emission standards relaxed as a way of attaining adequate mile-per-gallon ratings. The increased use of coal and synthetic fuels brings with it the potential of vitiating the nation's air quality. Emissions from increasing fossil fuel combustion combine with accumulations of carbon dioxide to form acid rain that has fallen on the Northeast depleting fish in mountain lakes and affecting crop production and forest yields.

Our water quality and reserves are also declining at a dangerous rate. Our ground water is being contaminated by abandoned waste dumps, unsafe landfills, polluted streams, and oil and gas well drilling techniques.

Some suggest we submerge environmental concerns to solve the energy, productivity, and economy issues. We must put in place policies and programs that will answer the needs of the future and not be oriented to short-term concerns without reference to what the consequences might be for future generations.

The Anderson Administration will establish the strict enforcement of the Clean Air Act of 1977 and the Water Pollution Control Act of 1972 as national priorities.

Through the EPA, the Anderson Administration will seek to reduce further industrial emissions and require the installation of best available control technology on existing coal-fired power plants.

The Anderson Administration will lobby against attempts to weaken standards or postpone the deadlines for reducing carbon monoxide and hydrocarbon levels in automobile exhausts.

The Anderson Administration will direct the EPA to phase out the substitution of taller smoke stacks for emission controls.

The Anderson Administration will seek to retain the section of the Clean Air Act that prohibits any "significant deterioration" of pristine air in our national parks and wilderness areas. (Removal of this provision would have allowed a giant coal-fired plant to be erected only nine miles from a major park in Utah.)

The Anderson Administration will direct the EPA to institute an exhaustive study of the effects of acid rain and methods for its prevention. (For further discussion of acid rain, see the Energy plank.)

A national program of water conservation will be initiated by the Anderson Administration. Environmental values will receive top priority in planning of water programs and projects.

Through the EPA, the Anderson Administration will strictly enforce federal standards for carcinogens in drinking water. If standards are not met by the utility or municipality serving a community, the consumers will be notified, and the utility required to meet the standards using appropriate technologies.

Wildlife — Ninety percent of all species which ever lived on Earth have now disappeared; almost all of them died out naturally. Recently, this process has changed. Man's actions now account for the extermination of numerous species. In 300 years man has eliminated 150 known species of mammals and birds, and an unknown number of reptiles, amphibians, and fish. Pressures from an increasing world population seeking room to live and resources necessary to support an ever rising standard of living are depleting the habitat of our wildlife.

A concern for wildlife conservation can seem frivolous in today's world, yet man has a tremendous self-interest in ensuring ecosystem stability and protecting the Earth's gene pool. Any reduction in the diversity of resources reduces our ability to respond to new problems and opportunities. In order to protect the wildlife of our lands and seas, the Anderson Administration will:

Strengthen the National Wildlife Refuge program

by limiting the secondary uses of the refuges: grazing, timber harvest, hunting, trapping, predator control, and pesticide use.

Expand and strengthen the current embargo on the importation of products derived from endangered wildlife.

Exercise the influence of the United States to encourage other countries to terminate the wholesale slaughter of whales, porpoises, seals, and other wildlife.

Enforce international whale conservation efforts through sanctions under the Pelly amendment to the Fisherman's Protective Act, which provides that any nation which undermines an international conservation treaty will have its nation's fishing products embargoed from entering U.S. ports under the direction of the Department of Commerce. Where a nation was in violation of an international conservation treaty and certified under the Pelly amendment, the Anderson Administration would employ the Packwood/Magnuson amendments to the Fishery Conservation and Management Act, which can expressly limit the amount of fishing allowed within the U.S. 200-mile limit.

Water Projects — Due to the pork-barrel nature of Army Corps of Engineers and other federally funded water projects, legislation in this area is often given a cursory review by Congress and usually passes with ease. As a result, many water projects are constructed without proper attention to their environmental impact.

The insatiable desire for ever cheaper electric power, without attention to cost-benefit ratios, will bring about the construction of numerous hydro-electric dams on previously free-flowing rivers and streams. This could have many adverse effects such as the destruction of valuable fish and wildlife habitats, the inundation of productive farmland, the displacement of rural populations, and loss of irreplaceable scenic and recreational areas.

The wetlands of our country are also in jeopardy. Land developers are now turning to areas that were previously difficult to develop, but are now attractive due to escalating land costs. Now that the technology and machinery exist to drain our marshes and wetlands easily, we are faced with the prospect of the destruction of these valuable ecosystems that provide habitats for many forms of flora and fauna. Wetlands are also a valuable component in our water cycle, providing natural waste treatment and a means by which we can store flood waters to recharge our groundwater supplies.

To assure that federal water projects respect environmental concerns the Anderson Administration will do the following:

Direct the Army Corps of Engineers to place a strong emphasis on the preservation and restoration of our nation's wetlands.

Pay careful attention to proposed federal water projects to see that their cost-benefit ratios did not under-estimate environmental impact. An example of a project that proves to be very cost-effective and that the Anderson Administration will support is the Charles River Watershed Project in North Carolina. This project establishes good floodplain management and protects valuable wetlands.

Re-evaluate the cost-benefit ratios of all navigation projects for barges that are less than 40 percent complete to determine if they are still profitable. If they no longer pass this profitability test, then the Administration will halt their construction.

Decrease federal funding of water project costs to encourage the states to assume a larger share of project costs.

Federal water project aid will be made conditional on state implementation of groundwater management laws.

Toxic Substances — Through the manufacture of chemical substances, our nation generates 77 billion pounds of hazardous waste each year. Such waste threatens our air, rivers, and ground water resources. The serious toxic contamination discovered in the Love Canal area of New York has understandably resulted in public suspicion, fear, and anger. Such reaction is not unwarranted. There is convincing and sobering evidence that chemical wastes until recently have been disposed of illegally or carelessly in a way that assures they will ultimately find their way into the environment. In many instances these chemicals once released cannot be controlled.

The U.S. government through EPA has the framework to control chemical products and wastes. (The Toxic Substances Control Act authorizes the government to collect information on chemicals that may damage health or the environment and to control them where necessary.) The Resource Conservation and Recovery Act provides for government control over hazardous wastes from their point of generation to final disposal.

Thus the U.S. government is beginning to collect information on all aspects of waste generation and to dispose of (or store) the wastes securely. There is growing public concern that the federal government's present level of commitment is not adequate for the task.

In many instances, the failure to take swift measures endangers the public's health. As a matter of public policy, we cannot delay action while we await conclusive evidence of toxic-related cancer, abortion, fatalities, and birth defects.

Federal policy must be focused on the prevention of toxic disasters. The following policies will be implemented to address this national environmental crisis:

The Anderson Administration will more aggressively enforce the Toxic Substance Control Act and the Resources Conservation and Recovery Act. This calls for rapid promulgation of the rules by the EPA and for the expansion of testing and monitoring. Within legislative mandates, the Anderson Administration will expand the existing testing and monitoring procedures.

The Anderson Administration will work toward enactment of a "Toxic Waste Superfund" program for the clean-up of improperly disposed of toxic materials.

The superfund will be built on taxes levied on the principal hazardous waste generating industries.

The industries to be taxed will be identified through a study by the EPA.

The individual tax rates will be determined by the quantity of waste produced by the company.

The "Toxic Waste Superfund" will be administered by the EPA.

The superfund will be used for:

The clean-up of improperly disposed of toxic materials.

Compensation to innocent victims as a remedy of last resort. It must be noted that a polluter is liable for injuries incurred as a result of its improper disposal of toxic waste. If the polluter is unknown, or if liability for damage cannot be expeditiously established, then the EPA will be able to award compensation to the victim if it can be proven that injuries resulted from the improper disposal of toxic wastes.

The Anderson Administration will promptly convene regional councils of governors and mayors to develop sensible regional solutions to the disposal site problem. These councils would make the hard choices that are needed, assisted by technical experts from federal, state, and local agencies, with input from private citizens.

The Anderson Administration will direct the EPA to grant funds to be used to help the councils ensure that these priority disposal sites are managed with the greatest care and skill. This would include provision of technology development funds where appropriate in order to pioneer new and more effective disposal techniques.

The Anderson Administration will institute temporary emergency bans on the usage of toxic substances, herbicides, and pesticides where there is extensive evidence and confirmatory information that the substance is causing serious adverse health effects on people and the environment. (The EPA imposed an emergency ban on the use of both 2,4,5–T and Silvex. They took the action due to evidence that these herbicides caused cancer, birth defects, and miscarriages. We support this emergency ban.)

The Anderson Administration will examine in detail the problem of the transport of hazardous chemicals. It will act quickly to reduce the danger to the public from this source. Safe traffic routes will clearly be a major component of this initiative.

IV. Guaranteeing Rights and Promoting Justice

Prosperity without justice, and security without basic rights, are incomplete. Indeed, any society that long denies basic rights and just treatment to all its citizens diminishes its unity and strength, and sows a crop of bitterness and rage. It is both the obligation and the interest of every society to deal fairly with all.

In modern American society, however, it must be remembered that economic wellbeing is considered a basic right of all Americans. Action in the field of civil rights today, therefore, has these basic priorities:

First, we must seek to provide employment opportunities for all. This is the purpose of our proposals here and elsewhere in the platform in the area of jobs.

Second, we must transform our laws so that they cover and protect all equally. This is the purpose of our proposals in the area of civil rights.

Third, we must ensure that all the laws we have are enforced fairly and equally. This is the purpose of our proposals in the areas of criminal justice.

Jobs and Justice

A just and progressive civil rights policy must be founded not only upon the enactment and enforcement of civil rights legislation, but must also be founded upon an economic policy that provides opportunities for employment and advancement.

Throughout this program we have set forth proposals that affect the employment status of minorities. These include strengthening Title VII of CETA, enacting a Youth Energy Projects Act, supporting the Youth Act of 1980, stimulating small businesses in declining areas, establishing urban enterprise zones, and rebuilding neighborhood confidence by promoting policies that encourage local initiative. We have proposed urban housing programs to increase the supply of low income housing, encouraging self-ownership, and removing restrictions on the use of HUD funds for the restoration of existing residential structures. We have proposed low income energy assistance needed to help families unable to meet skyrocketing residential energy and weatherization costs. Our investment proposals include tax credits for firms that renovate their existing structures (largely relevant to urban areas). We have proposed a job-creating Urban Investment Trust Fund to rebuild the basic infrastructure of our cities and a job-creating Community Transit Trust Fund to renovate and rebuild our transportation network. Jobs will be a central concern of an Anderson Administration.

In addition to these and other programs outlined in this program, we propose a strong initiative in the field of minority business.

The ownership of businesses and other capital assets is the best way in which members of minority groups can gain their deserved share of the American economy. However, minority-owned businesses face not only all of the problems of finance, overregulation and marketing facing all small businesses, but also the additional problems caused by a long history of discrimination. Thus, it is necessary to provide additional assistance to Black, Hispanic, American Indian and other minority entrepreneurs. Such assistance should be carefully tailored to provide help to businesses that create long-term productive jobs and stimulate economic growth. We endeavor to:

Place additional emphasis in the Minority Business Development Program upon assisting minority entrepreneurs in growth industries, such as energy production and conservation, electronics and communications.

Implement legislative setaside provisions for minority businesses, especially in areas that can improve the productivity of the minority community and the economy as a whole, including funds allocated for research and development activities.

Expand the Minority Business Technology Commercialization Program of the U.S. Department of Commerce in assisting minority entrepreneurs to participate in the process of the commercialization of new technologies, including those resulting from our space program.

Make the programs of the Small Business Administration more effective through streamlined procedures, monitoring of results and closer working with minority-owned banks.

Civil Rights

John Anderson's commitment to civil rights has never wavered throughout his years of government service. A vocal supporter of every major piece of civil rights legislation from the 1964 Civil Rights Act to the 1980 Fair Housing Act, he has remained steadfast in his loyalty to the principles of equal education, open housing, and employment for all. Governor Lucey has an equally long and distinguished civil rights record.

Although many are willing to make the claim that the battle for civil rights has been won and is over, we disagree. We are willing to applaud the progress thus far, but as long as we fail to see an Equal Rights Amendment ratified, as long as previous commitments to the rights of American Indians, Hispanics, Blacks, and other minorities are not honored; as long as we fail to extend those same commitments to the rights of the handicapped, immigrants, and others; as long as our fair housing laws are wantonly abused; and as long as groups such as the Ku Klux Klan and the Nazi party not only survive but actually gain nominations for public office, we are unwilling to call for a truce in the struggle for civil rights.

In most instances, the legislation necessary for the guarantee of civil rights is already in existence. Unfortunately, many of these laws, some of which have existed for a century, and some for two decades, are not being seriously upheld or enforced. Existing laws and statutes must be upheld and, if necessary, revised to enhance their enforcement. Only when we strictly enforce laws such as the Civil Rights Acts and uphold our fair housing laws will we realize an effective commitment to civil rights.

Housing — Title VIII of the 1968 Civil Rights Act declared that "it is the policy of the United States to provide, within constitutional limitations, for fair housing throughout the United States." But despite this, many Blacks, Hispanics, and other minorities are still denied equal housing opportunities.

We believe steps must be taken immediately to insure equal housing opportunities for all.

The Anderson Administration will seek immediate enactment of Fair Housing legislation, if H.R. 5200 is not enacted during the 96th Congress.

In 1968, John Anderson cast the deciding vote in the Rules Committee which brought the Open Housing bill to the House floor, and he helped lead the fight for its passage. We recognize that the original bill must be strengthened. Thus, we support the legislation currently before the Congress which would authorize HUD to order violators to cease discriminatory practices, and to assess civil penalties against those accused of violating the Fair Housing Act.

We believe adequate funding must be provided to enable HUD to conduct community-wide compliance reviews, monitor compliance agreements, and establish a viable program for interagency coordination with regard to fair housing. We must increase funding for the Department of Justice in order to ensure adequate prosecution of Title VII violators.

Affirmative Action — The mandate of our civil rights legislation cannot be fulfilled simply by prohibiting practices intentionally designed to deny opportunities. We believe that we must make an honest and positive effort to enforce the equal protection clause of our Constitution through the establishment of affirmative action programs.

We cannot be lax either in the monitoring or in the enforcement of affirmative action programs. Such programs have been in effect for only a brief interval of time compared to the years of oppression that preceded them. Over a century ago, the Supreme Court stated that when a person emerges from slavery to citizenship, he "ceases to be a special favorite of the laws." Such thinking, similar to the growing revisionism of today, helped to usher in a century of enforced segregation and discrimination. An Anderson Administration will never accept such a reactionary and unjustified view. It will be prepared to use the threat of terminating federal funds to offending institutions and municipalities much more extensively than previous administrations have been.

We also believe that the federal government should set the example in the application of minority hiring practices. An Anderson Administration will require full accountability from all government departments and agencies with regard to the implementation of affirmative action. We believe that the true test of an administration's intentions lies in its ability to place minorities in all branches of government, not just in those sections of government concerned with minorities. An Anderson Administration will seek to place minorities in all foreign as well as domestic branches of government.

Education

Since the *Brown vs. The Board of Education* decision, school districts have struggled with the problem of properly integrating their schools. We favor federal support for communities to devise their own methods to attain school desegregation. Those methods include redrawing zone boundaries, pairing and clustering of schools, and cooperative arrangements between school districts where feasible. However, if these strategies fail to achieve integration, we favor an intelligently devised busing plan as a last resort.

The Anderson Administration will absolutely oppose any attempts to pass a constitutional amendment prohibiting busing.

We recognize that court-ordered busing is the result of community failure to design a local remedy for school desegregation. An Anderson Administration will seek to enact the National Educational Opportunity Act introduced in the 95th and 96th Congresses by John Anderson. This legislation would provide federal funds to encourage local cooperation in enacting school desegregation programs.

Native Americans and Alaskan Natives

The obligation owed to Native Americans and Alaskan Natives by the federal government is not discretionary, but is based on prior legal commitments established through judicial and legislative pronouncements. However, in many instances, the federal government has failed or is failing to meet this nation's obligations to Native Americans and Alaskan Natives.

We have always been strong supporters of sovereign tribal rule, as guaranteed to Native Americans and Alaskan Natives by treaty, Supreme Court decisions, Congressional policy and Executive Order. Under an Anderson Administration, treaties will not be abrogated without the consent of all parties involved.

We believe that a strong Bureau of Indian Affairs is necessary to adequately protect the interests of Native Americans and Alaskan Natives within the federal government. Any reorganization of the Bureau should seek to distribute more power toward both the Agency and tribal level.

The federal government must work with Native Americans and Alaskan Natives to plan, develop and implement realistic economic development programs which will improve and strengthen their economic position and which will bring long-term employment opportunities to their people. Where Tribal and Alaskan Native lands contain considerable amounts of coal, uranium, natural gas and other natural resources the federal government should not be permitted nor should it permit private industry to exploit these resources in a manner detrimental to those tribes and Alaskan Natives.

We support the efforts of the Bureau of Indian Affairs' Federal Recognition Project.

An Anderson Administration will order enforcement of the Voting Rights Act and the Bilingual Education Act to assure that Native Americans and Alaskan Natives will receive voting information as well as sufficient educational materials in their native languages.

Life expectancy for Native Americans and Alaskan Natives is low. We propose an expansion of programs involving tribally controlled paraprofessionals and grassroots health services with an emphasis on preventive medicine.

Puerto Rico

The islands of Puerto Rico should be entitled to political self-determination. We support any decision the people of Puerto Rico make in a referendum whether the decision includes becoming a state, maintaining its status as a commonwealth, or establishing independence.

Sexual Orientation

We believe that discrimination due to sexual orientation should not be tolerated by the federal govern-

ment. An Anderson Administration would work to repeal the section of the Nationality and Immigration Act which excludes individuals from immigrating soley on the grounds of sexual orientation. We would issue an executive order baring discrimination based upon sexual orientation within the federal government. An Anderson Administration would encourage Congress to extend to the Civil Rights Commission the power to investigate acts of discrimination against individuals based upon their sexual orientation.

District of Columbia

We applaud past efforts to grant the District representational rights. We support ratification of the amendment which would grant D.C. voting rights in Congress.

Immigration

Immigration policy raises a number of difficult issues. We seek to balance the aspirations of the poor, hungry, and jobless in other lands while protecting the most disadvantaged members of our own society from special burdens.

An Anderson Administration will create an executive task force to review and, where appropriate, to implement the recommendations of the Select Commission of Immigration and Refugee Policy as soon as its report is made public. In so doing, it will constantly keep in mind the contributions made by generations of immigrants.

The two-thousand-mile border we share with Mexico presents unique problems, but unique opportunities for mutually beneficial cooperation as well. The immigration of undocumented Mexican workers affects the interests of many parties, not just those of our two governments. It affects local communities on both sides of the border; it affects the American worker as well as the undocumented Mexican worker; and it affects our own Hispanic-American community.

We believe that any attempt to close the border would be detrimental to our relations with Mexico. We are opposed to any policy which requires the carrying of work cards. Such a policy is inconsistent with this nation's fundamental commitment to civil rights.

We must deal with the issue of Mexican immigration within the context of other border issues. The existing mechanisms for handling specific problems in the border region have not been satisfactory. Therefore, an Anderson Administration would propose the creation of a joint Mexican-American commission to promote cooperative border development in an integrated fashion as described elsewhere in the platform.

Handicapped

While significant strides have been made toward ending discrimination against the handicapped, much remains to be done in terms of increasing employment and education opportunities, while also promoting freer access to public buildings and services. Several tasks remain to be done.

We must work to eliminate discrimination against the handicapped in housing by amending Title VIII of the Civil Rights Act to bar such discrimination.

We must insure compliance with Section 504 of the Rehabilitation Act of 1973 to increase the accessibility of public facilities for disabled Americans.

We must accelerate the spending of monies already authorized for independent living demonstration projects.

We must expand federal vocational and educational training provisions to include independent skill training programs for the disabled.

We must provide appropriate tax relief for private employers who remove architectural or other barriers to the hiring of the handicapped.

Justice for American Women

The time has come for all our institutions and leaders to seek justice for American women.

Full partnership for women in our society is essential to our self-respect as a nation and our moral standing as a world leader. In addition, rebuilding our nation depends on our capacity to utilize all the creativity, leadership, and technical skills available. Justice for women is not a luxury; it is a necessity.

The women's movement of this generation is a vital force in our society. Thousands of the ablest women are enlisted in this cause and have achieved great gains.

Federal legislation prohibiting discrimination in education, employment, credit, and housing has been passed. The Equal Rights Amendment has been ratified by 35 states representing 72 percent of the population. Thirteen states have added effective ERAs to their state constitutions. The Supreme Court has made tentative but ambiguous steps in the direction of interpreting the Fourteenth and Fifth amendments to extend to women equal protection of the laws.

Women of means can get legal, safe abortions.

Improvements have been made in marital property, divorce, and inheritance laws in a number of states.

The number of women mayors, city council members, and state legislators has steadily grown.

Half our college undergraduates are women, and 25 percent of our law and medical school enrollment.

Participation of girls and women in sports has skyrocketed.

Opportunities for women in non-traditional training and jobs have been opened up.

Government funding of child care facilities for low income women has increased.

Women have made gains in full acceptance in the military services, particularly in non-traditional occupations.

Some shelters for victims of rape and battered women have been established, and some federal government funding is being provided.

These gains came against great opposition and at great cost in time and money to literally thousands of women and many supportive men.

In spite of the impressive victories already won, women are nowhere near achieving full partnership in any of our institutions, including the family.

The ERA, which would provide legal equality, has not been ratified.

The ERA is sorely needed because federal law and most state laws are based on the English common law, under which married women were chattel under the control of their husbands. They were considered incompetent to control their children, their property, or their own lives. Although many piecemeal reforms have been made, the laws are still riddled with vestiges of the English common law. For example, one state code reads as follows: "The husband is the head of the family and the wife is subject to him; her legal civil existence is merged in the husband, except so far as the law recognizes her separately, either for her own protection, or for her benefit, or for the preservation of public order."

Under another state code, a widow may forfeit any rights in her deceased husband's estate if she is guilty of "misconduct." There is no similar provision applying to a widower.

In a number of states, a wife may not receive alimony if she is at fault. A husband, however, is not penalized for being at fault.

In several states, profits from a business run jointly by wife and husband are the property of the husband.

The ERA is needed to insure that states and the Federal government make a systematic effort to review and revise their codes to eliminate such laws as these.

Many other problems remain:

Stumbling blocks have been put in the way of those seeking reform of domestic relations laws to accord homemakers the value and dignity they so richly deserve;

Over one-half of divorced mothers are supporting their children without assistance from the father and only 4.6 percent of divorced women receive any alimony;

The right to choose whether to bear children is not available to many poor women, and sterilizations without informed consent are still being performed;

Women still earn on the average 59 percent of what men earn, and 80 percent of women in the labor force are still employed in the segregated low-paid occupations. Many of these occupations pay less than traditionally male jobs with less responsibility and requiring less skill and education. Too many of the children of working mothers have inadequate care. Only 1.6 million licensed day care slots are available for 6.9 million children under 6 with working mothers;

Our university faculties have been very resistant to employing and promoting women. Although, there are many more women Ph.Ds than fifteen years ago, the percentage of women faculty in universities has not improved significantly. Most of the improvement has come at four-year and two-year colleges in lower ranks;

Little progress has been made in participation of women in non-traditional vocational education programs;

Most battered women still have no refuge from violence, particularly women in small towns and rural areas;

The domestic relations laws of most states and the tax laws of the federal government are not based on the premise that the contributions of homemakers are equal in value and dignity to that of the providing spouse;

The federal government does not direct a fair share of employment and training opportunities to women;

Many federal government programs, such as alcohol and drug abuse programs, have not provided benefits to women in proportion to their needs. Health research has focused on women's reproduction leaving women out of studies on other aspects of health. In some programs, data are not kept by sex so that assessment of the impact on women cannot be made.

The Anderson Administration will strive to create a climate that will encourage all our leaders and institutions to join the effort to bring women into full partnership in our society.

Equal Rights Amendment — The Anderson Administration will strongly support the Equal Rights Amendment by giving its ratification a high priority. We will develop a joint strategy with state sponsors in unratified states and do our part to implement it. We will publicize the truth about the ERA and expose the distortions that are prevalent. We support the boycott of unratified states and urge private organizations to do so.

Reproductive Freedom — The Anderson Administration will:

Oppose government intrusion or coercion in the most private of decisions — to bear or not to bear children. We support freedom of choice for the individual;

Oppose any constitutional amendment prohibiting abortion and urge that federal programs providing funding for medical care of pregnancy and childbirth should include funding for abortion;

Strictly enforce federal regulations to insure that sterilization is voluntary;

Increase government funding of family planning services, including services for teenagers; and

Increase research to find more effective methods of contraception, with the hope the time will come soon when no woman finds it necessary to have an abortion.

Appointments — Recognizing that highly qualified women are not as visible as highly qualified men, the Anderson Administration will make a systematic effort to identify women for key positions, using the many women's organizations and other sources. Volunteer experience will be evaluated on its merits.

Enforcement of Anti-Discrimination Laws — Anderson's Administration will vigorously enforce anti-discrimination laws and executive orders, giving special attention to university tenure and promotion practices. We will oppose amendments that weaken such laws, including amendments that would limit women's opportunities to participate in sports. Appointees to positions responsible for enforcing such laws will be chosen on the basis of their capacity and commitment to full enforcement.

Participation of Women in Government Programs — Anderson's Administration will require that administrators of government programs collect data by sex and review the impact of these programs on women and the participation of women in policymaking. Corrective action will be required in those services, such as employment and training programs and alcohol and drug abuse programs, not enrolling women in proportion to their numbers in the populations served.

Health research will include women in the populations studied and women will serve on the committees designing studies and selecting grantees. It will be the Anderson Administration's policy that women be equitably represented on all grant-awarding and review boards, committees, and advisory panels.

Pay Equity — The Anderson Administration will support research on methods of achieving pay equity for women in traditionally women's occupations and the development of guidelines and legislation, if necessary, to promote this goal.

Child Care — The Anderson Administration will

support more extensive child care funding for children whose parent or parents are employed and cannot afford privately funded child care. We will support increased child care facilities for welfare mothers who want work or training for work.

Marriage—The Anderson Administration will seek modification of federal laws to conform with the principle that the contributions of wife and husband are of equal value and dignity. We will:

Urge elimination of gift and estate taxes on transfers between marital partners;

Recommend elimination of the "marriage tax" by permitting two-earner families to file as if single;

Develop proposals for revision of social security laws to provide equity for homemakers and wives employed outside the home;

Support enactment of the Homemaker Retirement bill of which John Anderson is a sponsor;

Support government assistance for displaced homemakers to help them enter or reenter paid employment;

Recommend legislation and appropriations to aid victims of domestic violence.

While the marital property, divorce, and inheritance laws are under state jurisdiction, the Anderson Administration will create a climate that will encourage fair treatment of women.

Registration/Draft/Military Service—The Anderson Administration opposes a peace time draft. If the Congress authorizes registration or a draft, we will urge inclusion of women.

The Anderson Administration will:

Support repeal of laws prohibiting women in combat, leaving to the Armed Services discretion in assigning personnel;

Elimination of discrimination against women in the military services, and opening up of more military occupations to women.

Health and Safety—Health insurance programs proposed by John Anderson's Administration or supported by it will include coverage of women's health needs, such as care for pregnancy and pregnancy-related disabilities and abortion. Coverage will be provided for single-parent families and divorced and widowed women, who too often have inadequate coverage.

Safety and health standards will protect the reproductive health of women and men, and Title VII of the Civil Rights Act will be strictly enforced in cases where women are indiscriminately removed from positions involving contact with toxic substances. The Equal Employment Opportunity Commission and the Labor Department will be directed to issue the too-

long-delayed guidelines immediately and proceed with enforcement.

Rural American Women—Women living in small towns and rural areas are particularly handicapped by distance from educational institutions, employment and counseling services, day care, job training programs, health services, battered women's and rape crisis centers, and alcohol and drug abuse treatment centers. John Anderson's Administration will endeavor in cooperation with representative organizations, to modify federal programs as necessary to provide equity for farm women and other women living in rural areas and small towns.

Minority and Ethnic Women—Special attention will be given to the needs of minority and ethnic women in all programs to combat discrimination and in programs to provide services to support women.

International—The Anderson Administration will:

Advocate ratification by the Senate of the UN Convention on Elimination of all forms of Discrimination Against Women, attaching if appropriate reservations to insure consistency with United States laws;

Appoint more women to U.S. delegations, on governing bodies of international agencies, and in the UN system.

Criminal Justice

Criminal Code Reform—An Anderson Administration will support a studied, incremental approach to criminal code revision rather than an omnibus approach that may sacrifice essential civil rights in the process of legislative bargaining.

We should set clear priorities and concentrate on revision in areas of key concern. These include:

Fair and uniform sentencing policies;

Equal protection of rights for all, including aliens, in every appropriate area;

More extensive coverage of white-collar crime.

Police/Community Relations—A police department must have the cooperation and good will of the residents of a community if it is to act in an efficient and effective manner. For cooperation to exist, residents must believe that the police force is acting on their behalf and is not an enemy to be feared and avoided.

An Anderson Administration would introduce legislation to Congress which would specifically authorize the Attorney General to take civil action against offending government and police departments so as to eliminate proven patterns and practices of misconduct in those departments. Anderson would also encourage efforts to increase staffing for the Department of Justice in the criminal division with a special emphasis placed on minority recruitment and hiring. Adequate staffing should also be provided for civil rights enforcement in the U.S. Attorney's office.

We also believe that those suspected of violating the law must be apprehended with a minimum of force. It should be the trial, not the arrest, that renders judgment and determines punishment. The federal government must use its powers of moral, legal and political persuasion to ensure that local justice is meted out in conformity with the standards of minimum force.

The Community Relations Service (CRS) which provides mediation and conciliation as opposed to litigation can be most useful in limiting racial tension. However, CRS is understaffed and underfunded. An Anderson Administration will seek to expand the staff beyond the 111 it now employs. Arbitration and mediation is a viable tool in police and community relations as well as in intra-community relations.

Prison Reform — There are approximately 314,000 offenders housed in state and federal prisons. At present, prisons are largely failing to rehabilitate those inmates and are instead creating impediments to rehabilitation. One-third of all prisoners released are back in prison within five years.

We support efforts being made by the courts to correct unconstitutional prison conditions created by the neglect of government officials. Such conditions can only prove to be a counter-productive force in our society. In addition, an Anderson Administration would authorize the Attorney General to institute civil suits on behalf of any inmate unable to get redress for deprivations of his or her federal constitutional and statutory rights.

We support legislation which would provide financial assistance to states for use in expanding educational and job training programs at correctional facilities.

Handgun Crime — The statistical profile of handgun crime constitutes a litany of death:

Handguns are used to commit nearly half of all the murders committed in the United States;

During the peak years of the Vietnam War, more Americans were killed by handguns than were killed in action in Vietnam;

Almost three out of every four law enforcement officers killed are victims of handguns;

Every hour, one American is killed by a handgun.

Despite these tragic realities, small but influential elements of our society have successfully fought handgun crime controls. More than a decade after the Eisenhower Commission called for handgun registration and the eventual universal licensing of handgun ownership, these goals elude us.

Some state and local governments have enacted laws to regulate handgun sales, distribution, and possession. These controls have effectively reduced handgun crimes, but their piecemeal enactment has resulted in localized benefits. In the absence of uniform activity by the states and municipalities, the national handgun problem cannot be solved. The deadly facts showing high rates of homicide by handguns mean that comprehensive federal legislation is needed now.

Before assuming office, candidate Carter "committed" his Administration to handgun control. After taking office, President Carter either forgot his promise or intentionally ignored it. The Carter Administration has not proposed any gun control legislation to the Congress and the death toll from handgun crimes continues to mount.

The Anderson Administration will do what the Carter Administration has failed to do: submit handgun legislation to both houses of Congress. The Anderson Administration will propose a Handgun Crime Control bill which will:

Stop the manufacture, sale, and transfer of "Saturday Night Specials," the cheap handguns so widely used by criminals;

Establish mandatory jail sentences for the commission of crimes with a handgun;

Reduce illegal purchases of handguns by requiring purchasing licenses;

Establish strict requirements for those who are licensed to sell or manufacture handguns;

Develop a more effective tracing system to track down misused handguns and curtail illicit handgun traffic;

Require manufacturers, dealers, and owners to report the theft or loss of handguns, and penalize those who fail to do so;

Establish liability for illegal transfer of any handgun subsequently used to kill or injure another person;

Improve enforcement of federal handgun laws;

Require licenses to carry handguns outside the home or place of business.

The enactment of legislation embodying these proposals will not eliminate handgun crimes completely, and it will take years to eliminate illegal handguns from society. Yet the longer this legislation is postponed, the higher the handgun death toll will climb. We must begin to enact remedies immediately.

Right to Privacy

Our right to privacy and freedom from government intrusion is one of our most fundamental rights. Now it is one of our most endangered rights. Improved communications technology allows increasing amounts of personal information to be transmitted and stored electronically. Many life-altering decisions are now based upon analyses of recorded data instead of personal interviews. The use of microwaves in telephone communications subjects our conversations to interception. Electronic funds transfer systems are capable of centralizing data on our financial transactions, but are also subject to possible abuse.

An Anderson Administration will draft legislation which more adequately protects our right to privacy. It will include provisions enabling citizens:

To have greater knowledge about data being collected about them;

To have the opportunity to correct erroneous information;

To be notified of adverse decisions based upon recorded information; and

To protect consumers' private financial records from unauthorized disclosure.

Recent court decisions concerning First and Fourth Amendment rights have increased the likelihood of government intrusion. An Anderson Administration will seek to enact legislation proposed in 1979 by John Anderson to prohibit law enforcement officials from obtaining search warrants to seize notes, photographs, and similar materials from groups or individuals not suspected of any criminal activity, except when necessary to prevent death or serious bodily injury.

Appointments

An Anderson Administration will work to increase the number of minorities and women at every level of our judicial system—as United States Attorneys, federal magistrates, federal judges, and United States Supreme Court Justices.

We completely reject any ideological "litmus test" of fitness for judicial positions as being wholly antithetical to the ideals of an independent and impartial judiciary.

V. SECURITY POLICY

FOREIGN POLICY

Introduction

The last two decades have seen a dramatic decline in the credibility and integrity of America's position in world affairs. We have witnessed the growth of Soviet military power, Soviet aggression in Afghanistan, and Soviet military and political thrusts in Southeast Asia and Africa. We have seen Americans taken hostage, our representatives abroad killed, and our embassies destroyed. We have seen a significant erosion of our own economic power, our industrial productivity and our scientific and technological base. With this decline has come a concurrent rise in our dependence on others—on the Arab states for our oil, on the Third World for other vital raw materials, on the Europeans to rescue our currency, and on China to balance Russia.

We are drifting downstream, learning to cope with each new demonstration of our weakness, unable to take the measures necessary for our long-run survival as a free and independent society.

We need clear and coherent answers and thoughtful leadership to revive the wellsprings of our strength so that we can regain our independence and restore our international position.

The first priority for American foreign policy quite simply must be to put our own house in order. Our economy and our technological base have always been the principal sources of our strength. Their decline is now the principal source of our growing weakness. The call, elsewhere in this program, for rebuilding our domestic strength is the starting point for our international recovery.

The next priority for American foreign policy is to restore and nurture our historic alliances, which have been neglected in the pursuit of global power balances that play our potential adversaries against each other. A common sense approach to foreign policy will look to our alliance systems as the bedrock of our long-range security.

The successful execution of these two prudent policies will go far toward restoring our international posture. Relying on these solid and secure foundations, we can better define our relationships with the Soviet Union, China, and the Third World.

The Soviet government will attempt to advance the reach of Soviet influence, whenever it is considered timely and promising. It will do so borne along by a large and skilled population, by deep and powerful historic currents of Russian nationalism, and by a comprehensive and flexible ideology. The Soviet Union is also beset with significant economic difficulties. It must contend with East European states always probing the limits of Soviet domination, and with a growing, united, and determined China. In dealing with the Soviets, we must be militarily strong, but seek whenever possible through negotiations to reduce fear and uncertainty. We should also pursue an even-handed policy between the Soviet Union and China, seeking to reduce our reliance upon their mutual antagonism as a major factor in our security position in Asia.

We must next reexamine our entire approach to the Third World, an area in which the United States has suffered great setbacks in the last two decades. We have treated Third World countries more as clients and as suppliers than as sovereign and independent states with their own needs, interests, and destinies. Our foreign policy must enunciate our ideals and promote our interests, but always within the bounds of respect for the sovereignty and independence of every nation, large and small.

We must also pay heed to human rights, not only to display our moral concern, but also to further human decency and to relieve pain and suffering. A strengthened America will launch a quiet offensive to help the refugee fleeing oppression, the Soviet citizen who wishes to leave his or her homeland, political prisoners all over the world, and American citizens languishing under barbarous conditions in foreign jails. We must also reach out to the hundreds of thousands of starving people in Cambodia, the Sahel, and other places throughout the world.

To succeed in these tasks, we must pay more attention to the conduct of our diplomacy. In recent years indecision and disunity have characterized the conduct of American diplomacy. There have been too many egregious examples where at best communications broke down and at worst important people with relevant viewpoints were deliberately excluded from the decision-making process. An Anderson Administration will not tolerate such practices.

In formulating our policy, we must abandon the false logic that dexterity is a substitute for genuine strength. We must rediscover the meaning of the word commitment and understand that flexibility for its own sake is a self-defeating enterprise. We must recognize that America, as the world's leading power, must set an example for others by providing a focus for stability in the world. And we must never again find ourselves in a position where we need others more than they need us.

Furthermore, in the conduct of our diplomacy, we must once again emphasize substance over symbol. No grand conceptualization is needed to understand the dimensions of our current difficulties. No moral crusade will ever be a substitute for a solid foundation of patient diplomacy. No glittering style can ever successfully replace a cautious prudence. And no amount of bullying—however aggressive—can ever disguise genuine weakness.

What Americans must insist upon and must achieve is a renewed economic power and moral authority linked to a reinvigorated partnership with our democratic allies. With it, Western civilization can confront the dangers and the challenges of the world from a position of quiet but unquestioned strength and courage.

Western Europe and the Atlantic Alliance

The strength of our relationship with Western Europe and the Atlantic Alliance is central to the successful conduct of our foreign policy. Our ties to Europe touch all facets of America's interests abroad: relations with the Soviet Union and China, Middle Eastern and Persian Gulf problems, development in the Third World, nuclear and conventional defense capabilities, arms control, energy dependency, human rights, and many others. These issues are addressed elsewhere in this program. What follows are the broad principles upon which an Anderson Administration will build its Western European policies. Also considered here are Western European issues not discussed elsewhere in this program.

For more than thirty years, the great and historic partnership between the United States and the nations of Western Europe succeeded in preserving the peace and in providing a climate within which European skills and energy were mobilized to produce unprecedented prosperity, stability, and progress.

There are today significant challenges to the transatlantic relationship. Chief among them are the loss of control over the supply and price of energy, the relative decline of the American economy in comparison to the economies of Europe, and the steady expansion of Soviet military capabilities. These will continue to cause rivalry and tension in transatlantic relations. We reemphasize our belief, however, that close relations between the United States and Western Europe are central to sustaining our freedoms and security.

To pursue and nurture successfully our Atlantic partnership in the next decade, we must have a strong sense of the basic principles that should guide our efforts.

First among these broad principles is the recognition that apart from deterring a physical attack upon the United States itself, there is no more important national interest than the maintenance of our Alliance with Western Europe. We can afford nothing less than a full measure of cooperation and partnership.

Second, we must recognize that the Alliance must be a union of equal partners. Each member must act as a leader in its own right. Each must be prepared to share fairly in the burdens of our joint endeavors, and to justify these sacrifices to its own people. Each must have the steadfastness to persevere in joint initiatives.

Third, we must be prepared to acknowledge that there will be times when European interests are not those embraced by the United States. But we must not use these differences to decry the state of the Alliance. A mature and balanced partnership can accommodate differences of opinion or approach.

Fourth, the United States must cease talking about consultation and actually begin to consult with its allies before embarking on ventures in which it expects them to participate. Reciprocally, our allies must acknowledge that they have a similar responsibility. We must be ever aware of the need to seek counsel, explore proposals, and air ideas in confidence with our allies, before we embark on a course of conduct which we would expect others to follow. We must seek to use those opportunities and organizations that now exist to better advantage. To assist in achieving this goal, we need to broaden the scope of the present summit meetings to cover a wider range of political and security problems as well as economic problems.

An Anderson Administration will also encourage the European Community's evolution toward political union. The first direct election of the European Parliament and the establishment of the European Monetary System are significant indications of a prospering European idea. We believe that the admission of Greece, Spain and Portugal to the European Community will both strengthen the European idea and the future of democracy in Southern Europe.

In the economic sphere, oil and energy policies, monetary problems, and the rise of protectionism continue to crowd the transatlantic agenda. These issues are of deep concern to Japan as well, for they affect all the industrial democracies in similar ways. In dealing with these issues, an Anderson Administration will adhere to two tenets. First, rebuilt American industries are the mainstay of our international economic relationships. We must rebuild our industrial base and increase the productivity of our workers to restore our competitiveness in world markets. Second, the United States and the Western nations must ensure that divergent economic interests do not impair our security relations. These differences, rather than isolating countries, can encourage greater efforts toward agreed-upon solutions to our various problems.

Consistent with our strong interest in augmenting the Atlantic Alliance, we welcome Greece's participation as a full member of the Alliance, and will support efforts at enhancing stability in the Eastern Mediterranean. We recognize the importance of the Aegean Islands to the security of Greece, and look forward to a just resolution of Aegean Island issues.

We believe that the continuing crisis in Cyprus, too long delayed in its resolution, must be settled through negotiations between Greece, Turkey, and the Cypriot people.

The principles embodied in United Nations Resolution 3212 and the Ten Point Agreement of 1979 provide the surest foundation for peace, security, and stability in the region. An Anderson Administration will be prepared to provide assistance in the rebuilding of the Cypriot community.

The Soviet Union

We have entered a new era in our relationship with the Soviet Union. The Soviet troops and tanks that poured into Afghanistan have banished to the history books the business as usual relations of the 1970's. The problem of how to deal with the Soviet Union is the greatest task our diplomacy will face in the years ahead.

Our relationship with the Soviet Union is competitive. They are our rival, not our partner, in the international arena. But the elements of our rivalry, while extremely serious, are neither total nor absolute, largely because our security interests are not completely separable. We share with the Soviet Union, and with all nations, a pre-eminent interest in avoiding a nuclear holocaust.

We must therefore establish a balance of prudent expectations in our relationship with the Soviet Union. An Anderson Administration will not hesitate to take serious measures to resist Soviet political and military thrusts, but we will exercise our power in a responsible manner. We will be energetic in seeking safeguards to reduce the risks of war, and we will do our utmost to demonstrate to the Soviets that their interests are best served by their own restraint.

Toward these ends, the Anderson Administration, as stated elsewhere in this program, will do what is required to maintain the invulnerability of our nuclear forces as the Soviets continue to improve the accuracy of their missiles. We will continue to improve our conventional forces. Without illusions, we will continue the SALT II process, and thereby lay the groundwork for SALT III.

Measured against the resources, skills, and capacities of the West, the Soviet Union is the far weaker force. The successes of the Soviet Union thus depend in great part on the degree of cohesion, firmness, and vigor which the Western world can exhibit. The Anderson Administration's efforts to rebuild the Western Alliance will therefore be a centerpiece of our efforts to conduct diplomacy toward the Soviet Union.

We strongly support the Helsinki process. The broadening of trade, as well as the expansion of scientific, technological, and cultural exchanges, will be dependent upon practices by the Soviet and East European governments which are consistent with basic human rights standards.

We respect the desires of the people of Eastern Europe to determine their own destinies, free of outside interference. We reaffirm our commitment to respect the territorial integrity and national sovereignty of Eastern European states and we expect the Soviet Union to respect that integrity and sovereignty as well.

Lastly, our relations with the Soviet Union must be seen in the broader setting of world policies. Activities by the Soviet Union and East European countries in Third World areas which endanger our interests must necessarily impede the broadening of our relationships. But we must not let our concerns about the Soviet Union distort our policies toward the nations of Africa, Asia, Latin America, and elsewhere. With our allies, we will encourage the forces of nationalism to find expressions not in demagoguery and military dictatorships, the breeding ground of revolutionary violence, but in moderate policies of social change.

We will oppose Soviet adventurism wherever necessary, but we will also seek opportunities for reducing fear, uncertainty, and misunderstanding through negotiations. Above all else, we must be clear, steady, and coherent in our dealings with the Soviet Union, leaving no doubt about our determination to maintain and advance our foreign policy interests.

Middle East

The attainment of peace and stability in the Middle East is a high priority of American foreign policy. In recent years, the cause of peace has advanced dramatically with the signing of the Camp David accords by Israel and Egypt. In the Persian Gulf, however, stability is threatened by the revolution in Iran, the Soviet invasion of Afghanistan, world dependence on Arab oil, and religious and ideological disputes among the regional actors. Our policy throughout the region must be directed towards the reduction of tensions and, with the support of our allies, the protection of Western interests.

American policy toward the Arab-Israel dispute must be conducted with the understanding that a solution to that conflict will not resolve the energy crisis, the instability of the oil producers, the turmoil in the Persian Gulf, the plight of the hostages in Iran or the occupation of Afghanistan. The United States must remain the guarantor of the Egyptian-Israeli Peace Treaty.

An Anderson Administration will not exert pressure on the parties involved nor interfere in the negotiations. The United States should not attempt to dictate the terms of a peace settlement with public rebukes of the negotiating parties, clandestine meetings with those who would abort the peacemaking process or submission of comprehensive proposals for peace that are not supported by the countries directly concerned.

America's political, economic and military commitment to Israel is fundamental to our strategic interests in the Middle East. Israel is committed, as we are, to democratic ideals and to a free and open way of life that respects human rights. We should utilize Israel's strategic and technical experience, its intelligence information and, in an emergency, its facilities. We will continue to provide military and economic assistance to Israel at a level sufficient to enable it to maintain its security as its potential adversaries expand their military capabilities, and to maintain its economy while accepting the high costs of withdrawal, relocation and peace.

The United States must remain committed to a meaningful peace. A lasting settlement must encompass the the principles affirmed in the Camp David accords, including reconciliation; the establishment of secure and recognized borders; fully normalized relations including trade, travel, communications and the exchange of ambassadors; and an end to military threats, political attacks and economic warfare.

The courageous efforts of President Sadat to achieve peace with Israel have encouraged the development of friendly relations between Egypt and the United States. This relationship with the Arab world's leading country should be vigorously promoted with assistance and diplomatic support, to demonstrate the value of the Camp David accords, to promote Western interests and to help maintain the balance of power in the region.

An Anderson Administration will continue to support the recognition of Palestinian rights, embodied in the Camp David accords, but will oppose the creation of a Palestinian state between Israel and Jordan. Such a state would be dominated by the Palestine Liberation Organization, would promote instability in the Middle East and would threaten other nations in the area as much as the security of Israel. We should look to Jordan to help significantly in resolving the Palestinian questions. The United States must continue its refusal to recognize or negotiate with the PLO until it repudiates terrorism, explicitly recognizes Israel's right to exist in peace, and accepts UN Security Resolutions 242 and 338 unchanged.

An Anderson Administration will weigh its public statements with care and put greater emphasis on quiet diplomacy through regular diplomatic channels. We will not, for example, stoop to the temptation to use UN votes as a means of interfering with the diplomacy of the peace process. An Anderson Administration will not label Israeli settlements as "illegal" and as "obstacles to peace." This prejudges and compromises negotiations from the outset. The question of the settlements can best be resolved by Egypt, Israel and the Palestinian residents of the West Bank and Gaza Strip.

The final status of East Jerusalem must be decided by negotiation. The United States must support the continuation of free and unimpeded access to Jerusalem's holy places by people of all faiths. Jerusalem must remain an open and undivided city. At the conclusion of the peacemaking process, the Anderson Administration will recognize Jerusalem as the capital of Israel and move the U.S. embassy there.

The Anderson Administration will exercise restraint in approving arms transfers to those nations which oppose the peace process and do not cooperate with our diplomatic efforts. The United States should actively use diplomatic channels to discourage those arms transfers by third parties which might contribute to regional instability.

The invasion of Afghanistan, the instability in Iran, and recent events in Saudi Arabia have provided the Soviet Union with an opportunity to achieve the political encirclement of the Persian Gulf and the states of the Arabian peninsula. Soviet activity in the Yemens, Syria, Libya, and Ethiopia increases the danger of this threat and offers immediate challenges to the United States. Efforts to increase our presence in the region should proceed with caution, and be made in close cooperation with our friends in the region and our European allies.

To give ourselves greater leverage in regional and great-power disputes, we must reduce our costly dependence on foreign oil. An Anderson Administration will embark on a comprehensive program of energy independence, outlined elsewhere in this platform.

Our principal objective in Iran is to secure the prompt and safe release of our embassy personnel still being held hostage by the Iranian government. We will use every measure of quiet diplomacy, bilateral and multilateral, to achieve this end.

East Asia and the Pacific

Japan — Our relationship with Japan stands at the center of American foreign policy toward East Asia. The bonds of history, though recently forged, are strong. Common interests bind us as well: Japan, next to Canada, is the single largest trading partner of the United States, and our treaty with Japan is the cornerstone of our security interests in East Asia.

We believe that two basic principles should guide our policy toward Japan: that a genuine American-Japanese partnership is fundamental to all else in the Pacific, and that economic and security elements in the partnership cannot be separated.

We recognize that Japanese defense expenditures raise critically difficult problems for both Japan and the nations of East Asia. Japan's role as an economically powerful, but lightly armed, nation significantly contributes to East Asian regional stability. A major shift in Japan's military role in the region could undermine, not enhance, that stability. An Anderson Administration will not press Japan to expand its military capabilities beyond the level which the Japanese believe their security requires and their constitution permits. Japan should contribute more to collective security, but this need not be through military measures. We will urge Japan to increase its economic assistance to other countries, and to expand its contribution to research and development of alternative energy resources. We will continue to renegotiate burden-sharing arrangements on the cost of American bases in Japan to reflect changes in the value of the yen and the dollar as well as increases in Japan's economic capabilities.

We will make no military or diplomatic moves in East Asia, particularly with regard to China and Korea, without advance consultation with Japan. We will demonstrate greater sensitivity to Japan's great dependence on imported energy supplies and to the vital role alternative energy sources can play in Japan's economy.

Japan's post-war economic ties to the United States have been fundamental to Japan's own progress and its expansion into regional and world economies. The ASEAN Nations (the Association of Southeast Asian Nations comprised of Indonesia, Malaysia, the Philippines, Singapore, and Thailand), with its population expected to increase from its present 230 million to 290 million in 1985, is one of the world's fastest-growing economic regions.

An Anderson Administration will explore ways of expanding America's role among the ASEAN group which also enhance our relationship with Japan. One approach to this end would be to extend current mechanisms for American-Japanese consultation now dealing with defense issues and bilateral trade to include funding for ASEAN projects.

Japan is at once our military ally and our economic rival. Three major issues have troubled American-Japanese trade relations from our perspective: the large current trade imbalance; the impact of Japanese exports on the American automobile industry; and access to Japan's domestic market.

The principal remedy for these problems is to restore the dynamism of the American economy to make it more competitive in the Japanese market. We will press for the removal of restraints on the importation of American goods by Japan, particularly in tele-communications equipment, computers, and semiconductors, areas in which the United States has a comparative advantage over Japan but has not had fair access to Japanese markets. We will encourage Japan to build additional industrial plants in the United States to retain jobs now being lost to industry in Japan.

China — The diplomatic breakthrough with China is a remarkable achievement of twentieth century diplomacy. An Anderson Administration will build on this achievement to develop closer relations with China diplomatically, economically, and culturally.

We have been reduced in recent years to a reliance upon the antagonism between Russia and China to bolster our security position in Asia. We believe that those who talk blithely about playing the fabled "China card" fail to recognize that China is not a card to be played, but a player with cards. China's interests may depart from our own or from those of our Asian allies. We cannot allow China to develop an "America card" for use in her relations with the Soviet Union or with other East Asian countries, who view China with a mixture of awe and fear.

An Anderson Administration will never place the United States in a position where we pressure any of our friends into reaching a dangerous accommodation with their historic antagonists. We must, therefore, never put ourselves in a position where Taiwan is the price for Chinese cooperation against Russia.

We will continue our present informal military and economic relations with Taiwan, at the same time giving quiet encouragement to the indirect trade relations developing between Taiwan and China. We strongly oppose restoring our relationship with Taiwan to governmental status. Such a course of action would be a disastrous setback for American foreign policy.

The Anderson Administration will take no steps to increase antagonism between Russia and China. It is therefore unwise at this time to become an arms supplier to China.

We will seek to bring China into discussions with the Soviet Union, Western Europe, and the United States on arms control. We will search for ways to encourage China's leaders to take measures to guard against accidental nuclear war, and to maintain strategic nuclear stability.

The Chinese government has announced plans for a ten-year economic plan of staggering proportions; the estimated total investment is some $600 billion, and includes construction of 120 large industrial projects. China is, however, a great distance from these goals, and its successful modernization will require the participation of all industrial nations.

The Anderson Administration will expand scientific, cultural, and particularly educational exchanges with China. We will also promote the growth of United States trade with China through such measures as assisting the American business community to expand its presence in China. We will discuss with China ways in which we can assist its efforts to generate foreign exchange to finance its imports. We believe that sales of technology to China should encourage the Chinese to continue to concentrate their efforts on improving its economic performance.

In broadening trade contacts with China, the Anderson Administration will adhere to two tenets. First, China will not provide America with a major market for many years to come. Second, we must extend credits to China and accord her full opportunities under the most favored nation principle at the same time we move forward in resolving our trade difficulties with Japan. If these difficulties are left unresolved, while trade with China expands, we run the risk of convincing our principal ally in East Asia that our support is truly feckless.

Southeast Asia — Southeast Asia has once again become an arena of military conflict and human suffering. The boat people from Vietnam and the millions of hungry Cambodians assisted through American-supported international programs are the victims of these conflicts.

We support swift humanitarian responses to the human tragedies of Southeast Asia. An Anderson Administration will place a high priority on American support for Red Cross/UNICEF humanitarian aid programs for Kampuchea. We will also support their insistence that no relief goods go to armed groups in Kampuchea nor those on the Thai border.

But humanitarian responses alone are not enough. Vietnam's occupation of Kampuchea and Chinese support for Pol Pot's guerrillas, China's threat to invade Vietnam again, and Soviet access to Vietnamese ports and airfields are parts of a deepening Southeast Asian crisis. The present trend is toward the consolidation of Vietnamese control over Kampuchea and greater involvement by both the Soviet Union and China in the region.

Our objectives will be the reduction of the Soviet military presence and political influence in Vietnam, the restoration of normal life in Kampuchea by an end to the fighting and the withdrawal of Vietnamese troops, and the assurance of Thailand's security.

To achieve these objectives we will encourage the ASEAN nations in their current negotiations with Vietnam. We will, while forging a new relationship with China, be attentive to Vietnam's concerns about China, just as we pay heed to the concerns of Thailand and other ASEAN nations about Vietnam itself.

We will also announce an end to United States support for the forces under Pol Pot's command. They represent a morally reprehensible regime and prolong the suffering of the Kampuchean people without offering any realistic prospect of helping to reach a compromise settlement of the conflict.

The United States should not vote for the seating of Pol Pot's regime at the UN, but instead support a vacant seat for Kampuchea until a government emerges with a proper claim to represent the Kampuchean people.

Korea — Geography and ideology have combined to make the division of Korea a danger to the peace of East Asia and the world. The United States is responsible for supporting South Korean security both through the presence of its combat forces in South Korea and its security treaty with South Korea. We reaffirm the importance of maintaining our commitment to defend South Korea against attack. We will not pursue unilateral withdrawal of American combat forces from South Korea, as was attempted by the Carter Administration in 1977–78. Those unilateral actions increased rather than allayed tensions throughout the region, raising new questions about America's seriousness of purpose and capacity for determined leadership.

The eruptions of anti-government protests demanding restoration of democratic freedoms and constitutional government in South Korea require far-sighted and coherent United States policies. Pressures for progress toward these political goals and opposition to physical repression by the military-dominated government have become far stronger than in past years. The government's attempt to suppress protest while failing to establish a timetable for elections and the removal of restrictions on democratic freedoms risks an unprecedented political explosion which might invite intervention by North Korea and trigger a new war.

The problem of security and political stability in South Korea cannot be separated, therefore, from the problem of political freedoms. An Anderson Administration will strengthen American efforts to persuade the military to change its policy. We will make it clear that the United States cannot remain passive in the present situation, given its own heavy responsibility for the defense of South Korea, and that it supports to the fullest extent possible the legitimate aims of those demanding democratic freedoms.

Toward North Korea, we will end the fruitless and dangerous isolation from the United States, moving forward, in consultation with South Korea and Japan, in such areas as cultural and academic exchanges.

The critical issue of stabilizing the Korean situation on a more lasting basis will be a daunting task. We will give active encouragement to North and South Korea to move toward a true accommodation, recognizing that the goal will not be achieved soon and that the issue is of deep concern to Japan and China, and to the Soviet Union.

Australia and New Zealand—Our friendship with Australia and New Zealand is deep and lasting. The ANZUS Treaty, the continuing symbol of our close ties, will remain a cornerstone of American security in the Pacific.

An Anderson Administration will consult with Australia and New Zealand on security issues of mutual concern. We should pursue a unified approach to strengthening ASEAN and in handling refugee problems in the region. We will consult with Australia and New Zealand before establishing any permanent spent nuclear fuel storage sites in the southern Pacific.

The United States shares with Australia and New Zealand important commercial and economic interests. An Anderson Administration will pay close attention to the issues created by Australian and New Zealand access to American markets.

South Asia

Since the end of World War II, United States foreign policy in South Asia has suffered from misunderstanding concerning the political, economic, and strategic importance of the region, the aims of its principal nations, and the nature of its regional conflicts. As a result, we have repeatedly failed to achieve our foreign policy objectives in the region, and we have helped to create the one condition we sought most to avoid—namely, the extension of Soviet influence into an area whose leaders and peoples are inclined toward friendship with the United States.

An Anderson Administration's policies toward South Asia will center around three interrelated realities.

First, India lies at the region's center in every sense of the word. None of the major conflicts in the region can be resolved consistent with our interests without considering the interests of India.

Second, there are two principal sources of tension in South Asia: the India-Pakistan conflict and the India-China conflict. Our policy in the 1980's must avoid the past mistake of embracing Pakistan and tilting away from India. We must help each recognize that their common regional security interests should outweigh local differences that have separated them in the past. We must, while developing the new relationship with China, be sensitive to India's concerns about China.

Third, the underlying bases for conflicts among the South Asian countries are indigenous and regional in character. They are distorted, not clarified, when viewed solely through the prism of American-Soviet relations.

The Carter Administration's unsuccessful rush to rearm Pakistan following the Soviet invasion of Afghanistan diminished our prestige, and revived Indian suspicions that the United States was building an informal alliance which threatened India's interests.

If the Soviet Union threatens Pakistan's territorial integrity—a threat that would also endanger India's security—we will consult with Pakistan, India, and other countries about steps to be taken to meet the Soviet challenge. An Anderson Administration will be prepared to consider seriously a request for arms by Pakistan in such circumstances.

We believe that any economic aid to Pakistan must genuinely help to maintain the country's integrity and economy, and should be designed to strengthen Pakistan's internal stability by improving the standard of living of its people. It should be concentrated in such areas as agrarian development and reform, road-building programs, rural electrification, and improved internal communication. But if Pakistan is to become truly secure, the government must be encouraged to broaden its political base, renew its commitment to constitutional government and fair elections, and move toward more stable relations with India.

An Anderson Administration will make a major effort to open a wider window to India, whose size, population, economic strength, military might, and relative political stability ensure that it will continue to exercise significant influence in the region. We will support India's independent role in world affairs. We will not abandon our commitments to other countries in the area for the sake of improved relations with India. But with quiet and patient diplomacy it is both possible and desirable to establish a more lasting and productive friendship with this enormous land.

To help achieve this goal, the Anderson Administration will encourage both India and China to continue efforts to settle their boundary controversies. We will assure the Indian government that the American naval forces in the Indian Ocean will not intervene in internal South Asian disputes.

Our interrelated policies toward Pakistan and India will require diligence and courage. Nowhere will this be more important than in forging a position on nuclear materials. First, we must encourage India in the moderate nuclear policies the country has pursued since its explosion of a nuclear device in 1974. We will link our nuclear materials export programs to the continuation of such policies. Second, we will help to create a sense of security for Pakistan in order to reduce its incentives to test a nuclear device.

Finally, we cannot accept as permanent any arrangement which incorporates Afghanistan into the Soviet orbit. An autonomous and independent Afghanistan must be our goal. An Anderson Administration will work with the government of India in efforts to influence the Soviet Union to withdraw its troops from Afghanistan in furtherance of the regional stability which we and our friends desire.

Africa

The United States must recognize that Africa will play a key role in world affairs in the years ahead. Today many African states are expressing increased independence in world affairs. Africa possesses an abundance of oil and other raw materials essential to the world economy, and represents an important potential export market for our manufactured goods. The success of global policies will increasingly depend on our ability to maintain good relations with African countries.

We must respect the right of Africans to determine their own destinies. An Anderson Administration's African policies will promote genuine stability in the continent by helping the nations of Africa to achieve social justice, political progress, and economic prosperity for their people.

We believe that the long-term interests of all the people in Namibia and South Africa will be served best by an orderly transition to majority rule in each country. The South African government's continued refusal to permit free elections in Namibia, or to share power with the black majority in its own country, threatens the stability of Africa. An Anderson Administration will look for peaceful means to increase pressures on South Africa to expedite the resolution of these conflicts.

South Africa is the only country in the world where all political, economic, and social rights are completely dictated by race. Apartheid, an all-encompassing legal system proclaiming the superiority of the white race, is an affront to human decency.

In an effort to bring a peaceful transition to majority rule in South Africa, an Anderson Administration will:

Continue efforts to bring an end to apartheid in South Africa through negotiations in regional and multilateral forums;

Continue Export-Import Bank restrictions on lending and credit guarantees for investments in South Africa;

Encourage compliance by all countries with the United Nations embargo on the export of military equipment to South Africa; and

Discourage investments in South Africa, whenever possible in cooperation with our allies.

South Africa's refusal to allow for the completion of a negotiated transition to majority rule in Namibia requires a number of immediate steps. An Anderson Administration will:

Work with other members of the Contact Group (Canada, France, West Germany, Britain) to seek a final agreement on Namibia based on UN Security Council Resolution 435, which has been accepted by both South West Africa People's Organization and the South African government;

Deny Export-Import Bank credit privileges to corporations making investments in Namibia based on rights secured from South Africa or the present Namibian authorities;

Support all UN efforts to speed the transition to majority rule in Namibia; if UN efforts prove ineffective, an Anderson Administration will work through other multilateral forums, particularly the Organization for African Unity (OAU), to bring majority rule to Namibia.

Territorial disputes, particularly those in the Western Sahara and in the Horn of Africa, threaten both the stability of the countries directly involved, and that of the entire region. In helping to resolve these disputes, an Anderson Administration will adhere to two principles. First, all settlements should be consistent with the principle of territorial integrity endorsed by the Organization of African Unity. Second, the United States should encourage OAU peacekeeping and peacemaking initiatives aimed at resolving these conflicts.

The Cuban and Soviet military presence in Africa is of deep concern to us. We believe that peace and political stability in Africa is best assured by African people and governments resolving their political disputes without the intervention of outside military forces. We will encourage the peaceful resolution of African disputes as the surest means of guaranteeing African regional stability.

American interests in Africa will best be served if our policies are designed to assist African nations develop their economies. Thus, an Anderson Administration will increase the effectiveness of our foreign aid by augmenting our programs and improving our disbursement practices (see Foreign Assistance).

We will give priority to assistance programs in those African countries which have made significant progress toward responsive, stable governments. Zimbabwe, for example, has recently undergone a peaceful transition to majority rule, but the United States has not yet offered assistance adequate to meet reconstruction needs. An Anderson Administration will also endeavor to build a close partnership with Nigeria, which has recently made an encouraging transition from military rule to a system of government whose constitution closely resembles our own.

Our government should also promote private investment in Africa which is essential to fostering peaceful progress.

The Western Hemisphere

A fundamental principle of our foreign policy is that relations with countries that are closest geographically and in interest and purpose are among the most important. We must give primacy to maintaining confidence and trust in these relations. Too often we have assumed, however, that good relations come naturally and without effort. They do not. They must be carefully nurtured through positive action to further and maintain mutual understanding and respect.

Canada—Facts of history, geography, economics, and security tie the United States closely to Canada. But our ties, no matter how strong, need constant attention. By failing to resolve differences when they

first appear, we run the risk of having them turn into more serious problems. There are four initiatives that the Anderson Administration will take toward Canada.

We will support the conclusion of a treaty on Atlantic fishing rights. Our countries began negotiations on fishing rights in August, 1977, culminating in a treaty signed on March 29, 1979. The Senate has yet to approve this treaty. But a fishing rights treaty which serves the long-term economic interests of American fishermen is desperately needed if we are to avoid the overfishing of the Georges Bank.

We will continue to engage the Canadians in a dialogue on trade issues of mutual concern, and will work to reach agreement on a comprehensive tax arrangement on trade between our two nations.

The United States and Canada must work together to ensure that both our nations have adequate future energy supplies. Our nations need to increase their cooperation in energy research and development projects. The Anderson Administration will work to expedite the construction of the Alaskan-Canadian natural gas pipeline, a cooperative effort which offers important benefits to both our nations. American investment in Canadian energy resource projects will help Canada achieve energy independence.

Our common border dictates that the United States and Canada develop a consistent approach to environmental problems. The United States is presently considering an increase in its use of coal as an energy source, particularly in the Northeast. This increase threatens to raise the level of sulphuric pollution in the atmosphere in Canada as well as in the United States. The proposed Garrison dam project would also have serious effects on the Canadian environment. Canada is thus justifiably concerned with these and other issues that affect the Canadian environment. As a responsible ally and neighbor, we must continue to consult Canada on these matters of mutual interest.

Latin America

For most of the 20th century, our hemispheric neighbors in Latin America have lived in the military, political, and economic shadow of the United States. This old, unequal relationship is now obsolete. Over the past decade, economic development and social change within the hemisphere have given our neighbors a new sense of self-confidence and national pride. Our Latin American relations will thus be increasingly complex in the years ahead. If we accept this challenge in a spirit of mutual respect and cooperation, our traditional friendships will be strengthened. If we turn away from the challenge, ignoring it or seeking to reassert the paternalism of the past, we will find ourselves increasingly isolated in our own hemisphere.

Mexico—We have no more important partner in Latin America than Mexico. Many of the most pressing bilateral issues between the United States and Mexico have major domestic implications on both sides of the border. Improving our relations will require careful, flexible negotiations which are sensitive to the legitimate interests of both nations, and that recognize the emerging industrial power of our southern neighbor.

The Anderson Administration will explore more fully the ways in which we can assist Mexico in its program of industrial development. Unless we are able to find fields for mutual cooperation, such as technology transfer, Mexico will naturally seek such assistance elsewhere. Unless we are responsive to the needs of Mexico's industrial development program, it will be difficult to secure Mexico's cooperation on such issues as energy and immigration.

One of the most complex and difficult issues is the immigration of undocumented Mexican workers to the United States. The immigration issue touches the interests of many parties, not only those of our two national governments. It affects local communities on both sides of the border; it affects the American worker as well as the undocumented Mexican worker; and it affects our own Hispanic-American community.

We recognize that there is no easy solution to the immigration problem. Any attempt on our part to close the border would be impractical and enormously expensive. And Mexico would see it as an unfriendly act.

An Anderson Administration will begin to deal with the issue of immigration within the context of other border issues. Migration in the border regions has produced local communities that straddle the border. We have not worked closely enough with Mexico to fashion policies that address the unique social problems that these border communities face. The existing mechanisms for handling specific social problems in the border region have not been satisfactory.

We propose that a joint American/Mexican Commission be created to promote cooperative social development in the border region. This Commission would concern itself with improving and integrating social services in the border areas. Among that Commission's tasks would be the strengthening of organizations like the U.S./Mexico Border Health Association. The joint Commission would establish a structure responsive to the basic unmet human needs in the border region.

Beyond the immediate human problems along our common border, there are many issues between our two countries that require and deserve a mechanism for continuing high level collaboration. The Anderson Administration will expand the State Department's current modest effort to collaborate with Mexico by formalizing a permanent consultative mechanism. An on-going, high-level dialogue on issues such as trade, agriculture, energy, migration, finance, and industry is essential to building the kind of partnership that should characterize our relations with Mexico in the 1980's and beyond.

Central America—The most dangerous threat to hemispheric peace today is the acute political crisis in Central America. We must recognize that the political violence in El Salvador, Guatemala, and Honduras is in part the product of real social problems and human rights violations, and that decades of poverty, inequality, brutality, and dictatorship have produced the volatile conditions with which we now must grapple.

The Anderson Administration will take initiative in urging the governments of these nations to broaden their political base, create truly democratic political institutions, and proceed with the necessary policies of social change without delay. We will refrain from supporting governments unwilling to undertake these necessary reforms. We cannot again afford to wait until a political crisis is full blown, as it is today in El Salvador, before we begin to seek solutions.

It would be a grave mistake to blame the current political crises in Central America on Cuban subversion. Cuba will seek to take advantage of instability in the region, but Cuba is not the sole cause of such instability. We must not allow our concerns about Cuba exclusively to shape our policy toward Central America, or any other part of the hemisphere. No amount of military aid can make a repressive government popular, and an unpopular government is never secure for long. The best antidote to Cuba's promotion of revolution is a region of sound, popular, democratic governments—not an armed camp of military dictators.

For four decades, the United States supported the corrupt and unpopular dictatorship of Anastasio Somoza in Nicaragua. Even though the revolution which drove Somoza from power last year enjoyed the support of virtually the entire populace, the United States tried, until the last moment, to prevent the revolutionary government from coming to power. The new Nicaraguan government is understandably suspicious of American intentions.

Nevertheless, Nicaragua and the United States have been able to maintain cordial relations over the past year. The new Government of National Reconstruction has committed itself to political pluralism. The government's program of reforms has created some tensions with the private sector, but both sides have thus far shown a willingness to compromise in the interests of national reconstruction.

We believe that providing economic aid to Nicaragua serves our national interest well. We support the $75 million aid package recently passed by the Congress. It will speed economic recovery and will also help sustain the current atmosphere of compromise and moderation within Nicaragua. To cut off economic assistance, as proposed in the Reagan platform, will undermine those political groups which have urged moderation, push the government towards more radical economic policies, and drive Nicaragua to seek closer ties with the Soviet Union.

In recent years Cuba has taken new initiatives in both Central America and the Caribbean. Cuba has provided some arms to revolutionaries in Central America, and has provided economic aid to some nations in the Caribbean.

We must not allow our concerns about Cuba to distort our policies toward the rest of the hemisphere. It would be a mistake to support repressive governments in Central America merely because Cuba opposes them; it would be a mistake to refuse aid to governments in the Caribbean merely because Cuba aided them.

At the same time, we will not tolerate direct military intervention by Cuba in Central America. There must be no Angolas in the Western hemisphere. We will also oppose any attempt by the Cubans to lead the nonaligned movement into the Soviet camp.

Others may wish to enter into relations with Cuba, but we ourselves cannot consider a normalization of relations until Cuba demonstrates a willingness to compromise on the many issues that divide us.

Caribbean — The economic situation in most of the Caribbean is particularly difficult today. The small-island economies which depend on world trade for many critical resources face severe trade imbalances because of the rising price of energy. This has led to a burgeoning foreign debt, inflation, and unemployment, all of which aggravate the already serious problem of poverty in most of the Caribbean.

These conditions have produced both a new potential for political unrest and a new willingness to experiment with different models of economic development. Jamaica, Grenada, and Guyana have adopted democratic socialist models which seek to blend socialist economies with parliamentary democracy.

As Cuba seeks to expand its influence on the region through its own economic assistance programs, the United States should respond, not with efforts to contain Cuba, but with efforts to build a strong basis of friendship between ourselves and our Caribbean neighbors. The complex social and economic problems of this region cannot be solved by military responses.

Increased economic assistance is an absolute neces-

sity for some of the Caribbean islands. While the Carter Administration has raised the level of U.S. assistance to the region, even more must be done. The ongoing deterioration in the region's terms of trade requires balance of payments assistance as well as development assistance.

To avoid creating an unhealthy bilateral dependency between the United States and those Caribbean economics that are most in need of external aid, much of the economic assistance provided by the United States should be channeled through multilateral institutions such as the Caribbean Development Bank.

Increased levels of aid cannot by themselves solve the economic problems faced by Caribbean countries. Other global and regional programs will be required if these states are to experience sustained growth. Effective commodity agreements, particularly for sugar, are needed to reduce the vulnerability of Caribbean economics to the vagaries of the world market. Initiatives toward regional economic cooperation and integration should be encouraged. International donors, including the United States, could support a regional shipping line to lower transportation costs and stimulate intra-regional trade. Similar cooperative ventures in such fields as food and energy should be encouraged as well.

South America — In South America, we must continue to strengthen our diplomatic relations with the continent's democracies. The Andean states of Venezuela, Colombia, Peru, and Ecuador are important allies in our quest for human rights and the restoration of democracy in the region. We must increase the co-ordination of our policy with theirs in responding to crises such as the recent military coup in Bolivia. Military officers in Bolivia and elsewhere must know that when they destroy a democratic government, they will meet not only the opposition of the United States, but also a solid front of opposition from all of the democracies of our hemisphere.

The existing military governments of the southern zone must understand that our commitment to human rights and democracy is firm. Until they demonstrate substantive progress in the field of human rights and towards the restoration of democracy, they can expect no improvement in their relations with the United States. Moreover, we must make clear to them that interference in the internal affairs of their neighbors is incompatible with hemispheric peace and security.

The current U.S. policy of denying foreign assistance to governments that systematically violate human rights is a laudible one and should be continued. But more must be done. In too many cases, American banks and corporations undercut our governmental policy by providing loans and investments to the very countries which are ineligible for governmental aid.

Our government must make greater informal efforts to bring public and private policy into better coordination.

The case of Chile is a special one. There is strong reason to believe that the Chilean military government was directly responsible for a brutal act of international terrorism perpetrated in the United States—the assassination of Orlando Letelier and the murder of Ronni Moffitt. The Chilean government has refused to cooperate with the U.S. in bringing the responsible parties to justice.

As the scourge of international terrorism spreads, the United States must take an unequivocal stand that it will not tolerate acts of terrorism in this country, especially when those acts are the responsibility of a foreign government. If Chile continues to refuse to cooperate in the prosecution of the Letelier-Moffitt case, the U.S. should consider additional measures to bring diplomatic and economic pressure on Chile.

Human Rights

To advocate human rights is to insist on respect for and protection of the rights and freedoms of persons—to be free from political persecution and torture, hunger, and deprivation; to enjoy freedom of thought, conscience, religion or belief.

We must not allow others to come to believe that our commitment to human rights is negotiable, or that it will be sacrificed at the first convenience. Of necessity, we must recognize the limits of our ability to improve the condition of human rights in other nations: the results will be long-term and gradual. But we shall never despair in promoting the full and free development of the individual.

A primary task of the Anderson Administration will be to sustain the framework of international peace and security within which human rights can be discussed, championed, and enlarged. The continuation of stable relations itself is therefore a crucial condition for the improvement of human rights in Eastern Europe and the Soviet Union.

We are angered that the number of Jews permitted to emigrate from the Soviet Union has plummeted, and we deplore the continued harassment of Jews in the Soviet Union. We are also deeply troubled with actions taken by authorities in the Soviet Union and Eastern European countries against individuals monitoring their nation's progress in complying with the Helsinki Accords. We reaffirm the conviction set forth in the Helsinki Accords of the "right of the individual to know and act upon his [human] rights and duties."

We must attend the second Helsinki review conference in Madrid, and we must insist upon a complete assessment of the degree to which the Soviet Union and the Eastern European nations have complied with the Helsinki Accords. We must make it clear before and during the Madrid conference that the imprisonment of Helsinki monitors and the punishment of countless others for their religious or political beliefs is violative of the Helsinki Accords and repugnant to the common tenets of civilizaton.

Under an Anderson Administration, the growth of American trade with the Soviet Union and Eastern European countries will require progress toward genuine respect for the right to emigrate. We see few, if any, justifications for denying the right of persons to change their citizenship from one country to another country willing to admit them.

An Anderson Administration will bring to bear on all countries, through bilateral and multilateral measures, every possible peaceful influence to prevent, to repair, or to end gross violations of human rights. Exceptions to our peaceful intercessions in support of human rights will be narrowly construed and strictly limited.

An Anderson Administration will:

Give strong diplomatic support for democratic governments; it will propose new foreign assistance legislation that would allow us to furnish these governments adequate and timely aid to help secure economic, social, and political rights for their people;

Limit economic and military assistance to nations that overthrow their democratic governments;

Deny military and economic assistance to governments that systematically violate human rights; and

Encourage corporations to conduct their activities and policies abroad in ways that are consistent with internationally recognized human rights standards.

The plight of refugees seeking haven in America requires urgent and diligent action. The Refugee Act of 1980 establishes the first comprehensive statutory basis for our refugee policy, providing for more equitable refugee admissions and assistance programs. The Anderson Administration will vigorously implement this important new legislation.

Equal justice and our commitment to human rights requires our establishing a sound and humane national immigration policy. John Anderson has repeatedly urged the Carter Administration to grant political asylum to the 10,000 Haitian refugees who have sought refuge in this country since 1971. Our immigration policies, laws, and practices must safeguard the civil rights of all Americans and the rights of those visiting our country for legitimate purposes. The Select Commission on Immigration and Refugee Policy chaired by Father Theodore Hesburgh will report to Congress by December on reforming our system of immigration and our refugee laws. Reform is greatly needed, and the Anderson Administration will move vigorously in this area.

The absence of bold leadership in the past four years has been nowhere more apparent than in the timorous responses of the Carter Administration to the tragedy in Cambodia. An Anderson Administration will press for adequate aid programs and will oppose any reduction in the monthly number of Indochinese refugees who may now be admitted to the United States.

An Anderson Administration will give active support to the private voluntary agencies, the Red Cross, and the various United Nations organizations in their unflagging efforts to provide relief and sustenance to hundreds of thousands of men, women, and children throughout the world who, fleeing war and famine, face disease and starvation. We must, where the need is especially urgent, speed up our timetable for contributing pledged funds. Humanitarian assistance, quickly provided, can mean the difference between life and death for thousands of people.

United Nations

The United Nations, now nearly 35 years old, continues work that needs to be done, but which the United States cannot begin to do by itself. The UN is helping to eradicate the ancient scourges of disease and malnutrition through public health programs. It is organizing help for refugees and migrants. It is monitoring world-wide environmental dangers. It is administering safeguards to discourage nuclear proliferation. It is maintaining truce supervisors and peacekeeping forces in the Middle East and elsewhere.

The Anderson Administration will play a vigorous role in supporting United States foreign policy objectives in the United Nations, through the General Assembly, the Security Council, and the specialized agencies. We will give strong support in the Congress to those UN programs which further our interests. The agenda is crowded:

Strengthening the peacemaking and peacekeeping capacities of the UN;

Helping Namibia, through a United Nations presence, in its transition from South African control to full independence;

Reaching an acceptable conclusion on the Law of the Sea negotiations;

Establishing a United Nations High Commissioner for Human Rights;

Sustaining the work of the International Labor Organization; and

Expanding United Nations efforts in controlling international terrorism.

We must also reassess our role in a number of United Nations activities.

Our contribution to the United Nations Development fund fell by one-third in real terms during the 1970's. We need to consider maintaining our financial contribution at historical levels. But more than money is needed. We should also make significant program contributions. Few economies have developed and applied technology to their productive processes so quickly as ours. We should make full use of our own economic development experiences in launching initiatives for United Nations development activities.

We have in recent years given greater attention to human rights concerns in our foreign policy, but incongruously we have failed to ratify a number of international human rights conventions widely accepted in the international community.

The Convention on the Prevention and Punishment of the Crime of Genocide has languished in the Senate for more than thirty years. It has been supported by every administration, Democrat and Republican. It should be promptly approved by the Senate. Other human rights agreements are in the Senate, including the Convention on the Elimination of All Forms of Racial Discrimination and the International Covenant on Civil and Political Rights. These covenants raise important constitutional issues. Our aim should be their ratification, attaching, where appropriate, reservations to insure that they are consistent with the United States Constitution.

The recent decision by the International Court of Justice calling for the release of our diplomatic personnel held hostage in Iran underlines the need to strengthen international legal institutions. If we expect other countries to accept the jurisdiction of the Court, we must be prepared to do the same by repealing the Connally Reservation.

We have seen in the Security Council action on Iran and in the General Assembly condemnation of the Soviet invasion of Afghanistan how the United Nations can advance the goal of world peace. We have seen in General Assembly resolutions on Israel and the Palestine Liberation Organization how our purposes can be impeded. Neither euphoria, born of success, nor cynicism, born of frustration, should guide our policies toward the United Nations.

The United Nations is a political institution. Our success in it will be in equal measure to the aggressiveness with which we promote our legitimate interests. But we must be unyielding in our efforts to prevent the humanitarian aims of the UN's nonpolitical organizations from being exploited for narrow national or ideological advantage. An Anderson Administration will strongly oppose efforts to stack committees and to bar nations from participating in regional or organizational activities.

We should not be dismayed at setbacks. Instead we must move to regain in the United Nations and in its specialized agencies that role which the strength, skills, and democratic practices of this nation suggest should be ours.

Foreign Assistance

The United States should return to its long tradition of extending assistance to the needy peoples and countries of the world. Funds channeled through American agencies and international organizations have been spent in the pursuit of a wide range of objectives, consistent with our humanitarian obligations and our political, economic, and security interests.

During the past decade, domestic support for foreign aid has waned. At present, the United States ranks 13th among industrialized nations in the percentage of GNP devoted to foreign assistance. There is a growing belief among voters that America can no longer afford to spend scarce resources on foreign assistance programs that seemingly produce few concrete results.

An Anderson Administration will seek to reverse this trend by heightening public awareness of the value of foreign aid programs. American foreign aid:

Increases world stability by supporting countries which are struggling to establish responsive political institutions, and prosperous economies;

Gives us continued access to raw materials by promoting steady economic development in Third World countries;

Provides business and jobs for Americans because roughly 75 cents of every development aid dollar is used to buy American products;

Promotes a vigorous export sector, which is a key element in American economic growth; and

Adds to the security of our nation by reinforcing alliances of strategic value.

These practical reasons for strengthening foreign aid programs reinforce humanitarian concerns. Foreign aid enables us to help alleviate the plight of the world's poor.

Our national interests, humanitarian obligations, and international responsibility demand that we provide more funds for foreign assistance. An Anderson Administration will harbor no illusions about foreign aid programs. The primary objective of foreign aid, to foster the development and modernization of Third World countries, is an extremely delicate task that often takes years. We should do all we can to ensure the success of development programs, but not lose faith if some development efforts meet with failure.

Foreign aid funds used to alleviate absolute poverty should be channeled through multilateral assistance programs wherever possible. By meeting basic human needs in nutrition, health, and education, we can provide people with the means to become self-reliant, and to participate in the building of their societies.

Long-term economic development will also play a major role in an Anderson foreign assistance program.

International and regional financial institutions provide capital essential for the development of Third World economies. An Anderson Administration will seek suitable assistance for the World Bank, the United Nations, and other institutions with similar goals to ensure that adequate capital is available for multilateral development programs.

The rising cost of oil has caused the current accounts deficit of non-oil-exporting developing countries to increase 400 percent in the last seven years. An Anderson Administration will encourage OPEC states to help Third World countries cope with an increasing burden of debt.

An Anderson Administration will emphasize economic assistance over military aid, consistent with our belief that security is built upon responsible political institutions and economic prosperity.

Specifically, an Anderson Administration will:

Increase the efficiency of the foreign assistance bureaucracy by placing the Agency for International Development (AID) once more directly under the supervision of the Secretary of State;

Establish a clearer separation of economic aid from military aid;

Re-evaluate present assistance allocation policies which tend to give small amounts of money to many different programs. The result is that some projects do not receive enough money to be fully successful.

As America moves into the 1980's, we cannot weaken our commitment to a sound policy of foreign assistance. A sensible foreign policy requires a strong assistance program. Misunderstanding, cynicism, and a leadership vacuum have led to neglect of this vital component of our national heritage and prosperity.

The Intelligence Agencies

Our intelligence community is passing through the darkest period of its history. The talents of the intelligence agencies have been sorely misused in the past and investigations by congressional committees have raised serious questions about the integrity and effectiveness of our intelligence effort.

Many claim that a strong intelligence service, with secrecy necessarily woven into the fabric of its activities, is basically antagonistic to the exercise of liberty in a free and open society. We disagree. The work of the intelligence agencies is a significant and necessary part of America's efforts to live securely and peacefully in the world. And we are confident that the intelligence agencies can accomplish their vital functions without impairing our basic rights and freedoms.

An Anderson Administration will strongly support congressional oversight of the intelligence agencies. We will request Congress to enact charter legislation to define the nature, breadth, and scope of intelligence activities. We will also support reduction in the number of congressional committees to which the intelligence agencies must report. Through its oversight committees, Congress should receive prior notification of all significant covert intelligence operations, and the principle of congressional access to intelligence agency information and material must be firmly established.

We believe that covert operations should be undertaken only for compelling reasons, and we will support legislation that prohibits assassination in peacetime and other practices by our intelligence agencies that are repugnant to our democratic traditions. We also favor a prohibition on the paid covert use for intelligence purposes of accredited American journalists, academicians, those following a full-time religious vocation, and Peace Corps volunteers. The Intelligence Oversight Board, too long ineffective, must meaningfully monitor the propriety of intelligence activities.

The ability of the intelligence agencies to provide accurate and timely assessments of actual and emerging international events requires urgent attention. Two areas must be immediately addressed. We must strengthen our ability to make a more discriminating use of intelligence-collecting resources and to engage in more thoughtful analysis. We must also vigorously promote better coordination of both agency information and counter-intelligence activities.

Finally, we share the widespread concern about the exposure of the identities of our intelligence agents abroad. An Anderson Administration will consider seeking legislation to bring criminal charges against individuals who, using secrets learned while employed in an intelligence agency, endanger lives by revealing an agent's identity. We affirm our conviction, however, that punishing writers who have not worked for an intelligence agency is inconsistent with First Amendment freedoms. Such measures would be a false promise of agent safety and national security.

Nuclear Non-Proliferation

For thirty-five years the United States has pursued policies intended to restrict the spread of nuclear weapons. The original objective of the program was to keep weapons design and fabrication techniques secret while promoting the use of nuclear power for peaceful purposes. As other countries developed research expertise, however, the focus shifted toward a framework of multilateral and bilateral agreements to renounce nuclear weapons development and apply internationally administered controls on the technology and supplies required to build atomic weapons.

The unchecked proliferation of nuclear weapons and weapons-grade material directly affects the security of the United States, by altering regional balances, and potentially threatening global stability. The destabilizing effects of nuclear proliferation are compounded by the danger of civil wars, irridentist ambitions, terrorist activities, and the failure of command and control systems.

An Anderson Administration will work in cooperation with other states to safeguard physically all nuclear materials from diversion and to restrain the spread of sensitive nuclear technology. We will devote particular attention to limiting the number of facilities which use or produce plutonium or weapons-grade uranium.

Reprocessing plants are particularly susceptible to the diversion of nuclear fuels since a commercial plant processes about 150 tons of plutonium annually and existing accounting techniques have significant "acceptable" error levels. Even if new technology was developed which could monitor fuel losses continuously to an accuracy of 1 percent, measurement uncertainties would still greatly exceed the amount needed to fabricate a bomb. We must therefore, rely increasingly on physical security measures to deter diversion of nuclear fuels, while also working to improve the measurement techniques which provide a crucial technical safeguard. An Anderson Administration will work to restrict the spread of reprocessing plants to additional countries since most states with "young" nuclear industries have no economic need for these facilities.

We believe that the United States must maintain a vigorous program of nuclear energy research and development if we are to retain our capacity to contribute technology, managerial skills, and operational experience to the broad range of nuclear activities relevant to the prevention or management of nuclear weapons proliferation. In particular, we must take a lead in supporting research to develop improved fuel cycle safeguard technology, including exact and continuous fuel rod assay systems for use in reprocessing plants. Nuclear weapons can be manufactured from diverted fuel in a matter of days, so exact and continuous international monitoring of the fuel flow and stocks in all civilian nuclear facilities should be a long-range objective of American diplomacy.

Though the detection of "trickle" diversion of fuels from reprocessing plants may never be possible, technological improvements and strict internationally supervised safeguards could make nuclear power and re-processing systems much more secure than they are today.

An Anderson Administration will use every techno-logical and managerial tool at its disposal to increase still further the distance between the military and peaceful uses of nuclear energy, and to secure nuclear fuel from diversion or misuse. For example, we will support basic research into alternative designs of the breeder reactor which do not use plutonium and we will consult closely with our European allies on all non-proliferation matters.

We must encourage all states to join in improving nuclear facility safeguards as a means of building con-fidence between nations and increasing the genuine security of nuclear fuel cycles. We will best be able to broaden the appeal of nuclear safeguards policies by emphasizing their technical aspects and avoiding pub-lic condemnations of our allies. We will promote in-ternal accounting improvements as a means of boost-ing quality control and reducing worker radiation hazards.

An Anderson Administration will support a strengthening of the safeguards and inspection author-ity of the International Atomic Energy Agency (IAEA). We will also encourage efforts to have the IAEA play a greater role in ensuring the physical se-curity of nuclear material. Standards for the physical protection of nuclear materials in transit, whether in-ternational or domestic, should be made as rigorous as current protective technology will allow.

We believe that the international community will gain from future efforts along the lines of the Interna-tional Nuclear Fuel Cycle Evaluation process and an Anderson Administration will support such efforts. Technically oriented meetings presently offer the best procedure for evaluating elements of civilian nuclear programs and building toward an international con-sensus on the issue.

The Non-Proliferation Treaty and the Treaty of Tlatelolco have helped to build confidence among participating states by establishing verification pro-cedures as well as a presumption against nuclear pro-liferation. Neither treaty has been signed by every pos-sible signatory, but the agreements have clearly had a beneficial effect and an Anderson Administration will search for further opportunities to expand the scope of the non-proliferation regime.

We believe that exports of nuclear technology should only be approved by the United States in in-stances where the proposed transfer clearly assists American non-proliferation goals. An Anderson Ad-ministration will enforce strict policies concerning the export of technical data, material, and technology and we will review the definition of relevant technologies to ensure that certain non-nuclear technology will be controlled if the technology, when combined with nu-clear technology, might lead to the further prolifera-tion of nuclear weapons.

An Anderson Administration will support the provi-sions of the 1978 Nuclear Non-Proliferation Act. We will seek to strengthen the commitments of all nuclear supplier states to refrain from the transfer of those fuel cycle components which were identified as "least pro-liferation resistant" at the International Nuclear Fuel Cycle Evaluation conference. We will call on all nu-clear supplier states to make known the agreed upon arrangements for disposal of spent fuel from nuclear facilities which they have supported in any way. We will propose negotiations towards an agreement which would involve the IAEA in the approval of design and construction plans for all nuclear facilities worldwide.

An Anderson Administration will take initiatives aimed at satisfying the legitimate research and devel-opment needs of countries with small nuclear pro-grams. This approach certainly introduces some minor proliferation risks, but it might prove to be the most effective means of avoiding additional unnecessary programs using weapons-grade fuels. We should init-iate joint research programs with scientists from such states, but should simultaneously ask their govern-ments to forego nuclear explosive research and accept all international safeguards.

We believe that the United States and other nuclear supplier nations should join with the IAEA, EURA-TOM, and national nuclear authorities to create a fund and technical advisory service to assist devel-oping nations to convert research facilities using weap-ons-grade fuel to fuels of lower nuclear weapons utility. An Anderson Administration will also increase the amount of foreign aid devoted to technical and fi-nancial assistance for developing countries which are interested in expanding their "soft path" energy resource programs.

Defense

Introduction — The fundamental purpose of Amer-ica's armed forces is to provide for our security and to sustain and advance our national policies. The years ahead will see old and new challenges to our achieving this purpose that will test the patience and wisdom of our people and our leaders.

The greatest of those challenges will continue to be the expansion of Soviet military strength, and the Kremlin's efforts to exploit its military capabilities against the West.

In strategic forces, the Soviets have reached essential equivalence with our own and continue to improve the accuracy of their missiles. In conventional forces, the

Soviet Union has greatly augmented its forces in Central Europe. It has sent thousands of ground troops into Afghanistan, and whether directly or through client states, has sought to extend its political and military influence in Southeast Asia, in the Persian Gulf region, and elsewhere.

The United States must therefore contend with the continued growth of Soviet military capabilities.

We must also attend to other challenges to our security, which lie outside the realm of our concerns with the Soviet Union.

In Central and Latin America, Africa, and throughout the region stretching from the Persian Gulf to the Pacific Ocean, nations and peoples are undergoing immense political, economic, and social changes. Change is inevitable. It is rapid, often unanticipated, and too frequently causes human tragedy on a vast scale. Regions and continents will not be won or lost by any single power. But our political, economic, and military interests in an interdependent world require consistent attention to the Third World through economic and political measures, and, where appropriate, through prudent and effective defense programs.

What must be done to meet these challenges?

Our first priority is to build a defense posture that demonstrates to the Soviet Union that it cannot gain strategic advantages over us.

We must take steps to protect the invulnerability of our nuclear forces.

We must have usable conventional forces to carry out the tasks dictated by defense needs.

We must proceed with arms control measures that enhance our security, but at the same time not fall prey to the illusion that arms control can or should carry the entire burden of preserving the military balance with the Soviet Union.

We must do our utmost to modernize our military personnel policies to retain the skilled men and women whom we need so much to implement our defense responsibilities.

We must spend what we need for defense, but we must apply the most exacting standards of efficiency and accountability to the way we spend defense dollars.

What matters is what we buy with our defense dollars, not how much we incrementally change our budget. We must discard simplicities which hold that spending more money will itself provide a solution to our security problems.

Moreover, we must never forget that arms by themselves are not sufficient to guarantee our security. As outlined elsewhere in this program, we must also restore our domestic economy, which, in the long run, is the true foundation of our international power. We must encourage further growth of our technological and scientific capacity. Spending unwisely for defense while we neglect the steps necessary to increase the productivity, innovation, and competitiveness of the American economy will buy us short-range comfort and long-range disaster.

Provision for our security also requires that we invigorate our alliances with Europe and Japan. If these alliances are preserved on the basis of a full measure of cooperation and partnership, the West will have more economic, industrial, and technological resources than any power or combination of powers that might challenge us. But we must also recognize that our alliances are unions of partners. Each must be prepared to share the burden of our joint endeavors fairly and to justify these sacrifices to its own people.

We cannot enter the international arena of the 1980's either poorly armed or fearful to do whatever is necessary to meet our commitments. There is the risk that the world will become a more hostile environment for the United States, and we must be prepared for this eventuality.

We need leadership to develop sound defense programs and strategies to implement them.

We need leadership to work constructively with Congress, orchestrating a balanced approach to national security.

We need leadership to provide steady coherence in the conduct of our joint affairs with our allies.

The Anderson Administration will meet the challenges to our national security as follows:

Strategic Forces — The nuclear weapons relationship with the Soviet Union is at the center of our military concerns.

Nuclear weapons, because of their enormous destructive power, their global reach, and the great speed with which they can reach their targets, have had a revolutionary impact on the security of nations. Throughout history, the chief purpose of armed forces has been to win wars. The chief purpose of nuclear weapons must be to prevent war.

For the past five administrations, Democrat and Republican, our nuclear strategy has been based on the principle of deterrence. Our principal objective is, not to wage nuclear war, but to prevent it.

An Anderson Administration will unambiguously reaffirm this traditional strategy. We must hold fast to the conviction that control of nuclear war is improbable, and that victory in nuclear war is meaningless. We re-emphasize our belief that the extensive deployment of weapons which threaten to destroy the other side's strategic weapons undermines the stability of the strategic balance and can be dangerous in a crisis, for each side will then have a strong incentive to fire its missiles before they are destroyed on the ground. We must maintain secure strategic forces capable of delivering measured, timely, proportionate, and, if necessary, overwhelming responses to any conceivable attack. We have such forces now. We must protect their ability to survive in the future.

One component of our strategic arsenal, our fixed, land-based missiles, is, however, becoming vulnerable to an all-out surprise attack by Soviet forces. We must recognize the danger but not be either paralyzed or imprisoned by it. We should remember that even after absorbing a massive first-strike against one portion of our nuclear deterrent, our strategic forces will be able to destroy enough of the Soviet Union's industries and military facilities to prevent its re-emergence as a major industrial or military power.

The fundamental question posed by the growing vulnerability of our land-based missiles is what comprises the most desirable mix of forces as the American arsenal is modernized in the 1980's. Should we preserve the three main components of our strategic forces, land-based missiles, bombers, and submarines? Or, as we move into the future, should we place greater reliance on bomber and submarine forces?

A possible solution would be negotiations with the Soviet Union that verifiably reduce the capacity of each party to threaten the other's land-based missiles. Unfortunately, the Soviets have so far rejected such negotiations. We must urgently seek to convince them that their intransigence is forcing us to consider options which may severely impair strategic stability.

The Carter Administration's specific cure for the vulnerability of our land-based missiles — the proposed mobile land-based MX system — is unsound. It will be enormously expensive (at least $50 billion, perhaps as much as $100 billion). There is reason to believe that the Soviet Union could destroy the system for less cost than we can build it. The proposed system will consume vast water and energy resources, and will disrupt, perhaps irreparably, the environment in the proposed missile site areas. It would invite Soviet military planners to aim nuclear weapons at thousands of new targets in the United States, and if SALT II is not ratified, the Soviets can develop all the necessary warheads and additional delivery vehicles to overwhelm the system as proposed.

American ingenuity can devise a more flexible and more cost-effective solution to the threat posed to our land-based missiles.

The Anderson Administration will give this matter the fresh and sober consideration it deserves through a comprehensive assessment of strategic doctrines, capabilities, and choices, free from either ideology or illusion.

What specific steps must be taken now to rebuild and modernize our strategic forces?

Our military command, control and communications systems should be made as survivable as our strategic weapons systems. For much less than it would cost to build the MX system proposed by the Carter Administration, we can insure that our command, control, and communications systems could survive any attack.

Our warning systems must be improved, as well as our ability to analyze data and make decisions under war-time conditions.

We can improve the basing systems for our aircraft and fleet ballistic missiles.

We must also move ahead with the current Trident submarine program. The technology embodied in the missile and in the submarine will enable us to be more secure and confident in the coming decades.

We should continue research into other missile-carrying submarines, including a larger number of smaller submarines, as additional means for enhancing our deterrent capabilities, as well as protecting our seaborne strategic retaliatory forces against future Soviet anti-submarine warfare capabilities.

We will continue modernization of the B–52 with air-launched cruise missiles, short-range attack missiles, and with improved navigational and other electronic systems. The B–52 is a formidable weapon of destruction. The Soviet Union obviously does not take it for granted. Neither should we.

We will continue existing research on new bomber forces, including those capable of launching cruise missiles.

Conventional Forces — The brutal invasion of Afghanistan has underscored that the Soviet Union persists in a foreign policy of opportunistic expansion. However, in allocating more money for conventional defense capabilities to help limit Soviet power, we must pause to assess our situation and to clarify our strategy.

Soviet improvements of their general purpose forces, real and potential, must be taken seriously. They must also be kept in perspective. The Soviet Union cannot be assured that with the outbreak of war in Central Europe, the East European countries would be compliant allies. And to the East, there is a united and hostile China, growing stronger.

In Europe, the size and quality of Western forces continue to make military aggression appear unattractive to the Soviet Union. The risk of nuclear escalation imposes even greater cautions. But to maintain a credible conventional deterrent, United States forces and those of our European allies will need to be improved, particularly to address the critical issue of depth in the alliance's central sector.

An Anderson Administration will:

Improve personnel effectiveness.

Increase operations and maintenance funding to improve overall force readiness. Too large a proportion of our equipment is not ready for action on short notice.

Pre-position more equipment in Europe. This would allow us to send reinforcements to Europe more quickly, and would have the added advantage of freeing airlift and sealift capabilities to meet threats to stability in the Persian Gulf region.

Reexamine the relation between support to combat roles in the Army to determine how the "tooth-tail" ratio can be increased to achieve greater efficiency of fire-power and use of logistic assets.

Improve weapons design systems. Advanced technology can and should be used to strike out in new directions. Too often, however, we forego simple, reliable, rugged weapons systems with clear missions in favor of expensive, complex systems which yield only marginal improvements. Multi-purpose weapons systems, while providing more flexibility, may suffer from four defects: (1) they are usually very expensive and, hence, fewer can be bought; (2) because fewer can be bought, additional resources are often needed to protect them; (3) they may be less suited to any given mission than simpler single-purpose systems; (4) this "gold-plating" invariably makes weapons more difficult to maintain, thereby compounding our manpower problems. An Anderson Administration will conduct a thorough assessment of military design and procurement practices to examine such problems as these and to establish a sounder basis for making judgments about the cost-effectiveness of weapons systems.

We welcome our allies' commitment to raise defense spending by 3 percent a year until 1984. An Anderson Administration will discuss with our European allies additional measures for increasing their conventional capabilities in concert with our efforts. These measures include:

The role of European reserves as combat-ready forces for use in the initial phases of combat. Most European reserves are meant to serve as individual replacements for casualties in units already in action. These reservists could be organized into actual combat formations to help cope with a Warsaw Pact armored breakthrough.

The condition of European war reserve stocks of ammunition, parts, and replacement equipment. There should be agreed stockage levels among the allies, as well as standardization and interoperability to share stockpiled materials in wartime.

The level of armaments in European ground forces.

The role of European civilian airline fleets in airlift operations, looking towards alterations in widebodied jets to increase the speed at which American reinforcements reach Europe.

Although the defense of Europe remains the central concern of our overseas conventional force capabilities, it is necessary to recognize that other areas of the world, notably the Middle East and the Persian Gulf, may require the continued deployment of American conventional forces in the foreseeable future. An Anderson Administration will not let our primary focus on European force requirements lead us to neglect our responsibilities in other areas of the world.

The Anderson Administration will develop political and military measures, wherever possible in cooperation with our allies and others, to limit Soviet influence in Third World areas, and to persuade the Soviets that unilateral action on their part will not be successful. Our conventional capabilities must also respond effectively to local situations that arise outside our relationship with the Soviet Union. Economic and political measures are the principal instruments for serving our security interests in these areas, but military forces can provide a necessary ingredient in our overall posture.

Our military forces in the Persian Gulf area should serve two purposes: to give confidence to friends and to deter Soviet action in the Persian Gulf region.

To achieve these goals, an Anderson Administration will improve the Marine Corps' tactical mobility and ground-based fire-power capabilities. We will take measures to deploy a regular naval presence in the Persian Gulf region, without impairing our naval strength elsewhere. We must be able to reinforce this presence rapidly with sufficient military power to contend successfully with Soviet incursions.

An Anderson Administration in its military acquisition practices will recognize that some parts of the world may require equipment that is different from equipment designed for operations in Europe.

An Anderson Administration will also encourage our Western allies and Japan to act in concert with us, whenever possible, in the Persian Gulf Region. The British, Dutch, French, and Australians either maintain bases in the Indian Ocean and/or regularly deploy naval units there. The security of the Persian Gulf area is vitally important to the economies of the West. The United States should not be alone in shouldering the burden of shared concerns.

We will discuss with our friends in the Persian Gulf region ways of pre-positioning equipment in their countries, and use of their air and naval facilities.

In all these measures, we will proceed cautiously, mindful that military capabilities and commitments must not become engines driving our foreign policy.

During the past twenty years, our general purpose naval forces have emphasized capabilities for offensive actions against Soviet sea and land targets. This must remain a significant mission for the Navy. But we believe that the Navy, as a flexible instrument of American statecraft, must give renewed and significant attention to its traditional responsibilities, namely, protecting the sealanes between the United States and our allies and protecting our interests in Third World areas. An Anderson Administration will develop a naval construction program to expand existing capabilities and to meet new challenges to our security interests in the 1980's and beyond.

The Draft and Military Personnel Policies — An Anderson Administration will oppose peacetime draft registration. The freedom to choose individual careers without the threat of government compulsion is a precious one. To protect it, we must make every effort to meet our military manpower needs without conscription.

The all-volunteer forces as currently maintained, however, are not adequate. The armed services are finding it difficult to recruit men and women to their ranks. The average educational competence of new recruits is declining. There is evidence that the military competence of our combat troops has deteriorated.

Career military personnel, whose professional skills are critical to our military effectiveness, are leaving the armed services at disturbing rates. Continued erosion of the size and quality of the armed forces will have serious repercussions for our national security. No more urgent task confronts our armed forces than meeting our military personnel needs.

Fairness to the men and women in the armed services and their families also argues for action. They deserve a quality of life equal to the importance of their responsibilities and the sacrifices we ask of them.

An Anderson Administration will:

Increase basic pay and allowances to compensate for losses since the start of the all-volunteer force;

Support breaking the link between military pay and that of civil service workers;

Provide bonuses for superior job performance by individuals as determined by unit commanders, as well as reenlistment bonuses for those individuals in occupational skills of critical importance to the armed forces;

Eliminate in many instances the "up or out" policy governing military promotions which requires many qualified enlisted personnel and officers to retire from the service even though they could continue to make useful contributions to our national security. We should create a pool of skilled individuals who may remain in the armed services outside the normal promotion path up to age 55 or 60;

Improve base housing, increase housing allowances, and expand social services such as day care facilities for military families;

Increase the cost-of-living allowances for individual service men and women in areas with especially high costs of living;

Grant allowances for all forces stationed overseas in places such as Germany, where, for example, the value of the dollar has declined 66 percent against the mark since 1970;

Adopt independent insurance fee schedule for medical services provided by private physicians to dependents of U.S. military personnel;

Develop a program of lateral entry enlistments for active duty and reserve forces for both enlisted and officer ranks;

Provide enlistment bonuses for those with education or technical training beyond high school;

Provide additional education to enlistees in exchange for an extension of the initial enlistment period;

Provide more extensive training to individual reservists including overseas deployments with active units for two-week periods where appropriate;

Reevaluate the issue of ceilings on the numbers of military dependents overseas.

These measures will cost money. But our nation can make no sounder defense investment. Moreover, these measures will save money in the long run. Reducing the outflow of experienced personnel will mean lower expenditures for recruiting, outfitting, and training. Additional monies can be saved by having the most experienced personnel continue to operate and maintain sophisticated weapons systems.

Arms Control — We face a critical juncture in the pursuit of a sound arms control policy aimed at limiting the levels and types of nuclear weapons as well as conventional forces. SALT II, the SALT process itself, technological threats to stability, the continuing proliferation of nuclear weapons, all demand our closest attention.

What are the fundamental elements of a sound and workable arms control policy?

Arms control agreements must enhance our basic security and must not compromise our ability to protect our national interests.

In our major arms control endeavors, we must insure that present and future agreements will preserve and reinforce the stability of the strategic balance.

Arms control agreements, particularly our accords with the Soviet Union, are not agreements between friends. We cannot rely on the good intentions, or promises on paper, of our adversaries. Arms control agreements must be based on adequate, effective verification.

We must develop new ways in which our NATO allies can participate fully, wherever possible, in the arms control process. Genuine consultation with our allies is essential if we are to deal imaginatively with the complex problems of theater nuclear weapons and the conventional military balance in Europe.

The Anderson Administration will take steps to complete the SALT II process, and thereby lay the groundwork for SALT III. We will propose immediate discussions with Moscow to consider possible supplementary measures to facilitate ratification of the pending treaty and to explore an agenda for the next round of negotiations on strategic weaponry.

The basic security interests of the United States are well served by ratifying the SALT II treaty. The treaty as negotiated is adequately verifiable, within the constraints imposed by national technical means of verification. Critics of the treaty have not shown how our nation would be more secure if we rejected it. In the absence of the SALT II constraints, the Soviets can expand their nuclear armaments to levels well beyond those provided in the treaty. We would have no choice but to match arms for arms in a renewed arms race. Fear and insecurity, the wellsprings of war, would be the constant lot of both countries.

In Europe, the Soviet Union is deploying nuclear missiles of sufficient accuracy to threaten land-based nuclear weapons in Europe. The Western Alliance should proceed with its plans to modernize its theater nuclear arsenal; at the same time, we should keep open the possibility of negotiations with the Soviet Union to limit theater nuclear forces.

The Anderson Administration will support efforts to negotiate a ban on the development, testing, and deployment of anti-satellite warfare systems. Until, however, the Soviet Union shows a willingness to enter serious negotiations in this area, we should continue research on an anti-satellite capability.

We favor conclusion of a short-term comprehensive Nuclear Test Ban Treaty among the United States, the Soviet Union, and the United Kingdom, with frequent review pending inclusion of all nuclear weapons states.

The United States should continue to seek agreements in such key areas as peaceful nuclear explosions, chemical warfare, and conventional arms transfer restraint.

Conclusion

We cannot help keep the peace, nor retain the confidence of our friends or the respect of our adversaries, if our military strength declines. We must do what is required to sustain the credibility of our nuclear forces, to rebuild our conventional forces, and to retain the services of our most capable military personnel. These actions must be pursued consistently and with common sense.

Our aim must be the wiser use of defense moneys to achieve for ourselves and our posterity a peaceful future, confident in America's ability to maintain a defense policy that will insure its security in the years ahead.

VI. How an Independent Can Govern

We have set forth a comprehensive program for America. But this is not enough. The American people want new ideas, but they also want effective government. The novel possibility of an Independent administration raises important questions about governing this nation—questions to which the American people deserve answers.

We believe that at this critical juncture, America needs an Independent President, and we believe that such a President can work successfully with a Congress organized along party lines to govern this nation.

We now need an Independent President, for two reasons:

The major parties have proved unequal to the task of formulating a realistic post-New Deal public philosophy. The Democratic Party is committed to extending the New Deal without providing the means to pay for it. The Republican Party has been captured by forces that offer a curious combination of consumption-oriented economics and pro-New Deal social policies. The Anderson-Lucey National Unity Campaign is based on a centrist philosophy that ties its program of social policies to those measures needed to rebuild the economic base upon which they can rest.

The traditional parties were reasonably effective mechanisms for distributing the dividends of economic growth. But during a period in which the central task of government is to allocate burdens and orchestrate sacrifice, these parties have proved incapable of making the necessary hard choices. We are prepared to tell the American people what we must do, and allocate the burdens in a manner sensitive to both economic efficiency and social equity.

Most of the key issues confronting the country now cross traditional party divisions. In the sphere of foreign and defense policy, the overwhelming majority believes that our military preparedness must be increased, that our long-standing alliances with Europe and Japan must be rebuilt, and that our manufactured goods must be free to compete on a fair basis in major world markets. In the domestic sphere, we agree that we must reindustrialize our economy, rebuild our cities, reduce unemployment, inflation, and energy consumption, safeguard our environment, and extend the full protection of civil rights to all who reside within our borders. Conversely, the issues that most passionately divide us—the controversy between capitalism and corporatism, and social issues such as ERA, abortion, and affirmative action—are debated within rather than between political parties.

The Anderson National Unity Campaign builds on this agreement. It transcends the irrelevant quarrels between an old liberalism and an even older conservatism, and it offers effective, coordinated means to achieve goals that enjoy overwhelming public support.

We believe, further, than an Independent President can be effective. We must, of course, acknowledge that the context in which presidents must act has become more complicated and restrictive during the past two decades. Sober observers have pointed to the decentralization of Congress, the fragmentation of political parties, the risk of single-issue constituencies, and the atomization of the electorate as major elements of this new situation. But we contend that in 1980 an Independent Anderson Administration can deal with it more effectively than can a major party administration.

We have four reasons for this contention.

An Anderson victory—in the teeth of the enormous institutional bias against independents—would be a dramatic signal to Congress that the nation wants and expects action, based on the new consensus the campaign has articulated.

Unlike other post-war independent candidacies, the Anderson campaign represents neither a region nor a dissident fringe, but rather a coalition of the center—the traditional basis for governing the American polity.

In the absence of Congressional cohesion and party discipline, the President's effectiveness rests largely on his ability to persuade significant numbers of legislators that his proposals are sensible and fair. John Anderson and Patrick Lucey are superbly equipped to do this. Mr. Anderson has spent two decades acquiring a working knowledge of the issues, from a national perspective. He is intimately acquainted with the intricate process by which ideas are translated into proposals, proposals into laws, and laws into deeds. And he knows the individuals who make the laws—their concerns, their language, their sensibilities. As President, Anderson would have the potential to work as effectively with the Congress as any post-war chief executive. Mr. Lucey has served as an effective Governor of a major state which contains virtually all the problems of industry, commerce, and agriculture that are found elsewhere in the United States.

Congress will work productively with any President who enjoyed the trust and confidence of the American people. A key determinant of this in modern politics is the President's ability to communicate with them, face-to-face and through the media. This ability does not depend upon the party application of the Presi-

dent, but upon the ability of the President to advocate and persuade.

We believe with Alexander Hamilton that: ". . . the true test of a good government is its aptitude and tendency to produce a good administration."

A good administration, in turn, has two requisites: good personnel, and prudent use of them.

As President, an Anderson Administration will strive to appoint talented individuals, without regard to party affiliation. They will be drawn from a broad range of backgrounds—government, business, labor, academia. Ideally, each will blend general intellectual or theoretical competence and practical experience—both in Washington and elsewhere.

The Administration will attach great weight to judicial appointments on every level. It will strive to ensure that only wise and experienced individuals be nominated for these crucial offices without regard to partisan affiliation. We believe that the greatest asset of the judiciary is the trust—even reverence—accorded to it by the American people, and that in the years ahead this high regard can be maintained only if the judiciary is perceived as broadly representative of the spirit of the nation. Accordingly, we will intensify the quest for women and members of minority groups from whom judges and Supreme Court Justices can be appointed.

As to the appropriate use of individuals within the modern Presidency, two great statesmen and electoral antagonists have between them succinctly propounded the correct policy. Adlai Stevenson once stated that there are only three rules of sound administration: pick good people, tell them not to cut any corners, and back them to the limit. And Dwight Eisenhower, whose genius for governance becomes more evident with every passing year, once reflected on his tenure in office in the following terms:

> The government of the United States has become too big, too complex, and too pervasive in its influence on all our lives for one individual to pretend to direct the details of its important and critical programming. Competent assistants are mandatory; without them the Executive Branch would bog down. To command the loyalties and dedication and best efforts of capable and outstanding individuals requires patience, understanding, a readiness to delegate, and an acceptance of responsibility for any honest errors—real or apparent—those subordinates might make.

We believe that the greatest administrative failure of the current administration is its failure to deal successfully with the Congress. At the heart of its failure lies its inability to engage in substantive, meaningful consultation. Such consultation has two components:

The involvement of relevant Congressional personnel in the drafting of legislative submissions; and

A constant two-way exchange on the progress of proposed legislation through the Congress.

An Anderson Administration will give relations with Congress the highest priority, assigning to this task experienced senior officials known to and trusted by the members of Congress.

In general, an Anderson Administration will act on the principle that a strong Presidency rests on a strong Congress. It will respect the traditional prerogatives of the Congress and it will attempt to foster unity rather than foment discord within the Congressional ranks. At the same time, an Anderson Administration will protect and vigorously employ the powers of the Presidency. Our Constitution envisages a perennial mixture of contest and harmony among the different branches of our government, through which the liberties of the people will be preserved and the general welfare promoted.

Conception of the Presidency

A successful presidency rests on a clear conception of the presidency. We believe that:

The President must be a problem-solver, whose every effort is directed toward the general welfare. The "general welfare" is not a rhetorical fiction, but rather a course of action that promotes individual well being while complying with the dictates of justice and fair play.

The President must be a policy-coordinator. Government fails unless its initiatives are mutually consistent, reflecting coherent priorities and a sense of direction. Standing at the apex of government, only the President is in a position to perform this task.

The President must give leadership to the Executive Branch. He should not recklessly attack federal personnel, most of whom are dedicated and hard working, but rather ensure that they receive clear signals to guide their endeavors.

A President cannot simply enunciate his preferences but must energetically follow through with determined efforts to translate them into policy. To this end, the President must avoid inflammatory public rhetoric while engaging in quiet persuasion and patient, persistent negotiation.

A President must tell the truth to the American people, even when it is unpalatable and unpopular. In current circumstances, only an individual prepared to be a one-term President, if necessary, can faithfully and conscientiously discharge his Constitutional responsibilities.

A President must exhibit constant resolve and steadfastness once he has made a decision and embarked on a course of action. He should not expect to please everyone; nor should he be deterred by criticism. And he should not attempt to govern the nation by public opinion polls, but should always act to further the long-term public good, as he sees that good.

The President must embody and express an appropriate historical perspective. He must strive to link significant public acts to the American political tradition, to give the American people a sense of continuity with their basic values and a feeling of participation in a meaningful common enterprise.

It has become fashionable to point to the many constraints within which modern presidents must operate. And some political leaders — including the present occupant of the Oval Office — have sought to lower our expectations of presidential performance and achievement.

We cannot deny the existence of constraints. But for the most part they are nothing new. They are built into the structure of the Constitution itself. In the past, great presidents have used the many powers of their office to overcome these obstacles, to promote the common defense and general welfare.

We believe that it is still possible to do this, with bold, farsighted, independent leadership. We believe that the program we have set forth is the basis for such leadership, and that we can effectively direct the affairs of this nation in the 1980's.

The essence of presidential responsibility is to assert the general interest over narrow interests; to make difficult choices among worthy, but conflicting, objectives; to strike policy balances that are wise and fair enough to earn the support of Congress and the nation.

No president can forecast in all respects the precise course he will follow on all issues. But it is incumbent upon candidates who seek your vote to state their view of the country's needs and to identify those initiatives they expect to undertake.

This we have attempted to do. Many distinguished Americans have contributed to the studies and position papers upon which it is based, but it is our own sketch of the priorities we believe should guide our country — not a mosaic of bargains among special interests or trade-offs among experts.

We seek a workable synthesis of policy and program, for the next administration must blend new ideas with old, innovative concepts with traditional values, proven approaches with tentative ones. In responding to the challenges we face, government must be frankly experimental in some fields, conventional in others. It must also be utterly ruthless in judging its performance and pruning its failures. These convictions will animate our administration.

We speak for a patriotism greater than party. And we invite patriots of all persuasions to join with us in shaping a government that can shape the future.

Republican Platform 1980

A PREAMBLE

The Republican Party convenes, presents this platform, and selects its nominees at a time of crisis. America is adrift. Our country moves agonizingly, aimlessly, almost helplessly into one of the most dangerous and disorderly periods in history.

At home, our economy careens, whiplashed from one extreme to another. Earlier this year, inflation skyrocketed to its highest levels in more than a century; weeks later, the economy plummeted, suffering its steepest slide on record. Prices escalate at more than 10 percent a year. More than eight million people seek employment. Manufacturing plants lie idle across the country. The hopes and aspirations of our people are being smothered.

Overseas, conditions already perilous, deteriorate. The Soviet Union for the first time is acquiring the means to obliterate or cripple our land-based missile system and blackmail us into submission. Marxist tyrannies spread more rapidly through the Third World and Latin America. Our alliances are frayed in Europe and elsewhere. Our energy supplies become even more dependent on uncertain foreign suppliers. In the ultimate humiliation, militant terrorists in Iran continue to toy with the lives of Americans.

These events are not isolated, or unrelated. They are signposts. They mark a continuing downward spiral in economic vitality and international influence. Should the trend continue, the 1980s promise to be our most dangerous years since World War II. History could record, if we let the drift go on, that the American experiment, so marvelously successful for 200 years, came strangely, needlessly, tragically to a dismal end early in our third century.

By far the most galling aspect of it all is that the chief architects of our decline—Democratic politicians—are without program or ideas to reverse it. Divided, leaderless, unseeing, uncomprehending, they plod on with listless offerings of pale imitations of the same policies they have pursued so long, knowing full well their futility. The Carter Administration is the unhappy and inevitable consequence of decades of increasingly outmoded Democratic domination of our national life. Over the past four years it has repeatedly demonstrated that it has no basic goals other than the perpetuation of its own rule and no guiding principle other than the fleeting insights provided by the latest opinion poll. Policies announced one day are disavowed or ignored the next, sowing confusion among Americans at home and havoc among our friends abroad.

Republicans, Democrats, and Independents have been watching and reading these signs. They have been watching incredulously as disaster after disaster unfolds. They now have had enough. They are rising up in 1980 to say that this confusion must end; this drift must end; we must pull ourselves together as a people before we slide irretrievably into the abyss.

It doesn't have to be this way; it doesn't have to stay this way. We, the Republican Party, hold ourselves forth as the Party best able to arrest and reverse the decline. We offer new ideas and candidates, from the top of our ticket to the bottom, who can bring to local and national leadership firm, steady hands and confidence and eagerness. We have unparalleled unity within our own ranks, especially between our Presidential nominee and our congressional membership. Most important, we go forth to the people with ideas and programs for the future that are as powerful and compelling as they are fresh. Together, we offer a new beginning for America.

Our foremost goal here at home is simple: economic growth and full employment without inflation. Sweeping change in economic policy in America is needed so that Mr. Carter's promise of hard times and austerity—his one promise well kept—can be replaced with Republican policies that promise economic growth and job creation. It is our belief that the stagflation of recent years not only has consigned millions of citizens to hardship but also has bottled up the enormous ingenuity and creative powers of our people. Those energies will not be released by the sterile policies of the past: we specifically reject the Carter doctrine that inflation can be reduced only by throwing people out of work. Prosperity will not be regained simply by government fiat. Rather, we must offer broad new incentives to labor and capital to stimulate a great outpouring of private goods and services and to create an abundance of jobs. From America's grassroots to the White House we will stand united as a party behind a bold program of tax rate reductions, spending restraints, and regulatory reforms that will inject new life into the economic bloodstream of this country.

Overseas, our goal is equally simple and direct: to preserve a world at peace by keeping America strong. This philosophy once occupied a hallowed place in American diplomacy, but it was casually, even cavalierly dismissed at the outset by the Carter Administration—and the results have been shattering. Never before in modern history has the United States endured as many humiliations, insults, and defeats as it has during the past four years: our ambassadors murdered, our embassies burned, our warnings ignored, our diplomacy scorned, our diplomats kidnapped. The Carter Administration has shown that it neither understands totalitarianism nor appreciates the way tyrants take advantage of weakness. The brutal invasion of Afghanistan promises to be only the forerunner of much more serious threats to the West—and to world peace—should the Carter Administration somehow cling to power.

Republicans are united in a belief that America's international humiliation and decline can be reversed only by strong Presidential leadership and a consistent, far-sighted foreign policy, supported by a major upgrading of our military forces, a strengthening of our commitments to our allies, and a resolve that our national interests be vigorously protected. Ultimately, those who practice strength and firmness truly guard the peace.

This platform addresses many concerns of our Party. We seek to restore the family, the neighborhood, the community, and the workplace as vital alternatives in our national life to ever-expanding federal power.

We affirm our deep commitment to the fulfillment of the hopes and aspirations of all Americans—blacks and whites, women and men, the young and old, rural and urban.

For too many years, the political debate in America has been conducted in terms set by the Democrats. They believe that every time new problems arise beyond the power of men and women as individuals to solve, it becomes the duty of government to solve them, as if there were never any alternative. Republicans disagree and have always taken the side of the individual, whose freedoms are threatened by the big government that Democratic idea has spawned. Our case for the individual is stronger than ever. A defense of the individual against government was never more needed. And we will continue to mount it.

But we will redefine and broaden the debate by transcending the narrow terms of government and the individual; those are not the only two realities in America. Our society consists of more than that; so should the political debate. We will reemphasize those vital communities like the family, the neighborhood, the workplace, and others which are found at the center of society, between government and the individual. We will restore and strengthen their ability to solve problems in the places where people spend their daily lives and can turn to each other for support and help.

We seek energy independence through economic policies that free up our energy production and encourage conservation. We seek improvements in health care, education, housing, and opportunities for youth. We seek new avenues for the needy to break out of the tragic cycle of dependency. All of these goals—and many others—we confidently expect to achieve through a rebirth of liberty and resurgence of private initiatives, for we believe that at the root of most of our troubles today is the misguided and discredited philosophy of an all-powerful government, ceaselessly striving to subsidize, manipulate, and control individuals. But it is the individual, not the government, who reigns at the center of our Republican philosophy.

To those Democrats who say Americans must be content to passively accept the gradual but inexorable decline of America, we answer: The American people have hardly begun to marshal their talents and resources or realize the accomplishments and dreams that only freedom can inspire.

To those Democrats who say we face an "age of limits," we ask: Who knows the limit to what Americans can do when their capacity for work, creativity, optimism, and faith is enhanced and supported by strong and responsive political leadership and ideals.

To those who, with Mr. Carter, say the American people suffer from a national "malaise," we respond: The only malaise in this country is found in the leadership of the Democratic Party, in the White House and in Congress. Its symptoms are an incompetence to lead, a refusal to change, and a reluctance to act. This malaise has become epidemic in Washington. Its cure is government led by Republicans who share the values of the majority of Americans.

Republicans pledge a restoration of balance in American society. But society cannot be balanced by the actions of government or of individuals alone. Balance is found at society's vital center, where we find the family and the neighborhood and the workplace.

America will not, however, achieve any of these goals on its present course nor under its present leadership. The uncharted course of Mr. Carter will lead surely to catastrophe. By reversing our economic decline, by reversing our international decline, we can and will resurrect our dreams.

And so, in this 1980 Republican Platform, we call out to the American people: With God's help, let us now, together, make America great again; let us now, together, make a new beginning.

FREE INDIVIDUALS IN A FREE SOCIETY

It has long been a fundamental conviction of the Republican Party that government should foster in our society a climate of maximum individual liberty and freedom of choice. Properly informed, our people as individuals or acting through instruments of popular consultation can make the right decisions affecting personal or general welfare, free of pervasive and heavy-handed intrusion by the central government into the decisionmaking process. This tenet is the genius of representative democracy.

Republicans also treasure the ethnic, cultural, and regional diversity of our people. This diversity fosters a dynamism in American society that is the envy of the world.

Taxes

Elsewhere in this platform we discuss the benefits, for society as a whole, of reduced taxation, particularly in terms of economic growth. But we believe it is essential to cut personal tax rates out of fairness to the individual.

Presently, the aggregate burden of taxation is so great that the average American spends a substantial part of every year, in effect, working for government.

Substantial tax rate reductions are needed to offset the massive tax increases facing the working men and women of this country. Over the next four years, federal taxes are projected to increase by over $500 billion due to the Carter Administration's policies. American families are already paying taxes at higher rates than ever in our history; as a result of these Carter policies, the rates will go even higher. The direct and indirect burden of federal taxes alone, imposed on the average family earning $20,000, has risen to $5,451 — over 27 percent of the family's gross income. During the Carter term, the federal tax alone on this family will have risen $2,000.

The Republican Party believes balancing the budget is essential but opposes the Democrats' attempt to do so through higher taxes. We believe that an essential aspect of balancing the budget is spending restraint by the federal government and higher economic growth, not higher tax burdens on working men and women.

Policies of the Democratic Party are taxing work, savings, investment, productivity, and the rewards for human ingenuity. These same tax policies subsidize debt, unemployment, and consumption. The present structure of the personal income tax system is designed to broaden the gap between effort and reward.

Therefore, the Republican Party supports across-the-board reductions in personal income tax rates, phased in over three years, which will reduce tax rates from the range of 14 to 70 percent to a range of from 10 to 50 percent.

For most Americans, these reduced tax rates will slow the rate at which taxes rise. This will assure workers and savers greater rewards for greater effort by lowering the rate at which added earnings would be taxed.

These reductions have been before the Congress for three years in the Roth-Kemp legislation. The proposal will not only provide relief for all American taxpayers, but also promote non-inflationary economic growth by restoring the incentive to save, invest, and produce. These restored incentives will in turn increase investment and help reinvigorate American business and industry, leading to the creation of more jobs. In fact, Governor Reagan and Congressional Republicans have already taken the first step. Working together, they have boldly offered the American people a 10 percent tax rate cut for 1981, which will stimulate growth in our economy, and a simplification and liberalization of depreciation schedules to create more jobs.

Once tax rates are reduced, Republicans will move to end tax bracket creep caused by inflation. We support tax indexing to protect taxpayers from the automatic tax increases caused when cost-of-living wage increases move them into higher tax brackets.

Tax rate reductions will generate increases in economic growth, output, and income which will ultimately generate increased revenues. The greater justification for these cuts, however, lies in the right of the individual to keep and use the money they earn.

Improving the Welfare System

The measure of a country's compassion is how it treats the least fortunate. In every society there will be some who cannot work, often through no fault of their own.

Yet current federal government efforts to help them have become counter-productive, perpetuating and aggravating the very conditions of dependence they seek to relieve. The Democratic Congress has produced a jumble of degrading, dehumanizing, wasteful, overlapping, and inefficient programs that invite waste and fraud but inadequately assist the needy poor.

Poverty is defined not by income statistics alone, but by an individual's true situation and prospects. For two generations, especially since the mid-1960s, the Democrats have deliberately perpetuated a status of federally subsidized poverty and manipulated dependency for millions of Americans. This is especially so for blacks and Hispanics, many of whom remain pawns of the bureaucracy, trapped outside the social and economic mainstream of American life.

For those on welfare, our nation's tax policies provide a penalty for getting a job. This is especially so for those whose new income from a job is either equal to, or marginally greater than, the amount received on welfare. In these cases, due to taxes, the individual's earned income is actually less than welfare benefits. This is the "poverty trap" which will continue to hold millions of Americans as long as they continue to be punished for working.

The Carter Administration and the Democratic Party continue to foster that dependency. Our nation's welfare problems will not be solved merely by providing increased benefits. Public service jobs are not a substitute for employable skills, nor can increases in the food stamp program by themselves provide for individual dignity. By fostering dependency and discouraging self-reliance, the Democratic Party has created a welfare constituency dependent on its continual subsidies.

The Carter Administration has proposed, and its allies in the House of Representatives actually voted for, legislation to nationalize welfare, which would have cost additional billions and made billions more dependent upon public assistance. The Democrats have presided over — and must take the blame for — the most monstrous expansion and abuse of the food stamp program to date. They have been either unable or unwilling to attack the welfare fraud that diverts resources away from the truly poor. They have sacrificed the needy to the greedy, and sent the welfare bills to the taxpayers.

We categorically reject the notion of a guaranteed annual income, no matter how it may be disguised, which would destroy the fiber of our economy and doom the poor to perpetual dependence.

As a party we commit ourselves to a welfare policy that is truly reflective of our people's true sense of compassion and charity as well as an appreciation of every individual's need for dignity and self-respect. We pledge a system that will:

—provide adequate living standards for the truly needy;

—end welfare fraud by removing ineligibles from the welfare rolls, tightening food stamp eligibility requirements, and ending aid to illegal aliens and the voluntarily unemployed;

—strengthen work incentives, particularly directed at the productive involvement of able-bodied persons in useful community work projects;

—provide educational and vocational incentives to allow recipients to become self-supporting; and

—better coordinate federal efforts with local and state social welfare agencies and strengthen local and state administrative functions.

We oppose federalizing the welfare system; local levels of government are most aware of the needs in their communities. We support a block grant program that will help return control of welfare programs to the states. Decisions about who gets welfare, and how

much, can be better made on the local level.

Those features of the present law, particularly the food stamp program, that draw into assistance programs people who are capable of paying for their own needs should be corrected. The humanitarian purpose of such programs must not be corrupted by eligibility loopholes. Food stamp program reforms proposed by Republicans in Congress would accomplish the twin goals of directing resources to those most in need and streamlining administration.

Through long association with government programs, the word "welfare" has come to be perceived almost exclusively as tax-supported aid to the needy. But in its most inclusive sense — and as Americans understood it from the beginning of the Republic — such aid also encompasses those charitable works performed by private citizens, families, and social, ethnic, and religious organizations. Policies of the federal government leading to high taxes, rising inflation, and bureaucratic empire-building have made it difficult and often impossible for such individuals and groups to exercise their charitable instincts. We believe that government policies that fight inflation, reduce tax rates, and end bureaucratic excesses can help make private effort by the American people once again a major force in those works of charity which are the true signs of a progressive and humane society.

Veterans

Republicans recognize the very special sacrifice of those who have served in our nation's armed forces. Individual rights and societal values are only as strong as a nation's commitment to defend them. Because of this our country must never forget its appreciation of and obligation to our veterans.

Today the veteran population numbers 30 million. This is the largest veteran population in our nation's history. We recognize the major sacrifices they have made for their fellow Americans.

We will maintain the integrity of the Veterans Administration. We will seek to keep it separate and distinct from other federal agencies as the single agency for the administration of all veterans' programs. In particular we feel it is of vital importance to continue and expand the health programs provided to veterans through the Veterans Administration hospitals. Here we see the need for increased access to care, especially for older veterans.

We further advocate continued and expanded health care for our Vietnam veterans and consider it vital for the Veterans Administration to continue its programs for the rehabilitation of the disabled as well as its job training efforts.

We are committed to providing timely and adequate adjustments in compensation for service-disabled veterans and the survivors of those who died as a result of their service. We are also committed to maintaining the pension program for those who have served during a period of war, for those who were disabled and impoverished, and for their widows and orphans.

We will support measures to provide for every veteran at death a final resting place for his remains in a national cemetery, and for costs of transportation thereto.

Veterans preference in federal employment in all departments and agencies will be continued and strictly enforced.

Retired military benefits deserve more than the cursory attention given them by a Department of Defense otherwise interested in on-going programs. We believe that such benefits should be administered by the Veterans Administration.

Private Property

The widespread distribution of private property ownership is the cornerstone of American liberty. Without it neither our free enterprise system nor our republican form of government could long endure.

Under Democratic rule, the federal government has become an aggressive enemy of the human right to private property ownership. It has dissipated savings through depreciation of the dollar, enforced price controls on private exchange of goods, attempted to enforce severe land use controls, and mistreated hundreds of thousands of national park and forest inholders.

The next Republican Administration will reverse this baneful trend. It will not only protect the cherished human right of property ownership, but will also work to help millions of Americans—particularly those from disadvantaged groups—to share in the ownership of the wealth of their nation.

Transportation—Personal Mobility

Americans enjoy greater personal mobility than any other people on earth, largely as a result of the availability of automobiles and our modern highway system. Republicans reject the elitist notion that Americans must be forced out of their cars. Instead, we vigorously support the right of personal mobility and freedom as exemplified by the automobile and our modern highway system. While recognizing the importance of fuel efficiency and alternate modes of transportation, we quickly acknowledge that for millions of Americans there is no substitute on the horizon for the automobile. We reaffirm our support for a healthy domestic automobile industry, complete with continued support for the highway trust fund, which is

the fairest method yet devised for financing America's highway system.

Republicans recognize the need for further improvement in highway safety. Projections indicate that highway fatalities may exceed 60,000 per year in the coming decades. Republicans support accelerated cost-effective efforts to improve highway, automobile, and individual driver safety.

Privacy

The essence of freedom is the right of law abiding individuals to life, liberty, and the pursuit of happiness without undue governmental intervention. Yet government in recent years, particularly at the federal level, has overwhelmed citizens with demands for personal information and has accumulated vast amounts of such data through the IRS, Social Security Administration, the Bureau of the Census, and other agencies. Under certain limited circumstances, such information can serve legitimate societal interests, but there must be protection against abuse.

Republicans share the concerns of our citizens as to the nature, use, and final disposition of the volume of personal information being collected. We are alarmed by Washington's growing collection and dissemination of such data. There must be protection against its misuse or disclosure.

The Republican Party commits itself to guaranteeing an individual's right of privacy. We support efforts of state governments to ensure individual privacy.

Black Americans

For millions of black Americans, the past four years have been a long trail of broken promises and broken dreams. The Carter Administration entered office with a pledge to all minorities of a brighter economic future. Today there are more black Americans unemployed than on the day Mr. Carter became President. The unemployment rate of black teenagers is once again rising sharply. And the median income of black families has declined to less than 60 percent of white family income.

Republicans will not make idle promises to blacks and other minorities; we are beyond the day when any American can live off rhetoric or political platitudes.

Our Party specifically rejects the philosophy of the Carter Administration that unemployment is the answer to inflation. We abhor the notion that our cities should become battlegrounds in the fight against inflation and that the jobs of black Americans should be sacrificed in an attempt to counterbalance the inflationary excesses of government. Nor are we prepared to accept the practice of turning the poor into permanent wards of the state, trading their political support for continued financial assistance.

Our fundamental answer to the economic problems of black Americans is the same answer we make to all Americans—full employment without inflation through economic growth. First and foremost, we are committed to a policy of economic expansion through tax-rate reductions, spending restraint, regulatory reform and other incentives.

As the Party of Lincoln, we remain equally and steadfastly committed to the equality of rights for all citizens, regardless of race. Although this nation has not yet eliminated all vestiges of racism over the years, we are heartened by the progress that has been made, we are proud of the role that our Party has played, and we are dedicated to standing shoulder to shoulder with black Americans in that cause.

Elsewhere in this platform, we set forth a number of specific proposals that will also serve to improve the quality of life for blacks. During the next four years we are committed to policies that will:

—encourage local governments to designate specific enterprise zones within depressed areas that will promote new jobs, new and expanded businesses and new economic vitality;

—open new opportunities for black men and women to begin small businesses of their own by, among other steps, removing excessive regulations, disincentives for venture capital and other barriers erected by the government;

—bring strong, effective enforcement of federal civil rights statutes, especially those dealing with threats to physical safety and security which have recently been increasing; and

—ensure that the federal government follows a non-discriminatory system of appointments up and down the line, with a careful eye for qualified minority aspirants.

Hispanic-Americans

Hispanics are rapidly becoming the largest minority in the country and are one of the major pillars in our cultural, social, and economic life. Diverse in character, proud in heritage, they are greatly enriching the American melting pot.

Hispanics seek only the full rights of citizenship—in education, in law enforcement, in housing—and an equal opportunity to achieve economic security. Unfortunately, those desires have not always been fulfilled; as in so many other areas, the Carter Administration has been long on rhetoric and short on action in its approach to the Hispanic community.

We pledge to pursue policies that will help to make the opportunities of American life a reality for Hispanics. The economic policies enunciated in this platform will, we believe, create new jobs for Hispanic teenagers and adults and will also open up new business opportunities for them. We also believe there should be local educational programs which enable those who grew up learning another language such as Spanish to become proficient in English while also maintaining their own language and cultural heritage. Neither Hispanics nor any other American citizen should be barred from education or employment opportunities because English is not their first language.

The Handicapped

The Republican Party strongly believes that handicapped persons must be admitted into the mainstream of American society. It endorses efforts to enable our handicapped population to enjoy a useful and productive life.

Too often in the past, barriers have been raised to their education, employment, transportation, health care, housing, recreation, and insurance. We support a concerted national effort to eliminate discrimination in all these areas. Specifically we support tax incentives for the removal of architectural and transportation barriers. We pledge continued efforts to improve communications for the handicapped and to promote a healthy, constructive attitude toward them in our society.

Women's Rights

We acknowledge the legitimate efforts of those who support or oppose ratification of the Equal Rights Amendment.

We reaffirm our Party's historic commitment to equal rights and equality for women.

We support equal rights and equal opportunities for women, without taking away traditional rights of women such as exemption from the military draft. We support the enforcement of all equal opportunity laws and urge the elimination of discrimination against women. We oppose any move which would give the federal government more power over families.

Ratification of the Equal Rights Amendment is now in the hands of state legislatures, and the issues of the time extension and rescission are in the courts. The states have a constitutional right to accept or reject a constitutional amendment without federal interference or pressure. At the direction of the White House, federal departments launched pressure against states which refused to ratify ERA. Regardless of one's position on ERA, we demand that this practice cease.

At this time, women of America comprise 53 percent of the population and over 42 percent of the work force. By 1990, we anticipate that 51 percent of the population will be women, and there will be approximately 57 million in the work force. Therefore, the following urgent problems must be resolved:

—total integration of the work force (*not* separate but equal) is necessary to bring women equality in pay;

—girls and young women must be given improved early career counseling and job training to widen the opportunities for them in the world of work;

—women's worth in the society and in the jobs they hold, at home or in the workplace, must be re-evaluated to improve the conditions of women workers concentrated in low-status, low-paying jobs;

—equal opportunity for credit and other assistance must be assured to women in small businesses; and

—one of the most critical problems in our nation today is that of inadequate child care for the working mother. As champions of the free enterprise system, of the individual, and of the idea that the best solutions to most problems rest at the community level, Republicans must find ways to meet this, the working woman's need. The scope of this problem is fully realized only when it is understood that many female heads of households are at the poverty level and that they have a very large percentage of the nation's children.

The important secret about old age in America today is that it is primarily a woman's issue, and those over 65 are the fastest growing segment of the population. With current population trends, by the year 2020, 15.5 percent of our population will be over 65; by 2035, women in this age group will outnumber men by 13 million.

In 1980, 42 percent of women between 55 and 64 are in the work force. Half of the 6 million elderly women who live alone have incomes of $3,700 or less, and black women in that category have a median income of $2,600. How do they survive with the present rate of inflation? The lower salaries they earned as working women are now reflected in lower retirement benefits, if they have any at all. The Social Security system is still biased against women, and non-existent pension plans combine with that to produce a bereft elderly woman. The Republican Party must not and will not let this continue.

We reaffirm our belief in the traditional role and values of the family in our society. The damage being done today to the family takes its greatest toll on the woman. Whether it be through divorce, widowhood, economic problems, or the suffering of children, the impact is greatest on women. The importance of support for the mother and homemaker in maintaining the values of this country cannot be over-emphasized.

In other sections of this platform, we call for greater equity in the tax treatment of working spouses. We deplore this marriage tax which penalizes married two-worker families. We call for a reduction in the estate tax burden, which creates hardships for widows and minor children. We also pledge to address any remaining inequities in the treatment of women under the Social Security system.

Women know better than anyone the decline in the quality of life that is occurring in America today. The peril to the United States and especially to women must be stressed. Women understand domestic, consumer, economic issues more deeply because they usually manage the households and have the responsibility for them. With this responsibility must also come greater opportunity for achievement and total equality toward solution of problems.

Equal Rights

The truths we hold and the values we share affirm that no individual should be victimized by unfair discrimination because of race, sex, advanced age, physical handicap, difference of national origin or religion, or economic circumstance. However, equal opportunity should not be jeopardized by bureaucratic regulations and decisions which rely on quotas, ratios, and numerical requirements to exclude some individuals in favor of others, thereby rendering such regulations and decisions inherently discriminatory.

We pledge vigorous enforcement of laws to assure equal treatment in job recruitment, hiring promotion, pay, credit, mortgage access and housing.

Millions of Americans who trace their heritage to the nations of Eastern, Central, and Southern Europe have for too long seen their values neglected. The time has come to go beyond the ritual election year praise given to Ethnic Americans. We must make them an integral part of government. We must make recognition of their values an integral part of government policy. The Republican Party will take positive steps to see to it that these Americans, along with others too long neglected, have the opportunity to share the power, as well as the burdens of our society. The same holds true of our Asian-American citizens from the cultures of the Orient.

As a party we also recognize our commitment to Native Americans. We pledge to continue to honor our trusted relationship with them and we reaffirm our federal policy of self-determination. We support the assumption by Indians, Aleuts, and Eskimos themselves of the decisions and planning which will affect their lives and the end of undue federal influence on those plans and decisions.

Puerto Rico has been a territory of the United States since 1898. The Republican Party vigorously supports the right of the United States citizens of Puerto Rico to be admitted into the Union as a fully sovereign state after they freely so determine. We believe that the statehood alternative is the only logical solution to the problem of inequality of the United States citizens of Puerto Rico within the framework of the federal constitution, with full recognition within the concept of a multicultural society of the citizens' right to retain their Spanish language and traditions. Therefore we pledge to support the enactment of the necessary legislation to allow the people of Puerto Rico to exercise their right to apply for admission into the Union at the earliest possible date after the presidential election of 1980.

We also pledge that such decision of the people of Puerto Rico will be implemented through the approval of an admission bill. This bill will provide for the island's smooth transition from its territorial fiscal system to that of a member of the Union. This enactment will enable the new state of Puerto Rico to stand economically on an equal footing with the rest of the states and to assume gradually its fiscal responsibilities as a state.

We continue to favor whatever action may be necessary to permit American citizens resident in the United States territories of the Virgin Islands and Guam to vote for President and Vice President in national elections.

Abortion

There can be no doubt that the question of abortion, despite the complex nature of its various issues, is ultimately concerned with equality of rights under the law. While we recognize differing views on this question among Americans in general — and in our own Party — we affirm our support of a constitutional amendment to restore protection of the right to life for unborn children. We also support the Congressional efforts to restrict the use of taxpayers' dollars for abortion.

We protest the Supreme Court's intrusion into the family structure through its denial of the parents' obligation and right to guide their minor children.

STRONG FAMILIES

The family is the foundation of our social order. It is the school of democracy. Its daily lessons — cooperation, tolerance, mutual concern, responsibility, industry — are fundamental to the order and progress of our Republic. But the Democrats have shunted the family aside. They have given its power to the bureaucracy,

its jurisdiction to the courts, and its resources to government grantors. For the first time in our history, there is real concern that the family may not survive.

Government may be strong enough to destroy families, but it can never replace them.

Unlike the Democrats, we do not advocate new federal bureaucracies with ominous power to shape a national family order. Rather, we insist that all domestic policies, from child care and schooling to Social Security and the tax code, must be formulated with the family in mind.

Education

Next to religious training and the home, education is the most important means by which families hand down to each new generation their ideals and beliefs. It is a pillar of a free society. But today, parents are losing control of their children's schooling. The Democratic congress and its counterparts in many states have launched one fad after another, building huge new bureaucracies to misspend our taxes. The result has been a shocking drop in student performance, lack of basics in the classroom, forced busing, teacher strikes, manipulative and sometimes amoral indoctrination.

The Republican Party is determined to restore common sense and quality to education for the sake of all students, especially those for whom learning is the highway to equal opportunity. Because federal assistance should help local school districts, not tie them up in red tape, we will strive to replace the crazyquilt of wasteful programs with a system of block grants that will restore decisionmaking to local officials responsible to voters and parents. We recognize the need to preserve within the structure of block grants, special educational opportunities for the handicapped, the disadvantaged, and other needy students attending public and private non-profit elementary and secondary schools.

We hail the teachers of America. Their dedication to our children is often taken for granted, and they are frequently underpaid for long hours and selfless service, especially in comparison with other public employees.

We understand and sympathize with the plight of America's public school teachers, who so frequently find their time and attention diverted from their teaching responsibilities to the task of complying with federal reporting requirements. America has a great stake in maintaining standards of high quality in public education. The Republican Party recognizes that the achievement of those standards is possible only to the extent that teachers are allowed the time and freedom to teach. To that end, the Republican Party supports deregulation by the federal government of public education, and encourages the elimination of the federal Department of Education.

We further sympathize with the right of qualified teachers to be employed by any school district wishing to hire them, without the necessity of their becoming enrolled with any bargaining agency or group. We oppose any federal action, including any action on the part of the Department of Education to establish "agency shops" in public schools.

We support Republican initiatives in the Congress to restore the right of individuals to participate in voluntary, non-denominational prayer in schools and other public facilities. We applaud the action of the Senate in passing such legislation.

Our goal is quality education for all of America's children, with a special commitment to those who must overcome handicap, deprivation, or discrimination. That is why we condemn the forced busing of school children to achieve arbitrary racial quotas. Busing has been a prescription for disaster, blighting whole communities across the land with its divisive impact. It has failed to improve the quality of education, while diverting funds from programs that could make the difference between success and failure for the poor, the disabled, and minority children.

We must halt forced busing and get on with the education of all our children, focusing on the real causes of their problems, especially lack of economic opportunity.

Federal education policy must be based on the primacy of parental rights and responsibility. Toward that end, we reaffirm our support for a system of educational assistance based on tax credits that will in part compensate parents for their financial sacrifices in paying tuition at the elementary, secondary, and postsecondary level. This is a matter of fairness, especially for low-income families, most of whom would be free for the first time to choose for their children those schools which best correspond to their own cultural and moral values. In this way, the schools will be strengthened by the families' involvement, and the families' strengths will be reinforced by supportive cultural institutions.

We are dismayed that the Carter Administration cruelly reneged on promises made during the 1976 campaign. Wielding the threat of his veto, Mr. Carter led the fight against Republican attempts to make tuition tax credits a reality.

Next year, a Republican White House will assist, not sabotage, congressional efforts to enact tuition tax relief into the law.

We will halt the unconstitutional regulatory vendetta launched by Mr. Carter's IRS Commissioner against independent schools.

We will hold the federal bureaucracy accountable for its harassment of colleges and universities and will clear away the tangle of regulation that has unconscionably driven up their expenses and tuitions. We will respect the rights of state and local authorities in the management of their school systems.

The commitment of the American people to provide educational opportunities for all has resulted in a tremendous expansion of schools at all levels. And the more we reduce the federal proportion of taxation, the more resources will be left to sustain and develop state and local institutions.

Health

Our country's unequalled system of medical care, bringing greater benefits to more people than anywhere else on earth, is a splendid example of how Americans have taken care of their own needs with private institutions.

Significant as these achievements are, we must not be complacent. Health care costs continue to rise, farther and faster than they should, and threaten to spiral beyond the reach of many families. The causes are the Democratic Congress' inflationary spending and excessive and expensive regulations.

Republicans unequivocally oppose socialized medicine, in whatever guise it is presented by the Democratic Party. We reject the creation of a national health service and all proposals for compulsory national health insurance.

Our country has made spectacular gains in health care in recent decades. Most families are now covered by private insurance, Medicare, or in the case of the poor, the entirely free services under Medicaid.

Republicans recognize that many health care problems can be solved if government will work closely with the private sector to find remedies that will enhance our current system of excellent care. We applaud, as an example, the voluntary effort which has been undertaken by our nation's hospitals to control costs. The results have been encouraging. More remains to be done.

What ails American medicine is government meddling and the strait-jacket of federal programs. The prescription for good health care is deregulation and an emphasis upon consumer rights and patient choice.

As consumers of health care, individual Americans and their families should be able to make their own choices about health care protection. We propose to assist them in so doing through tax and financial incentives. These could enable them to choose their own health coverage, including protection from the catastrophic costs of major long-term illness, without compulsory regimentation.

Americans should be protected against financial

disaster brought on by medical expense. We recognize both the need to provide assistance in many cases and the responsibility of citizens to provide for their own needs. By using tax incentives and reforming federal medical assistance programs, government and the private sector can jointly develop compassionate and innovative means to provide financial relief when it is most needed.

We endorse alternatives to institutional care. Not only is it costly but it also separates individuals from the supportive environment of family and friends. This is especially important for the elderly and those requiring long-term care. We advocate the reform of Medicare to encourage home-based care whenever feasible. In addition, we encourage the development of innovative alternate health care delivery systems and other out-patient services at the local level.

We must maintain our commitment to the aged and to the poor by providing quality care through Medicare and Medicaid. These programs need the careful, detailed reevaluation they have never received from the Democrats, who have characteristically neglected their financial stability. We believe that the needs of those who depend upon their programs, particularly the elderly, can be better served, especially when a Republican Administration cracks down on fraud and abuse so that program monies can be directed toward those truly in need. In the case of Medicaid, we will aid the states in restoring its financial integrity and its local direction.

We welcome the long-overdue emphasis on preventive health care and physical fitness that is making Americans more aware than ever of their personal responsibility for good health. Today's enthusiasm and emphasis on staying well holds the promise of dramatically improved health and well-being in the decades ahead. Additionally, health professionals, as well as individuals have long recognized that preventing illness or injury is much less expensive than treating it. Therefore, preventive medicine combined with good personal health habits and health education, can make a major impact on the cost of health care. Employers and employees, unions and business associations, families, schools, and neighborhood groups all have important parts in what is becoming a national crusade for better living.

Youth

The Republican Party recognizes that young people want the opportunity to exercise the rights and responsibilities of adults.

The Republican agenda for making educational and employment opportunities available to our youth has been addressed in detail in other sections of this platform.

Republicans are committed to the enactment of a youth differential in the minimum wage and other vitally needed incentives for the creation of jobs for our young.

In addition, we reaffirm our commitment to broaden the involvement of young people in all phases of the political process—as voters, party workers and leaders, candidates and elected officials, and participants in government at all levels.

We pledge, as we have elsewhere in this platform, efforts to create an environment which will enable our nation's youth:

—to live in a society which is safe and free;

—to pursue personal, educational, and vocational goals to the utmost of their abilities;

—to experience the support, encouragement, and strength that comes from maintenance of the family and its values; and

—to know the stimulus of challenge, renewal through encouragement, provision of opportunities, and the growth that comes from responsible participation in numerous aspects of our society.

Older Americans

Inflation is called "the cruelest tax." It strikes most cruelly at the elderly, especially those on fixed incomes. It strikes viciously at the sick and the infirm, and those who are alone in the world.

Inflation has robbed our elderly of dignity and security. An entire generation of responsible and productive citizens who toiled and saved a full working life to build up a retirement nest egg now finds that it cannot survive on its savings. Today's inflaton rates dwarf yesterday's interest rates, and the pensions and annuities of our elderly citizens cannot keep up with the rising cost of living. Millions of once-proud and independent elderly Americans face a future of welfare dependency and despair.

We propose to assist families, and individuals of all ages, to meet the needs of the elderly, primarily through vigorous private initiative. Only a comprehensive reduction in tax rates will enable families to save for retirement income, and to protect that income from ravaging inflation. Only new tax exemptions and incentives can make it possible for many families to afford to care for their older members at home.

Present laws can create obstacles to older Americans' remaining in the family home. Federal programs for the elderly, such as Medicare and Supplemental Security Income, must address, humanely and generously, the special circumstances of those who choose to stay with their families rather than enter a nursing home or other institution.

Social Security is one of this nation's most vital commitments to our senior citizens. We commit the Republican Party to first save, and then strengthen, this fundamental contract between our government and its productive citizens.

Republicans consider older Americans a community asset, not a national problem. We are committed to using the sadly wasted talents of the aged throughout our society, which sorely needs their experience and wisdom. To that end, and as a matter of basic fairness, we proudly reaffirm our opposition to mandatory retirement and our long-standing Republican commitment to end the Democrats' earnings limitation upon Social Security benefits. In addition, the Republican Party is strongly opposed to the taxation of the Social Security benefits and we pledge to oppose any attempts to tax these benefits.

Republicans have resisted Democratic electioneering schemes to spend away the Social Security trust funds for political purposes. Now the bill has come due, and the workers of America are staggering under their new tax burdens. This must stop.

Precisely because Social Security is a precious lifeline for millions of the elderly, orphaned, and disabled, we insist that its financing be sound and stable. We will preserve Social Security for its original purpose.

The problems of Social Security financing are only an aspect of the overriding problems of the economy which Democratic mismanagement has produced. There is but one answer, the comprehensive tax rate reduction to which Republicans are committed. To save Social Security, we have no choice but to redirect our economy toward growth. To meet this country's commitments to Social Security recipients, present and future, we need more people at work, earning more money, thereby paying more into the trust funds. That same growth can balance the federal budget with lower taxes, over time reducing inflation, which falls so cruelly on senior citizens whose income is fixed by the size of their public or private pension.

We pledge to clean up the much-abused disability system. We will also expand eligibility for Individual Retirement Accounts to enable more persons to plan for their retirement years.

The Welfare System

The Republican agenda for welfare reform has been discussed in a previous section, but we think it important to stress that central to it is the preservation of the families the system is designed to serve. The current system does not do this. Neither would guaranteed annual income schemes. By supplanting parental responsibility and by denying children parental guidance and economic support, they encourage and reward the fragmentation of families. This is unconscionable. The values and strengths of the family

provide a vital element in breaking the bonds of poverty.

Ultimately, the Republican Party supports the orderly, wholesale transfer of all welfare functions to the states along with the tax sources to finance them.

The Family Economy

It is increasingly common for both husbands and wives to work outside the home. Often, it occurs out of economic necessity, and it creates major difficulties for families with children, especially those of pre-school age. On one hand, they are striving to improve the economic well-being of their family; on the other, they are concerned about the physical and emotional well-being of their children. This dilemma is further aggravated in instances of single parenthood due to death or divorce.

Recognizing these problems, we pledge to increase the availability of non-institutional child care. We see a special role for local, private organizations in meeting this need.

We disapprove of the bias in the federal tax system against working spouses, whose combined incomes are taxed at a proportionately higher rate than if they were single. We deplore this "marriage tax" and call for equity in the tax treatment of families.

We applaud our society's increasing awareness of the role of homemakers in the economy, not apart from the work force but as a very special part of it: the part that combines the labor of a full-time job, the skills of a profession, and the commitment of the most dedicated volunteer. Recognizing that homemaking is as important as any other profession, we endorse expanded eligibility for Individual Retirement Accounts for homemakers and will explore other ways to advance their standing and security.

Family Protection

In view of the continuing efforts of the present Administration to define and influence the family through such federally funded conferences as the White House Conference on Families, we express our support for legislation protecting and defending the traditional American family against the ongoing erosion of its base in our society.

Handicapped People

Republicans will seek every effective means to enable families more easily to assist their handicapped members and to provide for their education and special medical and therapeutic needs. In the case of handicapped children particularly, flexibility must be maintained in programs of public assistance so that, whenever possible, these youngsters may remain at home rather than in institutions.

Targeted tax relief can make it possible for parents to keep such a child at home without foregoing essential professional assistance. Similarly, tax incentives can assist those outside the home, in the neighborhood and the workplace, who undertake to train, hire, or house the handicapped.

SECURE AND PROSPEROUS NEIGHBORHOODS

The quality of American neighborhoods is the ultimate test of the success or failure of government policies for the cities, for housing, and for law enforcement.

Obsessed with the demands of special interest groups and preoccupied with the design of expensive "comprehensive" programs, the Democrats in Congress and the Administration have lost sight of that simple but important criterion. They have proposed more social and fiscal tinkering with our cities and towns.

Republicans will address the real problems that face Americans in their neighborhoods day by day—deterioration and urban blight, dangerous streets and violent crime that make millions of Americans, especially senior citizens, fearful in their own neighborhoods and prisoners in their own homes.

In the summer of 1980, Americans suffer a rising national unemployment rate, now at nearly 8 percent, and double-digit inflation and interest rates. As Republicans meet in Detroit, the policies of the Carter Administration and the Democratic Congress have pushed the economy into recession and have resulted in unemployment approaching 20 percent in our host city.

The people of Detroit have worked long and hard to revitalize their city and the evidence of its rebirth is impressive. Their efforts have been severely set back by Carter Administration policies outside of this or any city's control. The grim evidence is manifested in jobs lost as a direct consequence of bankrupt economic policies which have fostered this recession. Republicans will address and resolve the real problems of today's economy, problems that destroy jobs and deny even the hope of homeownership to millions of American families. We are, moreover, committed to nurturing the spirit of self-help and cooperation through which so many neighborhoods have revitalized themselves and served their residents.

Neighborhood Self-help

The American ethic of neighbor helping neighbor has been an essential factor in the building of our nation. Republicans are committed to the preservation of this great tradition.

To help non-governmental community programs aid in serving the needs of poor, disabled, or other disadvantaged, we support permitting taxpayers to deduct charitable contributions from their federal income tax whether they itemize or not.

In contrast, the Democrats' assault against Meals-on-Wheels highlights their insensitivity to the neighborly spirit that motivates so many Americans. For over 25 years, voluntary Meals-on-Wheels organizations have been feeding needy homebound citizens—usually the elderly—with funding from local private charitable sources. Promising for the first time to "help" these neighborhood volunteer efforts in 1978, the Democratic Congress and administration instead used the carrot of federal funding and the stick of federal regulation to crowd out private ventures.

Government must never elbow aside private institutions—schools, churches, volunteer groups, labor and professional associations—in meeting the social needs in our neighborhoods and communities.

Neighborhood Revitalization

The city is the focus for the lives of millions of Americans. Its neighborhoods are places of familiarity, of belonging, of tradition and continuity. They are arenas for civic action and creative self-help. The human scale of the neighborhood encourages citizens to exercise leadership, to invest their talents, energies, and resources, to work together to create a better life for their families.

Republican economic programs will create conditions for rebirth of citizen activity in neighborhoods and cities across the land. In a Republican economic climate, America's cities can once again produce, build, and grow.

A Republican Administration will focus its efforts to revitalize neighborhoods in five areas. We will:

—cut taxes, increase incentives to save, restore sound money, and stimulate capital investment to create jobs;

—create and apply new tax incentives for employees and employers alike to stimulate economic growth and reduce red tape for business ventures. Local government will be invited to designate specific depressed areas as job and enterprise zones;

—encourage our cities to undertake neighborhood revitalization and preservation programs in cooperation with the three essential local interests: local government, neighborhood property owners and residents, and local financial institutions;

—replace the categorical aid programs with block grant or revenue sharing programs and, where appropriate, transfer the programs, along with the tax sources to pay for them, back to the state and local governments; and

—remain fully committed to the fair enforcement of all federal civil rights statutes and continue minority business enterprise and similar programs begun by Republican Administrations but bungled by over-regulation and duplicaton during the Carter Administration.

Republican programs will revitalize the inner cities. New jobs will be created. The federal government's role will be substantially reduced. The individual citizen will reclaim his or her independence.

The revitalization of American cities will proceed from the revitalization of the neighborhoods. Cities and neighborhoods are no more nor less than the people who inhabit them. Their strengths and weaknesses provide their character. If they are to grow, it is the people who must seize the initiative and lead.

Housing and Homeownership

Our citizens must have a real opportunity to live in decent, affordable housing. Due to the disastrous policies of the Carter Administration and the Democratic Congress, however, the goal of homeownership and all that aspiration entails is now in jeopardy. These irrational policies have been catastrophic to the housing industry. The highest home mortgage interest rates in the history of the United States have depressed housing starts to the lowest level since World War II. Democratic policies guarantee shortages in owner-occupied and rental housing.

As many as 1.4 million people who depend upon homebuilding for work may lose their jobs in this recession. Many already have. In addition to the toll taken on millions of American families, intolerable pressures will build on state, local, and federal budgets as tax revenues decline and expenditures increase to aid the unemployed.

We support financing and tax incentives to encourage the construction of rental housing as an essential addition to our housing inventory.

Prospective first-time home buyers simply cannot afford to buy. The affordability of housing has become a crisis. The high rates of inflation have driven mortgage payments, house prices, and down-payment requirements beyond the means of close to 80 percent of young American families. In order to assist the record number of young families who wish to become home buyers, we propose to implement a young family housing initiative, which would include several elements such as: urban homesteading, savings and tax reforms, and innovative alternate mortgage instruments to help meet monthly payment requirements

without federal subsidies. To assist older homeowners, again without federal subsidy, we urge more extensive availability of the reverse annuity mortgage which allows older homeowners to withdraw the substantial equity they have built up in their homes and thus supplement their retirement income. In order to slow increases in housing costs, regulations which artificially limit housing production and raise housing costs must be eliminated.

We favor expansion of the Republican-sponsored urban homesteading program as a means of restoring abandoned housing. This innovative program is locally administered, returns property to the tax rolls, and develops new ownership and stability within our neighborhoods.

The collapse of new home production and the distress of the housing finance system are closely related. The stop and go economic policies of the past year have created extreme volatility in financial markets which have made it impossible for thrift institutions to supply housing credit at a reasonable cost.

A set of policies aimed at higher and more stable levels of housing production will simultaneously reduce housing costs and unemployment in the economy. To assure a stable and continuous flow of funds for home mortgage financing, we pledge to allow responsible use of mortgage revenue bonds. We will work to change the tax laws to encourage savings so that young families will be able to afford their dreams.

Specifically, we will support legislation to lower tax rates on savings in order to increase funds available for housing. This will help particularly to make homeownership an accessible dream for younger families, encouraging them not to despair of ever having a home of their own, but to begin working and saving for it now. We oppose any attempt to end the income tax deductability of mortgage interest and property taxes.

Republicans will also end the mismanagement and waste that has characterized the Department of Housing and Urban Development during the Carter Administration. As presently structured, HUD programs present local governments and developers with a maze of bureaucracy, complicated applications, and inflexible requirements, often unsuited to local needs. Such programs often infringe upon the right of local government to retain jurisdiction over their own zoning laws and building codes. As a result, their cost is so high that relatively few of the needy are ultimately housed or helped. Republicans will replace many of HUD's categorical programs with decentralized block grants to provide more efficient and responsive housing assistance to the elderly, the handicapped, and the poor. In remaining programs, particular emphasis should be given to rehabilitation and preservation of existing housing stock as a priority in federal housing policy.

Crime

Safety and security are vital to the health and well-being of people in their neighborhoods and communities. Republicans are committed to ensuring that neighborhoods will be safe places in which families and individuals can live, and we support and encourage community crime fighting efforts such as neighborhood crime watch and court monitoring programs.

First, we believe that Republican economic proposals, more particularly those proposals which strengthen society and smaller communities discussed elsewhere in this document, will go a long way toward stabilizing American society.

Second, we support a vigorous and effective effort on the part of law enforcement agencies. Although we recognize the vital role of federal law enforcement agencies, we realize that the most effective weapons against crime are state and local agencies.

Just as vital to efforts to stem crime is the fair but firm and speedy application of criminal penalties. The existence and application of strong penalties are effective disincentives to criminal actions. Yet these disincentives will only be as strong as our court system's willingness to use them.

We believe that the death penalty serves as an effective deterrent to capital crime and should be applied by the federal government and by states which approve it as an appropriate penalty for certain major crimes.

We believe the right of citizens to keep and bear arms must be preserved. Accordingly, we oppose federal registration of firearms. Mandatory sentences for commission of armed felonies are the most effective means to deter abuse of this right. We therefore support Congressional initiatives to remove those provisions of the Gun Control Act of 1968 that do not significantly impact on crime but serve rather to restrain the law-abiding citizen in his legitimate use of firearms.

In recent years, a murderous epidemic of drug abuse has swept our country. Mr. Carter, through his policies and his personnel, has demonstrated little interest in stopping its ravages. Republicans consider drug abuse an intolerable threat to our society, especially to the young. We pledge a government that will take seriously its responsibility to curb illegal drug traffic. We will first and most urgently restore the ability of the FBI to act effectively in this area. Republican government will work with local law enforcement agencies to apprehend and firmly punish drug pushers and drug smugglers, with mandatory sentences where appropriate. We support efforts to crack down on the sale and advertising of drug paraphernalia. Private, non-profit drug abuse rehabilitation agencies have taken the lead in fighting drug abuse, and they deserve greater cooperation and flexibility from federal, state, and local agencies and grant programs. We pledge the enactment of legislation to ban the utilization of federal funds by grantees of the Legal Services Corporation to render their services in cases involving the pushing or smuggling of drugs as well as in cases of repeat offenders. We commend the religious leaders, community activists, parents, and local officials who are working with fervor and dedication to protect young Americans from the drug plague.

Urban Transportation

The complex problems of mobility, congestion, and energy resources demand creative solutions if we are to improve the living conditions of our urban areas. Many urban centers of our nation need dependable and affordable mass transit systems. The first line of responsibility must lie with the local governments. They must be given the latitude to design and implement the transportation system best suited to their singular circumstances. Republicans believe we should encourage effective competition among diverse modes of transportation. The role of the federal government should be one of giving financial and technical support to local authorities, through surface transportation block grants. Because of the long planning and construction times inherent in bus, rail, and other mass transit systems, a consistent and dependable source of revenue should be established.

Mass transportation offers the prospect for significant energy conservation. In addition, both management and labor agree that ease of access to the workplace is an important factor in employment decisions and industrial plant locations. Lack of adequate access is a major reason why businesses have moved out of crowded urban areas, resulting in lower tax bases for cities. To encourage existing businesses to remain in urban centers and to attract new businesses to urban areas, it is vital that adequate public and private transportation facilities be provided.

Rural Transportation

Republicans recognize the importance of transportation in the rural areas of America.

Public transit is becoming more significant to rural areas as the costs of energy rise. While public transit will not replace the importance of private vehicles in rural America, it can serve as a vital adjunct to transportation in the neighborhoods throughout rural America.

JOBS AND THE WORKPLACE

We propose to put Americans back to work again by restoring real growth without inflation to the United States economy. Republican programs and initiatives detailed in this platform will create millions of additional new jobs in the American workplace. As a result of Mr. Carter's recession, more than 8 million Americans are now out of work.

Sweeping change in America's economic policy is needed. We must replace the Carter Administration's promise of hard times and austerity—one promise which has been kept—with Republican policies that restore economic growth and create more jobs.

The Democratic Congress and the Carter Administration are espousing programs that candidate Carter in 1976 said were inhumane: using recession, unemployment, high interest rates, and high taxes to fight inflation. The Democrats are now trying to stop inflation with a recession, a bankrupt policy which is throwing millions of Americans out of work. They say Americans must tighten their belts, abandon their dreams, and accept higher taxes, less take-home pay, fewer jobs, and no growth in the national economy.

We categorically reject this approach. Inflation is too much money chasing too few goods. Shutting down our nation's factories and throwing millions of people out of work leads only to shortages and higher prices.

We believe inflation can only be controlled by monetary and spending restraint, combined with sharp reductions in the tax and regulatory barriers to savings, investments, production, and jobs.

The Need for Growth and Its Impact on Workers

The Republican Party believes nothing is more important to our nation's defense and social well-being than economic growth.

Since 1973, the U.S. economy has grown in real terms at a rate of only 1.9 percent a year. This is barely half of the 3.7 percent annual growth rate we experienced between 1950 and 1973 and well below the 4.6 percent growth rate we enjoyed between 1961 and 1969. If our economy continues to grow at our current rate of less than 2 percent a year, our Gross National Product (GNP) will barely reach $3 trillion by 1990.

But if we can regain the growth we experienced during the economic boom of the 1960s, our GNP will reach nearly $4 trillion by the end of the decade, nearly one-third higher.

With this kind of economic growth, incomes would be substantially higher and jobs would be plentiful. Federal revenues would be high enough to provide for a balanced budget, adequate funding of health, education and social spending, and unquestioned military preeminence, with enough left over to reduce payroll and income taxes on American workers and retirees. Economic growth would generate price stability as the expanding economy eliminated budget deficits and avoided pressure on the Federal Reserve to create more money. And the social gains from economic growth would be enormous. Faster growth, higher incomes, and plentiful jobs are exactly what the unemployed, the underprivileged, and minorities have been seeking for many years.

All working men and women of America have much to gain from economic growth and a healthy business environment. It enhances their bargaining position by fostering competition among potential employers to provide more attractive working conditions, better retirement and health benefits, higher wages and salaries, and generally improving job security. A stagnant economy, which Democratic policies have brought about, decreases competition among business for workers, discourages improved employee benefits, reduces income levels, and dramatically increases unemployment.

Savings, Productivity, and Jobs

Savings and investment are the keys to economic growth. Only that part of national income which goes into savings and which is not consumed by government deficits is available to finance real economic growth.

Americans now save less than any other people in the Western world because inflation and the high rates of taxation imposed by the Carter Administration and the Democratic Congress have destroyed their ability and incentive to save and invest. This has strangled economic growth, choked off private initiative, pushed up prices, and retarded productivity and job creation.

The sharp drop in the growth of American productivity is the main reason why Americans' average real weekly earnings are no more than they were 19 years ago. This problem has worsened to the point that workers earn 8 percent less in real purchasing power as the Carter term comes to a close than they did when it began.

The 25 years of Democratic domination of the Congress have cost us a generation of lost opportunities.

The Carter Administration in particular has opposed every Republican effort to restore the health of the economy through lower taxes and work efforts, savings, and the modernization of America's productive machinery.

Republicans are committed to an economic policy based on lower tax rates and a reduced rate of government spending.

Therefore, the Republican Party pledges to:

—reduce tax rates on individuals and businesses to increase incentives for all Americans and to encourage more savings, investment, output and productivity, and more jobs for Americans;

—provide special incentives for savings by lowering the tax rates on savings and investment income;

—revitalize our productive capacities by simplifying and accelerating tax depreciation schedules for facilities, structures, equipment, and vehicles;

—limit government spending to a fixed and smaller percentage of the Gross National Product; and

—balance the budget without tax increases at these lower levels of taxation and spending.

We also oppose Carter proposals to impose withholding on dividend and interest income. They would serve as a disincentive to save and invest and create needless paperwork burdens for government, business, industry, and the private citizen. They would literally rob the saver of the benefits of interest compounding and automatic dividend reinvestment programs.

Unless taxes are reduced and federal spending is restrained, our nation's economy faces continued inflation, recession, and economic stagnation. Tax rate reductions and spending restraint will restore the savings and investment needed to create new jobs, increase living standards, and restore our competitive position in the world.

Employment Safety-net

To those individuals who have lost their jobs because of the Carter recession we pledge to insure that they receive their rightfully earned unemployment compensation benefits.

The Republican Party recognizes the need to provide workers who have lost their jobs because of technological obsolescence or imports the opportunity to adjust to changing economic conditions. In particular, we will seek ways to assist workers threatened by foreign competition.

The Democratic Administration's inability to ensure fairness and equity between our nation and some of our trading partners has resulted in massive unemployment in many core industries. As we meet in Detroit, this Party takes special notice that among the

hardest hit have been the automotive workers whose jobs are now targeted by aggressive foreign competition. Much of this problem is a result of the present Administration's inability to negotiate foreign trade agreements which do not jeopardize American jobs. We will take steps to ensure competitiveness of our domestic industries to protect American jobs. But for workers who have already lost their jobs, we will provide assistance, incentives for job retraining and placement, and job search and relocation allowances. Toward this end, we will pursue specific tax and regulatory changes to revitalize America's troubled basic industries. We will also seek the aid of private individuals, businesses, and non-profit organizations to formulate creative new self-supporting answers to training and placement problems as well as nongovernmental sources of temporary financial support.

The Republican Party believes that protectionist tariffs and quotas are detrimental to our economic well-being. Nevertheless, we insist that our trading partners offer our nation the same level of equity, access, and fairness that we have shown them. The mutual benefits of trade require that it be conducted in the spirit of reciprocity. The Republican Party will consider appropriate measures necessary to restore equal and fair competition between ourselves and our trading partners.

The international exchange of goods and services must take place under free and unfettered conditions of market entry.

Training and Skills

Unemployment is a growing problem for millions of Americans, but it is an unparalleled disaster for minority Americans. As this country's economic growth has slowed over the past decade, unemployment has become more intractable. The gravity of the crisis is so severe that as we entered the present recession, unemployment was over 6 percent for the entire labor force but it was 33 percent for minority youth. In addition, the black unemployment rate was 10.8 percent and youth between the ages of 16 and 24 continued to account for about one-half of the total unemployed.

Despite the almost $100 billion spent on well-intended public sector employment and training programs, the structural unemployment problem continues to fester among minorities and young people. In addition to providing a growth climate for job creation, specific and targeted programs must be developed to alleviate these problems.

Since four out of every five jobs are in the private sector, the success of federal employment efforts is dependent on private sector participation. It must be recognized as the ultimate location for unsubsidized jobs, as the provider of means to attain this end, and as an active participant in the formulation of employment and training policies on the local and national level. Throughout America, the private and independent sectors have repeatedly helped in the creation of minority business through donated counseling and consulting services. They have encouraged equal opportunity hiring practices within their own industries and have built non-profit, self-supporting training centers where the products produced during training are sold to support the programs.

A coordinated approach needs to be developed which maximizes the use of existing community resources, offers adequate incentives to the private sector, focuses on both large and small business, and minimizes red tape.

In recognizing the seriousness of the youth employment problem, Republicans also realize that a job alone will do very little to move a disadvantaged young person beyond the poverty line. Republicans support the creation of comprehensive programs for disadvantaged youth which would offer pre-employment training, educational instruction, job placement, and retention services. Second, Republicans support efforts to establish and maintain programs which seek to match the needs of the private sector and our young people as efficiently and effectively as possible. We also support expansion of proven skill training practices, such as apprenticeship, as well as private schools and trade schools. These methods can provide quality training and point toward the acquisition of specific job skills leading to specific employment goals.

We will encourage and foster the growth of new organizations operated by public-private partnerships to help forge a closer link between the schools and private employers. These institutions can afford in-school and out-of-school disadvantaged youth with the opportunity to upgrade basic skills, acquire work habits and orientation to work, and move directly from successful completion of the program to private unsubsidized jobs.

We believe that present laws create additional barriers for unemployed youth. One of the keys to resolving the youth unemployment problem is to reduce the cost to private employers for hiring young people who lack the necessary skills and experience to become immediately productive. Unfortunately, current government policy makes it too expensive for employers to hire unskilled youths. We urge a reduction of payroll tax rates, a youth differential for the minimum wage, and alleviation of other costs of employment until a young person can be a productive employee.

Small Business

Small business is the backbone of the American economy, with unique strengths and problems which must be recognized and addressed. For more than half of all American workers, the workplace is a small business. Small business is family business both in the sense that many of them are owned and operated by single families, and also because most American families rely not only on the goods and services, but on the jobs produced there for their livelihood and standard of living.

Republicans have demonstrated their sensitivity to the problems of the small business community. The Carter Administration held a conference to learn what Republicans have long known. In the Congress, we have been working to pass legislation to solve small business problems and achieve the very goals later identified by that conference. A 1978 initiative by the late Representative Bill Steiger reduced the capital gains tax rates which were destroying capital formation in America. Under the leadership of Republicans in Congress, efforts to simplify and liberalize the restrictive depreciation schedule are a top priority. Another proposal long advocated by our Party is the drive to encourage the entrepreneur by reform of the regulatory laws which stifle the very life of business through fines, threats, and harassment. Republicans realize the immediate necessity of reducing the regulatory burden to give small business a fighting chance against the federal agencies. We believe that wherever feasible, small business should be exempt from regulations and, where exemption is not feasible, small business should be subject to a less onerous tier of regulation. We have offered legislation to reimburse small businessmen who successfully challenge the federal government in court. Republicans believe the number one priority for small business in America is the achievement of lower business and personal tax rates for small businessmen and women and we intend to work to secure them.

All of these initiatives will receive immediate attention from a Republican Administration and Congress. Without such changes as these, the small entrepreneur, who takes the risks which help make the economy grow and provides over 90 percent of all new jobs annually, will be an endangered species.

By fostering small business growth, we are promoting permanent private sector solutions to the unemployment problem. We will continue to provide for small business needs by enacting a substantial increase in the surtax exemption. The heavy estate tax burden imposed on the American people is threatening the life savings of millions of our families, forcing spouses and children to sell their homes, businesses, and family farms to pay the estate taxes. To encourage continuity of family ownership, we will seek to ease this tax burden on all Americans and abolish excessive inheritance taxes to allow families to retain and pass on their small businesses and family farms.

We will reform the patent laws to facilitate innovation and we will further this goal by encouraging a greater share of federal research and development be done by small business. Finally, we will reform those tax laws which make it more profitable to break up a small business or merge it into a conglomerate, than to allow it to grow and develop as an independent business.

Fairness to the Worker

The Republican Party is committed to full employment without inflation. We will seek to provide more jobs, increase the standard of living, and ensure equitable treatment on the job for all American workers by stimulating economic growth.

We reaffirm our commitment to the fundamental principle of fairness in labor relations, including the legal right of unions to organize workers and to represent them through collective bargaining consistent with state laws and free from unnecessary government involvement. We applaud the mutual efforts of labor and management to improve the quality of work life.

Wage demands today often represent the attempt of working men and women to catch up with government-caused inflation and high tax rates. With the blessing of the Democrat's majority in Congress, the Council on Wage and Price Stability has put a de facto ceiling of 7 to 8.5 percent on workers' wages, while the Administration devalues their paychecks at a rate of 13 to 15 percent. The government, not the worker, is the principle cause of inflation.

We recognize the need for governmental oversight of the health and safety of the workplace, without interfering in the economic well-being of employers or the job security of workers.

The Republican Party reaffirms its long-standing support for the right of states to enact "Right-to-Work" laws under section 14(b) of the Taft-Hartley Act.

The political freedom of every worker must be protected. Therefore the Republican Party strongly supports protections against the practice of using compulsory dues and fees for partisan political purposes.

Fairness to the Consumer

The Republican Party shares the concerns of consumers that there be full disclosure and fairness in the marketplace. We recognize that government regulation and taxes add significantly to costs of goods and services to the consumer, reducing the standard of living for all Americans. For example, safety and environmental standards, some of which are counterproductive, increase the average price of a new car by over $700. Compliance with those regulations alone costs motorists as much as $12 billion a year.

Fairness to the consumer, like fairness to the employer and the worker, requires that government perform certain limited functions and enforce certain safeguards to ensure that equity, free competition, and safety exist in the free market economy. However, government action is not itself the solution to consumer problems; in fact, it has become in large measure a part of the problem. By consistent enforcement of law and enhancement of fair competition, government can and should help the consumer.

An informed consumer making economic choices and decisions in the marketplace is the best regulator of the free enterprise system. Consumers are also taxpayers, workers, investors, shoppers, farmers, and producers. The Republican Party recognizes the need for consumer protection but feels that such protection will not be enhanced by the creation of a new consumer protection bureaucracy. Just as there can be no single monolithic consumer viewpoint, so the Republican Party opposes the funding of special self-proclaimed advocates to represent consumer interests in federal agency proceedings.

Fairness to the Employer

The Republican Party declares war on government overregulation. We pledge to cut down on federal paperwork, cut out excessive regulation, and cut back the bloated bureaucracy.

In addressing these problems we recognize that overregulation is particularly harmful to America's small businesses whose survival is often threatened by the excessive costs of complying with government rules and handling federal paperwork.

While we recognize the role of the federal government in establishing certain minimum standards designed to improve the quality of life in America, we reaffirm our conviction that these standards can best be attained through innovative efforts of American business without the federal government mandating the methods of attainment.

The extraordinary growth of government, particularly since the middle 1960s, has brought mounting costs to society which, in turn, have added to inflationary pressures, reduced productivity, discouraged new investment, destroyed jobs, and increased bureaucratic intrusion into everyday life.

Regulatory costs are now running in excess of $100 billion each year, or about $1,800 for every American family. Federal paperwork annually costs businesses from $25 to $32 billion. According to official figures, it takes individuals and business firms over 143 million man-hours to complete 4,400 different federal forms each year. Government regulation produces many indirect, immeasurable costs as well and has led to increased bureaucratization of industry. Regulation also restricts personal choices, tends to undermine America's democratic public institutions, and threatens to destroy the private, competitive free market economy it was originally designed to protect.

Government Reform

In the face of a crisis of overregulation, the Carter Administration and the Democrats who control Congress have failed to recognize the problems facing workers, employers, and consumers and seem unable to come to grips with the underlying causes. While belatedly supporting transportation deregulation programs initiated by previous Republican Administrations, they have embarked on ambitious new schemes to tighten Washington's hold on energy and education. They have ignored or sidetracked Republican proposals to eliminate wasteful and outmoded spending programs and regulations. They have combined to push through more legislation and create additional programs which expand the size and power of the federal bureaucracy at the expense of ordinary taxpayers, consumers and businesses. In contradiction to 1976 Carter campaign promises to cut back on regulation, the number of pages in the *Federal Register* devoted to new rules and regulations has increased from 57,072 in 1976 to 77,497 in 1979 and will approach 90,000 by the end of 1980.

The result of Democratic rule in both the White House and the Congress is that government power has grown unchecked. Excessive regulation remains a major component of our nation's spiraling inflation and continues to stifle private initiative, individual freedom, and state and local government automony.

The Republican Party pledges itself to a comprehensive program of government reform. We propose to enact a temporary moratorium on all new federal regulations that diminish the supply of goods and services and add significantly to inflation. Such a moratorium will be consistent with the goal of achieving a safe and healthy working environment. We shall work to reduce substantially the regulatory and paperwork burdens on small businesses.

We encourage management and labor to form joint safety and health committees to make the workplace a better place to produce goods and services. At the same time we believe that the arbitrary and high-handed tactics used by OSHA bureaucrats must end. OSHA should concentrate its resources on encouraging voluntary compliance by employers and monitoring situations where close federal supervision is needed and serious hazards are most likely to occur. OSHA should be required to consult with, advise, and assist businesses in coping with the regulatory burden before imposing any penalty for non-compliance. Small businesses and employers with good safety records should be exempt from safety inspections, and penalties should be increased for those with consistently poor performance.

AGRICULTURE

In no American workplace is there to be found greater productivity, cooperation, neighborly concern, creative use of applied science, information and relevant research, honesty, perseverence, hard work, and independence than on the farm and ranch.

The Republican Party takes pride in the ability of American farmers to provide abundant, high quality, and nutritious food and fiber for all our citizens including those most in need and to millions throughout the world, and at the same time to supply the largest single component in our export balance of trade.

Crisis in Agriculture

Four years of the Carter Administration and 25 consecutive years of a Congress controlled by Democrats have brought farmers and ranchers to the brink of disaster and the hardest times they have known since the Great Depression. In the last four years, more than 100,000 family farms have failed as farm income has plummeted. Even the present Administration's own figures show a decrease in real net farm income of some 40 percent in the last year alone—from $33 billion in 1979 to less than $22 billion projected for 1980.

The Democratic Party and the Carter Administration have abused their authority and failed in their responsibility to provide sound agricultural policies. Republicans pledge to make life in rural America prosperous again. We will:

—increase net farm income by supporting and refining programs to bring profitable farm prices with the goal of surpassing parity levels in a market-oriented agricultural economy;

—control inflation by adopting sound fiscal and monetary policies and by eliminating excessive and unnecessary federal regulations;

—expand markets at home by effectively utilizing the advantages of the energy potential for farm, forestry, and other biomass products. We encourage the continued innovative efforts in developing alcohol and other renewable energy sources and equipment for both on-farm and commercial use;

—aggressively expand markets abroad by effectively using the Eisenhower Food for Peace program and revolving credit incentives, working to remove foreign restraints on American products and encouraging the development of dependable new markets in developing countries;

—assure a priority allocation of fuel for U.S. agriculture, including food and fiber production, transportation, and processing; and

—combine efforts to encourage the renewable resource timber production capability of privately-owned forests and woodlands with a federal program committed to multiple-use (timber, recreation, wildlife, watershed and/or range management) where federal land has not been designated as wilderness.

Rural America

Attention to the quality of life in our rural areas is a vital necessity because rural Americans impart a special strength to the national character. It is our goal to assure that all rural citizens—whether they are farmers or not—have the same consideration in matters of economic development, in energy, credit and transportation availability, and in employment opportunities which are given to those who live in towns and cities. The opportunity for non-farm jobs enhances the ability of people to live and work in rural America in the decade ahead, and our dedication to a prosperous and energetic rural America is part and parcel of our commitment to make America great again.

Expand Export Markets

Agriculture's contribution to the U.S. trade balance makes it especially fitting that an aggressive market development program to establish dependable new markets for farm exports will be a vital part of the policies to restore profitability to American agriculture. Republicans will ensure that:

—international trade is conducted on the basis of fair and effective competition and that all imported agricultural products meet the same standards of quality that are required of American producers;

—the General Agreement on Tariffs and Trade becomes a meaningful vehicle for handling agricultural trade problems and grievances;

—an aggressive agricultural market development program and the streamlining of the export marketing system is given top national priority;

—government-to-government sales of agricultural commodities be eliminated, except as specifically provided by law;

—the future of U.S. agricultural commodities is protected from the economic evils of predatory dumping by other producing nations and that the domestic production of these commodities, so important to the survival of individuals and small rural communities is preserved; and

—the important and productive potential of the commercial seafood industry is given encouragement.

Farmer-Held Reserves

We support farmer-owned grain reserves, should they become necessary, and adamantly oppose government-controlled reserves.

Grain Embargo

We believe that agricultural embargoes are only symbolic and are ineffective tools of foreign policy. We oppose singling out American farmers to bear the brunt of Carter's ill-conceived, ineffective, and improperly implemented grain embargo. The Carter grain embargo should be terminated immediately.

Excessive Regulation of Agriculture

The crushing burden of excessive federal regulation such as many of those imposed on farmers, ranchers, foresters, and commercial fishermen by OSHA, EPA, the departments of Agriculture, Labor, Justice, Interior, and other government entities are unrealistic and unnecessary.

We pledge a sensible approach to reduce excessive federal regulation that is draining the profitability from farming, ranching, and commercial fishing. Especially high on the agenda for changes in policy under Republican leadership are such regulatory issues as the Interior Department's ineffective predator control policies, EPA and FDA's excessive adherence to "zero risk" policies relative to the use of pesticides, herbicides, antibiotics, food additives, preservatives, and the like.

Soil and Water Conservation

We believe the strong soil and water conservation stewardship to which farmers, ranchers, watermen, and rural Americans are devoted is exemplary, and encourage appropriate local, state, and federal programs to give conservation practices vitality. Voluntary participation with adequate incentives is essential to the effective conservation of our soil and water resources.

Water Policy

The conservation and development of the nation's water resources are vital requisites for rebuilding America's national strength. The natural abundance of water can no longer be taken for granted. The impending crisis in water could be far more serious than our energy problems unless we act now. A dynamic water policy, which addresses our national diversity in climate, geography, and patterns of land ownership, and includes all requirements across the spectrum of water use, including reclamation policy, will be a priority of the Republican Administration working with the advice and counsel of state and local interests. We must develop a partnership between the federal and state governments which will not destroy traditional state supremacy in water law. Further, there must be cooperation between the Executive Branch and Congress in developing and implementing that policy. Lack of such partnership has resulted in four years of bitter confrontation between the states and the obstructive policies of the Democratic Administration. The congress has been frustrated in its efforts to conserve and develop our water resources. Working together, the states and the federal government can meet the impending water crisis through innovative and alternative approaches to such problems as cleaning our lakes and rivers, reducing toxic pollution, developing multiple-use projects, and achieving a workable balance between the many competing demands on our water resources.

Agricultural Labor

Comprehensive labor legislation, which will be fair to American workers and encourage better relations with our neighbors in Mexico and Canada with whom we wish to establish a working North American Accord, is an essential endeavor. We deplore disruptive work stoppages which interrupt the supply of food to consumers.

Taxation

Federal estate and gift taxes have a particularly pernicious effect on family farms. Young farmers who inherit farm property are often forced to sell off part of the family farm to pay taxes. Once these taxes are paid, young farmers often must begin their careers deeply in debt. Our tax laws must be reformed to encourage rather than discourage family farming and ranching.

We deplore the imposition of present excessive estate and gift taxes on family farms. We support the use of lower, productivity-based valuation when farms are transferred within the family. Further, we believe that no spouse should pay estate taxes on farm property inherited from a husband or wife. We support the Republican tax cut proposal which provides accelerated depreciation and expanded investment tax credits to farm vehicles, equipment, and structures. Finally, we support legislation which would remove tax advantages foreign investors realize on the sale of U.S. forests, farmland, and other real estate.

Rural Transportation

It is essential to the well-being and security of our nation that an adequate rural transportation system be restored as a vital link between rural areas and their markets, both domestic and export. Overall, we pledge to eliminate those rules and regulations which are restrictive to the free flow of commerce and trade of agricultural products and encourage an environment that will enhance the private development and improvement of all modes of transportation to move agricultural production swiftly, safely, and economically. Recognizing the inherent advantages of each mode of transportation, the Republican Party will work to encourage and allow those advantages to be utilized on a balanced and equitable basis.

We believe the federal 55 miles per hour speed limit is counterproductive and contributes to higher costs of goods and services to all communities, particularly in rural America. The most effective, no-cost federal assistance program available would be for each state to set its own speed limit.

A Strong USDA

We pledge an Administration dedicated to restoring profitability to agriculture. A top priority will be the selection of a qualified and effective Secretary and policy staff who will speak up for American farmers—and a President who will listen.

America's preeminence in agriculture is rooted in a system of agricultural research, extension, and teaching—unique and unequalled in the world. Land Grant Universities focus on problems of national, regional, and local concern. Cooperative extension, operating in every county of the United States and its territories, brings the results of USDA and Land Grant University research to farmers and ranchers, rural women, consumers, agribusiness, and to youth through 4-H programs.

Food Safety

The Republican Party favors a legislative effort to revise and modernize our food safety laws, providing guidelines for risk assessment, benefit assessment, peer review, and regulatory flexibility which are consistent with other government health and safety policies.

Cooperatives

We believe farmer cooperatives and rural electric and telephone cooperatives provide essential benefits to farmers and the rural Americans they serve, and we support exclusive jurisdiction of USDA in the effective administration of the Capper-Volstead Act.

We Republicans pledge ourselves to work with farmers, ranchers, and our friends and neighbors to make America great again.

THE NATION

Though a relatively young nation among those of western civilization we are possessed of one of the oldest institutions of government extant. Steeped in the Judeo-Christian ethic and in Anglo-Saxon theories of law and right, our legal and political institutions have evolved over many generations to form a stable system that serves free men and women well. It governs a people of multifarious heritage dispersed across a great continent of marked geographical contrasts. It presides over a diverse economy that in its collective whole is the largest, most powerful and most resilient in the world. In the two centuries of its life, though it has from time to time been sorely tested by constitutional, economic, and social crises, it has stood and not been found wanting. Its timeless strength, coupled with and reinforced by the faith and good will, the wisdom and confidence of the people from whom it derives its powers, has preserved us as a nation of enormous vitality.

The intent of the Founders, embraced and reflected by succeeding generations of Americans, was that the central government should perform only those functions which are necessary concomitants of nationality, preserve order, and do for people only those things which they cannot do for themselves. The durability of our system lies in its flexibility and its accommodation to diversity and changing circumstance. It is notable as much for what it permits as for what it proscribes. Government must ever be the servant of the nation, not its master.

Big Government

Under the guise of providing for the common good, Democratic Party domination of the body politic over the last 47 years has produced a central government of vastly expanded size, scope, and rigidity. Confidence in government, especially big government, has been the chief casualty of too many promises made and broken, too many commitments unkept. It is time for change—time to de-emphasize big bureaucracies—time to shift the focus of national politics from expanding government's power to that of restoring the strength of smaller communities such as the family, neighborhood, and the workplace.

Government's power to take and tax, to regulate and require has already reached extravagant proportions. As government's power continues to grow, the "consent of the governed" will diminish. Republicans support an end to the growth of the federal government and pledge to return the decisionmaking process to the smaller communities of society.

The emergence of policies and programs which will revitalize the free enterprise system and reverse the trend toward regulation is essential. To sustain the implementation of such policy, it is necessary to raise the public awareness and understanding that our free enterprise system is the source of all income, government and private, and raise the individual's awareness of his or her vested interest in its growth and vitality.

The Republican Party believes that it is important to develop a growing constituency which recognizes its direct relationship to the health and success of free enterprise, and realizes the negative impact of excessive regulation. Education and involvement in the system are the best means to accomplish this. To this end, we will actively pursue new and expanding opportunities for all Americans to become more directly involved in our free enterprise system.

Government Reorganization

The Republican Party reaffirms its belief in the decentralization of the federal government and in the traditional American principle that the best government is the one closest to the people. There, it is less costly, more accountable, and more responsive to people's needs. Against the prevailing trend toward increased centralization of government under the Democrats, Republicans succeeded in the 1970s in initiating large scale revenue sharing and block grant programs to disperse the power of the federal government and share it with the states and localities.

Our states and localities have the talent, wisdom, and determination to respond to the variety of demands made upon them. Block grants and revenue sharing provide local governments with the means and the flexibility to solve their own problems in ways most appropriate for each locale. Unlike categorical grants, they do not lock states and localities into priorities and needs perceived by Washington. They are also more efficient because block grants and revenue sharing relieve both local government and the federal government from the costly and complicated process of program application, implementation, and review associated with the categorical grant system.

We pledge to continue to redouble our efforts to return power to the state and local governments. The regionalization of government encouraged by federal policies diminishes the responsiveness of state and local governments and impairs the power of the people to control their destiny.

While Republican efforts have been focused on sharing revenues and the powers that go with it, the Carter Administration has been preoccupied with the reorganization and consolidation of central authority. As a result, we have the Departments of Energy and Education, for example, but no more oil and gas, or learning, to show for it.

When we mistakenly rely on government to solve all our problems we ignore the abilities of people to solve their own problems. We pledge to renew the dispersion of power from the federal government to the states and localities. But this will not be enough. We pledge to extend the process so that power can be transferred as well to non-governmental institutions.

Government Reform

We favor the establishment of a commission of distinguished citizens to recommend ways of reorganizing and reducing the size and scope of the Executive Branch. Federal departments, agencies, and bureaus should be consolidated where possible to end waste and improve the delivery of essential services. Republicans pledge to eliminate bureaucratic red tape and reduce government paperwork. Agencies should be made to justify every official form and filing requirement. Where possible, we favor deregulation, especially in the energy, transportation, and communications industries. We believe that the marketplace, rather than the bureaucrats, should regulate management decisions.

The unremitting delegation of authority to the rulemakers by successive Democratic Congresses and the abuse of that authority has led to our current crisis of overregulation. For that reason, we support use of the Congressional veto, sunset laws, and strict budgetary control of the bureaucracies as a means of eliminating unnecessary spending and regulations. Agencies should be required to review existing regulations and eliminate those that are outmoded, duplicative, or contradictory. They must conduct cost-benefit analyses of major proposed regulations to determine their impact on the economy, on public health and safety, on state and local government, and on competition. We recommend legislation which would eliminate the present presumption of validity in favor of federal regulations. We also support legislation to require the federal government to provide restitution to those who have been wrongfully injured by agency actions. We oppose the use of tax monies of intervenors in the rule-making process.

We recognize that there are dangers inherent in the rapid growth of the federal bureaucracy, especially the arbitrary nature of its discretionary power and the abuses of procedural safeguards. Accordingly, we pledge to work for fundamental changes in the federal Administrative Procedures Act in order to give citizens the same constitutional protections before a government agency that they have in a courtroom. Among these reforms are requirements that agencies publish in the *Federal Register* all rules and statements of policy before they are adopted, that a person be guaranteed written notice and the opportunity to submit facts and arguments in any adjudicatory proceeding, that an agency decision be consistent with prior decisions unless otherwise provided by law, and that a person may seek judicial review without first exhausting his or her administrative remedies. At the same time we urge the Congress to strengthen its oversight to ensure that the agencies comply with the deadlines, report filing and other requirements mandated by law.

We propose to repeal federal restrictions and rewrite federal standards which hinder minorities from finding employment, starting their own businesses, gaining valuable work experience, or enjoying the fruits of their own labors.

Because there are too many federal employees in comparison to private sector employees, there should be no further increase in the number of civilian federal employees if that would increase the ratio of federal employees to private sector employees over the present ratio.

Election Reform

The Republican Party has consistently encouraged full participation in our electoral process and is disturbed by the steady decline in voter participation in the United States in recent years. We believe that the increased voter turnout during the past year in Republican campaigns is due to dissatisfaction with Democratic officials and their failure to heed popular demands to cut taxes, restrain spending, curb inflation, and drastically reduce regulation.

Republicans support public policies that will promote electoral participation without compromising ballot-box security. We strongly oppose national postcard voter registration schemes because they are an open invitation to fraud.

Republicans support public policies that encourage political activity by individual citizens. We support the repeal of those restrictive campaign spending limitations that tend to create obstacles to local grassroots participation in federal elections. We also oppose the proposed financing of congressional campaigns with taxpayers' dollars as an effort by the Democratic Party to protect its incumbent members of Congress with a tax subsidy. We prefer the present system of having the states and party rules determine the presidential nominating process to the concept of a uniform national primary which would only add to the already high costs of, and excessive federal intrusion into, presidential campaigns.

We support the critical roles of competitive political parties in the recruitment of candidates, the conduct of campaigns, and the development of broad-based public policy responsive to the people. We urge congress and state legislatures to frame their regulations of campaign finance, their nominating systems, and other election laws to strengthen rather than weaken parties.

Arts and Humanities

Recent Republican Administrations led the way in bringing together private support and governmental encouragement to effect a tremendous expansion of artistic and scholarly endeavor. The Carter Administration has crudely politicized these programs, lowering their standards of excellence and increasing federal control over them.

The Republican Party will restore the sound economy which is absolutely necessary for the arts and humanities to flourish. We will restore, as well, the integrity of federal programs in this area. Most important, to ensure the continued primacy of private funding for the arts, we reiterate our support of broader tax incentives for contributions to charitable and cultural organizations.

Transportation

America's transportation system must be designed to meet the requirements of the people, not to dictate what those requirements should be. Essential to any industrialized country is a transportation system which provides efficient and reliable service for both the movement of people and freight, urban and rural, domestic and foreign. Our nation has one of the finest transportation systems in the world but there is a danger that it will be unable to meet the future needs of a growing America.

Present levels of public and private investment will not preserve the existing system. For example, highways are deteriorating twice as fast as they are being rebuilt and inadequate rehabilitation will soon cost users more in reduced service levels than the cost of adequate rehabilitation.

The demand for transportation will grow dramatically in the next two decades with people-miles travelled increasing by over 50 percent and freight ton-miles more than doubling.

Government overregulation is inhibiting the return on investment necessary to attract capital for future growth and job creation.

A maze of federal agencies, Congressional committees, and conflicting policies is driving up costs and retarding innovation.

A lackluster energy policy, impeding production of oil, coal, and other forms of energy is endangering transportation's ability to keep up with demand.

Consequently, the role of government in transportation must be redefined. The forces of the free market must be brought to bear to promote competition, reduce costs, and improve the return on investment to stimulate capital formation in the private sector. The role of government must change from one of overbearing regulation to one of providing incentives for technological and innovative developments, while assuring through anti-trust enforcement that neither predatory competitive pricing nor price gouging of captive customers will occur.

Increased emphasis must be placed on the importance of having a well-balanced national transportation system where highways, passenger vehicles, buses, trucks, rail, water, pipelines, and air transportation each provide those services which they do best, while offering the widest range of reasonable choices for both passenger and freight movement. A sound transportation system is a prerequisite for the vision of America that Republicans embrace—a prosperous, growing nation where dreams can still come true.

Energy

Energy is the lifeblood of our economy. Without adequate energy supplies now and in the future, the jobs of American men and women, the security of their lives, and their ability to provide for their families will be threatened and their standard of living will be lowered. Every American is painfully aware that our national energy situation has deteriorated badly over the past four years of Democratic control. Gasoline prices have more than doubled. Our oil import bill has risen 96 percent. Our energy supplies have become increasingly vulnerable because U.S. oil production outside of Alaska is now 23 percent below 1973 levels. The threat of sudden shortages, curtailments, and gas lines has become a recurring reality.

This steady deterioration has not only compounded our economic problems of inflation, recession, and dollar weakness, but even more importantly, it has infected our confidence as a nation. Energy shortages, spiralling costs, and increasing insecurity are beginning to darken our basic hopes and expectations for the future.

The National Association for the Advancement of

Colored People has very accurately focused on the effects that a no-growth energy policy will have on the opportunities of America's black people and other minorities. The NAACP said that "a pessimistic attitude toward energy supplies for the future . . . cannot satisfy the fundamental requirement of a society of expanding economic opportunity."

In commenting on the Carter energy proposals the Association said, "We cannot accept the notion that our people are best served by a policy based upon the inevitability of energy shortage and the need for government to allocate an ever diminishing supply among competing interests. . . . The plan reflects the absence of a black perspective in its development."

Three and one-half years ago, President Carter declared energy the "moral equivalent of war" and sent Congress 109 recommendations for action, including the creation of a new Department of Energy. Since then, the federal budget for government's energy bureaucracy has grown to about $10 billion per year and more than 20,000 pages of new energy regulations and guidelines have been issued. But these have not fostered the production of a single extra unit of energy.

The Democratic Congress has joined in the stampede, taking action on 304 energy bills since 1977. As a result, the federal bureaucracy is busy from coast to coast allocating gasoline, setting building temperatures, printing rationing coupons, and readying standby plans to ban weekend boating, close factories, and pass out "no drive day" stickers to American motorists — all the time saying, "we must make do with less." Never before in the history of American government has so much been done at such great expense with such dismal results.

Republicans believe this disappointing cycle of shrinking energy prospects and expanding government regulation and meddling is wholly unnecessary. We believe that the proven American values of individual enterprise can solve our energy problems. This optimism stands in stark contrast to the grim predictions of the Democrats who have controlled Congress for the last 25 years.

They seem to believe not only that we are a nation without resources, but also that we have lost our resourcefulness. Republicans believe in the common sense of the American people rather than a complex web of Government controls and interventions that threaten America's ability to grow. We are committed to an alternative strategy of aggressively boosting the nation's energy supplies; stimulating new energy technology and more efficient energy use; restoring maximum feasible choice and freedom in the marketplace for energy consumers and producers alike; and eliminating energy shortages and disruptions as a roadblock to renewed national economic growth, rising living

standards, and a reawakening of the hopes and dreams of the American people for a better and more abundant future.

We believe the United States must proceed on a steady and orderly path toward energy self-sufficiency. But in the interim, our pressing need for insurance against supply disruption should not be made hostage to the whims of foreign governments, as is presently the case under the Carter Administration. We believe it is necessary to resume rapid filling of strategic oil reserves to planned levels of 500 million barrels in the short-term and ultimately to the one billion barrel level, and to insure that noncontiguous areas of the United States have their fair share of emergency oil reserves stored within their respective boundaries, as authorized by the Energy Policy and Conservation Act of 1975.

In order to increase domestic production of energy, Republicans advocate the decontrol of the price at the well head of oil and gas. We believe that the so-called windfall profits tax (which is unrelated to profit), should be repealed as it applies to small volume royalty owners, new oil, stripper wells, tertiary-recovery, and heavy crude oil, and that the phase-out of the tax on old oil should be accelerated. This tax legislation should be amended to include a plowback provision. We will seek decontrol of prices on all oil products and an end to government authority to allocate petroleum supplies except in national emergency. We also believe that market restrictions on the use of natural gas should be eliminated.

Coal, our most abundant energy resource, can bridge the gap between our other present energy sources and the renewable energy sources of the future. The coal industry has been virtually ignored by the Carter Administration and the Democratic Congress. In 1977, President Carter promised to double coal production by 1985. Instead, because of obstructionist actions of the Administration, coal production has increased by only 11 percent to date and future prospects are dim. Today, thousands of coal miners are out of work and without hope for the future.

Republicans support a comprehensive program of regulatory reform, improved incentives, and revision of cumbersome and overly stringent Clean Air Act regulations. This program will speed conversion of utility, industrial, and large commercial oil-burning boilers to coal to the greatest extent feasible, thus substantially cutting our dependence on foreign oil. This program must begin immediately on a priority basis and be completed at the earliest date possible.

To effectively utilize this vast resource, our coal transportation systems must be upgraded and the government controls on them relaxed. Government regulation regarding the mining and use of coal must be simplified. We will propose a policy which will assure that governmental restraints, other than necessary and reasonable environmental controls, do not prevent the use of coal. We also reaffirm that mined lands must be returned to beneficial use and that states, in accordance with past Congressional mandate, have the primary responsibility to implement rules concerning the mining of coal which are adapted to the states' unique characteristics.

Coal, gas, and nuclear fission offer the best intermediate solutions to America's energy needs. We support accelerated use of nuclear energy through technologies that have been proven efficient and safe. The safe operation, as well as design, of nuclear generating plants will have our highest priority to assure the continued availability of this important energy source. The design and operation of these plants can be guaranteed in less than the 10 to 12 year lead time now required to license and build them. We believe that the licensing process can and should be streamlined through consolidation of the present process and the use of standardized reactor designs.

The Three Mile Island incident suggests the need for certain reforms, such as in the area of operator training, but illustrates that properly designed and operated nuclear plants do not endanger public health or safety. We further encourage the research, development, and demonstration of the breeder reactor with its potential for safely contributing to our nation's future energy supplies.

Nuclear power development requires sound plans for nuclear waste disposal and storage and reprocessing of spent fuel. Technical solutions to these problems exist, and decisive federal action to choose and implement solutions is essential. The Democratic-controlled Congress and Administration have failed to address the spent fuel problem. A Republican Congress and Administration will immediately begin to implement plans for regional away-from-reactor storage of spent fuel with the goal of implementation of a program no later than 1984.

Republicans are committed to the rapid development of permanent storage facilities for nuclear wastes. Since waste disposal is a national responsibility, no state should bear an unacceptable share of this responsibility.

Republicans will also move toward reprocessing of spent fuel.

Republicans will continue to support the development of new technologies to develop liquid, gaseous, and solid hydrocarbons which can be derived from coal, oil shale, and tar sands. The decontrol of oil and gas prices will eliminate any necessity for government support for a synthetic fuel industry except possibly for limited demonstration projects. Clean air, water,

waste disposal, mine reclamation, and leasing rules must be made rational and final to accelerate private investment.

Gasohol is an important, immediately available source of energy that is helping to extend our petroleum reserves. We encourage development of a domestic gasohol industry.

We also believe the government must continue supporting productive research to speed the development of renewable energy technology, including solar energy, geothermal, wind, nuclear fusion, alcohol synthesis, and biomass, to provide the next generation of energy sources.

Conservation clearly plays a vital role in the consideration and formulation of national energy policy. Republicans reject, however, the position of the Democrats which is to conserve through government fiat. Republicans understand that free markets based on the collective priorities and judgments of individual consumers will efficiently allocate the energy supplies to their most highly valued uses. We also believe that the role of government is best performed by structuring creative cost-effective incentives to achieve energy efficiency and conservation.

We reject unequivocally punitive gasoline and other energy taxes designed to artificially suppress energy consumption.

Much inefficient energy use results from government subsidization of imported oil and holding the price of natural gas substantially below its market value. When the price of energy is held artificially low, there is no incentive for conservation. This kind of energy consumption stems not from the excesses of the public, but the foolish policy distortions of government. Every BTU of genuine energy "waste" in our economy would rapidly disappear if we immediately and completely dismantle all remaining energy price controls and subsidies.

A Republican policy of decontrol, development of our domestic energy resources, and incentives for new supply and conservation technologies will substantially reduce our dependence on imported oil. We reject the Carter Administration's incessant excuse that the high price of imported oil and OPEC are the primary cause of inflation and recession at home and a weak dollar and declining balance of payments abroad. The fastest way to bring international oil prices under control is to stop printing so recklessly the dollar in which those prices are denominated. Fully 60 percent of the world oil price increase since 1973 represents the depreciation of our dollars rather than an increase in the real price of oil.

Virtually all major environmental legislation in the past decade reflected a bipartisan concern over the need to maintain a clean and healthful environment.

While the new environmental policies have resulted in improving air quality, cleaner waters, and more careful analysis of toxic chemicals, the price paid has far exceeded the direct and necessary cost of designing and installing new control technology. In the energy area, the increased complexity of regulations, together with continual changes in the standards imposed, have brought about tremendous delays in the planning and construction of new facilities ranging from electric power plants to oil refineries, pipelines, and synthetic fuel plants.

Republicans believe that an effective balance between energy and environmental goals can be achieved. We can ensure that government requirements are firmly grounded on the best scientific evidence available, that they are enforced evenhandedly and predictably, and that the process of their development and enforcement has finality.

Republicans condemn the Democrats' withdrawal of a massive amount of the most promising federal lands from prospective energy development, including the rich potential of our Outer Continental Shelf. It has been estimated that by the end of the 1980s resources from government-controlled acreage could yield over two million barrels of oil per day and four trillion cubic feet of gas per year, the equivalent of nearly all of our imports from OPEC countries. It is clear that restrictive leasing policies have driven us further to depend on OPEC by severely impairing the exploration for, and development of, domestic oil, gas, and coal resources, thereby aggravating our balance of trade deficit and making our country less secure. Republicans will move toward making available all suitable federal lands for multiple use purposes including exploration and production of energy resources.

Republicans believe that in order to address our energy problem we must maximize our domestic energy production capability. In the short term, therefore, the nation must move forward on all fronts simultaneously, including oil and gas, coal, and nuclear. In the longer term, renewable resources must be brought significantly on line to replace conventional sources. Finally, in conjunction with this all-out production initiative, we must strive to maximize conservation and the efficient use of energy.

The return to the traditions that gave vitality and strength to this nation is urgent.

The free world — indeed western civilization — needs a strong United States. That strength requires a prospering economy. That economy will be secure with a vigorous domestic energy industry. That vigor can only be achieved in an atmosphere of freedom — one that encourages individual initiatives and personal resourcefulness.

Environment

The Republican Party reaffirms its long standing commitment to the conservation and wise management of America's renewable natural resources.

We believe that a healthy environment is essential to the present and future well-being of our people, and to sustainable national growth.

The nature of environmental pollution is such that a government role is necessary to insure its control and the proper protection of public health. Much progress has been made in achieving the goals of clean air, clean water, and control of toxic wastes. At the same time, we believe that it is imperative that environmental laws and regulations be reviewed, and where necessary, reformed to ensure that the benefits achieved justify the costs imposed. Too often, current regulations are so rigid and narrow that even individual innovations that improve the environment cannot be implemented. We believe, in particular, that regulatory procedures must be reformed to expedite decisionmaking. Endless delay harms both the environment and the economy.

We strongly affirm that environmental protection must not become a cover for a "no-growth" policy and a shrinking economy. Our economy can continue to grow in an acceptable environment.

We believe that agricultural policy should give emphasis to the stewardship of the nation's soil and water resources. The permanent loss of productive farm land is a growing problem and we encourage states and local communities to adopt policies that help maintain and protect productive agricultural land as a national asset.

Immigration and Refugee Policy

Residency in the United States is one of the most precious and valued of conditions. The traditional hospitality of the American people has been severely tested by recent events, but it remains the strongest in the world. Republicans are proud that our people have opened their arms and hearts to strangers from abroad and we favor an immigration and refugee policy which is consistent with this tradition. We believe that to the fullest extent possible those immigrants should be admitted who will make a positive contribution to America and who are willing to accept the fundamental American values and way of life. At the same time, United States immigration and refugee policy must reflect the interests of the nation's political and economic well-being. Immigration into this country must not be determined solely by foreign governments or even by the millions of people around the world who wish to come to America. The federal government has a duty to adopt immigration laws and follow enforcement procedures which will fairly and effectively implement the immigration policy desired by American people.

The immediate adoption of this policy is essential to an orderly approach to the great problem of oppressed people seeking entry, so that the deserving can be accepted in America without adding to their hardships.

The refugee problem is an international problem and every effort should be made to coordinate plans for absorbing refugee populations with regional bodies, such as the Organization of American States and the Association of Southeast Asian Nations, on a global basis.

The Judiciary

Under Mr. Carter, many appointments to federal judgeships have been particularly disappointing. By his partisan nominations, he has violated his explicit campaign promise of 1976 and has blatantly disregarded the public interest. We pledge to reverse that deplorable trend, through the appointment of women and men who respect and reflect the values of the American people, and whose judicial philosophy is characterized by the highest regard for protecting the rights of law-abiding citizens, and is consistent with the belief in the decentralization of the federal government and efforts to return decisionmaking power to state and local elected officials.

We will work for the appointment of judges at all levels of the judiciary who respect traditional family values and the sanctity of innocent human life.

Taxes and Government Spending

Elsewhere in this platform, we have pledged for the sake of individual freedom and economic growth to cut personal income tax rates for all. Republicans believe that these tax rate reductions should be complemented by firm limitations on the growth of federal spending as provided by the Roth-Kemp Bill. The Republican Party therefore, pledges to place limits on federal spending as a percent of the Gross National Product. It is now over 21 percent. We pledge to reduce it. If federal spending is reduced as tax cuts are phased in, there will be sufficient budget surpluses to fund the tax cuts, and allow for reasonable growth in necessary program spending.

By increasing economic growth, tax rate reduction will reduce the need for government spending on unemployment, welfare, and public jobs programs. However, the Republican Party will also halt excessive government spending by eliminating waste, fraud, and duplication.

We believe that the Congressional budget process has failed to control federal spending. Indeed, because of its big spending bias, the budget process has actually contributed to higher levels of social spending, has prevented necessary growth in defense spending, and has been used to frustrate every Republican attempt to lower tax rates to promote economic growth.

The immediate burden of reducing federal spending rests on the shoulders of the President and the Congress. We believe a Republican Congress can balance the budget and reduce spending through legislative actions, eliminating the necessity for a Constitutional amendment to compel it. However, if necessary, the Republican Party will seek to adopt a Constitutional amendment to limit federal spending and balance the budget, except in time of national emergency as determined by a two-thirds vote of Congress.

Government Lending

Not only has the Democratic Congress failed to control spending, but in the last 10 years federal credit assistance programs have soared out of control.

Many federal loan guarantees and related credit programs are off-budget. As a result, no one knows the nature and extent of our obligations or the effect such practices have on our economy. The best estimate is that outstanding federal credit is now close to $600 billion.

Runaway government lending can be just as dangerous as runaway federal spending.

The Republican Party will establish a workable federal credit policy that will bring order to the reckless lending practices of the past.

Inflation

We consider inflation and its impact on jobs to be the greatest domestic threat facing our nation today. Mr. Carter must go! For what he has done to the dollar; for what he has done to the life savings of millions of Americans; for what he has done to retirees seeking a secure old age; for what he has done to young families aspiring to a home, an education for their children, and a rising living standard, Mr. Carter must not have another four years in office.

In his three and one-half years in office, Mr. Carter has presented and supported policies which carried inflation from 4.8 percent in 1976 to a peak of 18 percent during 1980.

He has fostered a 50 percent increase in federal spending, an increase of more than $200 billion, boosting spending in an era of scarce resources, and driving up prices.

He has through both inaction and deliberate policy permitted or forced tax increases of more than 70 percent, more than $250 billion, directly increasing the cost of living and the costs of hiring and producing. This has crippled living standards, productivity, and our ability to compete in the world. It has led to reduced output, scarcity, and higher prices.

He has imposed burdensome regulations and controls on production which have reduced the availability of domestic goods and energy resources, increased our dependence on imports, particularly in the energy area, driven down the value of the dollar, and driven up prices.

He has permitted continuing federal budget deficits and increased federal borrowing, forcing higher interest rates and inflationary money creation, increasing prices.

The inflation policies of the Carter Administration have been inconsistent, counterproductive, and tragically inept. Mr. Carter has blamed everyone from OPEC to the American people themselves for his crisis of inflation—everyone, that is, but his own Administration and its policies which have been the true cause of inflation.

Inflation is too much money chasing too few goods. Much can be done to increase the growth of real output. But ultimately price stability requires a non-inflationary rate of growth of the money supply in line with the real growth of the economy. If the supply of dollars rapidly outstrips the quantity of goods, year in, year out, inflation is inevitable.

Ultimately, inflation is a decline in the value of the dollar, the monetary standard, in terms of the goods it can buy. Until the decade of the 1970s, monetary policy was automatically linked to the overriding objective of maintaining a stable dollar value. The severing of the dollar's link with real commodities in the 1960s and 1970s, in order to pursue economic goals other than dollar stability, has unleashed hyper-inflationary forces at home and monetary disorder abroad, without bringing any of the desired economic benefits. One of the most urgent tasks in the period ahead will be the restoration of a dependable monetary standard—that is, an end to inflation.

Lower tax rates, less spending, and a balanced budget are the keys to maintaining real growth and full employment as we end inflation by putting our monetary policy back on track. Monetary and fiscal policy must each play its part if we are to achieve our joint goals of full employment and price stability.

Unfortunately, Mr. Carter and the Democratic Congress seek to derail our nation's money creation policies by taking away the independence of the Federal Reserve Board, the same people who have so massively expanded government spending should not be allowed politically to dominate our monetary policy. The independence of the Federal Reserve System must be preserved.

The Republican Party believes inflation can be controlled only by fiscal and monetary restraint, combined with sharp reductions in the tax and regulatory disincentives for savings, investments, and productivity. Therefore, the Republican Party opposes the imposition of wage and price controls and credit controls.

Controls will not stop inflation, as past experience has shown. Wage and price controls will only result in shortages, inequities, black markets, and ultimately higher prices. We reject this short-sighted and misguided approach.

PEACE AND FREEDOM

At the start of the 1980s, the United States faces the most serious challenge to its survival in the two centuries of its existence. Our ability to meet this challenge demands a foreign policy firmly rooted in principle. Our economic and social welfare in the 1980s may depend as much on our foreign and defense policy as it does on domestic policy. The Republican Party reasserts that it is the solemn purpose of our foreign policy to secure the people and free institutions of our nation against every peril; to hearten and fortify the love of freedom everywhere in the world; and to achieve a secure environment in the world in which freedom, democracy, and justice may flourish.

For three and one-half years, the Carter Administration has been without a coherent strategic concept to guide foreign policy, oblivious to the scope and magnitude of the threat posed to our security, and devoid of competence to provide leadership and direction to the free world. The Administration's conduct of foreign policy has undermined our friends abroad, and led our most dangerous adversaries to miscalculate the willingness of the American people to resist aggression. Republicans support a policy of peace through strength; weakness provokes aggression.

For three and one-half years the Carter Administration has given us a foreign policy not of constancy and credibility, but of chaos, confusion, and failure. It has produced an image of our country as a vacillating and reactive nation, unable to define its place in the world, the goals it seeks, or the means to pursue them. Despite the Administration's rhetoric, the most flagrant offenders of human rights including the Soviet Union, Vietnam, and Cuba have been the beneficiaries of Administration good will, while nations friendly to the United States have suffered the loss of U.S. commercial access and economic and military assistance.

The threat to the United States and its allies is not only a military one. We face a threat from international terrorism. Our access to energy and raw material resources is challenged by civil unrest, Soviet-sponsored subversion, and economic combinations in restraint of free trade. Our first line of defense, our network of friendly nations and alliances, has been undermined by the inept conduct of foreign affairs.

American policy since World War II has rested upon the pillars of collective security, military and technological superiority, and economic strength, and upon the perception by our adversaries that the United States possesses the will to use its power where necessary to protect its freedom. These tenets have enabled a commonwealth of free and independent nations to enjoy the benefits and confidence that come from expanding economic interchange in peace and bilateral and multilateral support in time of war. The entire structure of peace was guaranteed by American and allied military power sufficient to deter conflict, or to prevail in conflict if deterrence should fail.

The Administration's neglect of America's defense posture in the face of overwhelming evidence of a threatening military buildup is without parallel since the 1930s. The scope and magnitude of the growth of Soviet military power threatens American interest at every level, from the nuclear threat to our survival, to our ability to protect the lives and property of American citizens abroad.

Despite clear danger signals indicating that Soviet nuclear power would overtake that of the United States by the early 1980s, threatening the survival of the United States and making possible, for the first time in post-war history, political coercion and defeat, the Administration *reduced* the size and capability of our nuclear forces.

Despite clear danger signals indicating that the Soviet Union was using Cuban, East German, and now Nicaraguan, as well as its own, military forces to extend its power to Africa, Asia, and the Western Hemisphere, the Administration often undermined the very governments under attack. As a result, a clear and present danger threatens the energy and raw material lifelines of the Western world.

Despite clear danger signals indicating that the Soviet Union was augmenting its military threat to the nations of Western Europe, American defense programs such as the enhanced radiation warhead and cruise missiles, which could have offset that buildup, were cancelled or delayed—to the dismay of allies who depend upon American military power for their security.

The evidence of the Soviet threat to American security has never been more stark and unambiguous, nor has any President ever been more oblivious to this threat and its potential consequences.

The entire Western world faces complex and multidimensional threats to its access to energy and raw material resources. The growth of Soviet military power

poses a direct threat to the petroleum resources of the Persian Gulf now that its military forces deployed in Afghanistan are less than 300 miles from the Straits of Hormuz, through which half the free world's energy supplies flow.

Soviet efforts to gain bases in areas astride the major sea lanes of the world have been successful due to their use of military power, either directly or indirectly through Cuban and other Soviet bloc forces. Since the Carter Administration took office in 1977, the Soviets or their clients have taken over Afghanistan, Cambodia, Ethiopia, and South Yemen, and have solidified their grasp on a host of other nations in the developing world. The Soviet noose is now being drawn around southern Africa, the West's most abundant single source of critical raw materials.

The failure of the United States to respond to direct threats to its security has left American citizens vulnerable to terrorist assaults as well. American diplomatic personnel have been subject to seizure and assault by terrorists throughout the world without drawing a meaningful Administration response.

No failure of the Administration has been so catastrophic as its failure of leadership. Mired in incompetence, bereft of strategic vision and purpose, the President's failure to shoulder the burden of leadership in the Western alliance has placed America in danger without parallel since December 7, 1941. The United States cannot abdicate that role without inducing a diplomatic and eventually a military catastrophy.

Republicans realize that if the challenges of the 1980s are not met, we will continue to lose the respect of the world, our honor, and in the end, our freedom. Republicans pledge to meet these challenges with confidence and strength. We pledge to restore to the United States and its people a government with conviction in our cause, a government that will restore to our great nation its self-respect, its self-confidence, and its national pride.

NATIONAL SECURITY

Defense Budget Trends

In the late 1960s, the Republicans returned to the White House, inheriting a war in Southeast Asia. Because of this war, they also inherited a Fiscal Year (FY) 1968 defense budget which, if calculated in constant 1981 dollars to account for inflation, had risen to over $194 billion from $148 billion in FY 1961, the last Eisenhower year. By the beginning of the second Nixon Administration, U.S. forces were totally disengaged from Southeast Asia. The FY 1974 defense budget had dropped back to $139 billion, and the country had reaped its desired "peace dividend" of an over $50 billion reduction in annual defense spending. During this period, between 1969 and 1973, the Democrats who controlled congress, led by Senators Mondale and Muskie, cut almost $45 billion from Nixon defense requests. Until 1975, Congress continued to ignore long-range defense needs, and made severe cuts in Republican defense proposals. The Ford Administration, however, succeeded in reversing this trend. From a low point of $134 billion in FY 75, the FY 76 defense budget rose, in response to President Ford's request, to $139 billion; and in FY 77 it rose again to $147 billion.

Despite the growing sentiment for a stronger defense, candidate Carter ran on a promise of massive cuts in U.S. defense spending, one promise he has kept. In his first three years in the White House, Mr. Carter reduced defense spending by over $38 billion from President Ford's last Five Year Defense Plan. Now, in his last year in office, faced with the total collapse of his foreign policy, and with his policy advisers and their assumptions disgraced, he has finally proposed an increase beyond the rate of inflation in defense spending. But this growth for 1981 will be less than 1 percent.

We deplore Mr. Carter's personal attempts to rewrite history on defense budgets. His tough speeches before military audiences cannot hide his continuing opposition to Congressional defense increases. The four chiefs of the armed services have each characterized the Carter defense program as "inadequate" to meet the military threat posed to the United States. We associate ourselves with the characterization by Democratic Congressional leaders of the President's behavior on defense as "hypocritical." We would go further; it is disgraceful.

Mr. Carter cut back, cancelled, or delayed every strategic initiative proposed by President Ford. He cancelled production of the Minuteman missile and the B-1 bomber. He delayed all cruise missiles, the MX missile, the Trident submarine and the Trident II missile. He did this while the Soviet Union deployed the Backfire bomber and designed two additional bombers equal in capability to the B-1, and while it deployed four new large ICBMs and developed four others.

Mr. Carter postponed production and deployment of enhanced radiation (neutron) warheads while the Soviet Union deployed the SS-20 mobile missile and the Backfire bomber against Western Europe. He cut President Ford's proposed shipbuilding plan in half. He vetoed a nuclear aircraft carrier. He did this while the Soviet Union pursued an aggressive shipbuilding program capable of giving them worldwide naval supremacy in the 1980s unless current trends are reversed immediately. Mr. Carter opposed efforts to correct the terribly inadequate pay rates for our military personnel and stood by as the alarming exodus of

trained and skilled personnel from the services quickened. At the same time, the Soviet Union increased its military manpower to a level of 4.8 million, more than double that of the U.S.

Recovery from the Carter Administration's neglect will require effort, but Americans know that effort is the unavoidable precondition to peace and economic prosperity. The Soviet Union is now devoting over $50 billion more to defense annually than the United States, achieving military superiority as a result. We have depleted our capital and must now devote the resources essential to catching up. The Secretary of Defense has stated that even if we were to maintain a constant increase in our spending of 5 percent in real terms, it would require 40 years for us to catch up.

Republicans commit themselves to an immediate increase in defense spending to be applied judiciously to critically needed programs. We will build toward a sustained defense expenditure sufficient to close the gap with the Soviets, and ultimately reach the position of military superiority that the American people demand.

Defense Strategy

More is required than reversing our military decline alone. We have seen in recent years how an Administration, possessed of dwindling but still substantial strength, has stood paralyzed in the face of an inexorable march of Soviet or Soviet-sponsored aggression. To be effective in preserving our interests, we must pursue a comprehensive military strategy which guides both the design and employment of our forces. Such a strategy must proceed from a sober analysis of the diverse threats before us.

Republicans approve and endorse a national strategy of peace through strength as set forth in House Concurrent Resolution 306. We urge speedy approval of this legislation by both the U.S. House of Representatives and the U.S. Senate as a means of making clear to the world that the United States has not forgotten that the price of peace is eternal vigilance against tyranny. Therefore we commend to all Americans the text of House Concurrent Resolution 306, which reads as follows: The foreign policy of the United States should reflect a national strategy of peace through strength. The general principles and goals of this strategy would be:

— to inspire, focus, and unite the national will and determination to achieve peace and freedom:

— to achieve overall military and technological superiority over the Soviet Union;

— to create a strategic and civil defense which would protect the American people against nuclear war at least as well as the Soviet population is protected;

— to accept no arms control agreement which in any way jeopardizes the security of the United States or its allies, or which locks the United States into a position of military inferiority;

— to reestablish effective security and intelligence capabilities;

— to pursue positive non-military means to roll back the growth of communism;

— to help our allies and other non-Communist countries defend themselves against Communist aggression; and

— to maintain a strong economy and protect our overseas sources of energy and other vital raw materials.

Our strategy must encompass the levels of force required to deter each level of foreseeable attack and to prevail in conflict in the event deterrence fails. The detailed analysis that must form the intellectual basis for the elaboration of such a strategy will be the first priority of a Republican Administration. It must be based upon the following principles.

Nuclear Forces

Nuclear weapons are the ultimate military guarantor of American security and that of our allies. Yet since 1977, the United States has moved from essential equivalence to inferiority in strategic nuclear forces with the Soviet Union. This decline has resulted from Mr. Carter's cancellation or delay of strategic initiatives like the B-1 bomber, the MX missile, and the Trident II submarine missile programs and from his decisions to close the Minuteman production line and forego production of enhanced radiation weapons.

As the disparity between American and Soviet strategic nuclear forces grows over the next three years, most U.S. land-based missiles, heavy bombers, and submarines in port will become vulnerable to a Soviet first-strike. Such a situation invites diplomatic blackmail and coercion of the United States by the Soviet Union during the coming decade.

An administration that can defend its interest only by threatening the mass extermination of civilians, as Mr. Carter implied in 1979, dooms itself to strategic, and eventually geo-political, paralysis. Such a strategy is simply not credible and, therefore is ineffectual. Yet the declining survivability of the U.S. ICBM force in the early 1980s will make this condition unavoidable unless prompt measures are taken. Our objective must be to assure the survivability of U.S. forces possessing an unquestioned, prompt, hard-target counterforce capability sufficient to disarm Soviet military targets in a second-strike. We reject the mutual-assured-destruction (MAD) strategy of the Carter Administration which limits the President during crises to a Hobson's choice between mass mutual suicide and surrender. We propose, instead, a credible strategy which will deter a Soviet attack by the clear capability of our forces to survive and ultimately to destroy Soviet military targets.

In order to counter the problem of ICBM vulnerability, we will propose a number of initiatives to provide the necessary survivability of the ICBM force in as timely and effective a manner as possible. In addition, we will proceed with:

— the earliest possible deployment of the MX missile in a prudent survival configuration;

— accelerated development and deployment of a new manned strategic penetrating bomber that will exploit the $5.5 billion already invested in the B-1, while employing the most advanced technology available;

— deployment of an air defense system comprised of dedicated modern interceptor aircraft and early warning support systems;

— acceleration of development and deployment of strategic cruise missiles deployed on aircraft, on land, and on ships and submarines;

— modernization of the military command and control system to assure the responsiveness of U.S. strategic nuclear forces to Presidential command in peace or war; and

— vigorous research and development of an effective anti-ballistic missile system, such as is already at hand in the Soviet Union, as well as more modern ABM technologies.

For more than 20 years, commencing in the mid-1950s, the United States has maintained tactical nuclear weapons in Europe for the purpose of assuring against deep penetrations into the West by the Soviet forces. Since 1977, however, the Administration has allowed our former superiority to erode to the point where we now face a more than three-to-one disadvantage.

A Republican Administration will strive for early modernization of our theater nuclear forces so that a seamless web of deterrence can be maintained against all levels of attack, and our credibility with our European allies is restored. In consultation with them we will proceed with deployments in Europe of medium-range cruise missiles, ballistic missiles, enhanced radiation warheads, and the modernization of nuclear artillery.

Conventional Forces

The greatest single result of our loss of nuclear parity has been the manifest increase in the willingness of the Soviet Union to take risks at the conventional level. Emboldened by the Carter Administration's failure to challenge their use of surrogate Cuban forces in Africa and the later Soviet presence in Angola, Ethiopia, and South Yemen, the Soviets, for the first time in post-war history, employed their own army units outside of the Soviet bloc in a brutal invasion on Afghanistan. The invasion presents chilling evidence of the mounting threat and raises fundamental questions with respect to United States strategy.

We believe it is not feasible at this time, and in the long term would be unworkable, to deploy massive U.S. ground forces to such areas as the Persian Gulf on a permanent basis as we do in Europe and elsewhere. A more effective strategy must be built on the dual pillars of maintaining a limited full-time presence in the area as a credible interdiction force, combined with the clear capability to reinforce this presence rapidly with the forces necessary to prevail in battle. In addition, the strategy must envision military action elsewhere at points of Soviet vulnerability—an expression of the classic doctrine of global maneuver.

The forces essential to the support of such a strategy must include a much-improved Navy, the force most suitable for maintaining U.S. presence in threatened areas and protecting sea lines of communication. In addition, we will require a substantial improvement in the air and sea mobility forces and improved access to regional installations. A Republican Administration will propose their substantial improvement, to include the establishment of a permanent fleet in the Indian Ocean. We will also improve contingency planning for the use and expansion of our commercial maritime fleet, and a new rational approach to emergency use of our civil aircraft fleet.

The budget cuts imposed by Mr. Carter on the Army and his restoration of the supremacy of systems analysis in the Pentagon have resulted in slowdowns, deferrals and cost increases in nine vitally needed Army procurement programs in armor, firepower, air defense, and helicopters. These critical and long-delayed modernization programs must be restored to economical production rates and must be speeded into the field. Of equal importance is the need to bring our stocks of ammunition, spare parts and supplies—now at woefully inadequate levels—to a standard that will enable us to sustain our forces in conflict.

In addition to the strategic programs needed for our Air Force, we pledge to restore tactical aircraft development and procurement to economical levels and to speed the achievement of 26 modernized wings of aircraft able to conduct missions at night, in all weather conditions, and against the most sophisticated adversary.

We pledge to increase substantially our intra- and inter-theater airlift capability and to increase our aerial tanker fleet through procurement and speedy modernization.

Of all the services, the Navy and Marines have suffered most from Mr. Carter's cuts. Their share of the defense budget has shrunk from 40 to 33 percent during the Carter Administration. Mr. Carter slashed President Ford's 157 ship, five-year construction program to 83. He has slowed the Trident submarine and requested only one attack submarine each year in spite of a Soviet three-to-one advantage. He vetoed the Fiscal Year 79 Defense Authorization Bill because it included an aircraft carrier which a year later Congress forced him to accept. For the fourth straight year he has requested fewer than half the number of 325 aircraft needed annually to stay even with peacetime attrition and modernization requirements. He has requested fewer than one-third of the amphibious ships needed just to keep the current level of capability for the Marines, and he has opposed Marine tactical aircraft and helicopter modernization.

The current Chief of Naval Operations has testified that, "We are trying to meet a three ocean requirement with a one-and-a-half ocean Navy." Republicans pledge to reverse Mr. Carter's dismantling of U.S. Naval and Marine forces. We will restore our fleet to 600 ships at a rate equal to or exceeding that planned by President Ford. We will build more aircraft carriers, submarines and amphibious ships. We will restore Naval and Marine aircraft procurement to economical rates enabling rapid modernization of the current forces, and expansion to meet the requirements of additional aircraft carriers.

Defense Manpower and the Draft

The Republican Party is not prepared to accept a peacetime draft at this time. Under Mr. Carter, the all-volunteer force has not been given a fair chance to succeed. The unconscionable mismanagement and neglect of personnel policy by the Carter Administration has made a shambles of the all-volunteer force concept.

Perhaps the most compelling vulnerability of our forces results from the dramatic exodus of the core of highly skilled men and women who form the backbone of our military strength. This loss is the direct result of neglect by the Commander-in-Chief.

The sustained malign neglect of our military manpower is nothing short of a national scandal. This Administration's active assault on military benefits and military retirement has been accompanied by an enforced pay-cap set at half the inflation rate. The average military family has lost between 14 percent and 25 percent in purchasing power over the past seven years.

Officers and skilled enlisted personnel are leaving in droves, and 250,000 of our servicemen qualify for public assistance. Many of our career people earn less than the minimum wage. The services are currently short 70,000 senior enlisted personnel. This scandal is the direct result of Mr. Carter's willful downgrading of the military and inept mismanagement of personnel policy. As a top priority, the Republican Party pledges to end this national disgrace.

We pledge to restore a national attitude of pride and gratitude for the service of our men and women in the armed forces. We will act immediately to correct the great inequities in pay and benefits of career military personnel. Specifically, we support immediate action to:

—provide for an increase in military pay targeted in particular toward the career grades now experiencing the greatest attrition;

—increase enlistment and reenlistment bonuses;

—improve continuation bonuses for aviators;

—increase per diem travel allowances;

—increase the allowance for moving mobile homes;

—provide family separation allowances for junior personnel; and

—expand benefit entitlement under the CHAMPUS program.

A Republican Administration will index military pay and allowances to protect military personnel from absorbing the burden of inflation. We pledge that the profession of arms will be restored to its rightful place as a preeminent expression of patriotism in America.

In order to attract recruits of high ability, a Republican Administration will act to reintroduce G.I. Bill benefits for those completing two years active service. We will press for enactment of legislation denying federal funds to any educational institution that impedes access of military recruiters to their students. We regard as a serious loss the decision of many of our finest institutions of higher learning to discontinue their military officer training programs. The leadership of our armed forces must include the best trained minds in our nation. Republicans call upon our colleges and universities to shoulder their responsibilities in the defense of freedom. We will investigate legislative inducements toward this end. We will not consider a peacetime draft unless a well-managed, Congressionally-funded, full-scale effort to improve the all-volunteer force does not meet expectations.

Reserve Forces

The armed forces of the U.S. are today critically dependent upon our nation's Reserve components for both combat arms and combat support. The Army Reserve and National Guard provide one-third of the Army's combat divisions, 80 percent of its independent combat brigades, one-half of its artillery battalions, and one-third of its special forces groups. The Navy Reserve provides 90 percent of the Navy's ocean mine sweeping and two-thirds of its mobile construction battalions. The Air Force Reserve and Air National Guard provide all of our strategic interceptors, 60 percent of our tactical airlift, and one-third of our tactical fighters. Reserve and National Guard units may be mobilized for even the smallest of conflicts and many such units today are expected to deploy immediately with the active duty units they support.

Today, however, the reserves are ill equipped, underpaid, and undermanned by several hundred thousand personnel. Proper equipment, realistic, challenging training, and greater full-time support must be made available. We must ensure that all Americans take note of the proud and vital role played by the Reserve and National Guard components of the armed forces of the United States.

Readiness and Industrial Preparedness

History records that readiness for war is the surest means of preventing it. Lack of preparedness is the most dangerously provocative course we can take. Yet funding requests for sufficient fuel, spare parts, ammunition, and supplies for U.S. war reserves have been cut each year for the past four years from the minimum quantities the armed services have stated they need. This has left the U.S. Armed Forces at their lowest state of preparedness since 1950, seriously compromising their ability to sustain a military conflict.

Crippling shortages of spare parts, fuel, and ammunition compromise the ability of the armed forces to sustain a major military conflict. Some critical types of ammunition could not support combat operations for more than a week although we are committed to holding a 90-day inventory of major ammunition types. In addition, critical facilities such as airfields, ammunition depots, maintenance installations, and living quarters for our troops are in serious disrepair. The backlog of deferred maintenance and the underfunded purchase of vital combat consumables is so vast that years of effort will be required to rebuild U.S. forces to the required level of readiness.

The problem of maintaining the day-to-day combat readiness of U.S. armed forces is compounded by the reduced ability of American industry to respond to wartime contingencies. Reduced acquisition of equipment for the modernization of the armed forces and the Carter Administration's failure to maintain combat readiness have eroded the incentive of American industry to maintain capacity adequate to potential defense requirements.

Republicans pledge to make the combat readiness of U.S. Armed Forces and the preparedness of the industrial base a top priority.

Research and Development

Research and Development (R&D) provides a critical means by which our nation can cope with threats to our security. In the past, the United States' qualitative and technological superiority provided a foundation for our military superiority. Yet we are now on the verge of losing this advantage to the Soviet Union because of Mr. Carter's opposition to real increases in the R&D effort. Delays imposed on the R&D process now allow 7 to 10 years or more to elapse between the time when a new weapon system is proposed and when it becomes available.

The Soviet Union now invests nearly twice as much in military research and development as does the United States. This disparity in effort threatens American technological superiority in the mid-1980s and could result in Soviet breakthroughs in advanced weapon systems.

Republicans pledge to revitalize America's military research and development efforts, from basic research through the deployment of weapons and support systems, to assure that our vital security needs will be met for the balance of the century. We will seek increased funding to guarantee American superiority in this critical area and to enable us to deal with possible breakthroughs in anti-missile defense, anti-satellite killers, high-energy directed systems, and the military and civilian exploitation of space.

America's technological advantage has always depended upon its interaction with our civilian science and technology sector. The economic policy of the Carter Administration has severely encumbered private research and development efforts, thereby depriving both our civil and military sectors of the fruits of scientific innovation.

Underfunding of beneficial government-sponsored research efforts in basic and applied scientific research has disrupted the benefits of years of effective effort. In particular, America's preeminence in the exploration of space is threatened by the failure of the Carter Administration to fund fully the Space Shuttle program (with its acknowledged benefits for both the civil and military applications) as well as advanced exploration programs. Republicans pledge to support a vigorous space research program.

Management and Organization

The Republican Party pledges to reform the defense programming and budgeting management system es-

tablished by the Carter Administration. The ill-informed, capricious intrusions of the Office of Management and Budget, and the Department of Defense Office of Program Analysis and Evaluation have brought defense planning full circle to the worst faults of the McNamara years. Orderly planning by the military services has become impossible. Waste, inefficiency, and paralysis have been the hallmarks of Carter Administration defense planning and budgeting. This has resulted in huge cost overruns and in protracted delays in placing advanced systems in the field.

National Intelligence

At a time of increasing danger, the U.S. intelligence community has lost much of its ability to supply the President, senior U.S. officials, and the Congress with accurate and timely analyses concerning fundamental threats to our nation's security. Morale and public confidence have been eroded and American citizens and friendly foreign intelligence services have become increasingly reluctant to cooperate with U.S. agencies. As a result of such problems, the U.S. intelligence community has incorrectly assessed critical foreign developments, as in Iran, and has, above all, underestimated the size and purpose of the Soviet Union's military efforts.

We believe that a strong national consensus has emerged on the need to make our intelligence community a reliable and productive instrument of national policy once again. In pursuing its objectives, the Soviet Union and its surrogates operate by a far different set of rules than does the United States. We do not favor countering their efforts by mirroring their tactics. However, the United States requires a realistic assessment of the threats it faces, and it must have the best intelligence capability in the world. Republicans pledge this for the United States.

A Republican Administration will seek to improve U.S. intelligence capabilities for technical and clandestine collection, cogent analysis, coordinated counterintelligence and covert action.

We will reestablish the President's Foreign Intelligence Advisory Board, abolished by the Carter Administration, as a permanent non-partisan body of distinguished Americans to perform a constant audit of national intelligence research and performance. We will propose methods of providing alternative intelligence estimates in order to improve the quality of the estimates by constructive competition.

Republicans will undertake an urgent effort to rebuild the intelligence agencies, and to give full support to their knowledgeable and dedicated staffs. We will propose legislation to enable intelligence officers and their agents to operate safely and efficiently abroad.

We will support legislation to invoke criminal sanctions against anyone who discloses the identities of U.S. intelligence officers abroad or who makes unauthorized disclosures of U.S. intelligence sources and methods.

We will support amendments to the Freedom of Information Act and the Privacy Act to permit meaningful background checks on individuals being considered for sensitive positions and to reduce costly and capricious requests to the intelligence agencies.

We will provide our government with the capability to help influence international events vital to our national security interests, a capability which only the United States among the major powers has denied itself.

A Republican Administration will seek adequate safeguards to ensure that past abuses will not recur, but we will seek the repeal of ill-considered restrictions sponsored by Democrats, which have debilitated U.S. intelligence capabilities while easing the intelligence collection and subversion efforts of our adversaries.

Terrorism

In the decade of the seventies, all civilized nations were shaken by a wave of widespread, international terrorist attacks. Time and again, nations and individuals have been subjected to extortion and murder at the hands of extremists who reject the rule of law, civil order, and the sanctity of individual human rights. Terrorism has been elevated to the level of overt national policy as authorities in Iran, encouraged by the Soviet Union, have held 53 Americans captive for more than eight months. Comprehensive support of international terrorist organizations has been a central, though generally covert, element of Soviet foreign policy.

Republicans believe that this tragic history contains lessons that must serve as the basis for a determined international effort to end this era of terrorism. We believe that certain principles have emerged from incidents in which states have defeated terrorist attacks, and we believe the United States should take the lead in a multilateral drive to eliminate the terrorist threat. A first requirement is the establishment of a military capability to deal promptly and effectively with any terrorist acts. We cannot afford, as in the abortive Iranian rescue mission, to allow months to pass while we prepare responses.

The United States must provide the leadership to forge an international consensus that firmness and refusal to concede are ultimately the only effective deterrents to terrorism. The United States should take the lead in combating international terrorism. We must recognize and be prepared to deal with the reality of expanded Soviet sponsorship of international terrorist movements. Development of an effective anti-terrorist military capability and establishment of a Congressional and Executive capability to oversee our internal security efforts will no longer be neglected.

The Role of Arms Control in Defense Policy

The Republican approach to arms control has been markedly different from that of the Democratic Party. It has been based on three fundamental premises:

—first, before arms control negotiations may be undertaken, the security of the United States must be assured by the funding and deployment of strong military forces sufficient to deter conflict at any level or to prevail in battle should aggression occur;

—second, negotiations must be conducted on the basis of strict reciprocity of benefits—unilateral restraint by the U.S. has failed to bring reductions by the Soviet Union; and

—third, arms control negotiations, once entered, represent an important political and military undertaking that cannot be divorced from the broader political and military behavior of the parties.

A Republican Administration will pursue arms control solely on the principles outlined above.

During the past three and one-half years, the Carter Administration's policy has been diametrically opposed to these principles. First, by its willful cancellation or delay of essential strategic military programs such as the B-1, the MX missile, and the Trident submarine, it has seriously damaged the credibility and effectiveness of the U.S. deterrent force. Second, by not insisting upon corresponding concessions from the Soviet Union it has, in effect, practiced unilateral disarmament and removed any incentives for the Soviets to negotiate for what they could obviously achieve by waiting. The Republican Party rejects the fundamentally flawed SALT II treaty negotiated by the Carter Administration.

The Republican Party deplores the attempts of the Carter Administration to cover up Soviet non-compliance with arms control agreements including the now overwhelming evidence of blatant Soviet violation of the Biological Warfare Convention by secret production of biological agents at Sverdlovsk.

In our platform four years ago, we stated that, "The growth of civilian nuclear technology and the rising demand for nuclear power as an alternative to increasingly costly fossil fuel resources, combine to require our recognition of the potential dangers associated with such development." We called for the formation of new multilateral arrangements to control the export of sensitive nuclear technologies. Unfortunately, the Carter Administration has failed to provide the leadership and creative diplomacy essential to forging effective international safeguards and cooperation in this vital area. In particular we oppose and deplore the pending delivery to India of nuclear material which can be directed to the manufacture of weapons.

The Republican Party reaffirms its commitment to the early establishment of effective multilateral arrangements for the safe management and monitoring of all transfers and uses of nuclear materials in the international market.

Foreign Policy

U.S.-Soviet Relations

The premier challenge facing the United States, its allies, and the entire globe is to check the Soviet Union's global ambitions. This challenge must be met, for the present danger is greater than ever before in the 200-year history of the United States. The Soviet Union is still accelerating its drive for military superiority and is intensifying its military pressure and its ideological combat against the industrial democracies and the vulnerable developing nations of the world.

Republicans believe that the United States can only negotiate with the Soviet Union from a position of unquestioned principle and unquestioned strength. Unlike Mr. Carter we see nothing "inordinate" in our nation's historic judgment about the goals, tactics, and dangers of Soviet communism. Unlike the Carter Administration, we were not surprised by the brutal Soviet invasion of Afghanistan or by other Soviet violations of major international agreements regulating international behavior, human rights, and the use of military force. And, unlike the Carter Administration, we will not base our policies toward the Soviet Union on naive expectations, unilateral concessions, futile rhetoric, and insignificant maneuvers.

As the Soviet Union continues in its expansionist course, the potential for dangerous confrontations has increased. Republicans will strive to resolve critical issues through peaceful negotiations, but we recognize that negotiations conducted from a position of military weakness can result only in further damage to American interests.

A Republican Administration will continue to seek to negotiate arms reductions in Soviet strategic weapons, in Soviet bloc force levels in Central Europe, and in other areas that may be amenable to reductions or limitations. We will pursue hard bargaining for equitable, verifiable, and enforceable agreements. We will accept no agreement for the sake of having an agreement, and will accept no agreements that do not fundamentally enhance our national security.

Republicans oppose the transfer of high technology to the Soviet Union and its Eastern European satellites such as has been done in the past permitting development of sophisticated military hardware which threatens the United States and our allies. The Carter Administration has encouraged the most extensive raid on American technology by the Soviet bloc since World War II. The Soviet Union has gained invaluable scientific expertise in electronics, computer sciences, manufacturing techniques, mining, transportation, aviation, agriculture, and a host of other disciplines. This has contributed to the ability of the Soviet Union to divert investment and manpower from their civilian economy to their armed forces. The fruits of Soviet access to American technology will improve the performance of the Soviet military establishment for years to come. The matter is compounded by the practice of subsidized financing of much of the Soviet bloc's acquisition of American technology through U.S. financial institutions.

Republicans pledge to stop the flow of technology to the Soviet Union that could contribute, directly or indirectly, to the growth of their military power. This objective will be pursued by a Republican Administration with our allies and other friendly nations as well. We will ensure that the Soviet Union fully understands that it will be expected to fulfill all of the commercial and diplomatic obligations it has undertaken in its international agreements.

We oppose Mr. Carter's singling out of the American farmer to bear the brunt of his failed foreign policy by imposition of a partial and incompetently managed grain embargo. Because of his failure to obtain cooperation from other grain exporting countries, the embargo has been a travesty and a substitute for policy. We call for the immediate lifting of this embargo.

We reaffirm our commitment to press the Soviet Union to implement the United Nations Declaration on Human Rights and the Helsinki Agreements which guarantee rights such as the free interchange of information and the right to emigrate. A Republican Administration will press the Soviet Union to end its harassment and imprisonment of those who speak in opposition to official policy, who seek to worship according to their religious beliefs, or who represent diverse ethnic minorities and nationalities.

Republicans deplore growing anti-semitism in the Soviet Union and the mistreatment of "refuseniks" by Soviet authorities. The decline in exit visas to Soviet Jews and others seeking religious freedom and the promulgation of ever more rigorous conditions inhibiting their emigration is a fundamental affront to human rights and the U.N. Charter. Republicans will make the subject of emigration from the Soviet Union a central issue in Soviet-American relations. Human rights in the Soviet Union will not be ignored as it has been during the Carter Administration. As a party to the Helsinki Conference Final Act, a Republican Administration will insist on full Soviet compliance with the humanitarian provisions of the agreement.

Republicans pledge our continued support for the people of Cuba and the captive nations of Central and Eastern Europe in their hope to achieve self-determination. We stand firmly for the independence of Yugoslavia. We support self-determination and genuine independence for new captive nations of Africa and Latin America threatened by the growing domination of Soviet power.

A Republican Administration will end the sustained Carter policy of misleading the American people about Soviet policies and behavior. We will spare no efforts to publicize to the world the fundamental differences in the two systems and will strengthen such means as the International Communication Agency, the Voice of America, Radio Free Europe, and Radio Liberty actively to articulate U.S. values and policies, and to highlight the weaknesses of totalitarianism.

We pledge to end the Carter cover-up of Soviet violations of SALT I and II, to end the cover-up of Soviet violation of the Biological Warfare Convention, and to end the cover-up of Soviet use of gas and chemical weapons in Afghanistan and elsewhere.

NATO and Western Europe

Since its inception three decades ago, the North Atlantic Treaty Organization has expressed the collective will of free nations to resist totalitarian aggression. As a cornerstone of the Western Alliance, NATO has stood on the firm foundations of American strategic strength, joint Allied defense efforts, and cooperative diplomacy based on shared interest and close consultations. The Republican Party recognizes that NATO serves the vital interests of the entire Western world and over the years we have continued to give the Alliance our undiminished and bipartisan support.

Republicans deplore the current drifts toward neutralism in Western Europe. We recognize that NATO and our Western Allies today face the greatest array of threats in their history, both from within and from without. Through its inept policies, the Carter Administration has substantially contributed to the evident erosion of Alliance security and confidence in the U.S. A Republican Administration, as one of its highest priorities and in close concert with our NATO partners, will therefore ensure that the United States leads a concerted effort to rebuild a strong, confident Alliance fully prepared to meet the threats and the challenges of the 1980s.

The chief external threat to NATO is that of developing Soviet military superiority. In a period of supposed "detente," the NATO nations have too often cut back or delayed essential defense programs and too often placed excessive hopes in arms control negotiations, while the Soviet-dominated Warsaw Pact has been transformed into the world's most powerful offensive military force.

Three-and-a-half years of Carter Administration policies have resulted in an increased threat to vital Alliance security interests. Mr. Carter's unilateral cancellations, reductions, and long delays in the B-1, Trident, MX, cruise-missile, and shipbuilding programs have increased the vulnerability of the U.S. strategic triad and have contributed to a developing strategic imbalance which undermines the foundation of Western deterrent and defense capabilities. His fundamentally flawed SALT II treaty would have codified Western inferiority. His reversals on the development and deployment of the "enhanced radiation" or neutron weapon, his treatment of future theater nuclear force modernization negotiations, and his manner of dealing with terrorist actions directed against Americans abroad, further undermined Alliance solidarity and security.

These Carter Administration inconsistencies have caused disunity in the Alliance. We have seen confusion in the fields of trade, fiscal, and energy policies. The lack of close coordination regarding Iran, the Middle East, Afghanistan, the Olympic boycott, nuclear proliferation, East-West trade, human rights, North-South issues, and a host of other international issues affecting Alliance interests, has reinforced Allied concerns. Republicans are concerned that these Carter Administration actions have increased Allied temptation to conduct independent diplomacy and to seek accommodation in the face of pressure from the Soviet Union. In this regard, we categorically reject unilateral moratoria on the deployment by the U.S. and NATO of theater nuclear weapons. Further, Republicans will oppose arms control agreements that interfere with the transfer of military technology to our allies.

In pledging renewed United States leadership, cooperation, and consultation, Republicans assert their expectation that each of the allies will bear a fair share of the common defense effort and that they will work closely together in support of common Alliance goals. Defense budgets, weapons acquisition, force readiness, and diplomatic coordination need to be substantially increased and improved. Within Europe as well as in areas beyond Europe which affect the shared vital interests of the Alliance, we will seek to increase our cooperative efforts, including increased planning for joint actions to meet common threats.

The Republican Party recognizes the vital importance of countries defending the flanks of NATO.

We will search for an early resolution of problems that currently inhibit the effective participation of all the nations of NATO's southern flank and we call for the integration of Spain into the North Atlantic Alliance.

Middle East, Persian Gulf

In the past three years, the nations of the Middle East and Persian Gulf have suffered an unprecedented level of political, economic, and military turmoil. The Soviet Union has been prompt in turning these sources of instability to its advantage and is now in an excellent position to exploit the chaos in Iran and to foment similar upheavals in other countries in the region. Today, the countries of the Middle East and Persian Gulf are encircled as never before by Soviet advisers and troops based in the Horn of Africa, South Yemen, and Afghanistan. Moreover, the Soviets have close political and military ties with other states in the region.

The Soviet goal is clear — to use subversion and the threat of military intervention to establish a controlling influence over the regions' resource-rich states, and thereby to gain decisive political and economic leverage over Western and Third World nations vulnerable to economic coercion. The first signs of Soviet success in this undertaking are already evidenced in the recent proposal by European countries to associate the Palestinian Liberation Organization in the West Bank autonomy talks.

Republicans believe that the restoration of order and stability to the region must be premised upon an understanding of the interrelationship between Soviet and radical Palestinian goals, the fundamental requirements of stable economic development and marketing of the area's resources, and the growing ferment among Islamic radical groups. Republicans believe that a wise and credible United States policy must make clear that our foremost concern is for the long-term peaceful development of all states in the region, not purely a self-serving exploitation of its resources. Our goal is to bring a just and lasting peace to the Arab-Israeli conflict.

With respect to an ultimate peace settlement, Republicans reject any call for involvement of the PLO as not in keeping with the long-term interests of either Israel or the Palestinian Arabs. The imputation of legitimacy to organizations not yet willing to acknowledge the fundamental right to existence of the State of Israel is wrong. Repeated indications, even when subsequently denied, of the Carter Administration's involvement with the PLO has done serious harm to the credibility of U.S. policy in the Middle East and has encouraged the PLO's position of intransigence. We believe the establishment of a Palestinian State on the West Bank would be destabilizing and harmful to the peace process.

Our long and short-term policies for the area must be developed in consultation with our NATO allies, Israel, Egypt, and other friends in the area, and we will spare no effort in seeking their consultation throughout the policy process, not merely demanding their acquiescence to our plans.

The sovereignty, security, and integrity of the State of Israel is a moral imperative and serves the strategic interests of the United States. Republicans reaffirm our fundamental and enduring commitment to this principle. We will continue to honor our nation's commitment through political, economic, diplomatic, and military aid. We fully recognize the strategic importance of Israel and the deterrent role of its armed forces in the Middle-East and East-West military equations.

Republicans recognize that a just and durable peace for all nations of the region is the best guarantee of continued stability and is vital to deterring further Soviet inroads. Peace between Israel and its neighbors requires direct negotiations among the states involved. Accordingly, a Republican Administration will encourage the peace process now in progress between Egypt and Israel, will seek to broaden it, and will welcome those Arab nations willing to live in peace with Israel. We are encouraged by the support given to the Middle East peace process by Sudan and Oman and the progress brought about by the strong and effective leadership of their governments.

We applaud the vision and courage of Egyptian President Anwar Sadat and we pledge to build our relationship with Egypt in cultural affairs, economic development, and military cooperation.

Republicans recognize that the Carter Administration's vacillations have left friend and foe alike unsure as to United States' policies. While reemphasizing our commitment to Israel, a Republican Administration will pursue close ties and friendship with moderate Arab states. We will initiate the economic and military framework for assuring long-term stability both in the internal development of regional states and an orderly marketplace for the area's resources. We will make clear that any reimposition of an oil embargo would be viewed as a hostile act. We will oppose discriminatory practices, including boycotts, and we will discourage arms sales which contribute to regional instability.

Republicans believe that Jerusalem should remain an undivided city with continued free and unimpeded access to all holy places by people of all faiths.

The Americas

Latin America is an area of primary interest for the United States. Yet, the Carter Administration's policies have encouraged a precipitous decline in United

States relations with virtually every country in the region. The nations of South and Central America have been battered by the Carter Administration's economic and diplomatic sanctions linked to its undifferentiated charges of human rights violations.

In the Caribbean and Central America, the Carter Administration stands by while Castro's totalitarian Cuba, financed, directed, and supplied by the Soviet Union, aggressively trains, arms, and supports forces of warfare and revolution throughout the Western hemisphere. Yet the Carter Administration has steadily denied these threats and in many cases has actively worked to undermine governments and parties opposed to the expansion of Soviet power. This must end.

We deplore the Marxist Sandinista takeover of Nicaragua and the Marxist attempts to destabilize El Salvador, Guatemala, and Honduras. We do not support United States assistance to any Marxist government in this hemisphere and we oppose the Carter Administration aid program for the government of Nicaragua. However, we will support the efforts of the Nicaraguan people to establish a free and independent government.

Republicans deplore the dangerous and incomprehensible Carter Administration policies toward Cuba. The Administration has done nothing about the Soviet combat brigade stationed there, or about the transfer of new Soviet offensive weapons to Cuba in the form of modern MIG aircraft and submarines. It has done nothing about the Soviet pilots flying air defense missions in Cuba or about the extensive improvements to Soviet military bases, particularly the submarine facilities in Cienfuegos, and the expanded Soviet intelligence facilities near Havana.

Republicans recognize the importance of our relations within this hemisphere and pledge a strong new United States policy in the Americas. We will stand firm with countries seeking to develop their societies while combating the subversion and violence exported by Cuba and Moscow. We will return to the fundamental principle of treating a friend as a friend and self-proclaimed enemies as enemies, without apology. We will make it clear to the Soviet Union and Cuba that their subversion and their build-up of offensive military forces is unacceptable.

Republicans recognize the special importance of Puerto Rico and the United States Virgin Islands in the defense of freedom in the Caribbean. We believe that Puerto Rico's admission to the Union would demonstrate our common purpose in the face of growing Soviet and Cuban pressure in that area.

Republicans recognize the fundamental importance of Mexico and restoration of good working relations with that country will be of highest priority. A new Republican Administration will immediately begin high-level, comprehensive negotiations, seeking solutions to common problems on the basis of mutual interest and recognizing that each country has unique contributions to make in resolving practical problems.

Republicans pledge to reestablish close and cooperative relations with the nations of Central and South America and repair the diplomatic damage done by the Carter Administration. We pledge understanding and assistance in the efforts of these nations, and their neighbors, to deal seriously with serious domestic problems.

We pledge to ensure that the Panama Canal remains open, secure, and free of hostile control.

The reservations and understandings to the Panama Canal treaties, including those assuring the United States of primary responsibility of protecting and defending the Canal, are an integral part of those treaties and we will hold Panama to strict interpretation of the language of the treaties, clearly established by the legislative history of Senate adoption of amendments, reservations, and understandings at the time of Senate approval of the treaties.

We would remind the American taxpayers that President Carter gave repeated assurances that the Panama Canal treaties would not cost the American taxpayers "one thin dime" and we emphasize the fact that implementing the Panama Canal treaties will cost them $4.2 billion.

We will work closely with Canada as our most important trading partner in the hemisphere. We will foster the deep affinity that exists between our two nations and our policies will be based on mutual understanding and complete equality.

We will seek a North American Accord designed to foster close cooperation and mutual benefit between the United States, Canada, and Mexico.

A new Republican Administration will, in close cooperation with its neighbors, seek to work together to build prosperity and to strengthen common efforts to combat externally produced revolution and violence.

Asia and the Pacific

The United States is and must remain a Pacific power. It is in our vital interest to maintain U.S. guaranteed stability in the area. Republicans recognize the dangerous shifts in power that have accelerated under the current Democratic Administration. The balance on the Korean peninsula has shifted dangerously toward the North. Soviet naval forces in Asia and the Pacific have steadily increased and are now at least equal to U.S. Naval forces there. Unilateral cancellation by the United States of the mutual defense pact with Taiwan and the abrupt announcement of withdrawal of U.S. ground forces from Korea, have led countries throughout the region to question the value of alliance with the United States.

A new Republican Administration will restore a strong American role in Asia and the Pacific. We will make it clear that any military action which threatens the independence of America's allies and friends will bring a response sufficient to make its cost prohibitive to potential adversaries.

Japan will continue to be a pillar of American policy in Asia. Republicans recognize the mutual interests and special relationships that exist between the two countries in their commitment to democracy and in trade, defense, and cultural matters. A new Republican Administration will work closely with the Japanese government to resolve outstanding trade and energy problems on an equitable basis. We strongly support a substantially increased Japanese national defense effort and reaffirm that our long-range objectives of military security and a balancing of the expanded Soviet military presence in the region are of mutual interest.

Republicans recognize the unique danger presented to our ally, South Korea. We will encourage continued efforts to expand political participation and individual liberties within the country, but will recognize the special problems brought on by subversion and potential aggression from the North. We will maintain American ground and air forces in South Korea, and will not reduce our presence further. Our treaty commitments to South Korea will be restated in unequivocal terms and we will reestablish the process of close consultations between our governments.

We reaffirm our special and historic relationships with the Philippines, Singapore, Malaysia, Indonesia, Thailand, New Zealand, and Australia. Republicans will recognize the long friendship with these countries and will cultivate and strengthen our diplomatic and trade relationships.

We deplore the brutal acts of Communist Vietnam against the people of Cambodia and Laos. We recognize that the suffering of refugees from these ravaged countries represents a major moral challenge to the world and one of the great human tragedies of modern times. A Republican Administration will work actively to bring relief to these suffering people, especially those who have sought refuge in Thailand. We value the special contribution the people of Thailand have made to the refugees by opening their borders and saving hundreds of thousands of them from death, and we pledge to provide full economic aid and military material to assist Thailand in repelling Vietnamese aggression.

We believe that no expanded relations with Communist Vietnam should be pursued while it continues its course of brutal expansionism and genocide. We pledge that a Republican Administration will press for full accounting of Americans still listed as missing in action.

Recognizing the growing importance of the People's Republic of China in world affairs, Republicans—who took the historic initiative in opening the lines of communication with that nation—will continue the process of building a working relation with the PRC. Growing contacts between the United States and the People's Republic of China reflect the interests of both nations, as well as some common perceptions of recent changes in the global military balance. We will not ignore the profound differences in our respective philosophies, governmental institutions, policies, and concepts of individual liberty.

We will strive for the creation of conditions that will foster the peaceful elaboration of our relationship with the People's Republic of China. We will exercise due caution and prudence with respect to our own vital interests, especially in the field of expanding trade, including the transfer of sophisticated technology with potential offensive military applications. The relationship between the two countries must be based on mutual respect and reciprocity, with due regard for the need to maintain peace and stability in Asia.

At the same time, we deplore the Carter Administration's treatment of Taiwan, our long-time ally and friend. We pledge that our concern for the safety and security of the 17 millon people of Taiwan will be constant. We would regard any attempt to alter Taiwan's status by force as a threat to peace in the region. We declare that the Republican Administration, in strengthening relations with Taiwan, will create conditions leading to the expansion of trade, and will give priority consideration to Taiwan's defense requirements.

Africa

The Republican Party supports the principle and process of self-determination in Africa. We reaffirm our commitment to this principle and pledge our strong opposition to the effort of the Soviet Union and its militant allies to subvert this process. Soviet bases, tens of thousands of Cuban troops, and Soviet-bloc subversion are unacceptable.

We recognize that much is at stake in Africa and that the United States and the industrial West have vital interests there—economically, strategically, and politically. Working closely with our allies, a Republican Administration will seek to assist the countries of Africa with our presence, our markets, our know-how, and our investment. We will work to create a climate of economic and political development and confidence. We will encourage and assist business to play a major role in support of regional industrial development programs, mineral complexes, and agricultural self-sufficiency.

Republicans believe that African nations, if given a choice, will reject the Marxist, totalitarian model being forcibly imposed by the Soviet Union and its surrogates including Cuban and Nicaraguan troops as well as East German secret police. We believe that they know the Communist powers have relatively little to offer them and that, for the most part, the African peoples are convinced that the West is central to the world stability and economic growth on which their own fortunes ultimately depend.

A Republican Administration will adhere to policies that reflect the complex origins of African conflicts, demonstrate that we know what U.S. interests are, and back those interests in meaningful ways. We will recognize the important role of economic and military assistance programs and will devote major resources to assisting African development and stability when such aid is given on a bilateral basis and contributes directly to American interests on the continent.

In Southern Africa, American policies must be guided by common sense and by our own humanitarian principles. Republicans believe that our history has meaning for Africa in demonstrating that a multiracial society with guarantees of individual rights is possible and can work. We must remain open and helpful to all parties, whether in the new Zimbabwe, in Namibia, or in the Republic of South Africa. A Republican Administration will not endorse situations or constitutions, in whatever society, which are racist in purpose or in effect. It will not expect miracles, but will press for genuine progress in achieving goals consistent with American ideals.

Foreign Assistance and Regional Security

The United States has included foreign assistance and regional security as a major element of its foreign policy for four decades. Properly administered and focused, foreign assistance can be an effective means of promoting United States foreign policy objectives, and serve to enhance American security by assisting friendly nations to become stronger and more capable of defending themselves and their regions against foreign subversion and attack.

The threat posed to individual third world nations is beyond the means of any one of them to counter alone. A Republican Administration will seek to strengthen and assist regional security arrangements among nations prepared to assume the burden of their defense.

No longer should American foreign assistance programs seek to force acceptance of American governmental forms. The principal consideration should be whether or not extending assistance to a nation or

group of nations will advance America's interests and objectives. The single-minded attempt to force acceptance of U.S. values and standards of democracy has undermined several friendly nations, and has made possible the advance of Soviet interests in Asia, the Middle East, Africa, and in the Western Hemisphere in the past four years.

American foreign economic assistance is not a charitable venture; charity is most effectively carried out by private entities. Only by private economic development by the people of the nations involved has poverty ever been overcome. U.S. foreign economic assistance should have a catalytic effect on indigenous economic development, and should only be extended when it is consistent with America's foreign policy interest. America's foreign assistance programs should be a vehicle for exporting the American idea.

A Republican Administration will emphasize bilateral assistance programs whenever possible. Bilateral programs provide the best assurance that aid programs will be fully accountable to the American taxpayer, and wholly consistent with our foreign policy interests.

The effort of the Carter Administration to diminish the role of American military assistance and foreign military sales in our foreign policy has had several negative effects:

—it has resulted in the export of many thousands of American jobs as the Soviet Union, Britain, and France have taken sales prohibited to American manufacturers;

—it has reduced the ability of friendly nations to defend their independence against Soviet-sponsored subversion, resulting in several cases, in abject takeovers by overtly pro-Soviet regimes; and

—it has weakened the fabric of the U.S. alliance structure by making the U.S. appear to be an unreliable ally, a trend which can only lead to the undesirable attempt by nations fearful of their security to seek to acquire their own nuclear weapons.

Decisions to provide military assistance should be made on the basis of U.S. foreign policy objectives. Such assistance to any nation need not imply complete approval of a regime's domestic policy. Republicans pledge to strengthen America's presence abroad by well-constructed programs of military assistance to promote national and regional security.

The manipulation of foreign arms sales has been one of the most seriously abused policy initiatives of the Carter Administration. The establishment of arbitrary ceilings on foreign sales, and the complex procedural and policy guidelines governing such sales have impeded the support of U.S. foreign policy objectives abroad. Friendly and allied nations alike have had to turn elsewhere for arms. This has stimulated the growth of a new arms industry in developing nations.

Republicans pledge to reform and rebuild U.S. military assistance and foreign arms sales policies so that they will serve American interests in promoting regional security arrangements and the individual defense needs of friendly nations.

International Economic Policy

The American economy has an abundance of human and material resources, but nevertheless, it is part of a larger global economy. Our domestic prosperity and international competitiveness depend upon our participation in the international economy. Moreover, our security interests are in part determined by international economic factors. Yet the Carter Administration has largely ignored the role of international economics in relations between the United States and friendly nations throughout the world. The Administration has conducted its international economic policy at cross-purposes with other dimensions of its foreign policy, resulting in strains within the Western alliance and a general decline in the domestic prosperity. Under a Republican Administration, our international economic policy will be harmonized with our foreign and defense policies to leave no doubt as to the strategy and purpose of American policy.

The economic policy of the Carter Administration has led to the most serious decline in the value of the dollar in history. The ability of Americans to purchase goods and services or to invest abroad has been diminished by Carter Administration policies devaluing the dollar. Republicans will conduct international economic policy in a manner that will stabilize the value of the dollar at home and abroad.

The Republican Party believes the United States must adopt an aggressive export policy. For too long, our trade policy has been geared toward helping our foreign trading partners. Now, we have to put the United States back on the world export map. We helped pull other countries out of the post-World War II economic chaos; it is time to remedy our own crisis. Trade, especially exporting, must be high on our list of national priorities. The Republicans will put it there and will promote trade to ensure the long-term health of the U.S. economy.

Exports can play a key role in strengthening the U.S. economy, creating jobs and improving our standard of living. A $15 billion increase in exports can increase employment by 1,000,000, the Gross National Product by $37 billion per year, and private investment by $4 billion per year. Nevertheless, the Carter Administration has placed exporting at the bottom of its priority list. The present Administration's trade policies lack coordination, cohesiveness, and true commitment to improving our export performance. Rather than helping to create strong exporters in the United States and thereby create more jobs for Americans, the Carter Administration's trade policies have discouraged traders. At best, the Administration has adopted a passive approach to trade, merely reacting to changing world economies rather than actively seeking to promote a global structure that best addresses America's needs. As a result, we lag seriously behind our foreign competitors in trade performance and economic strength. Export promotion will be a central objective of international economic policy in a Republican Administration.

A Republican Administration will emphasize a policy of free trade, but will expect our trading partners to do so as well. The failure of the Carter Administration energetically to pursue negotiations designed to improve the access of American exports to foreign markets has contributed, in part, to protectionist sentiment.

Domestic problems—over-burdensome government regulations, excessive taxation, inflationary monetary policy, and an unstable economy—have contributed to the protectionist sentiments as well. We realize that protectionist legislation has engendered retaliation by America's trading partners in the past resulting in "beggar thy neighbor" policies that had such disastrous consequences in the 1930s.

Republicans are committed to protect American jobs and American workers first and foremost. The Republican Party believes in free trade, and we will insist that our trade policy be based on the principles of reciprocity and equity. We oppose subsidies, tariff and non-tariff barriers that unfairly restrict access of American products to foreign markets. We will not stand idly by as the jobs of millions of Americans in domestic industries, such as automobiles, textiles, steel, and electronics are jeopardized and lost. We pledge to strengthen trade agreements and to change the Carter economic policies that have undermined the capability of American agriculture and industry to compete abroad.

Republicans believe that this nation's international trade balance can be improved through the elimination of disincentives for exporters. Statutory and regulatory requirements that inhibit exports should be reviewed and, where practical, eliminated. We further recognize that government can play a role in promoting international trade by establishing incentives for exports, especially those for small and medium size business. We pledge also to work with our trading partners to eliminate subsidies to exports and dumping.

The ability of the United States to compete in foreign markets is hampered by the excessive taxation of Americans working abroad who contributed to our domestic well-being by promoting international trade. Increased exports to our trading partners result in jobs and a rising standard of living at home. Carter Administration policy has the effect of discouraging the presence of American businessmen abroad due to the unfairly high level of taxation levied against them. A Republican Administration will support legislation designed to eliminate this inequity so that American citizens can fully participate in international commerce without fear of discriminatory taxation.

The Security of Energy and Raw Materials Access

The security of America's foreign sources of energy and raw material supply can no longer be ignored. The United States imports 50 percent of its domestic petroleum requirements, and depends upon foreign sources for 22 of the 74 non-fuel raw materials essential to a modern industrial economy. Nine of the most critical raw materials are almost entirely (i.e., more than 90 percent) located abroad. In contrast, the Soviet Union imports only 2 critical minerals at a level in excess of 50 percent of domestic consumption.

Reducing reliance on uncertain foreign sources and assuring access to foreign energy and raw materials requires the harmonization of economic policy with our defense and foreign policy. Domestic economic and regulatory policy must be adjusted to remove impediments to greater development of our own energy and raw materials resources. Democratic policies for federal land management, taxation, monetary policy, and economic regulation have served to increase America's dependence on foreign sources of energy and raw materials. Republicans pledge to work to eliminate domestic disincentives to the exploitation of these resources.

Multilateral negotiations have thus far insufficiently focused attention on U.S. long-term security requirements. A pertinent example of this phenomenon is the Law of the Sea Conference, where negotiations have served to inhibit U.S. exploitation of the sea-bed for its abundant mineral resources. Too much concern has been lavished on nations unable to carry out sea-bed mining with insufficient attention paid to gaining early American access to it. A Republican Administration will conduct multilateral negotiations in a manner that reflects America's abilities and long-term interest in access to raw material and energy resources.

Resource access will assume an important place in defense and economic planning under a Republican Administration. Since America's allies are, in most cases, more dependent than the U.S. on foreign sources of energy and raw materials, they too have a vital interest in the defense of their access to these critical resources. Republicans pledge to promote allied defense cooperation to assure protection from military threats to overseas resources.

Socialist Platform 1980

PROGRAM FOR THE 80S: HUMANIZE AMERICA!

Our focus in the 80s is the immediate halt in preparation for war; disarmament for survival; the development of safe energy programs; and a full-employment economy.

We emphasize an immediate increase in the use of technical assistance, food and other resources, to the developing nations.

Americans can take back the power to solve our problems by beginning the transfer of power from a small handful of interlocking corporations back to our neighborhoods and democratic unions.

More decentralized functions of government are essential to democratic socialism. Unrepresentative, unresponsive, top-heavy governments discourage citizen participation — particularly by hoarding the information needed by citizens for informed decision-making.

Our aim is the social ownership and democratic control of the major means of production and distribution. Democratic socialism is the extension of democracy from the ballot box to the workplace and the community, the eradication of race and sex discrimination, and the recognition of the right of every individual to maximum personal development, health care, economic security, and the humane use of science and technology.

DOMESTIC POLICY

The Economy

The militarization of America not only increases the prospect of war abroad and repression at home, it is also the wellhead of inflation. The military budget, scheduled for $175 billion in 1980, devours the productive effort of the work force and scarce materials, for products which at best become useless and obsolete and at worst endanger us through nuclear leakage, accidental explosion, or war. Buying power is introduced into the economy without corresponding goods and services.

Mutual disarmament will free the billions of dollars needed to meet basic human needs. The present military budget could easily be cut by 25 percent. We could use such a cut as the basis for calling on both China and the Soviet Union to follow our example.

We favor strong emphasis on programs of conversion to peace production.

Full Employment

Our program will guarantee the right of every person to a meaningful job. We oppose the plans of Democrats and Republicans to reduce inflation by maintaining an official unemployment rate of 6 to 8 percent, a plan which worsens racial and sexual divisions and divides the working class.

Housing

Most Americans have no hope of getting adequate, affordable housing unless they inherit a home. Rent control is an immediate stop-gap measure to halt the rent inflation caused by housing shortages.

We need to shift now to a program of non-profit housing, including limited-equity cooperatives and neighborhood housing corporations through which tenants will control their non-profit homes. Massive federal financing can be supplemented by the creation of state and cooperative banks to invest public money and pension funds in housing and energy needs.

A massive program to meet housing needs and establish renewable energy systems, including the insulation and solar retro-fit of existing homes, could be a major component of a full-employment program.

Energy

Our society can no longer afford private ownership of energy production and distribution, or the subversion of transportation policy for the profit of the auto and oil industries. Energy and transportation must be organized on a non-profit and decentralized basis, with a national plan of energy use in the interest of all: we support proposals for energy reduction through conservation.

Nuclear power is so dangerous and expensive that it must be eliminated. We call for the decommissioning of all operating nuclear plants, the permanent end of future construction, and a ban on export of nuclear technology. We support the massive demonstrations which helped focus public attention on this matter.

Health

We in the United States spend 9 percent of our Gross National Product on health care, but we do not get the best care for this investment, and many do not get any care at all.

We must put control of our health care in the hands of consumers and health care workers, the people who are really concerned with cost and quality. We stand for the establishment of health and safety committees in the workplace. We call for a community-controlled National Health Service to provide free medical and dental care for all, financed by a progressive income tax and operated on a non-profit basis. We oppose health care schemes which permit unlimited profit to the medical industry and which give immense profit and power to insurance companies.

Preventive care, patient information rights, and the right to choose birth alternatives are basic elements of a democratic health system.

The Dellums Health Act (H.R. 2969), which incorporates these goals, should be passed.

Inflation

There is no protection against inflation until the military budget and corporate profiteering are brought under control. We need to index pension payments to the cost of living to protect older people from disaster. Price control is needed for the essential components of the cost of living: rent, food, clothing, heat and energy until adequate supplies are available.

We as socialists call for a democratically planned economy where power over prices belongs to all the people and is not used to set prices for the benefit of the few.

Taxation

Current tax laws accurately reflect the power of the business community to control tax legislation and to protect themselves at the expense of the average citizen.

Despite the unfair regressive nature of our present tax structure, there are powerful and influential forces which would take advantage of the protest aroused by presently discriminatory taxes to further slant the tax structure to the advantage of upper-income recipients.

We support the institution of a truly progressive income tax with rates from 1 to 50 percent and no allowance for any deductions, credits or exemptions.

We stand for a restructuring of the inheritance tax laws to restrict the continuation of financial dynasties which enables succeeding generations to continue the exploitation of workers and consumers.

We support the right of conscientious objection to paying any form of a military tax, and support the passage of the World Peace Tax Fund Bill.

Self-Employed and Small Businesses

The self-employed and small businesses have an important role to fulfill in modern society but are vulnerable to the exploitative power of large corporations, suppliers, wholesalers, banks and other credit institutions. Voluntary, non-profit, membership-controlled cooperatives would strengthen the self-employed and small business enterprises and provide outlets, supplies and credit, and mean higher living standards and greater economic security for these groups.

Urban Problems

The private theft of publicly-created values has created an urban environment that is uncomfortable, dirty, dangerous, alienating, and inhumane.

We support public finance of neighborhood mutual-aid societies to re-humanize our cities through the co-operative and powerful effort of the people who live there.

Agriculture

We support the family farmer and encourage the new movement of younger people back to farming.

Farmers and farm workers need to be freed from the domination of the Board of Trade and corporate agribusiness. Farm workers must have the right to unionize. Cooperative farming holds the promise of high production with democracy.

We support 100 percent parity for all food and fiber agricultural products, with the recognition that by no means is this to be regarded as the ultimate solution to the problems of the American farmer.

All of our lives depend ultimately on the land; therefore, we must think of the long-term effects of our farming methods under the concept of stewardship, not an "ownership" that provides the right to exploit the land. We support soil conservation efforts.

Food should never be used to further foreign policy objectives.

Banks and Credit

Banks and other financial institutions, through control of credit and the supply of money, dominate the economy, direct production and often exercise control over industrial, commercial, municipal and other governmental functions. Given their vital role, banking and finance must be placed under social ownership so that they will serve all society. We oppose the high interest rates of the Federal Reserve Board. We encourage the establishment of co-operative banks.

Unions

A key freedom for workers is the right to form a union, independent of employer domination and influence. Without unions, workers' living standards would be driven down to sweatshop levels, the worker would be deprived of all protection from arbitrary discharge and would face a condition of near-serfdom. Together with the right to organize into unions, the right to strike is paramount for the worker, whether blue or white-collared; whether in the public or private sector; whether civilian or military. Unions, like all other institutions, should be legally required to be free of discrimination because of race, religion or sex. Unions should be controlled by their memberships, with fair and frequent elections of officers.

We support federal employees in the effort to obtain the political rights guaranteed to all other Americans and therefore call for repeal of the Hatch Act.

We support shop democracy and therefore reject the so-called right-to-work law.

The Socialist Party vigorously urges/supports the unionization of all working people, especially the "unorganizable." In that sense, we seek the unionization of students, housewives, prison inmates, the unemployed, and enlisted personnel in the armed forces.

Runaway Shops

We call for a Freedom of Information Act for Labor and Consumers, requiring disclosure of plans to close and relocate plants to reduce the dangers of runaway plants and unemployment. An Act of this nature would reveal information on plant safety and the quality of goods and services, and be a needed step to establish higher quality and safety of products and services.

We support a punitive tax on runaway industry and compensation for the workers and communities affected.

Workers' Control

A goal of the Socialist Party is workers' control of all industry through democratic organization of the workplace, with workers making all the decisions now made by management. The Socialist Party proposes a society of free, continuing, and democratic participation through shop councils, and through councils for the management of each industry by workers and others most affected by it, including consumers.

Spheres of life other than industry should also have popular control. These are the bases for democratic socialism, and can be achieved only through radical social change.

As partial advances worthy of support, we favor steps which undermine "management prerogatives" and institutionalize power in the hands of working people and their democratic organization. These include worker administration of the health and safety program, and the unqualified right of safety committees to stop dangerous operations; the election of immediate supervisors; the recognition of at least as many shop stewards as there are first-line supervisors; and the right to hold meetings, including union meetings, on company premises. Finally, there should be a sufficient number of worker-elected members of the board of directors, preferably chosen through the union, to make major decisions of the corporation.

Handguns

The Socialist Party calls for a firmly worded and enforced federal law requiring the registration of handguns.

Environment

As socialists we recognize that production for private profit results in environmental destruction. Only a love and respect for the environment and a democratically planned stewardship of natural resources can eliminate further destruction of the environment. We support such measures as conversion to renewable energy sources, mass transit, recycling and bottle-deposit laws, strong restrictions on promotional advertising, and preservation of wilderness areas.

Human Rights

As socialists we believe in and work toward the fulfillment of human rights for all individuals and groups. (Not only do we define human rights as the generally accepted ideas of freedom of speech, assembly and belief, but we declare that any definition of human rights must include the very basic rights of adequate food, clothing, shelter and health care.

Civil rights and civil liberties must be defined not only in class and/or economic terms, but also in social, cultural and psychological terms. We call for a radical change of society so that all exploitation is abolished.

Political Freedom

As democratic socialists, we are committed to the rights of free speech, free press, free assemblage, freedom of religion, and other provisions of the Bill of Rights.

As the conflict between the classes becomes more intense, sophisticated forms of McCarthyism appear and

come to the fore. We propose public control of the FBI, and local police agencies, and abolition of the CIA. Harassment and surveillance of dissidents as well as infringements of legal due process as fundamental rights should be resisted. We are opposed to Senate Bill 1722 (Kennedy-Thurmond Bill) as a step backward in civil liberties and human rights.

Racial Equality

Socialists stand for equal rights for all Americans. We are deeply aware that America's standard of living is built in part on the labor of Black slaves—unpaid labor which brought no rewards to Blacks. We know that in virtually every case, whether the Native American community, the Chicano community, the Latino community, or the Asian community, minorities have provided a pool of cheap labor for industry. We strongly support affirmative action programs. We do not believe the racism so deeply embedded in the structure of American life can be easily ended but we are committed to the creation of a pluralistic America, multi-racial, with equality for all. Among the most potent weapons in this struggle is full employment.

We must support efforts to raise consciousness necessary to alleviate the racist demands within our society.

We are firm opponents of any organization, movement, or individual that espouses inequality, and will oppose any at every opportunity.

Feminism

True feminism is human liberation. Socialism is part of that struggle. The Socialist Party-USA recognizes that the struggle against male domination and patriarchy must go hand in hand with any struggle against capitalism. The Socialist Party re-affirms its steadfast opposition to all forms of sexism and exploitation, and re-declares its existence as a socialist and feminist organization.

We are militant in our support of the rights of women and the Equal Rights Amendment, recognizing that this alone will not assure women equality. We support fundamental changes in our societal structure to facilitate this equality. We support massive expansion of day care opportunities, recognizing that children are the responsibility of society. We should not give exclusive marital sanction to heterosexual couples or nuclear families. There must be a socialization and re-distribution of work in the home. The contribution of homemakers must be recognized, and the special labor rights of women extended to men. Workers in the home must be assured of equal social security benefits. We demand full implementation of affirmative action programs. We urge women to become active in unions and other organizations to improve their working life. Reproductive rights must be guaranteed. We support education in the community about violence against women and men. We support establishment of community programs and shelters for abused and battered spouses and children.

Gay Rights

Lesbians and gay people are entitled to equality in jobs and housing; to all parental and legal rights; and to open participation in all phases of community life.

We support all efforts to increase understanding and co-operation among persons and groups of differing sexual orientations and to combat inaccurate and degrading stereotypes.

Crime and Punishment

Poverty is a fundamental cause of common crime. Real crime reduction will result from full employment programs and adequate income maintenance systems. We call for equal prosecution of business and white-collar crime, and legalization of so-called victimless crimes. Drug use is a medical and social problem, not a subject for arrest, prosecution and imprisonment.

Prisons have proved counter-productive for most offenders. We favor expanded work-release programs and the elimination of behavior modification (brain washing) programs. We call for the release of all prisoners of conscience and support freedom of religion in prisons. We oppose the death penalty.

Recognizing that the problem of repeat offenders lies not only in the individual but also in the prison system and society, we support prison reform and community correctional alternatives.

Asylum

We should provide asylum for those seeking refuge from political repression and economic hardship, and extend to undocumented workers recognition of rights accorded to United States citizens.

Youth and Age

Because future citizens are the responsibility of the whole society, we oppose abuse, exploitation, or abridgement of due process for young persons by any agency or person whatsoever. We are opposed to discrimination against persons in employment and credit because of advanced age. We support an increase in home services for older people so that they may remain independent in the community as long as possible.

Cultural Freedom

We must provide opportunities for all Americans to participate in meaningful arts activities. We must move to halt the alienation of Americans from their creative realizations. We must work against the present idea of professionalism in the arts as propagated by the current economic elite. We resist this division of people from spirit. The arts should have increased funding on the local level to establish community arts centers to give all people the opportunity to participate in, and the pride to enjoy, their individual creative talents.

Handicapped

We oppose discrimination against persons who are mentally or physically handicapped, disabled, or impaired. They should have equal rights to jobs and housing, and full legal rights as citizens. In addition, we support laws requiring that public facilities be designed to enable handicapped persons to travel and pursue employment, recreation and private affairs.

FOREIGN POLICY

Foreign Affairs

We are now on the brink of an international crisis. The Administration has set forth a dangerous new doctrine in the Middle East and Persian Gulf area under which the U.S. has declared its unilateral right to militarily intervene in that area in violation of the UN charter and the inherent right of self-determination. The U.S. and Soviet Union threaten the self-determination of the nations in the Middle East and in the Persian Gulf as the U.S. seeks to maintain its access to oil and the Soviet Union its political control over Afghanistan.

In the face of the cynical alliances and acts of aggression by China, the Soviet Union and the U.S. in recent history, Americans must work for a foreign policy that is democratic and humane. Therefore, we call for conservation of resources instead of seizing resources in other countries, plus fairness and responsibility in Third World affairs.

The most recent example of the failure of U.S. policy has been Iran, where the Shah of Iran, installed by the CIA in 1953, killed tens of thousands of Iranians with U.S. weapons. This policy led to the tragic and counterproductive seizure of U.S. hostages. We favor the full normalization of relations with Iran.

We should begin disarmament and the withdrawal of U.S. troops from foreign bases, and termination of arms sales to other countries. We believe no country should have troops stationed outside its borders.

Let us start disarmament with the most lethal weapons, nuclear weapons. Let us urge other nations to join us. Our example will be the turning point. The force of growing dissent in the Soviet Union and China will gain influence and strength from our example.

With the unprecedented credibility our stand for peace and disarmament will give us, we should encourage the Third World to disengage themselves from the major power blocs and join in demanding commensurate action by China and the Soviets, including Soviet withdrawal from Afghanistan. We also urge the dissolution of the NATO and Warsaw pacts.

Treaties with the Native American nations within our borders must be respected as treaties with sovereign nations.

We support a "New International Economic Order" to assure a fairer price for raw materials from underdeveloped countries. We urge the working people of all countries to institute popular control over their country's resources. We pledge our support both in direct aid and in opposition to capitalist retaliation.

We should set as a goal, to provide 1 percent of our Gross National Product to aid Third World development, as the UN has recommended and as several countries with social democratic governments have done. The agencies of the UN should be used as the main vehicles of such aid. We should swiftly deliver humanitarian aid to Nicaragua, Iran, Vietnam, Cambodia, Laos, and other countries hurt by U.S. corporate or military interference. As provided by the 1973 Paris peace accords, we should provide reconstruction aid to the peoples of Indochina, based on need and not on politics. We call for recognition of the Democratic Republic of Vietnam.

We oppose the shipment of weapons to any nation in the Middle East. We support the right of the State of Israel to exist in peace, and we recognize the right of the Palestinian people to a Palestine state to be established in Gaza and the West Bank. We are opposed to the terrorism of both the PLO and the Israeli strikes into Lebanon. We believe that a resolution of the conflicts in the Middle East cannot be achieved without direct dialogue with the PLO.

We pledge to work for the withdrawal of U.S. corporate and bank support for the outlaw apartheid regime in South Africa.

We support legislation outlawing reckless practices by U.S. corporations in the Third World, including promotion of infant formula and "dumping" of dangerous and banned products onto Third World markets.

Draft

We oppose military registration, national service, and the draft, and support a program of unconditional amnesty for all draft resisters or military deserters. In addition, we are appalled by the neglect of Vietnam veterans, and support increased benefits and adequate care for the medical and emotional problems resulting from military service.

Socialist Workers Platform 1980

Every day Washington drags us closer to war. Closer to sending American youth to fight and die in a foreign land.

From the Iran crisis to threats against Cuba, from support to racist regimes in southern Africa to secretly sending U.S. "advisers" to Thailand—the Carter administration is aggressively pushing to reassert the U.S. "right" to police the world.

Along with war moves come calls by the generals and the Democratic and Republican politicians to reinstitute the draft.

Carter's go-ahead to deadly new weapons systems—the MX missile, the Cruise missile, and Trident submarine—is a grim reminder that any new Vietnam-type war could quickly escalate into a nuclear holocaust.

The Democratic and Republican warhawks try to convince working people that "our" national honor is at stake.

But there is nothing honorable about maintaining in power bloody tyrants—like the ex-Shah of Iran—who outlaw unions and torture dissidents. American workers have no interest in fighting against the people of Iran, or Cuba, or Nicaragua—or any other country where workers and farmers are struggling to get the giant U.S. corporations off their backs and build a better future for their children.

The truth is that American workers have nothing to gain from going to war—and seeing once again an endless chain of flag-draped coffins returning our brothers and sons home.

The offensive by U.S. rulers abroad is matched by their offensive against working people at home.

The quality of life for most Americans is going downhill. Double-digit inflation—fueled by the government's record-high war spending—eats up our paychecks. The ranks of the unemployed are swelling. Especially hard hit are young people, millions of whom face a future of never finding steady work.

Suffering the most are those at the bottom of the ladder—Blacks, Chicanos, and Puerto Ricans. Affirmative action and school desegregation are under racist attack. Anti-Black and anti-union terrorism from the Ku Klux Klan goes on, while cops look the other way.

Ratification of the Equal Rights Amendment is in danger. Abortion rights are being sabotaged by Congress and the courts.

Huge corporations have set out to crush the ability of the unions to defend working people's livelihoods. U.S. Steel, Chrysler, and others lay people off and threaten plant shutdowns to blackmail workers into accepting wage and benefit cuts. Contrived bankruptcies are used by the railroads to slash jobs and erode safe working conditions. Union-busting violence is on the rise.

The government throws its weight more and more openly behind the employers — from Carter's 7 percent wage "guidelines" at a time of 14 percent inflation, to the growing use of Taft-Hartley, "right to work" and other anti-union laws to victimize workers who organize or strike.

Our problem is that the Rockefellers, DuPonts, Mellons, Morgans, and a handful of other superrich families have the power to lay off millions of workers, endanger us all with nuclear radiation, rob us blind at the gas pumps, or plunge the country into war — all for the sake of their profits!

But they are a tiny minority. They rule the country through their two parties, the Democrats and Republicans.

The Socialist Workers Party believes that working people should stop relying on these two capitalist parties. The time has come for labor to use its power in the political arena, to organize its own political party, based on the unions, to fight for the interests of the vast majority.

In the 1980 elections, the SWP is campaigning for the following elementary rights:

THE RIGHT TO A JOB

Full employment can be achieved by:

— An emergency public works program to provide jobs through construction of housing, schools, hospitals, mass transit, and other social needs. Priority should be given to projects in the workers' neighborhoods, where they are most needed — especially in Black and Latino communities. The huge sums needed for this program should come from eliminating the war budget.

— The work week should be cut to thirty hours, with no reduction in take home pay, in order to spread the available work.

— As long as anyone is unemployed — including youth looking for their first job — they should get unemployment compensation at union wages.

THE RIGHT TO AN ADEQUATE INCOME, PROTECTED AGAINST INFLATION

Wages must be protected against inflation with cost-of-living escalator clauses, so that wages go up — promptly and fully — with each rise in living costs. All pensions, Social Security, welfare, and veterans' benefits should be raised to union wage scales and be protected with cost-of-living clauses. Working people should not be taxed. The capitalists, who have billions, should be the ones to pay.

Working farmers, who are gouged by the banks on the one hand and squeezed by the food trusts on the other, should be allowed to make a decent living. The government should guarantee small farmers the full cost of production, plus a decent income.

THE RIGHT TO FREE EDUCATION THROUGH COLLEGE, TO FREE MEDICAL CARE, AND TO A SECURE RETIREMENT

Education, health, and security should not be privileges of the rich.

Tuition and living expenses should be furnished to all who want to attend college or trade school. Everyone, from birth to old age, should be guaranteed free medical care through a full program of socialized medicine. All retired and disabled people should receive government-financed benefits at full union wages.

THE RIGHT TO A CLEAN, SAFE ENVIRONMENT

Nuclear power threatens the future of humanity. All nuclear power plants should be shut down — now!

The energy trusts and other giant corporations poison our neighborhoods and work places. They tell us if we want jobs we must accept the destruction of the environment. But we have a right to jobs, and to health and safety, too.

Factories that refuse to safeguard the health or safety of workers on the job or in surrounding communities must be nationalized and run in the public interest. Union safety committees must have the right to shut down any job site that is not safe.

THE RIGHT OF OPPRESSED NATIONAL MINORITIES TO CONTROL THEIR OWN AFFAIRS

Blacks, Chicanos, Puerto Ricans, and other oppressed nationalities have a right to an equal education. Busing should be defended and expanded to desegregate the public schools. Bilingual programs also must be expanded and upgraded.

Affirmative-action programs to help overcome years

of discrimination on the job and in education must be extended and enforced.

Racist and right-wing terrorists must be prosecuted for their crimes against Blacks and Latinos. Police brutality and frame-ups in the ghettos and barrios must be halted.

The Right of Women to Full Social, Economic, and Political Equality

To help ensure equality under the law, the ERA should be adopted and implemented without further delay. Women must have the right to decide if and when to have children. This includes the right to abortion and contraception on demand, as well as protection from forced sterilization.

The growing numbers of women workers need government-financed, free child-care centers. Maternity leaves with full pay must be provided. Barriers keeping women out of job classifications must be removed, and women must receive equal pay for equal work.

The Right to Freedom from Government Repression, Spying, and Harassment

As big business and its government tighten the squeeze on working people, our basic rights and liberties are under attack.

Working people need an expansion of our democratic rights—not a cutback. All laws that permit government interference in the unions or that bar any workers from striking or engaging in political activities should be repealed. The use of FBI and police spies and provocateurs must be halted. Repressive legislation must be abolished, along with all cruel and unusual punishment—including the death penalty.

Full democratic and human rights should be extended to gay people, to foreign-born workers, to handicapped people, to prisoners, GIs, and to the young and the elderly.

The Right to Decide Political Policies that Affect Our Lives

We have a right to know the full truth about the decisions that affect our lives:

—Publish all secret treaties and agreements Washington has made with other countries!

—Open the CIA files! Tell the truth about how the U.S. put the Shah in power and kept him on the throne for twenty-five bloody years, how Washington intervened secretly in Chile to overthrow the elected Allende government, and how it has kept in power racist and repressive regimes from South Africa to South Korea.

—Let the people debate and vote in a referendum before the country is dragged into another war. Let us have the right to say no to policies that can lead to nuclear holocaust!

The Right to Know the Truth About and Decide on Economic and Social Policies

When the corporations claim they can't afford wage increases, or have to lay off workers, they should be forced to *open their books.* Make the energy, food, auto, and steel monopolies show their records to democratically-elected union committees so that we can see their real profits, production statistics, political payoffs, and tax swindles.

Working people have a right to control conditions on the job. We have the right to regulate the pace of work in the safest and least dehumanizing way.

In particular, the energy industry, which is today holding the working people of this country hostage to its demands for higher prices and more profits, must immediately be taken out of private hands and nationalized. The criminal secrecy about supplies, reserves, and refining capacity must be ended. The energy industry should be administered by an elected board, operating out in the open, under the vigilance of the unions and consumer groups. Books and records must be open, meetings public, everything on the table.

The unions of today have been crippled by a conservative and bureaucratic leadership. They will have to be strengthened and transformed to take on the fight for these goals.

—The struggle for *union democracy* is the key to unleashing union power. Workers must have the right to elect all officers, to know the terms of and vote on all contracts, and to democratically decide and implement policies to defend our own interests.

—*Solidarity* is the basis of labor's strength. Solidarity with other unions on strike, with organizing drives and battles for union recognition. Solidarity with workers and unionists in other countries, such as Nicaragua, who are striving to rebuild their country. And solidarity with all the oppressed and exploited in this country.

The strategy of the rulers is to divide working people by creating a class of outcasts—oppressed minorities, women, foreign-born workers, the youth, the unemployed—those they hope the relatively better-off white male workers will view as "them" rather than "us." Full support to the struggles of the oppressed is the only way to counter these attempts to undermine working-class solidarity.

—*Independent working-class political action* is essential to defend labor against the ruling-class attacks on our rights and living standards. We are handcuffed so long as our unions remain tied to the Democratic and Republican parties — the parties of the ruling rich.

To have any voice in government, to wage any effective fight for political policies in the interest of the majority of the American people, we need an independent labor political party.

Increasing numbers of people view the antics of the Democratic and Republican politicians with indignation and disgust. An independent labor party, based on the power of the unions, would get an enthusiastic response from working people and our allies — farmers, women, Blacks and Latinos, and other victims of the two-party system.

Launching such a party would be a giant step forward for the struggle to sweep aside the capitalist parties and bring to power a workers' government, a government of the majority.

This is what the Socialist Workers Party is campaigning for.

Join the SWP and join the struggle!

Workers World Platform 1980

The Workers World Party election campaign has developed a program to solve the problems of the working class, a program that has to be fought for in order to be won. Over the past election year, Workers World Party has reached tens of millions with this clear program of determined struggle against the bosses, bankers, and landlords. It has agitated around immediate demands to alleviate the cruel conditions being imposed on the people and at the same time has raised a socialist perspective as the answer to capitalist crisis and decay.

1. Jobs for all; Stop plant shutdowns; For workers' control of industry

2. End racism and all national oppression; Stop police brutality; Smash the KKK and Nazis; Honor the Native treaties; Independence for Puerto Rico

3. Stop the Pentagon's war plans; No draft, no war, no way!

4. People before profits; No nukes; For a people's takeover of the oil industry

5. Rebuild the cities; Roll back rents; Use the Pentagon budget for schools, hospitals, housing

6. Defend labor's rights; Abolish all anti-labor laws; Organize the unorganized

7. End sexism; Full rights for gays and lesbians; Pass the ERA; For a national gay rights bill

8. Equal opportunity for the disabled, elderly; Amnesty for undocumented workers

9. Jobs, not jails; Voting rights for all poor and working people

10. Protection for the jobless; End inflation, no "passalongs" to consumers; Eliminate taxes for all incomes under $25,000

11. Solidarity with workers' struggles abroad

Fight for a system that would end racism, exploitation, and all forms of oppression; Fight for socialism!

Subject Index

Key to Political Parties

A   American (1972-1980)
AI   American Independent (1968-1980)
C   Workers (Communist) (1976-1980)
CP   Citizens (1980)
D   Democratic (1840-1980)
LIB Libertarian (1972-1980)

N   National Statesman (1980)
NU National Unity (1980)
R   Republican (1856-1980)
S   Socialist (1904-1980)
SW Socialist Workers (1948-1980)
WW Workers World (1980)

Index of Names